*Themes and Structures:
Studies in German Literature
from Goethe to the Present*

A Festschrift for Theodore Ziolkowski

Studies in German Literature, Linguistics, and Culture

Edited by
James N. Hardin
(*South Carolina*)

Themes and Structures

Studies in German Literature from Goethe to the Present

Edited by
Alexander Stephan

CAMDEN HOUSE

Copyright © 1997 by
CAMDEN HOUSE, INC.

Published by Camden House, Inc.
Drawer 2025
Columbia, SC 29202 USA

Printed on acid-free paper.
Binding materials are chosen for strength and
durability.

All rights reserved,
including the right of reproduction in electronic or any other form.
All rights to this publication will be vigorously defended.

Printed in the United States of America
First Edition

ISBN: 1–57113–087–x

Library of Congress Cataloging-in-Publication Data

Themes and Structures: studies in German literature from Goethe to
   the present: a festschrift for Theodore Ziolkowski / edited
   by Alexander Stephan. – 1st ed.
      p.   cm. – (Studies in German literature, linguistics, and
culture (Unnumbered))
   Includes bibliographical references and index.
   ISBN 1–57113–087–x (alk. paper)
   1. German literature—History and criticism. I. Stephan,
Alexander, 1946–   . II. Ziolkowski, Theodore. III. Series:
Studies in German literature, linguistics, and culture (Unnumbered).
PT236. T44   1997
830' .9—dc21   97–2585
                                                                                       CIP

ACKNOWLEDGMENTS

The editor wishes to thank particularly President Harold T. Shapiro of Princeton University, whose generous grant from the President's Fund made this publication possible.

Contents

Alexander Stephan — 1
    Introduction

Geoffrey Atherton — 5
    "Edle Einfalt und stille Größe": Greek Art, Roman Eyes?

Walter D. Wetzels — 21
    Physics for the Ladies: Early Literary Voices
    and Strategies for and against the
    Popularization of Copernicus and Newton

Clark Muenzer — 39
    Transplanting the Poem: Goethe, Ghosts, and the
    Metamorphosis of an Elegy

Hildburg Herbst — 78
    Unterhaltungen deutscher Ausgewanderten,
    Political and Otherwise

Paola Mayer — 94
    Friedrich Schlegel's *Theorie der Entstehung der Welt*:
    A Romantic Cosmogony

Ellis Finger — 114
    The Poetry of Friedrich Rückert in the
    Songs of Schubert, Schumann, and Mahler

Kathryn Shailer Hanson — 135
    The Transitory Individual: Tieck's
    Der Runenberg and Handke's *Die Wiederholung*
    as Allegories of Aging

Otto W. Johnston — 149
    Chromatic Symbolism in Gottfried Keller's
    Romeo und Julia auf dem Dorfe

Maria Tatar — 164
"Das war ein Stück Arbeit!":
Jack the Ripper and Wedekind's Lulu Plays

George C. Tunstall — 188
Some Reflections on the Form and Motivic
Structure of Hofmannsthal's "Die Beiden"

James M. Skidmore — 208
Responding to the Crisis in Leadership:
Ricarda Huch's *Der wiederkehrende Christus*

Scott Abbott — 222
Postmetaphysical Metaphysics? Peter Handke's *Repetition*

Kathleen L. Komar — 234
Kassandra as a Rebel Against War:
The Theme of Heroism in Christa Wolf's
Re-Vision of the Trojan War

David Dollenmayer — 254
The Search for "Another Face of Germany"
in Kay Boyle's *The Smoking Mountain*

Alan Keele — 269
Walter Kempowski:
Tinker, Tailor, Chronicler... *Spy?*
A Note on the Margins of Fact and Fiction

Cecile Cazort Zorach — 281
Home Territory: The New Germany
in Recent American Fiction

Notes on Contributors — 309

Selected Writings by Theodore Ziolkowski — 313

Index — 323

INTRODUCTION

Alexander Stephan

This volume is presented to Theodore Ziolkowski, Class of 1900 Professor of Modern Languages at Princeton University, by his students on the occasion of his sixty-fifth birthday. True to his principles as a teacher, the book raises no monument to a special theory or school of literary study. Instead, each essay in its way testifies to the relationship of the students with their mentor. Often an approach or a topic is based upon one of Ziolkowski's writings; in other cases, only insiders may recognize which seminar gave rise to an offering. Still other pieces witness that Ziolkowski always encouraged his students to free themselves from models and pursue their own path. All the essays have in common that they were produced in respect for a teacher and colleague who was — as one contributor states — "the best single thing that happened to me in my career."

Ziolkowski preferred to forgo a classic *Festschrift*. He has no leaning to personality cults, especially not one that surrounds himself. And he is so firmly established among the leading post-war scholars of German that formal laudations from colleagues are superfluous, as is a *tabula gratulatoria*.

Instead, Ziolkowski consented to a different undertaking, one much closer to his heart: a volume of essays by his Ph.D. students. As every one of us who contributed to this project knows, "his" students from Yale, Columbia, and more than thirty years at Princeton stand — along with his research — in the center of his interests. His seminars are conducted with his students in mind, and are so carefully prepared and well thought out that future teachers can readily take them as models for their own classes. He patiently strives to impart the foundations of scholarship to doctoral candidates, so that they may remain flexible and competitive in the crisis-prone environment that threatens our discipline. A survey of former students revealed that our "Doktorvater" has a special talent for finding the right words for his protégés at times of personal difficulty. Reliable and tireless, he makes himself available to provide advice or expertise when they are needed.

Ziolkowski made the decision to study *Germanistik* in the early fifties, a time when the Nazi era still cast its deep shadows over all things German. Influenced by his own teachers at Yale, especially Hermann J. Weigand, he was among the small group of American Germanists who had to hold their own against the older, experienced exiles and immigrants from Europe. Since then he has been an active critic, observer and commentator on the methodological debates that have animated our field, from the politicization of literature in the sixties to the Hesse cult of the Flower Children to the debate on postmodernism. Yet the themes of his books and essays testify that he remained faithful over the years to himself and to his own areas of study.

Most of Ziolkowski's writings have long been standard works. His Hesse research, for example — books, editions, collections, and essays — is more than enough, in quality and quantity, to make up a scholar's life work. In addition there are the genre studies of the elegy and the novel, works of thematic research, pieces on modern Virgil criticism. The broad scope of *German Romanticism and Its Institutions* indicates the range of disciplines outside German which Ziolkowski addresses. This is true, as well, of his most recent book, *The Mirror of Justice*, which treats how Western law is reflected in literature from the classical Greeks to the present.

Regardless of which century, which national literature, which forms, themes or authors he engages at any one moment, Ziolkowski has a strong resilience to ideological narrow-mindedness or hidebound thinking. It is not his way to jump onto every methodological bandwagon that rolls by. The library always stands at the center of his ideal university. Surfing the Worldwide Web is not, for him, a substitute for reading and writing, and clearly he does not regard all data and publications as of equal value merely because all are increasingly accessible and come in similar packaging.

This is not to say that Ziolkowski produces esoteric scholarship. He wrote about Heinrich Böll and Max Frisch at a time when living authors were still excluded from study in university seminars. Already as a young scholar he avoided reproducing abstract, German-style *Germanistik* in the United States. Long before this was recognized in Europe, he taught, and showed by practice, that good scholarship can be written in a comprehensible form. By publishing in *TV Guide*, he stepped outside the academic world. With interest he observed how the counterculture of the time responded to his publications about Hesse and suggested that "Saint Hesse" was actually best understood by those hippies who "far from copping out ... leave the university to tutor children in the slums." But above all — and our volume may reflect this — he has always supported his students in their choice of the theory that guided their work — from Wellek and Warren to Marx and Lukács and to Derrida and Foucault — regardless of whether he personally agrees with the premises and results of their chosen method. But one thing is not open to question in his seminars, or in the more than thirty dissertations he has supervised: whatever the topic and whoever the intellectual influences may be, the scholarship must be impeccable, the sources researched, the reading done in depth, and work put into the language and style. In short, if not brilliance, at least an outstanding effort is expected from all.

But Ziolkowski has never asked more from his students than he does from himself. His curriculum vitae is evidence of his intellectual commitment: a Ph.D. from Yale at the age of twenty-five (earned when he had a family and three children, all of whom have since grown up to become established university professors in their own right); two monographs in the six years during which he served as chair of the German Department at Princeton, and three books and close to thirty scholarly pieces during his thirteen years as dean of Princeton's Graduate School. To these must be added six more books, scholarly editions, translations, lectures and several hundred book reviews, fellowships from the Guggenheim Foundation among others, honorary memberships of academies in Göttingen and Austria, book awards, a term as president of the Modern Language Association, service on the editorial boards of various publications, and honors and appointments from countless bodies ranging from Princeton University Press and the Internationale Vereinigung für Germanische Sprach- und Literaturwissenschaften to the German-American Academic Council.

Clearly, Theodore Ziolkowski's work as scholar and administrator has left a lasting mark on our field. By us, his students, he is remembered as a challenging, dedicated and fair teacher.

A. S.
June 1997

GEOFFREY ATHERTON

"Edle Einfalt und stille Größe": Greek Art, Roman Eyes?

In 1755, Johann Jachim Winckelmann published a small tract with the large title *Gedanken über die Nachahmung der griechischen Werke in der Malerei und Bildhauerkunst*. In it Winckelmann set down the arguments why the ancient Greeks, through a fortuitous coincidence of nature and culture, were unable to execute a work of art that was not beautiful, and so remain the school for the cultivation of taste throughout the ages. The great example that he chose for his case was the Laocoon statue. It was in relation to this statue that, when attempting to sum up the essential attributes of Greek beauty, he hit upon the happy phrase "edle Einfalt und stille Größe." These few words served to establish the essential attributes of the classical conception of beauty or "das Schöne" of German aesthetics in the eighteenth century and, at the same time, to make that ideal of beauty the historical possession of a particular people and a particular time.

The combination of an enthusiasm for the beautiful and for the Greeks gave Winckelmann a good claim to be the spiritual progenitor of the intense Graecomania which so distinguished the generations of Germans immediately after him. The counterpart of this new enthusiasm was a disinclination towards all things Roman. In part Winckelmann's argument dictated the necessity for this corollary. In order for Winckelmann's Greece to emerge with a distinctive profile from under the shadow of Rome, he was compelled to reject the current notion that the Latin heritage assimilated the Greek world and brought it to completion. "Es ist die romanische Welt und ihre fast unumschränkte Herrschaft in Europa, gegen die Winckelmann seine neue ursprüngliche Sicht des Griechentums kraftvoll durchsetzt.... Mit einem gewaltsamen Ruck und aus innerer Leidenshaft stellt Winckelmann das Steuer um vom Römertum hin zum Griechentum.... Antike war seit Renaissance schlechthin römische Antike."[1] Only by contrasting the one with the other could Winckelmann develop a sense of historical difference.

---

[1] Walter Rehm, *Griechentum und Goethezeit* (1936; Munich: Lehnen, 1952) 23–24.

The Latin world entered Winckelmann's pamphlet in the figure of Vergil. Winckelmann illustrated his point about the Greek beauty of the Laocoon statue by demonstrating the antithesis of that beauty. He cited incidentally the famous passage from the second Book of the *Aeneid* which recounts the death of Laocoon and his sons.[2] He condemned the Vergilian passage for its lack of any true artistic feeling: namely, that Vergil should permit his Laocoon to issue *clamores horrendos,* a "schreckliches Geschrei" in Winckelmann's words, betrayed the fact that he had no innate sense of the beautiful.[3] Vergil had failed to grasp that the greater the physical tumult of the body, the greater the contrast with the steadfast composure of the soul: to shriek in protest is neither simple and great, nor serene and noble. At its very inception, the German enthusiasm for all things Greek was paralleled by its equally unique counterpart: the discovery of the Latin heritage as second-rate and derivative.[4]

Vergil may fairly be considered as representative of the "romanisch-abendländische Kulturidee," which Walter Rehm views Winckelmann as controverting.[5] Arguably, on that account, Vergil remained intellectually and culturally closer to Winckelmann and the Germans of the eighteenth century than could a Greece, secure in a harmony of nature and culture, which they could not hope to possess, except vicariously in their imagination. Vergil as a poet and thinker represented a period of culture in antiquity which knew itself to be the heir of a long and rich tradition. It was a civilization acutely aware of its belated position not merely in the literary and intellectual world but also in the historical world. From that tradition it also possessed the habits of mind and philosophical cate-

---

[2]"Incidentally" because the remark has the character of an aside in the *Gedanken*, nor does Winckelmann make any mention of Vergil in either the *Florenzer Manuskript* (1757?) or the *Geschichte der Kunst des Altherthums* (1764). The omission of Vergil from his later descriptions and the meagerness of the original reference notwithstanding, the Vergilian association echoes strongly. Lessing, ostensibly writing his *Laokoon oder über die Grenzen der Mahlerei und Poesie* (1766) in response to Winckelmann's *Geschichte der Kunst*, nonetheless begins with exactly this point of difference between Vergil's account and the statue. One might even sense some of the daring of Winckelmann's comment in the outraged shock contained in Lessing's admission: "Ich bekenne, daß der mißbilligende Seitenblick, welchen er auf den *Virgil* wirft, mich zuerst stutzig gemacht hat," Gotthold Ephraim Lessing, *Gesammelte Werke*, ed. Wolfgang Stammler, vol. 2 (Munich: Hanser, 1959) 787.

[3]Johann Joachim Winckelmann, *Gedanken über die Nachahmung der griechischen Werke in der Malerei und Bildhauerkunst*, ed. Ludwig Uhland (Stuttgart: Reclam, 1990) 20.

[4]Rehm 23ff; cf. also Conrad Wiedemann, "Römische Staatsnation und griechische Kulturnation: Zum Paradigmawechsel zwischen Gottsched und Winckelmann," *Akten des VII. Internationalen-Germanisten-Kongresses*, Ed. Albrecht Schöne. Göttingen (1985), vol. 9, 173–78.

[5]Rehm 22.

gories to consider these matters with some power of insight. This was one basis of affinity between the Rome of Vergil and Germany of the eighteenth century which likewise faced the difficulty of absorbing a tradition while staking out its own place within it.

Another affinity was the position of the modern national cultures in relation to antiquity. They were the offspring of the Latin West. They issued forth from the mixture of late pagan culture and Christianity during the Roman Empire. Vergil was in this world a figure of a stature so immense that he earned the title "Vater des Abendlandes."[6] One need only think of Dante's Vergil to be reminded of this. Dante chose Vergil to be his guide up through the entrance of the earthly paradise, a symbol both of the distance natural reason, unaided by the Grace of Revelation, could carry the virtuous pagan and of the degree to which Christianity was the rightful heir to pagan antiquity.[7] Or alternatively one may recollect that Vergil's fourth *Eclogue* gained the title of the "Messianic Eclogue," as it was viewed as a pagan prophecy of the birth of Christ.[8] Vergil was a Janus figure who belonged to the Christian future as much as to the pagan past.

The "romanisch-abendländische Kulturidee" found more pragmatic support in the privileged position of the Latin language in education and general culture as well as in the preeminence which the Humanists of the Renaissance conceded to classical authors. These advantages combined to elevate Vergil to a position rivaled, perhaps, only by Horace or Cicero. Familiarity with his poetry formed so large a part of the educational curriculum that almost every scholar or poet of importance came into contact with him in the original. Even if the latter part of the eighteenth century was reluctant to look with favor on his manner of composition or the subject matter of his works, this lack of overt interest did not prevent Vergil from remaining a living presence to the mind of the educated. He formed an inextricable part of the intellectual climate in which they were raised. The legacy of Latin culture remained a lens through which everyone had to look even if he sought to examine a Greek object; and Winckelmann provided an example of this in the *Gedanken über die Nachahmung*.[9]

[6] The phrase is from the title of Theodor Haecker's book, *Vergil, Vater des Abendlandes* (1931; Zurich: Arche Verlag, 1946), in which he argues Vergil's claim to that epithet.

[7] Cf. Domenico Pietro Antonio Comparetti, *Vergil in the Middle Ages*, trans. E.F.M. Benecke (New York: Macmillan & Co., 1895) 195–231; and also Ernst Robert Curtius, *Europäische Literatur und lateinisches Mittelalter* (Bern: Francke, 1948) 25–27, 352–83.

[8] Cf. Eduard Norden, *Die Geburt des Kindes: Die Geschichte einer religiösen Idee* (Leipzig: Teubner, 1924).

[9] In recent years the Laocoon statue, its provenance and interpretation, has provoked renewed interest among scholars. Foremost among them is Bernard Andreae with two books on the subject: *Laokoon und die Gründung Roms*, Kulturgeschichte der antiken Welt 39 (Mainz: Zabern, 1988) and *Laokoon und die Kunst von Pergamon: Die Hybris*

An observer beholding the statue for the first time would be struck by the impression of petrified motion, of the writhing serpents, the intertwined limbs, the contorted bodies, the anguished faces, and, above all, of immense suffering and outright pain. It is unlikely that the description of "serene grandeur" or "stille Größe" would spring to mind. Perhaps some intimation of nobility might suggest itself to him before such obvious suffering; but that such seething confusion would be "simple" seems an improbable response.[10] Why then should these attributes have impressed themselves on Winckelmann as he gazed upon a plaster copy in the Großer Garten at Dresden in the early 1750s? The discrepancy between the statue and Winckelmann's description perplexes E. M. Butler greatly, but she can find no answer to it beyond:

> Nothing accounts so satisfactorily for Winckelmann's extraordinary blindness as the natural explanation that, dazzled by the flash of a great revelation, he saw the distinctive qualities of Greek art as he looked at this supposedly genuine specimen. He was in fact in a trance; and like many another clairvoyant, he was uttering truths which did not apply to the object before him, but were associated with it in his mind.[11]

But why should that statue prove to have been the lightning rod for Winckelmann's "flash of a great revelation"? In Dresden, he had other Greek statues in repose which would have offered a better illustration of his insight. Winckelmann saw Greek art, but looked with Roman eyes. He did not approach the statue without preconceptions, and these in turn came from an interpretative tradition. To answer Butler's query briefly: Vergil was the source of that tradi-

---

der Giganten (Frankfurt am Main: Fischer, 1991). He argues that the Vatican statue is a copy of a bronze orginal from Pergamum. German Hafner takes a wholly different position in *Die Laokoon-Gruppen: Ein gordischer Knoten*, Akademie der Wissenschaften und der Literatur 5 (Stuttgart: Steiner, 1992). He argues that the statue referred to by Pliny's famous comment (*Naturalis Historia*, bk. 36, chap. 37) is not the Vatican statue, rather it refers to a lost statue which antedates the *Aeneid*. The Vatican statue, on the other hand, was sculpted in response to the Vergilian epic. Bettina Preiß gives a detailed account of the art-historical and aesthetic-literary reception of the statue since its rediscovery in 1506 along with reproductions of much of the source material: see Bettina Preiß, *Die wissenschaftliche Beschäftigung mit der Laokoongruppe* (Bonn: VDG Verlag, 1992). Slightly before these, yet offering a readable and concise account of the statue and the vicissitudes since its rediscovery is Georg Daltrop, *Die Laokoongruppe im Vatikan: Ein Kapitel aus der römischen Museumsgeschichte und der Antiken-Erkundung*, Xenia: Konstanzer Althistorische Vorträge und Forschungen 5 (Constance: Universitätsverlag Konstanz, 1982).

[10] Hafner argues for the aptness of "edle Einfalt und stille Größe," *Die Laokoon-Gruppen*, 39–41.

[11] E. M. Butler, *The Tyranny of Greece over Germany* (New York: The Macmillan Co., 1935) 47.

tion, and Winckelmann came by his inspiration in part from him. He took from Vergil the notion that the scene before his eyes was to be associated with a moment of supreme passion, a great pathos.[12] He also borrowed from Vergil the assumption that this pathos had something to do with Stoic steadfastness, even if he understood that Stoicism in relation to very different conceptions of greatness.[13]

But what of Winckelmann's knowledge of Vergil? As a child, Winckelmann was precocious and a voracious reader of the ancients. Carl Justi relates that at the small Latin school in Stendal which Winckelmann attended until the age of seventeen, he sang for his bread and tuition as one of the "Kurrendaner." At the same time he often contrived to memorize Greek and Latin vocabulary; or, when compelled to take part in the games of his peers by the need to be agreeable, he would slip a book into his pocket for something to read. What he read must have been very restricted, at least to judge by the inventory of the school library that Justi gives. It consisted of a handful of books, princi-

---

[12] This point does not prejudice the question of the wording. An earlier association of the phrase "edle Einfalt" with ancient Greece and an urgent need for the muse to return to the purer springs of that Grecian nature may be found in the *Lyrische Gedichte* of Johann Peter Uz. In the preface to the edition of 1749, he speaks of "der edlen Einfalt, dem ungekünstelten Ausdrucke, oder der schönen Natur der Alten" and repeats the phrase in the opening stanza of *Lobgesang des Frühlings:*

> Wie lang hat meine Muse schon,
> Die Witz und edle Einfalt ehret,
> Am blumenvollen Helikon,
> Den Musen Griechenlands begierig zugehöret!

Winckelmann replaces "Witz" with "stille Größe" and opposes Greek to Roman antiquity unlike Uz, who regards them as part of a seamless whole. Both the preface and the poem are cited according to Johann Peter Uz, *Sämtliche poetische Werke*, ed. A. Sauer, Deutsche Litteraturdenkmale des 18. und 19. Jahrhunderts in Neudrucken 33 (Stuttgart: Göschen, 1890) 5 and 7 respectively.

[13] Stoicism neither exhausts the scope of the ideals and ideas which animate Winckelmann's writings, nor is it clearly separated from them; rather one must keep in mind the interdependence of his conception of history, his style, his vision of humanity, the beautiful and freedom, on which various points see: Horst Rüdiger, "Winckelmanns Geschichtsauffassung: Ein Dresdner Entwurf als Keimzelle seines historischen Denkens," *Euphorion*, 62.2 (1968) 99–116; Bernd Bräutigam, "Poetizität und der Ursprung literarischer Ästhetik im 18. Jahrhundert," *Neuere Studien zur Aphoristik und Essayistik*, ed. Giulia Cantarutti and Hans Schumacher, Berliner Beiträge zur neueren deutschen Literaturgeschichte, vol. 9 (Frankfurt am Main: Lang, 1986) 223–49; and Eberhard Wilhelm Schulz, "Winckelmanns Schreibart," *Studien zur Goethezeit: Erich Trunz zum 75. Geburtstag*, ed. Hans-Joachim Mähl and Eberhard Mannack (Heidelberg: Carl Winter, 1981) 233–55.

pally the works of Latin authors and included notably an incunabulum of Vergil.[14]

One need not rely on this as evidence of familiarity with the Vergilian text. Aware that nothing is more fatal to a reputation than silence and nothing attracts attention better than controversy, Winckelmann arranged for the second edition of his *Gedanken über die Nachahmung* in 1756 to appear with an anonymous piece strongly critical of his *Gedanken* and still another piece, a rebuttal of the criticism; both of which he wrote himself. In these three essays, Winckelmann adopted the practice common among the learned of adorning their efforts with *sententiae*: short, pithy quotations from the classical authors used to point the moral and display the erudition of the writer. The number he took from Horace was equal to that of all the rest taken together. Of those from Vergil, six are from the *Aeneid* — and only from Books 1 and 6 — and one from the *Georgics*. Furthermore, in common with the age, they were as often as not slightly misquoted, a testament to the fact that they were frequently cited from memory.

This may sufficiently demonstrate Winckelmann's knowledge of Vergil, though it fails to argue any deeper debt. For evidence of that one must turn to Winckelmann's descriptions of the statue itself. During the course of his career, Winckelmann described the statue three times. The first, and the best known, description occurred in the *Gedanken über die Nachahmung*, the second in the *Florenzer Manuskript* (1757?), and the last in the *Geschichte der Kunst des Alterthums* (1764).[15] In the first, Winckelmann makes the Laocoon statue the example of "edle Einfalt und stille Größe." He stresses in the short description the pain of Laocoon, evident in the definition of the musculature and in the contortions of the body, in order to contrast the physical tumult with the resolute composure of the soul: hence his wish to interpret Vergil's *clamores horrendos* as mistaken. There is, however, no actual description of the statue. Winckelmann contents himself with indicating a few signs of the body which reflect physical suffering: "Schmerz... in allen Muskeln und Sehnen des Körpers" and "dem schmerzlich eingezogenen Unterleibe."[16] The brevity of the description along

---

[14]Cf. Carl Justi, *Winckelmann und seine Zeitgenossen*, ed. Walter Rehm, 5th ed., vol. 1 (Cologne: Phaidon Verlag, 1956) 29f.

[15]Carl Justi discovered a miscellany of writings by Winckelmann in Florence which included among the letters and rough sketches a description of the statues in the Belvedere. He published a selection of them in "Ein Manuscript über die Statuen im Belvedere" (in: *Preussische Jahrbücher* 28 [1871]: 581–609) together with some notes on their composition and place within Winckelmann's writings. He dates the descriptions to the year 1757. For the description of the Laocoon statue, see 586–88.

[16]Winckelmann, *Gedanken*, 20–21. In addition to claiming that the Laocoon statue represents the principle *par excellence*, Winckelmann also maintains that it is the perfect instance of the technical standard of the ideal proportions of the human body estab-

with the suggestive use of "Schmerz" and "schmerzlich" has more the character of an assertion than a descriptive account. From his description one would not know that the statue is a group of three figures, as he fails even to mention the sons. The second description is much more detailed and includes all parts of the statue, the sons not exempted. The body is minutely detailed with the particulars of the hair, nose, nostrils, mouth and others parts all meticulously recorded; yet this succession of details, lacking a connective interpretation, is disjointed. If the character of the first description is assertive, then that of the second is static.

The final description is a combination of the first two; each detail becomes the result of the external violence of nature and the internal resistance of the spirit. The "aufgetriebene[.] Stirn" expresses the "mit Stärke bewaffnete[n] Geist," and the chest is arched forward "durch den beklemmten Othem und durch Zurückhaltung des Ausbruches der Empfindung."[17] The result of the continual movement in the prose, from the inner condition to the outer effect and back again, is to make the description dramatic, to move from the immobility of the stone, through the interpretative review of the details, to the dramatic tension of the whole. In doing this Winckelmann moves much closer to Vergil.

Vergil's account of Laocoon's fate, at the same time that it is dramatic, is also calculated to heighten the pathos of the event. The point at which Winckelmann's debt to Vergil becomes clearest is in the passage:

> Sein eigenes Leiden aber scheint ihn weniger zu beängstigen, als die Pein seiner Kinder, die ihr Angesicht zu ihrem Vater wenden und um Hülfe schreyen: denn das väterliche Herz offenbaret sich in den wehmüthigen Augen,[18]

when compared to the lines:

> *et primum parva duorum*
> *corpora natorum serpens amplexus uterque*
> *implicat et miseros morsu depascitur artus;*
> *post ipsum auxilio subeuntem ac tela ferentem.*
> (*Aen.* 2, 213–216)[19]

---

lished by Polyclitus and that it was also historically acknowledged as such by the Romans (4).

[17]Johann Joachim Winckelmann, *Geschichte der Kunst des Alterthums*, ed. Heinrich Meyer and Johann Schulz, vol. 6 (Dresden, 1815) 104–5.

[18]Winckelmann, *Geschichte der Kunst*, vol. 6, 105.

[19]All citations from Vergil are from *P. Vergilii Maronis Opera*, ed. R.A.B. Mynors (1969; Oxford: Clarendon, 1990). I give the whole passage for the sake of comprehension:

In both passages the duties of the father are contrasted with the imperative of self-preservation. And in both, the word "help" accentuates the drama of the moment; the one imagines cries of help from the mouths of the sons, the other tells us that it is rather the father *auxilio subeuntem*.[20] The change between Vergil's father, who hurries unbidden to render futile assistance to his sons, and Winckelmann's suggestion that the father responds to his children's cry for help is of great importance as a point of interpretation.

That Laocoon should, in Vergil's account, hasten to his sons' assistance heightens the pathos of the scene by emphasizing his selfless pursuit of his duty,

> *Laocoon, ductus Neptuno sorte sacerdos,*
> *sollemnis taurum ingentem mactabat ad aras.*
> *ecce autem gemini a Tenedo tranquilla per alta*
> *(horresco referens) immensis orbibus angues*
> *incumbunt pelago pariterque ad litora tendunt;*
> *pectora quorum inter fluctus arrecta iubaeque*
> *sanguineae superant undas, pars cetera pontum*
> *pone legit sinuatque immensa uolumine terga.*
> *fit sonitus spumante salo; iamque arua tenebant*
> *ardentisque oculos suffecti sanguine et igni*
> *sibila lambebant linguis uibrantibus ora.*
> *diffugimus uisu exsangues. illi agmine certo*
> *Laocoonta petunt; et primum parua duorum*
> *corpora natorum serpens amplexus uterque*
> *implicat et miseros morsu depascitur artus;*
> *post ipsum auxilio subeuntem ac tela ferentem*
> *corripiunt spirisque ligant ingentibus; et iam*
> *bis medium amplexi, bis collo squamea circum*
> *terga dati superant capite et ceruicibus altis.*
> *ille simul manibus tendit diuellere nodos*
> *perfusus sanie uittas atroque ueneno,*
> *clamores simul horrendos ad sidera tollit:*
> *qualis mugitus, fugit cum saucius aram*
> *taurus et incertam excussit ceruice securim. (Aen. 2, 201–24)*

The initial portion of the Laocoon episode occurs in *Aen.* 2, 40–56.

[20]If one holds that the statue antedates the epic, and Vergil may reasonably be supposed to have seen it in Rome (cf. Bernard Andreae, *Laokoon und die Kunst* 82–85), then one may well object, why should it surprise that from the same powerful statue two different viewers should arrive at similar understandings of it? This is anachronistic on two accounts. Firstly, in Winckelmann's day the matter of priority was no more settled than it is today. To Winckelmann's assertion in *Geschichte der Kunst* that the statue came before the epic, Lessing devotes two sections of his *Laokoon* treatise (XXVI-XXVII; *GW*, vol. 2, 940–53) to proving the contrary and Vergil's originality. Secondly, Vergil's text was the artifact first known and the one in relation to which the statue was measured when it was rediscovered in 1506. It therefore forms the basis for the reception of the statue.

even as the moment of his death is at hand. Indeed Vergil's composition of the entire episode is designed to accentuate the importance of Laocoon by drawing the attention of his audience to his figure and retaining it. The narrative, at this juncture, has no other justification. If one tries to make sense of the sequence of the action as Vergil relates it, one stumbles on repeated inconsistencies. Laocoon had earlier offended the god to whom the wooden horse was dedicated with his attempt to warn the Trojans against accepting the horse into their city by throwing a spear into its side. In punishment two serpents rise up from the sea as Laocoon sacrifices a bull at Neptune's altar, and

> *illi agmine certo*
> *Laocoonta petunt; et primum parva duorum.*
> (*Aen.* 2, 212–213)

At the sight of these monstrous serpents, prudence prevails and all flee, abandoning Laocoon to his fate. Among the fleeing would presumably be the sons, who, we know, are at some distance from Laocoon since he must hasten to their aid. If that is the case, why should serpents specifically *agmine certo Laocoonta petentes* be deflected from their divinely appointed task and make a deviation to devour a pair of spectators?

The logic of the story is clearly not dictated by narrative requirements; rather it is necessitated by the needs of drama: by the wish to heighten the pathos of Laocoon's fate. The telling of the story should sweep, not lead, the listener along. Laocoon, the priest of Neptune, attempted to warn his fellow citizens of their danger, a warning which they ignored despite the fact that the side of the horse rang out hollowly under the impact of the blow. Their failure was a sign that the gods had averted their eyes from the Trojans. Nonetheless, Laocoon continued to execute his duties, sacrificing to the gods and attempting to rescue his children even though he knew the action to be futile. He died in the performance of a human being's three defining activities in antiquity: as a priest, he fulfilled the responsibilities of a mortal to the gods; as a citizen, those of the individual towards society; as a *paterfamilias*, those of the individual to the family. Laocoon's fault was not a personal one in the modern sense of the word, nor was his fate a personal one. That his children should be slaughtered before his eyes merely elevated the horror and pathos of the moment for the Romans, who felt it the gravest rupture of the natural order that children, the future representatives of the *gens*, should die before their parents. The punishment of Laocoon also foreshadowed the fate of Troy; as Laocoon and his family were extirpated root and branch, so too would Troy be destroyed. The power of the portrayal is such that greatness and nobility are not inappropriate words to describe the stature of Laocoon's heroism.

The sense of duty on which the tragedy hinges is very Roman. Likewise, the masterful evocation of the human cost of it is very Vergilian. The episodes of the *Aeneid* are replete with such examples, as is the entire conception of the epic.

The understanding of it lies at the core of such words as *pius* and *grandanimus*. It is however a notion alien to the interests of the eighteenth century and contrary to its sensibility. Goethe, for example, is at loss to explain the presence of the Laocoon episode:

> Man ist höchst ungerecht gegen Virgilen und die Dichtkunst, wenn man das geschlossenste Meisterwerk der Bildhauerarbeit mit der episodischen Behandlung in der Aeneis auch nur einen Augenblick vergleicht. Da einmal der unglückliche vertriebene Aeneas selbst erzählen soll, daß er und seine Landsleute die unverzeihliche Torheit begangen haben, das bekannte Pferd in ihre Stadt zu führen, so muß der Dichter nur darauf denken, wie die Handlung zu entschuldigen sei? Alles ist auch darauf angelegt, und die Geschichte des Laokoons steht hier als ein rhetorisches Argument, bei dem eine Übertreibung, wenn sie nur zweckmäßig ist, gar wohl gebilligt werden kann. . . .
>
> So steht also die Geschichte Laokoons im Virgil bloß als Mittel zu einem höhern Zwecke, und es ist noch eine große Frage, ob die Begebenheit an sich ein poetischer Gegenstand sei?[21]

Formally Goethe's point is valid: Vergil must account for the fall of Troy. But then any writer must move his plot from A to B. That Goethe should fail utterly to understand its poetic justification indicates how incomprehensible its presuppositions have become both to him and to his age. In a letter to Schiller (23/12/1797), Goethe expresses even more categorically the same opinion, speaking this time of the whole episode of the fall of Troy: "Virgils rhetorisch sentimentale Behandlung kann hier nicht in Betracht kommen."[22] The point that does come across clearly to Goethe and his age is that the episode exudes a meretricious pathos, an indulgence in feeling which, bereft of any deeper justification, is empty, a purely rhetorical display of great technical virtuosity. It remains an affect unredeemed by any intimation of grandeur or nobility in Goethe's estimation; here was a great pathos in want of an explanation.[23]

---

[21]Johann Wolfgang Goethe, "Über Laokoon" (1797/98), *Sämtliche Werke nach Epochen seines Schaffens*, ed. Klaus H. Kiefer et al. (Münchener Ausgabe), vol. 4/2 (Munich: Hanser, 1986) 87–88, of 20/1 vols. to date, *SW*, ed. Karl Richter et al. (Munich: Hanser, 1985-). All citations from Goethe are from this edition.

[22]Goethe, *SW*, vol. 8/1, 472.

[23]It was Richard Heinze's detailed examination of exactly how Vergil constructed his narrative that led to a revaluation of Vergil in Germany at the turn of the twentieth century. The first portion of his study is devoted to this episode: cf. *Virgils epische Technik*, 3rd ed. (1915; Stuttgart: WBG, 1989), 1–81. On exactly this point, the older criticism was declared obsolete: "Damit werden die klassischen Deutungen (Lessing, *Laokoon*; Schiller, *Über das Pathetische*; Goethe, *Über Laokoon*; Herder, *Kritische Wälder*) hinfällig," in Karl Büchner, *P. Vergilius Maro: Der Dichter der Römer* (Stuttgart: Druckenmüller, 1957) 327.

Goethe's observation is identical to that of Winckelmann. He too felt the pathos of the Vergilian episode and transferred it to the statue while giving it a new justification. Winckelmann's lingering over the details of Laocoon's suffering, his dwelling on the children's cries "um Hülfe" and on the "väterliche Herz" revealed in "den wehmütigen Augen" seizes on the feeling of the Vergilian account for the same purpose: namely for the sake of magnifying through emotion the importance of the moment. "Im Gesichte des Laocoons," there stands revealed the human spirit. Crucial to that spirit is that life should not force from it an admission of its own negation:

> So wie die Tiefe des Meers allezeit ruhig bleibt, die Oberfläche mag noch so wüten, ebenso zeiget der Ausdruck in den Figuren der Griechen bei allen Leidenschaften eine große und gesetzte Seele.[24]

To demonstrate that the statue and, by extension, the Greeks, possessed a true greatness of spirit which others have misunderstood, he argued that a cry was tantamount to an admission of negation. Vergil permits Laocoon to emit a cry contrary to the dictates of the beautiful; the mouth of the statue, according to Winckelmann, does not admit the possibility of a cry. Winckelmann draws support for this contention from Jacopo Sadoleto, who is the only other candidate in this hermeneutic circle.[25]

Following the rediscovery of the statue in 1506, Sadoleto wrote in that same year a poem entitled *De Laocoontis statua*.[26] Winckelmann cites it as his source for the contention that Laocoon utters "ein ängstliches und beklemmtes Seufzen."[27] In point of fact Sadoleto mentions that Laocoon utters first a *gemi-*

---

[24] Winckelmann, *Gedanken*, 20.

[25] The texts most important for the interpretation of the Laocoon statue are Pliny's comment (cf. fn. 9), the episode from Vergil and a poem by Jacopo Sadoleto, which, according to Andreae, ushers in, after the initial phase of wonderment, "die zweite Phase...die der an Sadoletus anknüpfenden literarischen Auseinandersetzung mit dem Werk im Zeitalter der deutschen Klassik. Das auslösende Ereignis ist die Abfassung von J.J. Winckelmanns Schrift *Gedanken*..." (Andreae, *Laokoon und die Gründung*, 14). Preiß provides an extensive analysis of the innumerable references before Winckelmann to the statue found mostly, though by no means exclusively, in travel guides and letters (*Die wissenschaftliche Beschäftigung*). Hafner gives the most easily accessible and clearest account of the discovery of the Laocoon and the initial reaction to it complete with copies of the above mentioned texts and translations of them (*Die Laokoon-Gruppen*, 9–20). Cf. also Daltrop, *Die Laokoongruppe*. For the remnants of other ancient portrayals of Laocoon before Vergil's see Andreae, *Laokoon und die Gründung*, 149–51.

[26] Lessing prints the poem in its entirety in a footnote to *Laokoon* (*GW*, vol. 2, 825–27), from which note all citations of the poem are taken. The poem is also reprinted by Hafner, *Die Laokoon-Gruppen*, 15–17.

[27] Winckelmann, *Gedanken*, 20.

tum ingentem, then, as pain and exhaustion mount, a *murmur anhelum*, neither of which can be construed as "ängstlich," "beklemmt" or a "Seufzen." Instead Sadoleto's imagination seems so fired by the Vergilian account that his enthusiasm presents things to his eyes not to be found in the statue. Perhaps thinking of the gore and black poison bespattering Vergil's Laocoon (poison is always black, a proleptic sign of corruption), he envisions that the snakes' constrictions with their pressure *liuentesque atro distendunt sangiune uenas* —but the statue is of white marble. Or again, when relating the fate of the younger son, he preserves the sequence of the action from Vergil: first the son, then the father. Vergil states that the father sees the serpent consuming (*depascitur*) the limbs of his sons; Sadoleto tells us that the serpent has shredded the boy's limbs, consumed his chest, and now supports the expiring body in its coils. He even repeats the Vergilian word, *depasta*. Such a description bears only a loose relation to the statue that one can actually see with one's eyes. "Hievon sieht man nichts in der Gruppe," as Goethe notes in reference to this portion of Sadoleto's description.[28] Of equal interest, he attributes the source of the error to Sadoleto's misfortune of allowing himself to be influenced by Vergil. The degree to which the Vergilian account prejudices the eyes of the observer, he acknowledges in the details, but not in the conception: namely that the suffering bears witness to a great pathos for a purpose.

Sadoleto assumes the drama of the story, but the explanation of that drama in relation to the statue does not interest him. Rather Sadoleto elaborates at length on the magnitude of the body's suffering, even including some details of a struggle against the serpents. He does not, however, elevate it to an expression of the inner spirit. Of importance for Winckelmann, Sadoleto also states that the younger son, the one on the left, summons his father as he dies: *suprema genitorem uoce cientis*. The use of *cieo* not only makes more pronounced the poignant drama of the situation, but it also inverts the Vergilian account which mentions no summoning shrieks from the children, only a father hastening to their aid without prompting. Of the other son, he notes that he *horret ad adspectum miseri patris* before dissolving into tears. It is the sons who weep for the father, not he for them; the adjective *miserus* is applied to the father, not the children as in Vergil's version, and there is no mention of any help, although the younger son does cry out in death to the father.[29]

---

[28] Goethe, "Propyläen. Eine periodische Schrift" (1799; more commonly "Anzeige der Propyläen"), *SW*, vol. 6/2, 134.

[29] The suggestive power of the Vergilian phrase *Laocoonta auxilio subeuntem* continues undiminished. The translation offered next to the poem in the Hanser edition of Lessing's *Laokoon* gives for the Latin:

> *iamque alterius depasta <serpens> cruentum*
> *Pectus suprema genitorem voce cientis...*

Winckelmann takes the emphasis on the father's physical suffering and the sentimental portrayal of the sons by Sadoleto and combines it with the pathos of Vergil or, if one prefers, with the pathos of the interpretative tradition. He elevates the manifest suffering of the Laocoon group to a question of the fundamental attributes of the human spirit and of Greek art. Nonetheless, his use of the phrase "um Hülfe schreyen" attests the subtle persistence of the Vergilian hermeneutic. Sadoleto mentions only a last cry of the son to his father, Vergil mentions only a father hastening to the aid of his children, Winckelmann puts the help of the father into the mouth of the son.[30]

Winckelmann's account transforms the older pathos associated with the statue. He discharges it from its ancient colors and presses it into modern service. What he borrows from the Vergilian Laocoon is his stoic steadfastness, that is, the conception of a destructive confrontation between the individual and the world and the desirability of meeting that confrontation with resolve. No longer does the nobility and grandeur of Laocoon serve a Latin understanding of the

---

the German:

> ...schon zerbeißt sie die Brust des einen, der mit letzter Stimme den Erzeuger zu Hilfe ruft.... (827)

Cieo means to cause to move, and then by degrees: to stir, stimulate, call, summon. There is no reason, looking at the statue, why the boy should wish either to stimulate his father or to summon him. His father, inches away, does not need summoning, nor does it seem possible that he should be stimulated to still greater exertion. The same is true of the translation offered more recently in the "Stellenkommentar" to *Laokoon* in Gotthold Ephraim Lessing, *Werke*, ed. Wilfried Barner et al., vol. 5/2 (Frankfurt am Main: Deutscher Klassiker Verlag, 1990) 769: "Und schon ist die blutiger Brust des einen zerfressen, der, indem er mit versagender Stimme den Vater zu Hilfe ruft." Hafner's translation of the last portion of the lines in question, "der den Vater ruft mit ersterbender Stimme" (*Die Laokoon-Gruppen*, 17), while more accurate, still does not resolve the problem of *cieo* as it ignores the causative sense of the verb. To make sense of *cieo* one requires the Vergilian gloss, and the translations reflect this.

[30] The question of the expression on the faces of the figures is of interest. They are all in essence identical with the exception of Laocoon's being larger and more carefully executed. Each head is tilted in relation to the shoulders, the eyebrows are canted upwards and inward causing the forehead to wrinkle, the hair is tousled and matted, and the mouth is open slightly, allowing for sound and interpretation. The common treatment of expression suggests that one is dealing with an established artistic convention (cf. Andreae, *Laokoon und die Kunst*, 5–35). Winckelmann would seem to have taken the notion of the children crying out from Sadoleto but the notion of help and the father's distress from Vergil, both of which elements serve to heighten the pathos and, in Winckelmann, to underline the magnanimity of Laocoon. It is also ironic to note that Winckelmann is prepared to call the sound the dying child utters a "Schrei" when his mouth is no more open than that of Laocoon.

world. Virtue is not measured by the degree to which one fulfills the obligations of the human community. Instead grandeur and nobility of spirit exemplify humanity in its "natural" state, or, in that odd synonym of the eighteenth century, in its Greek state.

That the suffering of Laocoon sits uneasily with a conception of the beautiful as a unity within difference, a harmonious whole composed of variegated parts, remains unobserved in the eighteenth century.[31] Only the differentiation of the beautiful through the development of the companion concept of the sublime permits the exploration of the tension between the visibly "baroque" statue and visual serenity, on the one hand, and, on the other hand, between the beautiful and the disfigurement of extreme suffering; between, on the one hand, Winckelmann's dictum "edle Einfalt und stille Größe" and the insistence "da, wohin der größte Schmerz gelegt ist, zeiget sich auch die größte Schönheit," on the other hand; both of which statements are made in relation to the same statue.[32] Lessing returns Laocoon's pathos and his suffering to its proper context by association when he considers it in relation to suffering in tragedy and takes Sophocles's *Philoctetes* as his example. The connection remains implicit until Schiller takes up the matter of pathos directly in relation to tragedy in *Über das Pathetische* (1793):

---

[31] Simon Richter makes this observation the starting point for his recent book, *Laocoon's Body and the Aesthetics of Pain: Winckelmann, Lessing, Herder, Moritz, Goethe* (Detroit: Wayne State UP, 1992). He begins: "By Butler's account the Laocoon is merely the accidental object of Winckelmann's visionary aesthetics. It could as easily have been the Belvedere Apollo, the Antinous, or any other classical statue. But Winckelmann's descriptions of these other statues never attained the theoretical significance of the Laocoon nor were they in any way as productive of discourse" (11). He argues that the association is not accidental, since the discourse of pain decenters the classical aesthetical concept of the beautiful. If, however, the dynamic of the Laocoon description stems from Vergil's dramatic pathos and does not belong to the concept of harmonious beauty, then suffering is a moral instance, not a subtext of mutilation. Richter mentions that pain forms a part of the concept of tragedy from the time of Aristotle but does not explore the connection, preferring instead to regard pain as a marginalized subtext (cf. 33 and 61) and search for unconscious motivations: "The discourse from outside, that is, the historical and the biographical, is theory's body" (43). It is of interest that he omits Schiller in the list of authors he considers in his title. A similar process of discursive othering is pursued by Kevin Parker, "Winckelmann, Historical Difference, and the Problem of the Boy," in: *Eighteenth Century Studies*, vol. 25.4 (1992): 523–44.

[32] Winckelmann, *Geschichte der Kunst*, 106.

> Das erste Gesetz der tragischen Kunst war Darstellung der leidenden Natur. Das zweyte ist Darstellung des moralischen Widerstandes gegen das Leiden.[33]

Oddly, in view of the stated interest in tragedy, Schiller gives as his most extensive example of this dynamic not some incident from drama but the Laocoon episode from Vergil. In doing so, he confirms the categories of analysis from Winckelmann and Lessing: he stresses that Laocoon depicts humanity as subject to nature, as "leidende Natur," and also humanity as having an ideal nature capable of opposing the physical impositions of the body. The starkness of the dichotomy in the Vergilian depiction obviously appeals to Schiller's Kantian predilection for the sharp separation of the noumenal and the phenomenal, since he bothers to introduce Laocoon into the same context in *Das Ideal und das Leben* (1795).[34] At the same time, Schiller's emphasis on the moral freedom of humanity assimilates the treatment of the Laocoon pathos to the sublime, an aesthetic category more appropriate to it.[35] Schiller moves the Laocoon incident, and thereby Vergil, closer to the interest of the late eighteenth century in the sublime as an experience which compels the individual to recognize the incommensurability of nature according to his subjective categories and to contemplate the isolation of humanity from nature. Schiller, however, fails to pursue his analysis beyond observing the ferocity of nature, on the one hand, and the freedom of spirit on the part of Laocoon on the other. He too does not shift to consider what is the moral purpose pursued by Laocoon, contenting himself with merely affirming its presence. Perhaps to have expected Schiller to ponder the motivation of the Laocoon scene within the context of the ancient epic is too much. Ultimately Vergil does not conceive of the sublime as a moment of separation, nor is his solution of a fate realizing itself historically in the dominance of Rome as a universal community of any great appeal to Schiller. Instead he remains closely dependent on Winckelmann's idea of nature and humanity's relation to it as he exploits the Laocoon episode for his purposes. And Winckelmann's interpretation is in its presuppositions, though not in its conclusions, dependent on the Vergilian account.

---

[33]Friedrich Schiller, "Über das Pathetische," *Werke*, ed. Benno von Wiese, Nationalausgabe (Weimar: Hermann Böhlaus Nachfolger, 1962), vol. 20, 199.

[34]For an examination of Schiller's relation to Winckelmann see Ludwig Uhlig, "Schiller und Winckelmann," *Jahrbuch für internationale Germanistik*, 17.1 (1985): 131–146; and Rehm 191–228.

[35]The final paragraph of Schiller's treatise *Vom Erhabenen* (1793) in the section on the "Pathetischerhabene" is almost identical in its formulation to the sentence cited above from *Über das Pathetische*: "Aus diesem Grundsatz fließen die beiden Fundamentalgesetze aller tragischen Kunst. Diese sind *erstlich*: Darstellung der leidenden Natur; *zweytens*: Darstellung der moralischen Selbstständigkeit im Leiden" (*Werke*, vol. 20, 195).

Winckelmann's sharp turn from the Romans to the Greeks may owe its impetus to the necessity of distinguishing his vision of ancient Greece from the subsequent spread of ancient culture to Rome, but that ostensible rejection does not gainsay the fact that he had first to pass through Rome both physically and intellectually to reach his beloved Greece. Precisely because the Greeks were so thoroughly enmeshed in a Roman embrace, Winckelmann had no well-defined set of analytical distinctions independent of that tradition with which to work as he began to extricate the Greeks from that embrace. He found himself compelled unwittingly to work with those bequeathed to him. One may endorse Rehm's statement that "Winckelmann war tatsächlich der Grieche in Rom, derjenige, der von Rom aus Athen und den 'griechischen Geschmack' entdeckte und verkündete und damit das Römische in der Kunst und in der Menschenbildung bekämpfte" as an accurate summary of Winckelmann's intention and effect, but not of his means of accomplishing that end.[36] He may have fled to Greece but he took Rome with him. The Laocoon statue could become the catalyst for his "flash of revelation" because of its associations with the literary tradition definitively shaped by Vergil. The transposition of a literary tradition onto an art-object accounts for the fruitful ambiguity of "edle Einfalt und stille Größe." If one considers the phrase in its aesthetic-literary context, then the notions of Stoicism, suffering, sublimity, pathos, moral will, all inherent in the Vergilian text, come to the fore, as, for example, in Schiller. If one considers it in its art-historical context, then the insistence that the pose of the body reflect more directly the tranquillity of the soul comes to the fore; a condition which, for those of us who come after Winckelmann, seems best fulfilled by the sculpture of classical Greek antiquity, if of any period. As a result the Laocoon statue can only seem from this perspective increasingly "baroque" and a most puzzling, indeed inexplicable example of serenity and grandeur. In this vein, one would concentrate on the physical pain manifest in the statue, as Goethe does, to cite but one example. Both of these positions may draw support from Winckelmann's contradictory statement, as first one side, first the literary text, and then the other, the artistic object itself, is foremost in his mind.

---

[36]Rehm 26.

WALTER D. WETZELS

Physics for the Ladies: Early Literary Voices and Strategies for and against the Popularization of Copernicus and Newton

The idea of making facts, methods, and epistemological concepts of the sciences available to a broader readership began to become a reality during the seventeenth century, and it established itself as a special literary genre during the eighteenth century, occupying a privileged place near or, as some would claim, at the very center of the European Enlightenment. Of course, the popularization of science has accompanied the development of science proper ever since, in the form of many literary genres such as poems, dialogues, plays, letters, biographies and novels, to mention just the traditional printed varieties. Historically, at least two basic conditions for the popularization of the Copernican and later the Newtonian New Science became apparent after Galilei's *Dialogue Concerning the Two Chief World Systems* of 1632 (if one wishes a date). First, with Galilei's popularization of the Copernican system in the vernacular, and carefully composed as a dialogue, not as a treatise, the hermetic tradition of science ended. An open knowledge of nature, in principle accessible to everybody, was shown to be possible. Second, the *Dialogue* was a response to a perceived need, indeed the manifestation of a mission to spread scientific knowledge beyond the circle of experts and the learned elite. Taken together, these conditions characterized the onset of European Enlightenment, the emancipatory movement to free the human mind for a rational understanding of history as well as nature. At a later stage, the New Physics of Newton was obviously the most successful example of the new rationality which had liberated itself from the orthodoxy of authority and was to become the model of the new thinking in all areas of reassessment and inquiry. Thus, popularizing the New Science beginning with Copernicus and culminating in Newton was at the very core of the enterprise — as which the movement of European Enlightenment saw itself. There is also a broader sense in which an investigation into the early history of the popularization of the natural sciences is an important and rewarding undertaking. Along with the development of the sciences, it was and it is through the popular dissemination of this development that a public consciousness developed about the decisive and therefore problematic role of the sciences in the process of civilization itself.

For the Enlightenment, truth, reason, progress towards the good of humankind manifested themselves paradigmatically in the sciences, and most clearly and convincingly in the New Physics. It had become clear that access for everyone to these values was an entitlement for the individual, as well as a historical necessity. The belief in the intrinsic sense and the continuous progress of the rational understanding of reality was at the same time a belief in the unlimited and democratic didactic potential of reason itself, regardless of expertise and privilege.

On the following pages I shall limit myself to what are arguably the two most successful early popularizations of the Copernican and Newtonian physics: Bernard de Fontenelle's *Conversations on the Plurality of Worlds* of 1686, and Francesco Algarotti's *Il Newtonianismo per le Dame* of 1737, the latter explicitly and gratefully modeled after the former.[1] In both cases, it should be mentioned, Gottsched, probably the most prolific and influential popularizer of the Early Enlightenment in Germany, provided the translations into German.

I

Bernard le Bovier de Fontenelle published the first edition of his *Entretiens sur la pluralité des mondes* when he was thirty-one. The fourteenth edition of these *Conversations on the Plurality of Worlds*, still published under his personal supervision, appeared in 1742.[2] It was not the first, but by far the most successful popularization of the new astronomical system of Copernicus during Fontenelle's long life (he died just one month short of his one-hundredth birthday in 1757) to reach the general reading public not only of the late seventeenth, but all through the eighteenth and into the early nineteenth century, when Jérôme

---

[1] Bernhard le Bovier de Fontenelle, *Conversations on the Plurality of Worlds*. Trans. by H. A. Hargreaves, introduction by Nina Rattner Gelbart (Berkeley, Los Angeles, Oxford: University of California Press, 1990). All quotations are from this newest translation and are given in the text with page numbers. Francesco Algarotti's *Il Newtonianismo per le Dame, overro Dialoghi sopra la Luce e i Colori* (Naples, 1737) is quoted from the English translation: Francesco Algarotti, *Sir Isaac Newton's Philosophy explained for the use of the Ladies. In six Dialogues on Light and Colours*. From the Italian of Sig. Algarotti by Elisabeth Carter (London, 1739). Again the quotations in the text are by page numbers of this edition.

[2] The "Translator's Preface" of the edition provides a survey and valuable specifics of the various editions which appeared during Fontenelle's lifetime. H. A. Hargreaves also discusses her choice of the very first edition of 1686 as the basis for her translation, although any number of others, expanded and modernized by the author himself, might have been chosen.

de LaLande, then the director of the Paris Observatory, finally decided to write his own popular version of the new astronomy, *Astronomie des dames* (1820). Fontenelle's instant and continuous success had spread throughout Europe in numerous translations, reprints, pirated prints; it inspired many imitators.

The enormous success which the work enjoyed was due, as I see it, to two factors: first its form, and then the suggestion that the notion of a plurality of worlds could be and should be associated with the notion of these other worlds' being populated like the earth. With all the appeal to the imagination, this latter idea was also highly controversial with respect to the Christian faith. Before taking a closer look at these evening dialogues between a scientifically educated gentleman and a Marquise at her summer residence, it is worthwhile to remember that the work under consideration was first published within a year of Newton's *Principia*. In other words, it deals with the heliocentric system of Copernicus versus the geocentric system of Ptolomy, but it does not know anything as yet of Newton's New Physics and the notion of gravitation. Instead, its explanatory model for the planetary orbits around the sun is the Descartian notion of vortices. In other words, the new astronomy it teaches is pre-Newtonian; but the Copernican revolution in the understanding of the universe was still far from generally known, much less accepted beyond the scientifically educated or informed reading public. It was therefore very much in the didactic spirit of the Enlightenment that Fontenelle conceived of his five (later six) conversations: first on the Copernican system, then two evenings on the Moon, then on Descartes's vortices, and finally on the fixed star as other suns. The sixth evening discussion, added already to the second edition in 1687, presents essentially a summary of the first five. Some of the many editions to be published later were corrected and updated by Fontenelle himself, especially those of 1708 and 1742.

In the Preface, Fontenelle characterizes his enterprise as follows: "I've attempted to bring it to the point where it's neither too dry for men and women of the world nor too playful for scholars" (3). He also is quite explicit as to why he chose a *woman* as a partner in these dialogues, although it is clear that they are meant for men and women alike. He says: "I've placed a woman in these *Conversations* who is being instructed, one who has never heard a syllable about such things. I thought this fiction would serve to make the work more enticing, and to encourage women through the example of a woman who, having nothing of an extraordinary character, without ever exceeding the limitations of a person who has no knowledge of science, never fails to understand what's said to her, and arranges in her mind, without confusion, vortices and worlds. Why would any woman accept inferiority to this imaginary Marquise, who only conceives of those things of which she can't help but conceive" (4). Fontenelle had calculated correctly: the work became the most popular book on science in general and the new astronomy in particular among the emerging and rapidly increasing female readership of the period far into the eighteenth century.[3] There is, however, more at work here than a consideration of a promising market for the book. The educated woman seems in *fact* and as a *"fiction"* (as Fontenelle put it) an ideal student of this particular enterprise. The author could start with a *tabula rasa* as far as knowledge of natural philosophy is concerned, her education having been in the arts and belles-lettres. That is to say, the teacher spoke to an able and uncluttered mind that harbored no prejudices. It was a nimble and logical mind (Fontenelle speaks of the "vivacity of her intelligence" 7), who follows an argument easily (sometimes also critically) and accepts nothing but the logically inevitable conclusions. And it happens in these dialogues that it is the Marquise who admonishes her partner to return to the line of argumentation when he casually and sometimes flirtatiously deviates from the course of the discussion in order to render his presentations more enjoyable, less single-mindedly, to entertain as well as instruct, or rather to do both at the same time.

It would be wrong, therefore, to see these conversations in the lineage of the Socratic dialogue. Fontenelle certainly and consciously chooses the ideal literary form for didactic purposes: the dialogue. Yet his conversations do not show the rigorous, relentless pursuits of Plato's dialogues, which attempt to call into question the very language used, the concepts employed; they undermine assumptions, in order to lead to the realization that Socrates' opponent did, in fact, not understand the presuppositions, implications, or consequences of his pronouncements. They are a work of demolition. The gentleman whom Fontenelle introduces is a man of the world; broadly educated but by no means a scientist because that would be a form of learned barbarism to his mind. He is witty and seeks to convey knowledge casually; he easily wanders off the argument in order to make some ironic or critical remarks about society, the taste of the times, or simply to flatter the lady. If Fontenelle had had a model in mind at all, it would have been more likely a graceful form of Galilei's *Dialogue Concerning the Two Chief World Systems* rather than Plato.[4]

The first conversation, "The First Evening," begins with an almost romantic depiction of the end of a day, the beginning of nightfall, and then of the night. The beauty of the nightly sky with its stars is evoked; the night which veils again all that has the day unveiled, while revealing all that was invisible during the day. The diffuse images of a world by day and those of another world at night (more quiet, softer, directing us to the heavens) give rise to what Fontenelle calls

---

[3] Ursula Pia Jauch has counted thirty-three editions until 1764 in French alone. Ursula Pia Jauch, *Damenphilosophie and Männermoral. Von Abbé de Gérard bis Marquis de Sade. Ein Versuch über die lächelnde Vernunft.* (Vienna: Passagen Verlag, 1990) 20. Fontenelle's work is almost always the recommended text on natural science in the many reading lists designed specifically for women.

[4] This characterization of the Socratic method should of course be taken only as the roughest of approximations.

"many pleasantly confused thoughts in us" (10). The important notion here is that the first condition under which new insights might be gained is a confusion or destabilization of our existing, normal state of mind. Only a willing suspense of this normality creates the possibility of something new to be experienced. And in an ingenious anticipation of the issues to be discussed, he weaves into his romantic evocation of the pleasures of the night the remark: "Our thoughts are freer because we're so foolish as to imagine ourselves the only ones abroad to dream" (10). It is an *anticipation* because the focus of the discussion soon to begin is the notion that the moon (like the earth) is inhabited; indeed that all other planets are, and finally that the planets in all the other solar systems orbiting around *their* suns are. Therefore, the implication which is later made explicit is that others, too, dream us, or dream of us here on *this* star. The reverie about the virtues of the night ends with an even clearer expression of the theme about to be treated. The Marquise has just accused the sun of concealing and overpowering the stars, when her partner cries out: "I can never forgive it for making me lose sight of all those worlds" (10). Instantly, the Marquise is wide-awake: "What do you mean, worlds?" The plural is here a simple, yet very clever grammatical device not only to introduce Copernicus's revolutionary displacement of the earth from the center of the universe, but also a signal of the existential and, of course, the religious implications for humans. Later, he speaks of Copernicus's violent hands, which "pluck up the earth and send her far from the center of the universe," "he destroys and breaks into pieces old cycles and spheres" (10).

It is by conjecture only, as Fontenelle makes clear, that we surmise the moon and other stars to be inhabited. But the inference is not an idle speculation; it is based on observations which show that there are clear similarities between the stars, which similarities we can observe through the telescope: such as rotation about their axis, an orbit around the sun, moons, certain surface features which seem similar to lakes and mountains, etc. Yet, on the other hand, nobody has ever observed that those surface-features, in the case of the earth's moon, ever change. Wouldn't one expect to see certain features change depending on the condition of the atmosphere? Don't clouds, for example, obscure features of the earth's surface at times? Then, perhaps, there is no atmosphere on the moon, and if not, how could the moon be inhabited? The questions of whether or not the moon had an atmosphere was a hotly debated issue in the scientific community through most of the eighteenth century, long after the question of possible inhabitants had been laid to rest, except in utopian fiction. The Marquise is being drawn into a real scientific debate; she realizes something about the interplay of a hypothesis based on analogy and a scientific theory (or philosophy) based on observation. Fontenelle also articulates with laconic irony the drive behind and the dilemma of the human mind that attempts to understand nature: "All philosophy is based on two things only: curiosity and poor eyesight" (11). Nevertheless, not only does the Marquise receive a solid and fairly comprehensive factual introduction into modern astronomy, she also gets a notion of the new scientific method, and she is led as well to understand a scientific principle of enormous importance, namely that the simplicity of the new world view has won out over the ever-increasing complexity of the old one. She finally is made aware of the human condition underlying all endeavors to comprehend the world: an intellectual curiosity which will later also be labeled hubris, and an existential or biological limitation (poor eyesight is the metaphor) which will later be used to persuade human beings to forego what was not meant for them to know and see. These were, of course, the main arguments of Christian orthodoxy, anticipated already by Fontenelle himself, as we will see.

The rhetorical registers employed by Fontenelle are impressive. What cannot be shown either by direct observation (there simply isn't a telescope at hand) on these leisurely evening walks or by mathematical deduction (a discipline totally alien to the Marquise and probably not very familiar to her mentor, either), is explained by the ancient methods of comparison: simile and analogy, or by exemplifying a general theory with a specific case, or by the transformation of an abstract concept into a vivid image, a metaphor, or by rendering a problem by narrating its history. The whole traditional arsenal of didactic rhetoric is mobilized, but always in such a way that the ancient maxim is observed: *prodesse et delectare*. For example, Fontenelle compares the notion of a person who considers the earth to be immovable to the illusion of a passenger on a ship who is not able to comprehend that *he* is moving, not the water. When the Marquise remarks that this passenger could be helped by pointing out to him the changing scenery on the bank of the river, her mentor agrees and remarks that the "banks" of the planet earth by which one can tell and measure its movement are the fixed stars. Earlier he had compared the spectacle of astronomy to an opera, except that natural philosophers, unlike the audience of an opera, are not satisfied with what is in plain view. Rather, they want to understand "the wheels and counterweights" (11) which make the performance possible. If natural philosophy presents now, in "a kind of auction" of new ideas (15), as the Marquise very aptly puts it, a rather mechanical world view, it appears at least in the image of an intricate, superb clock, where every part perfectly works together with every other part in grandiose simplicity (12). It is noteworthy that the Marquise, while observing the rather mechanical nature of the new world view, recognizes the new beauty of perfection that superb mechanics can exhibit. Noteworthy, too, is the image of a perpetual auction of ideas as the action which drives scientific progress (and perhaps more than that). The auction of ideas of which the Marquise speaks conveys two very important ingredients of scientific discovery: openness and competition for the best explanation. In the end, the Marquise embraces the Copernican system as the clearly superior model of the universe, and her teacher gracefully admits her to the circle of natural philosophers who have seen the truth, and who are therefore called upon to spread it.

However, even after everything else is settled in favor of the Copernican system and Descartes's vortices, the notion of these many other worlds' being populated like ours remains, despite many plausible physical inferences; even despite the admonition that *denying* inhabitants to other stars would be nothing else but human vanity, this sensitive point remains tantalizingly open. It is clearly the most tempting and perhaps even most haunting question, that obviously drives both the curiosity and the irritation of the reader. And Fontenelle exploits this issue to the fullest while also anticipating the predictable reaction of some of his readers. He says in his Preface: "There are the scrupulous people who will think there is a danger in respect to religion in placing inhabitants elsewhere than on Earth... But what may be surprising to you is that religion simply has nothing to do with this system, in which I fill an infinity of worlds with inhabitants... The descendants of Adam have not spread to the Moon nor sent colonies there. Therefore the men on the Moon are not sons of Adam" (5–6). This is a clever, but a somewhat tautological argumentation, and it furthermore begs the question. A few lines later he pleads with disarming modesty that one must not burden his work with explications and terms which "are too serious and dignified to be placed in a book as unserious as this" (6). Who would do that, after such an elegant and diplomatic retreat? Well, some did: the Catholic Church placed the *Entretiens sur la pluralité des mondes* on the index of prohibited books one year after its first appearance, namely 1687. That was perhaps no surprise; what *is* surprising, though, is that as late as 1752 a series of "Letters against Fontenelle" was published in Venice in an Italian journal called *Lettere moderne* by an anonymous friend of the Church.[5] Fontenelle was 95, and the Copernican system had been incorporated into the grand design of Newton's New Physics on the basis of numerous and irrefutable experiments and observations, and systematized into an all-encompassing, logically compelling mathematical theory. The writer of these letters, again to a lady living at her country estate, tells her to be suspicious of an author who can express himself with such deceptive elegance, and who doesn't mention God, the creator of the whole universe, even once. The writer also observes, sometimes with a certain measure of justification, that the credibility of the arguments often is not based on the facts, but on the phrasing of the playful, seductive wit of the author. Sensing correctly that his lady feels quite attracted by Fontenelle's dialogues, the writer warns that works like this should only be put into the hands of those who can

---

[5]These letters are quoted from a German translation which appeared in the *Allgemeines Magazin der Natur, Kunst und Wissenschaften* (Leipzig: Gleditsche Handlung, 1753) anonymously under the title "Briefe wider Herrn Fontenelles Gespräche von mehr als einer Welt" (118–201). The subtitle mentions as source only an Italian journal *Lettere Moderne* (Venecia, 1752). I am grateful to the Herzog August Bibliothek in Wolfenbüttel for assistance in my research. Unfortunately, I have not been able to locate the Italian original. The translation from the German version into English is my own. What follows is a summary of the main points of the text.

read them properly. Weapons, butcher knives, and strong medications are to be handled only by those who can do so professionally. The hand of the Church must shield the unprepared from corruption by the kind of knowledge that puts them in harm's way. According to this writer, seven-eighths of the intellectual curiosity which Fontenelle had declared as one of the two necessary conditions for philosophy is the result of education, company, and, last but not least, of books. Apparently, all potentially dubious entities. Our real, that is, natural curiosity is very limited (one-eighth at his counting), and can be satisfied easily. The whole enterprise of modern natural philosophy has its origins in the attempt to order reality according to our imagination, and it tempts us to mistrust divine revelations as laid down in what the writer of these letters calls the "System of Moses." Hubris, in other words, is at the root of modern science, the desire to know what we are not meant to know and don't need to know. The notion, incidentally, that modern science is an attempt "to order reality according to our imagination" (132), provided the term imagination is understood properly, is not necessarily an inept characterization. However, the anonymous writer fails to mention the role of the ultimate test for such imagination, the experiment. And the recourse to the Mosaic system is simply the ancient recourse to authority as the ultimate test for truth.

Not that all arguments of Fontenelle's opponent are from well-known Christian, fundamentalist positions; some take on the rather shaky comparisons between earth and moon on their debatable scientific merits, and the reader realizes that the writer is fairly well acquainted with astronomy, although he detests what he calls its "sinister geometry" (130). This is probably a reference to the applications of calculus in geometry. And the writer is very leery of things beyond the capability of the human eye and that only telescopes can reveal. Astronomers should turn their gaze away from the heavens, and should listen to and observe what happens right here on our "poor earth" (146). Therefore: "Praise to the honest man Moses who was content with having assured us that the Earth stands still, and beyond that allowed the planets to move as God wanted them to move without concerning himself with their various orbits. Indeed, all we need is to calculate the eclipses and the changes of the seasons, which is necessary in order to plant our fields properly. With that we know enough" (151). A remarkable but familiar mixture: advocating a certain social responsibility of science; settling for the astronomy of the Old Testament; justifying scientific pursuits for basic human survival only, leaving the intricacies of the universe to its creator. (The utilitarian aspect of eclipses escapes me, unless they were interpreted as ominous signs of a power not only to be respected but also feared.) Above all hovers the ancient verdict of unguided reason as hubris.

However, Fontenelle's critic is keenly aware of the real threat, and the real issue which the new astronomy raises, emancipated from biblical and all other traditional philosophical authority. He wants to get to the heart of the matter by asking his lady very directly: "Do you want this whole world to have been created by God or not?" (163) In other words, he squarely confronts his lady with a choice between Moses on the one hand, and Copernicus on the other. It is a genuine and basic either-or, a radicalism that stands in stark contrast to Fontenelle's obliging diplomacy. Yet, in a sense, it is more serious, and definitely shows a troubled awareness of the true revolution in science that has taken place with its promises and its perils: a system of the universe in which the human being looks in vain or has to look again for place and purpose.

II

When Newton died in 1727, Alexander Pope wrote the famous epitaph:

> Nature, and Nature's Laws lay hid in Night.
> God said, *Let Newton be!* and all was *Light*.

As no one had done before him, Newton had first enlightened, though by no means popularized, natural philosophy through his *Principia*, first published in 1687, and then — less forbiddingly mathematical and in English — through his *Opticks*, first published in 1704. Francesco Algarotti's *Il Newtonianismo per le Dame* was one of the first, and by all accounts the most famous popularization of Newton's *Opticks*. Its first Italian edition appeared in 1737; the first French edition in 1738; the first English in 1739, and the first German in 1745, translated not from the original Italian, but from the French version. The model for Algarotti's work is, as has been mentioned, Fontenelle's *Entretiens sur la pluralité des mondes* of 1686, and the French translator notes with satisfaction that the Italian author had properly praised the French "Chef-d'oeuvre inimitable" of this particular genre.[6] He attests to the erudition, the *esprit*, the pleasant and illuminating method of presentation and "a charming dexterity to render the theses and experiments of Newton" without geometry or "embarrassing calculations" (V). De Castera, the French translator, also makes some critical observations, to be sure: the first is directed toward Algarotti's partisanship for British science and scientists to the detriment of the French scientific tradition, especially that of Descartes and Malebranche; the second has to do with style, more precisely with long-winded phrases. Indeed, Algarotti shows nothing but veneration for Newton and the British, and nothing but disdain (*mépris souverain*)

---

[6]The French version is: *Le Newtonianism pour les dames, ou Entretiens sur la lumiere, sur les couleurs, et sur l'attraction,* Traduit de l'Italien de M. Algarotti par M. Dupperon de Castera. Tome I, II (Paris, 1738). The translations are from the first English version by E. Carter (see note 1) who included de Castera's preface in her translation. (I should mention that this section on Algarotti's work has its origin in a paper which I gave at the Bristol meeting of the International Society for Eighteenth Century Studies. A summary of the brief paper appeared under the title "Newton for the Ladies: Algarotti's Popularization of Newton's Optics." *Studies on Voltaire and the Eighteenth Century*, vol. 304. [Oxford: The Voltaire Foundation, 1992] 1152–55.)

for Descartes and older schools of rationalism. He calls them, because of their tendency toward speculative system-building, "novelistic minds" (*esprits Romanesques*), exposing themselves to the "insults of observations and experiments" (VII). However, the French defense of Descartes's legacy of rational thought is perhaps less important than the criticism leveled against the style in parts of Algarotti's work. Features of proper discourse are, of course, central to the issue of a popularization of science for the educated lay audience. De Castera remarks that at times the Italian is too diffuse, with phrases which are too long and convoluted. One would expect that sort of critique coming from a tradition of stylistic beauty which is based on brevity, conciseness, clarity, the *mot propre*. More importantly, one should notice that there is not the slightest doubt about the capacity of that kind of normal, clear human discourse to render scientific facts and scientific thinking adequately. The criticism about the occasional lack of lucidity and conciseness affirms implicitly that the humanistic and the scientific realm still belong to the same linguistic universe. The French translator refers with some relish to the explicit promise the Italian author had given in his preface: "I have taken the utmost Care to avoid those perplexed and long Periods closed by the Verb, which only serve to run the Reader out of Breath, and are besides repugnant to good Sense, and much less agreeable to the Genius of our Language than is generally believed" (X). De Castera observes that the author begins with two sentences of which the first runs eight, the second seven lines. Altogether, as De Castera remarks, he saved a total of ten pages by clearing up Algarotti's style. Should one call this pedantic arrogance or rather a consciousness that the formal linguistic quality of the text translates into effective instruction?

Algarotti prides himself on having written clearly and concisely, and at the same time on having allowed himself "Images and Turns of Wit" (IX), so that his work became "neither Grammar nor Sonnet" (XVI), yet served very much the cultivation of the mind. Surprisingly, he formulates his central problem of transforming scientific discourse into a literary one as the difficulty in how "to recivilize this savage Philosophy" (VI). There is a curious paradox at work here: Newton's science is by any standard an extraordinary achievement of the human mind, yet it is also considered here as outside of the province of civilization, i.e., outside of civilized discourse. The monasticism of mathematics, the inhuman or nonhumanistic rigor of deductive logic together with the all-consuming pursuit of nature's secrets through relentless experimentation are seen as alien, alienating, that is to say, barbaric. That being the case, the popularizing of science becomes for the author the noble task of bringing home an endeavor gone awry or at least estranged from the mainstream of human civilization.

The setting is a summer palace or retreat on a peninsula at the Adriatic Sea. The lady is a marchioness as with Fontenelle; the dialogues take place in a parklike garden. This setting provides both the actual ambiance and the symbolism for the enterprise of popularizing, i.e., *civilizing* of Newton's physics.

The term *vulgarization* would be quite misleading since the recapturing of science from its barbaric isolation is an endeavor to reintegrate it into human culture. The noble lady who is the partner in these six dialogues taking place over a leisurely five-day period is described as having the "Charms of Wit," "refined sentiments," "and the most polite Imagination" (expected attributes), but also as combining them with an "uncommon strength of Judgement" and a "learned curiosity" (4). The author speculates that such rare accomplishments might be the reason "that learning in Ladies does not meet with so universal an Applause from the World as their Beauty" (5).

The point of departure for the entire enterprise that follows is, to the reader's surprise, *poetry*. But it is there and in the arts where the traditional education of the ladies of nobility are to be found, where sentiments and competence can be naturally assumed. The author evokes the splendor of Italian, French, English poetry, and cites Alexander Pope to her, quoting the cryptic lines:

> The seven-fold Light
> Whence every pleasing Charm of Colour springs,
> And forms the gay variety of Things (11).

Newton's prismatic colors, embedded in these lines, are presented as a challenge for literary interpretation, that is, in an ambiance in which the marchioness is accustomed to move. In fact, she knows these lines, and has always found them as enigmatic as Chinese hieroglyphics. She demands an explanation right away, but is told that it would be wiser to follow the example of the theater, where in a play the persons come to know each other only at the end. A plot has to evolve first, and only at the end will it shed light on the whole. The plot in this case is Algarotti's historical sketch of Natural Philosophy from ancient times to almost the recent period. Indian mysteries and Egyptian hieroglyphics are only hinted at. But the philosophy of Greece, while not so much treated in its details, comes in for a revealing criticism of its mode and its substance, because both were detrimental to experiment and observation. The *mode* was that of privileging rhetoric. The natural roots were "extirpated by the Eloquence of a Man whose Discourses were distinguished by a certain grave and elegant Pleasantry, which made him Master of the most powerful Arts of Persuasion, and who had been judged by the Oracle the wisest among Mortals" (21). And the new *substance* of philosophy became ethics. It is worth quoting how Algarotti perceived the unfortunate turn of philosophical thinking which Socrates brought about: "He asserted that we have nothing to do with what is above us, and strove to reclaim our Curiosity and Studies from natural to moral Objects; from the Combinations of the Universe to the little Chaos of human Extravagances, and from that Rapture with which we are transported by the Contemplation of our own Emptiness" (21–22). The many schools of philosophy and theology that followed are characterized by the "Noise of empty Words and the

Tyranny of Names" and dismissed as being led by "gray-headed Children" who "amused themselves only in fighting with Bubbles" (27). This is the exposition and perhaps the first act of the intellectual drama Algarotti unfolds for his marchioness. It is then only with Galilei that the perspective is turned toward the outside world again and the foundation is laid for reliable systems based on observation and experimentation. And it is only from there that the derivation of the underlying laws of nature proceeds. Not that everyone after Galilei built on these foundations: Descartes, unfortunately, the last great systematizer, built a "rational System concerning *Light* and *Colour*, when he was entirely ignorant of so many of their Qualities, which Sir *Isaac Newton* afterwards discovered by Observations" (33). In Algarotti's words: The "idle Enigmas of the learned Ignorance of past Ages" are still with us (35). Beginning with the ultimate source of all light on earth, the marchioness inquires: Would not the sun's capacity for emitting light be exhausted one day? With this inquiry, she articulates a well-known and widely discussed problem, which in turn shows that she is different from the largely passive, vivacious yet ignorant partner in the dialogues in which Algarotti's model Fontenelle had presented his marquise. Here, as in many other instances, the new marchioness is shown to be clear-headed, persistent, insisting on the facts when her partner cannot resist a flattery, and always exhibiting a keen intellectual curiosity. In order to allay her concerns about a sun eventually exhausted of its light- and life-giving power, Algarotti cites the theory that light is perhaps being replenished by comets or other stars falling back into the sun, and, as if to shore up this philosophical speculation with some poetic imagination, alludes to Milton's *Paradise Lost* where the angel "assures us, that the Sun draws his Aliment from humid Exhalations, and in a regular Manner takes his Supper every Night with the Ocean" (42). Later on, a skeptical marchioness will say: "You give me Consequence and Verses, when I want Evidence and Explications" (45). Clearly, the lady is beyond the traditional expectations which her mentor still finds fitting and sufficient. The differences between explanations through suggestive images and rational thought combined with evidence have become more evident to the student than her teacher is aware of.

It is only after the systems of the past are dismissed, including that of Descartes, which Fontenelle had promoted so eloquently, but also some of the classical poetry which misrepresent actual phenomena of nature, that the crucial discussion of Newton's optics can begin in the Second Dialogue: the discussion of reflection and refraction. Building up the new thinking seems to begin with the destruction or rather with the ironic but radical dismissal of the old.

The transition is worth noticing, too: the First Dialogue ends with the unresolved paradox of apparent and real color. Is the blush on the cheek of the lady real or is this color only in our mind transmitted from the retina? The question which effectively undermines part of the reality of the world of our senses goes unanswered for the time being, because it is dinner time, and the soup must not get cold. The marchioness and the reader are kept in suspense through the mandated ritual of an evening meal until the next dialogues, in which all natural bodies are then unceremoniously reduced to their basic qualities of extension, impenetrability, motion, and form — color being only in the eyes of the beholder. Both the lady and her mentor comment on the world of illusion which our senses present us as color, as taste, as the sensations of hot and cold, as the beautifully smooth surface of the skin of the lady's hand. But just look at it under a microscope: a landscape full of craters and slime, and unspeakable creatures. However, while the deceit of the senses has to be pointed out properly and even drastically, in polite company one doesn't dwell on the barrenness or ugliness of the world. Moreover, this very deception is at the same time the source of something peculiarly positive. The marchioness remarks that our senses "continually make us believe Things, which a more refined Sense, or our Reason afterwards contradict" (78). Her mentor comments: "It is to the Silence of our Reason, and the want of more refined Senses that we owe our Perception of Pleasure. And he gave a very just Definition of our Happiness, who affirmed, that the most tranquil Possession of Pleasure consists in our being agreeably deceived" (78–80). Yet the corollary to this insight must not be forgotten either: *understanding* this state of affairs reveals a new dimension of the creative potential of the human being; in Algarotti's words: "the Taste of the Pine-Apple, the pleasing Verdure of a Meadow, and even the Light of the Sun which animates and revives the whole Universe, are all our own" (85). Thus it is only through the scientific exploration of the objects that the real source of their sensual enrichment becomes apparent. Deprivation is a blessing in disguise, but it is the insight into the *interplay* of appearance and the underlying reality which enables us to live with and in both realms as full human beings.

Taking his cues for optics from poetry as he had done it in the very beginning with Alexander Pope, the author spices his scientific discussion of the refraction and reflection of light with verses from the Italian poet Tasso and later from Milton. Tasso had spoken of an unbroken ray of light in a stream, a pardonable poetic license, unless, as the mentor points out with ironic, yet polite pedantry, the poet "would be understood to speak of those Rays which fall perpendicularly upon the water" (115). Of course, the poet Tasso is unlikely to have known or cared about the changing angles of refraction when light proceeds from one medium to another. But Algarotti not only makes the marchioness wonder about "seeing ourselves deformed and crooked when in a Bath" (119), he is meeting her on familiar, namely literary grounds as he confronts her with this phenomenon of optics. Similarly, the reflection of light rays is presented superbly via Milton's verses in *Paradise Lost* in which Eve is charmed by her own image as she gazes at herself for the first time in a pond. In Book IV of *Paradise Lost*, we read the charming scene of Eve awakening after her creation:

> That day I often remember, when from sleep
> I first awaked, and found myself reposed
> Under a shade of flowers much wondering where
> And what I was, whence thither brought, and how.
> Not distant far from thence a murmuring sound
> Of water issued from a cave and spread
> Into a liquid plain, then stood unmoved
> Pure as the expanse of heaven, I thither went
> With unexperienced thought, and laid me down
> On a green bank, to look into the clear
> Smooth lake, that to me seemed another sky.
> As I bent down to look, just opposite,
> A shape within the watery gleam appeared
> Bending to look on me, I started back
> It started back, but pleased I soon returned,
> Pleased it returned as soon with answering looks
> Of sympathy and love; there I had fixed
> Mine eyes till now, and pined with vain desire,
> Had not a voice thus warned me: "What thou seest,
> What there thou seest fair creature is thyself,
> With thee it came and goes." (lines 449–67)

She then follows the voice that had warned her and continues:

> "Till I espied thee, fair indeed and tall,
> Under a platane, yet me thought less fair,
> Less winning soft, less amiably mild,
> Than that smooth watery image; back I turned,
> Thou following criedst aloud, "Return fair Eve,
> Whom fliest thou?" (lines 477–82)

The enhancement, indeed enchantment of reality through reflection endows the optical phenomenon under discussion with the magic of poetry. Yet the marchioness does not appear to be taken by the charm of the situation; instead she voices her moral concern about the possible hidden meaning of these verses. "Does not this Passage of *Milton* convey some malicious Insinuation, said the Marchioness? And is it not his real Meaning that the Sight of a Husband gives a Woman less Pleasure than even an Image or a Shadow" (124–125). It would be intriguing to delve into the complex psychology of narcissism in conflict with the surrender to the Other, to a husband designated by the Deity himself, but it would lead to a digression too expansive even for this genre. Brief digressions, incidentally, witty asides, general philosophical comments are not only tolerated in the discourse of popularizing science, they are intended to show the human mind at ease, civilized, and sovereign. And after this foray in what Milton might have intended to say, there follows a long and intense explanation of the way convex lenses, like the ones in our eyes, through refraction form an image of an object which is upside-down and inverted as to right and left. Later on, this leads to a discussion of the structure of the human eye, near- and farsightedness, blindness, the mysterious connection between the images formed on the retina and, through the optical nerve, the brain. Why do we see only *one* object although the two eyes form two images on the retina; and why do we see objects right-side-up although they appear upside-down on the retina? Tricky questions, not just about optics, but about vision, and therefore about the fundamental processes through which we perceive reality, physically and mentally. The answers are given not simply by stating the scientific fact, but also by describing experiments. In the case of vision, physiological experiments with persons afflicted with particular vision disabilities or defects serve as illustrative examples. Not only are the facts of the new sciences presented, but also the spirit of the new empiricism as contrasted to traditional speculation is evident.

I am passing over the discussion of the two most important instruments to come out of the new sciences: the telescope and the microscope, each opening literally new worlds, and together expanding enormously the realm of human sensory and intellectual experience. What is great; what is small in size or duration? And how, then, can one approach the ancient question of infinity via the quantitatively infinitely large and the infinitely small? Newton's new calculus, the mathematics of the infinite, is highlighted as the culmination of the efforts of finding a rational approach to the problem, but it is, of course, not treated.

The dialogue turns back to optics proper, to the question of what light, after all the Deity of the Enlightenment, is: waves propagated through and by an ether or particles moving through empty space? Malebranche and Huygens had favored the wave-model of light, which was particularly inviting because of its analogy with the vibrations or waves of sound. Newton, too, had allowed himself to speculate about the analogy of different colors and different sounds, about the seven intervals in an octave and the seven colors in the spectrum: red, orange, yellow, green, indigo, blue, and violet. Algarotti guides the lady effortlessly through many pleasing correspondences between sound and light, "the Harpsichord of Colours, and the Music of the Eyes" (222). The analogies seem overwhelming, and the marchioness is only too ready to embrace the idea of the 'brotherhood' of the two, i.e., of light as a wave-phenomenon. But her mentor has a surprise in store. With a keen sense for drama, he uses the very analogy which seemed as appealing as it seemed convincing to bring about the downfall of the model: "If an undulating Motion happens to meet with any obstacle in its Way, this does not stop its Progress, for it bends on all Sides and continues to propagate itself in Spite of the Obstacle that opposed it" (229). One can hear the sound of a French horn on the other side of a hill, and a stone thrown into the water creates waves which continue around any obstacle. Therefore, if light were a wave, no shadow would be cast by an object, and the reader is to remember: we are in Italy in the summer. The analogy falls apart; light is not like sound. The catharsis is completed by the surrender to Newton's system of optics with its central experiment, actually a host of related experiments, of the refraction of light through a prism into the elementary colors of the spectrum: Alexander Pope's enigmatic verses of the seven-fold light finally can be deciphered. And in order to show that a genuine learning process has taken place, the author has the marchioness spend a sleepless night in which the essence of the Newtonian counterexperiment occurs to her: If white light consists of the colors shown in the spectrum, shouldn't one be able to gather these colors back together into white light? But she can't think of a way to accomplish it. Still, her mentor praises her good thinking and explains to her that Newton had indeed performed the experiment with a convex lens uniting the colors back into white light.

Many more optical phenomena are discussed in the light of Newton's optics: Why do objects appear white or black to us? Because they reflect all the colors or none at all. Why should a lady, getting ready for the opera, change her make-up and watch the color of her dress for the occasion? Because the spectral colors of candlelight differ from those of sunlight; the yellow portion of the spectrum is wider. The composition of the emitted light being different, it follows that the light reflected by the face or the dress is going to be different. And all of this follows logically and is predictable: a system of thought which corresponds to reality.

Algarotti's great achievement in his popularization of Newton for a lady lies in his ability to render his evidence with elegance, reducing complex phenomena and thoughts to their essence; it lies in his ability to place his physics in the cultural and physical context of his student's experience and at the same time to recreate for her and with her active participation the great intellectual drama of science through the centuries with its climax in Newton's New Physics.

III

My concluding remarks will address a feature which is obviously common to Fontenelle's *Conversations*, to his anonymous Christian critic, to Algarotti's work and many others who followed the famous French model in either the form of the dialogue or the letter: the choice of a female partner. I already indicated in what sense the educated woman seemed to these male authors the ideal student. Diderot in his essay "Sur les femmes"[7] summarizes succinctly the advantages of a dialogue with a woman by drawing on certain natural dispositions

---

[7]See the discussion in Lisa Gasbarrone, "Voices from Nature: Diderot's Dialogues with Women." *Studies on Voltaire and the Eighteenth Century*, vol. 292. (Oxford: The Voltaire Foundation at the Taylor Institution, 1991) 259–91. I am quoting Diderot from this article.

of women, and by turning the relative ignorance of most educated women in matters of philosophy, be it moral or natural philosophy, into a definite advantage. He remarks on their "natural curiosity, their capacity for heightened awareness, and a relative ignorance of intellectual tradition that predisposes women" to accept the truth as soon as it is revealed to them (262). Lisa Gasbarrone, in her probing article, continues: "Their lack of formal education makes women more receptive to ideas founded in nature rather than in philosophical convention" (262). And this quality "which makes women more receptive to nature's truth also serves to make them more resistant to conventionally established authority" (262). This interpretation of Diderot's views, while emphasizing a variation of the traditional tenet that women are somehow instinctively close to nature, also makes clear that this is far from being an impediment. Rather, it can be a privileged position which makes women unencumbered by the orthodoxies of the past and enables them to think free of the authority of tradition and open to what nature reveals through experimentation and logical reasoning.

A final point, it seems to me, has to be made, not in regard to these many "fictional" women who appear in countless dialogues and letters meant to popularize the natural sciences, but in regard to real women in science. Paula Findlen,[8] in a very illuminating article about such women in Italy, makes some interesting observations about the social context in which science was being "circulated" (170). She relates the amusing and revealing story of Giambattista Vico instructing his oldest daughter Luisa in the kitchen (174). This must be one of the most concrete examples of what the author had pointed out earlier: "Domesticating science was a means of civilizing it" (168). In this context one should remember that Algarotti had considered natural science, if not brought back from its formalistic isolation into civilized discourse, a form of barbarism.

However, beyond the kitchen and the salon (where the new science was becoming a conversation topic), there was still another realm in which some learned women played an important role as intermediaries between the scientists and the larger reading public, namely as translators and authors of textbooks. Again, Paula Findlen's article offers valuable information and astute observations which go beyond her particular focus on learned women in Italy. A few prominent examples must suffice here to point to a phenomenon which shows women in the interface between actual science and the public sphere during the eighteenth century. Both a translation and a textbook occupy a space from which transfer and transport of the new findings and the new thinking in the natural sciences from their realm of origin to a new realm of their reception can take place. The authors of these transcultural and didactic endeavors also occupy

---

[8] See Paula Findlen, "Translating the New Science: Women and the Circulation of Knowledge in Enlightenment Italy," *Configurations*, vol. 3, Spring 1995 (Baltimore: The Johns Hopkins University Press, 1995) 167–206.

a unique space in that they have the opportunity to transmit and to teach without the responsibility which comes with genuine and original authorship. Yet it was through translations and textbooks that women gained their initial access to the world of the new sciences. In her article, Paula Findlen reminds the reader that it was the Marquise du Châtelet who first translated Newton's *Principia* into French and added extensive commentary to the text. But the Marquise also published a famous textbook on physics, *Institutions of Physics* (1740). Similarly, and certainly less well-known, Giuseppa Eleonora Barbapiccola translated Descartes's *Principia philosophiae* into Italian (1722); and an Italian mathematician, Maria Gaetana Agnesi, was the author of the widely used and translated (into French!) textbook, *Analytical Institutions for the Use of Italian Youth* (1748).

Finally, the enterprise of the early popularization of Copernicus and Newton can be seen and interpreted not only and not even mainly as an auxiliary exercise to science, as an aid with many flaws in the transfer of genuine science to some form of general, but necessarily diluted understanding. It can, and it has been eloquently and entertainingly depicted as a philosophy of a new kind: as *Damenphilosophie*.[9] This is not traditional philosophy, or Copernicus, or Newton, or physics or chemistry for ladies, but a philosophy *sui generis* which challenges this male-dominated discipline through spirited irony, through an ignorance of irreverence; by questioning with a smile, but also with a cause; by exposing barren fixations and the pompous boredom of much of traditional philosophy with elegant, yet unsettling naiveté. Fontenelle's and Algarotti's works, as well as those of others who aim at popularizing the sciences or any other system of knowledge in this new perspective, reveal then, through the very dialogue with their *female* partners, then as much about the internal problems in structure and orientation of the system, as they communicate some of the new insights into the external world. Popular *Damenphilosophie*, as Ursula Pia Jauch puts it at one point as a *bon mot*, is an experimental philosophy which does not in the classical fashion ask *Why*, rather it operates with the question *Why not?* (29).

---

[9] I have taken this term and the concluding observations from a very refreshing, well researched, stylistically highly unorthodox, and altogether unusually enlightening work by Ursula Pia Jauch, *Damenphilosophie and Männermoral. Von Abbé de Gérard bis Marquis de Sade. Ein Versuch über die lächelnde Vernunft.*

CLARK MUENZER

Transplanting the Poem: Goethe, Ghosts, and the Metamorphosis of an Elegy

> Lang und schmal ist ein Weg. Sobald du ihn gehest, so wird er
> Breiter; aber du ziehst Schlangengewinde dir nach.
> Bist du an's Ende gekommen, so werde der schreckliche Knoten
> Dir zur Blume, und du gib sie dem Ganzen dahin.
> (FA 2:230)[1]

Setting the Symbolic Stage

In the early spring of 1787 Goethe found himself happily situated in Palermo. He had drafted a sketch for resurrecting Homer's *Nausicaa* in a play on April 16 and had even worked out several of the scenes. On the following day, amidst the vernal splendor of the Sicilian paradise, however, his mood was changed. "Es ist ein wahres Unglück," he complained, "wenn man von vielerlei Geistern verfolgt und versucht wird!" (HA 11:374). Because he was distracted by all kinds of phantoms, he could not sustain his work on the "dichterischen Träume" (HA 11:266) from Homer's world, which would be published as a fragment forty years later in the fourth volume of the *Ausgabe letzter Hand*. From the very spot where the Garden of Alcinous[2] had presumably once thrived, "erhaschte mich ein anderes Gespenst," he recalled in his letter on April 17,

---

[1] Goethe's works are usually cited according to the following editions by volume and page number: FA=*Sämtliche Werke. Briefe, Tagebücher und Gespräche*, in 40 vols., eds. Henrik Birus, Dieter Borchmeyer, et al. (Frankfurt: Deutscher Klassiker Verlag, 1987–); HA=*Goethes Werke. Hamburger Ausgabe*, in 14 vols., ed. Erich Trunz (Hamburg: Christian Wegner Verlag, 1948–60); AA=*Gedenkausgabe der Werke, Briefe und Gespräche*, in 24 vols., ed. Ernst Beutler (Zurich: Artemis, 1948–60); and WA= *Werke*, in 133 vols., publ. under the auspices of der Großherzogin Sophie (Weimar: Böhlau, 1887–1919).

[2] Cf. Christoph Jamme, "Vom 'Garten des Alcinous' zum Weltgarten. Goethes Begegnung mit dem Mythos im aufgeklärten Zeitalter," *Goethe-Jahrbuch* 105 (1988), 93–114, for an alternative reading of this *topos*.

das mir schon diese Tage nachgeschlichen. Die vielen Pflanzen, die ich sonst nur in Kübeln und Töpfen, ja die größte Zeit des Jahres nur hinter Glasfenstern zu sehen gewohnt war, stehen hier froh und frisch unter freiem Himmel, und indem sie ihre Bestimmung vollkommen erfüllen, werden sie uns deutlicher. Im Angesicht so vielerlei neuen und erneuten Gebildes fiel mir die alte Grille wieder ein, ob ich nicht unter dieser Schar die Urpflanze entdecken könnte. (HA 11:266)

While at home in the intemperate north, Goethe had pursued his interest in exotic plants only in the obscure light of the ducal hothouses, where specimens were artificially entombed in glass, as well as isolated and confined in buckets and pots. On his island paradise, however, the pristine illumination of southern skies at first promised to enhance the powers of his observing eye. The fresh growth there appeared so sharply contoured and perfectly defined that he felt epistemologically encouraged to arrange the wealth of botanical material within his view into a system where differences of anatomical detail would both count and be counted.[3] Yet Goethe's Ganymedian dream of seamless continuity and universal comprehension was also haunted from the outset by a whim that he could not shake. For the transplanted specimens that he thought he had abandoned by fleeing to Italy were still pursuing him as a "Schar,"[4] or host of botanical forms. And though, according to his anecdote, he tried resisting their pursuit by configuring the instigating *Urpflanze* as a "Grille," it became quickly apparent that the chase was not yet over. The captivating "Muster" (HA 11:266) of all plants had entered his field of vision to stay, and it would continue defining his program of botanical inquiry for years to come.

What the ghosts in the public gardens compelled Goethe to abandon in 1787 was "natural history,"[5] which for the systematic botany of much of the

---

[3] I will use "epistemology" throughout in Richard Rorty's sense of finding some common ground of commensuration. According to his *Philosophy and the Mirror of Nature* (Princeton: Princeton UP, 1979), "the desire for a theory of knowledge is a desire for constraint—a desire to find 'foundations' to which one might cling, frameworks beyond which one must not stray, objects which impose themselves, representations which cannot be gainsaid" (315).

[4] Johann Christoph Adelung's *Grammatisch-kritisches Wörterbuch der Hochdeutschen Mundart*, 2nd. ed. (Leipzig: Breitkopf und Härtel, 1798), 3:1356–59, offers an immense range of etymologies and meanings for this word, including "Zischlaut," "Geschrey," "Kriechen" (1357), "Flüssigkeit," "Schwester," "Kranz," "Gefäß," "nebeneinander befindliche Dinge einer Art," "Menge" (1358), and "Geräusch" (1359).

[5] For more on the crucial shift, during the latter part of the eighteenth century, from "natural history" to a nascent science of developmental biology, cf. James L. Larson, *Interpreting Nature: The Science of Living Form from Linnaeus to Kant* (Baltimore and London: The Johns Hopkins UP, 1994); Wolf Lepenies, *Das Ende der Naturgeschichte: Wandel kultureller Selbstverständlichkeiten in den Wissenschaften des 18. und 19. Jahrhunderts* (Frankfurt am Main: Suhrkamp, 1978); Timothy Lenoir, *The Strategy of Life:*

eighteenth century meant Linnaeas's nomenclatures. As Foucault and others have suggested,[6] these tabular classifications locked each plant into a timeless grid, where species were objectively named, and the entire kingdom exhaustively arranged, on the basis of the discretely articulated parts of individual specimens. Through the early 1790s, however, Goethe gradually adopted, along with a number of other German scientists, a new program of investigation and discovery that used teleological categories, like natural purposiveness, as the basis for studying the complex organization of living things. A Kantian paradigm[7] thus gradually replaced the Linnaean paradigm of natural history in Goethe's intellectual formation as a botanist.[8]

Teleology and Mechanics in Nineteenth Century German Biology (Dordrecht, Boston, and London: D. Reidel, 1982). For Goethe's role in this program of inquiry cf. Hartmut Böhme, "Goethes Erde zwischen Natur und Geschichte: Erfahrungen von Zeit in der Italienischen Reise," *Goethe-Jahrbuch* 110 (1993), 209–26; Hartmut Böhme, "Lebendige Natur: Wissenschaftskritik, Naturforschung und allegorische Hermetik bei Goethe," in *Natur und Subjekt* (Frankfurt am Main: Suhrkamp, 1988); Karl J. Fink, *Goethe's History of Science* (Cambridge: Cambridge UP, 1991); Dieter Käfer, *Methodenprobleme und ihre Behandlung in Goethes Schriften zur Naturwissenschaft* (Cologne and und Vienna: Böhlau Verlag, 1982); Klaus H. Kiefer,*Wiedergeburt und Neues Leben: Aspekte des Strukturwandels in Goethes 'Italienischer Reise'* (Bonn: Bouvier, 1978); Stephen Koranyi, *Autobiographik und Wissenschaft im Denken Goethes* (Bonn: Bouvier, 1984); Uwe Pörksen, "Wissenschaftssprache und Sprachauffassung bei Linné und Goethe," in *Deutsche Naturwissenschaftssprachen: Historische und kritische Studien* (Tubingen: Günter Narr Verlag, 1986) 72–96; and Elisabeth von Thadden, "Das Ende der Naturgeschichte," in *Erzählen als Naturverhältnis—'Die Wahlverwandtschaften:' Zum Problem der Darstellbarkeit von Natur und Gesellschaft seit Goethes Plan eines 'Roman über das Weltall'* (Munich: Wilhelm Fink, 1993), 38–48. Von Thadden's bibliography, 233–43, is very useful.

[6]In addition to the works listed in the preceding note, cf. Michel Foucault, "Classifying," in *The Order of Things: An Archaeology of the Human Sciences* (New York: Random House, 1970) 125–65.

[7]Cf. Goethe's use of the term "Vorstellungsart" in his "Einwirkung der neueren Philosophie" (FA 24:445).

[8]Lenoir and Lessoin extensively treat Kant's role in the study of living things. In addition to the works already cited, cf. the following studies on Goethean biological and botanical thought: Ronald H. Brady, "Form and Cause in Goethe's Morphology," in *Goethe and the Sciences: A Reappraisal*, eds. Fredrick Amrine, Francis J. Zucker, and Harvey Wheeler (Dordrecht and Boston: D. Reidel, 1987) 257–300; Theodor Butterfass, "Goethe und die Wissenschaft von der Pflanze," in *Allerhand Goethe: Seine wissenschaftliche Sendung aus Anlaß des 150. Todestags und des 50. Namenstags der Johann-Wolfgang-Goethe-Universität in Frankfurt am Main*, eds. Dieter Kimpel and Jörg Pompetzki (Frankfurt and New York: Peter Lang, 1985) 165–80; Heidi Krueger, "Allegory, Symbol, and Symbolic Representation in Goethe's Aesthetic and Scientific

Goethe once described how crucial this shift during the 1790s had been for his thinking in several brief essays that he drafted in the context of his renewed interest in Kant around 1817.[9] He had begun his first, intensive studies of the *Kritik der Urteilskraft* in 1790–91, shortly after its publication and the nearly contemporaneous publication of his own treatise on plant metamorphosis.[10] Furthermore, although he had completed the *Versuch* before becoming familiar with Kant's analysis of aesthetic and teleological judgments, the philosopher's nod toward an "intellectual archetype" had underscored his own reliance on an analogous, intuitive power of judgment, which he called "anschauende Urteilskraft." By moving deductively through such categories as primal form and type to the observable particulars of nature, this synthetic faculty had enabled him to undertake Kant's "Abenteuer der Vernunft" and successfully reconstruct his knowledge of living beings.[11]

As a botanist, then, we find Goethe rethinking and restating the mechanical relationship in Linnaeas between parts and whole through the regulative idea of the *Urpflanze*, including its self-transforming *Blatt* and foliating process of

---

Writings," Yale University, 1984; Dorothea Kuhn, *Typus und Metamorphose: Goethe-Studien* (Marbach: Deutsche Schillergesellschaft, 1988); Adolf Portmann, "Goethe and the Concept of Metamorphosis," in *Goethe and the Sciences: A Reappraisal*, eds. Fredrick Amrine, Francis J. Zucker, and Harvey Wheeler (Dordrecht and Boston: D. Reidel, 1987) 133–45; N. Puszkar, "Goethes Metamorphose der Pflanzen: Innere Form und sozialer Organismus," *Études Germaniques* 45 (1990), 10–24; Peter Sprengel, "Die *Urpflanze*: Zur Entwicklung von Goethes Morphologie in Italien," in *Ein unsäglich schönes Land: Goethes "Italienische Reise" und der Mythos Siziliens*, ed. Albert Meier (Palermo: Sellerio, 1987) 122–35.

[9]"Einwirkung der neueren Philosophie," "Anschauende Urteilskraft," "Bedenken und Ergebung," and "Bildungstrieb" were published together in the second issue of the first volume of the *Hefte zur Morphologie* in 1820. Cf. FA 24:441–52.

[10]For Goethe's relation to Kant cf. Koranyi, 32ff., Géza von Molnár, *Goethes Kantstudien: Eine Zusammenstellung nach Eintragungen in seinen Handexemplaren der "Kritik der reinen Vernunft" und der "Kritik der Urteilskraft"* (Weimar: Hermann Böhlaus Nachfolger, 1994); Ferdinand Weinhandl, *Die Metaphysik Goethes* (Darmstadt: Wissenschaftliche Buchgesellschaft, 1932; 1965). Günter Peters, *Die Kunst der Natur: Ästhetische Reflexion in Blumengedichten von Brockes, Goethe und Gauthier* (Munich: Fink, 1993) 209–41, treats Goethe's reading of Kant's third critique and the elegy "Die Metamorphose der Pflanzen" in detail. This excellent study, which addresses many issues of interest here, has gone a long way in rescuing the poem from its classification as a straightforward didactic work.

[11]"Hatte ich doch erst unbewußt und aus innerem Trieb auf jenes Urbildliche, Typische rastlos gedrungen, war es mir sogar geglückt, eine naturgemäße Darstellung aufzubauen, so konnte mich nunmehr nichts weiter verhindern das *Abenteuer der Vernunft*, wie es der Alte von Königsberge selbst nennt, mutig zu bestehen" (FA 24:448).

Metamorphose. By experiencing the plant, synthetically, through the successively emergent totality of the leaf's self-regulating transformations, he would learn to "see" the spectacular growth in the gardens at Palermo—in more revealing terms than those of Linnaean nomenclature—as the reciprocal relationship between parts and whole that, according to Kant, patterned all purposive formation.[12] If plant life as such (the organism) developed through sites (the nodes) where old parts reappeared in new configurations, then the separate organs, which themselves are reincarnations of the leaf, could be meaningfully linked to one another, according to Goethe's hermeneutics of nature, as the reciprocally related parts of an emerging whole.

Along these lines, the Sicilian "Weltgarten" was a turning point for Goethe in two senses. First, his route south from Rome in search of the ancient Greek origins of modern Italian culture would soon double back from Palermo to the eternal city and thence to Weimar, where he would work for nearly half a century to construct a new, German classicism. In a more fundamental way, however, having reached a provisional goal of his spiritual adventure in the summarizing standpoints of the *Odyssey* and the *Urpflanze*, he would return to his northern home—with its less congenial spooks—intellectually reborn as a poet-scientist. Goethe thus wrote to Herder on May 17, 1787, that he had at last equipped himself with a structure of thought ("Modell") that promised to unlock ("Schlüssel") the secret of all natural, aesthetic, and social formation ("alles übrige Lebendige") in a system of consequential organization and infinite temporal extension. The foliage in Palermo had initially frustrated his divinely appointed role as a classical botanist to dispense names in God's timeless order of things. But it had also comprised a composite image ("Gebilde") of renewal that would enable him to reconstruct the plant and its history of extended foliation as a protean structure of survival.[13]

As the hidden, temporalized pattern out of which all plant life could emerge, the *Urpflanze* was appropriately located on Goethe's journey within the haunted gardens of Palermo, where the ancient "Garten des Alcinous" had reemerged to survive as a "Weltgarten."[14] Just as discrete experimental observations in Goethe's 1792 essay on scientific inquiry are serially arranged as a single grand experiment in order to stage a complex natural event ("Begebenheit"),[15] the vegetative world of the public park "appeared" within an arena of transition and change where the play of life was sustained as the "Bildung und Umbildung

---

[12]"Anschauende Urteilskraft" (FA 24:447).

[13]Cf. Goethe's letter to Herder of May 17, 1787 as cited in the *Italienische Reise* (HA 11:322–23). Each plant imaginable contains within it the condition of possibility of all future plant growth.

[14]"Gestört war mein guter poetischer Vorsatz, der Garten des Alcinous war verschwunden, ein Weltgarten hatte sich aufgetan" (HA 11:267).

[15]Cf. "Der Versuch als Vermittler von Objekt und Subjekt" (HA 13:17).

organischer Naturen."[16] How otherwise, Goethe mused, could he know "daß dieses oder jenes Gebilde eine Pflanze sei, wenn sie nicht alle nach einem Muster gebildet wären?" (HA 11:266). That is, the mass of botanical shape and color around him would make sense only if it could be constituted as a single event, or complex process, of dynamic composition. He had first looked upon the stage of the "Weltgarten" wanting to investigate "worin denn die vielen abweichenden Gestalten voneinander unterschieden seien" (HA 11:266–67). But he left its theater in search of the regulating unity that had produced the kaleidoscopic diversity before his eyes:

> Und ich fand sie immer mehr ähnlich als verschieden, und wollte ich meine botanische Terminologie anbringen, so ging das wohl, aber es fruchtete nicht, es machte mich unruhig, ohne daß es mir weiterhalf. (HA 11:267)

In other words, rather than trapping himself within the grids of Linnaean classifications and names, Goethe concluded his visit to the gardens by crossing the borders of "natural history."[17] Wandering Odysseus-like through the uncharted regions of organic formation, he would henceforth hone his intuitive intelligence by repeatedly challenging himself—as both a scientist and a poet—to re-enact the life (and death) drama of the wondrously creative plant.[18]

Goethe's adventures over the next forty-five years in the nodal regions of botanical growth, propagation, and survival regularly landed him in spots, like Palermo's "Weltgarten," where the complex reciprocity of the old and the new played itself out.[19] It seems appropriate, therefore, that he should mark the start of his search for the *Urpflanze* in a place that the ancients had depicted as a gateway to Persephone's underworld[20] and that eighteenth century travel accounts had featured as the most Homeric and, hence, the most archaic and historically layered site within Italy.[21] Against this wavering background of

---

[16]Cf. Goethe's title-page to the *Hefte zur Morphologie* (FA 24:399). For more on the use of the stage as a metaphor in both "Euphrosyne" and "Die Metamorphose der Pflanzen," cf. Peters, 180–90 and 190–96.

[17]Foucault 131.

[18]"Die Urpflanze wird das wunderlichste Geschöpf von der Welt, um welches mich die Natur selbst beneiden soll" (HA 11:324).

[19]For more on the issue of temporal reciprocity, cf. the "Betrachtungen über Morphologie" (FA 24 361–62), as well as the following Goethe poems in Schiller's 1799 *Musen-Almanach*: "Am 1. Oktober 97;" "Stanzen;" and "An meine Lieder."

[20]Cf. Frederick R. Amrine, "Goethe's Italian Discoveries as a Natural Scientist: The Scientist in the Underworld," in *Goethe in Italy, 1786–1986: A Bi-Centennial Symposium, November 14–16, 1986, University of California, Santa Barbara: Proceedings Volume*, ed. Gerhart Hoffmeister (Amsterdam: Rodopi, 1988) 55–76.

[21]Cf. Stuart Atkins, "Goethe's Nausicaa: A Figure in Fresco," in *Essays on Goethe*, eds. Jane K. Brown and Thomas P. Saine (Columbia, SC: Camden House, 1995) 121.

emergence and disappearance, however, it is also surprising that the host of shadowy forms from the "Weltgarten" should be altogether absent, when three years after the Sicilian descent, Goethe's first major botanical study was published.

The schematic arrangement of *Versuch die Metamorphose der Pflanzen zu erklären* into a series of one-hundred-twenty-three concise paragraphs, together with its system of consecutive numbering, lend the treatise the outward appearance of abstract argument and conclusive proof. But like the renovated *Faust* fragment—which was newly published in the same year—the study was meant to initiate and sustain a kind of botanical "Weltgespräch,"[22] and so it continued to test Goethe's thinking even long after its first, unsuccessful, run in 1790. Indeed, over time the informing ideas of his inquiry underwent a series of metamorphoses themselves that would recapitulate the "recapitulative" experience of plant metamorphosis and so cumulatively attest to the persistent conflagration of plants and ghosts in his mind.[23]

Goethe's first attempt at such an "experimental" restatement produced the well-known plant elegy of 1798, which until recently was widely viewed as a didactic poem.[24] When he substituted classical meters and elegiac distichs for the

---

[22]Goethe completed all three framing introductions to *Faust* between 1797 and 1800. In the last one of these, a now famous line connects the garden motif to Goethean cosmology, as well as to *Metamorphose* as a decorative framing of time: "Weiß doch der Gärtner, wenn das Bäumchen grünt,/Daß Blüt und Frucht die künftigen Jahre zieren" (lines 18–19) (HA 3:18). Since this composite frame, in a sense, does not close at the end of the play, it functions in a way analogous to the "interlocuted" plant elegy of 1798. Cf. discussion entitled "The Flowers of Interlocution" at the end of this essay. For more on the missing "Epilog" in *Faust*, cf. Benjamin Bennett, *Goethe's Theory of Poetry: 'Faust' and the Regeneration of Language* (Ithaca and London: Cornell UP, 1986) 313ff. The composition dates for the introductions are "Zueignung" (June, 1797), "Prolog im Himmel" (around 1800), and "Vorspiel auf dem Theater" (1797–98).

[23]Cf. "Der Versuch als Vermittler von Objekt und Subjekt" (HA 13:19–20), where Goethe describes the formation of scientific traditions in similar terms as a corrective device against hastily formed conclusions. Cf. also Fink, especially 127–42.

[24]Peters's extensive discussion most adequately respects the poem's complex hermeneutical strategies,163–241. Cf. also Günther Müller, "Johann Wolfgang Goethe: 'Die Metamorphose der Pflanzen,'" in *Die deutsche Lyrik:Form und Geschichte. Interpretationen*, vol. 1, *Vom Mittelalter bis zur Frühromantik*, ed. Benno von Wiese (Düsseldorf: August Bagel Verlag, 1956) 251–71; Klaus Oettinger, "Unschuldige Hochzeit. Zu Goethes Elegie 'Die Metamorphose der Pflanzen,'" *Deutschunterricht* 38 (1986): 69–78; Gertrud Overbeck, "Goethes Lehre von der Metamorphose der Pflanzen und ihre Widerspiegelung in seiner Dichtung," *Publications of the English Goethe Society* 28 (1959): 38–59; Klaus Prange, "Das anthropologisch-pädagogische Motiv der Naturauffassung Goethes in dem Lehrgedicht 'Metamorphose der Pflanzen,'" *Literatur in*

numbers and paragraphs of his botanical treatise, however, he was not—I suggest—just making his old point about metamorphosis more pleasing or accessible by offering it in verse. Rather, by anthologizing "Die Metamorphose der Pflanzen," together with some other poems, in a periodical publication that commemorated the passing of the year 1798 and the emergence of a centennial year-of-passage 1799, Goethe was also extending his point about the patterned sequence of life's rising and falling rhythms.[25] Furthermore, he was doing this with a rhythmic monument that would become through its subsequent publication history a composite, or summarizing, "experience of a higher order."[26] In accord with Goethe's understanding of metamorphosis as the self-reflexive, or reduplicating, pattern of all vital processes, therefore, I will track the story of his reconstructive poem about plants by locating and describing the changing intellectual fields where it emerged and reemerged during the thirty-odd years between its first publication in Schiller's *Musen-Almanach für das Jahr 1799* and its final appearance during the poet's lifetime as one of the "Gott und Welt" poems (1827) within his testamentary *Ausgabe letzter Hand*.[27] If a "secret law" or "geheimes Gesetz" (line 6)[28] lies buried within this poem in perpetual progress, it must be uncovered in the *corpus* of transmission[29] through which its textual life (like the life of the foliating plant) was sustained as a sacred riddle, or "heiliges Rätsel" (line 7), of interpretation.

Wissenschaft und Unterricht 8 (1975): 123–33; Karl Richter, "Wissenschaft und Poesie 'auf höherer Stelle' vereint: Goethes Elegie 'Die Metamorphose der Pflanzen,'" in *Gedichte und Interpretationen*, ed. Wulf Segebrecht. (Stuttgart: Reclam, 1984) 153–68.

[25]"Im Hexameter steigt des Springquells silberne Säule/Im Pentameter drauf fällt sie melodisch herab" (FA 1:558). "Das elegische Silbenmaß," according to Goethe's letter to Schiller on July 21, 1798, dynamically extends itself outward—"[läßt] sich nach allen Seiten hin bewegen" (WA IV, 13:222).

[26]Cf. "Der Versuch als Vermittler von Objekt und Subjekt:" "Eine solche Erfahrung, die aus mehreren andern besteht, ist offenbar von einer höhern Art" (HA 13:18).

[27]Cf. Peters, "Das Schauspiel der Natur: Die 'Metamorphose der Pflanzen' im Kontext ihrer Veröffentlichungen," 176–201. Cf. also Mariane Wünsch, *Der Strukturwandel in der Lyrik Goethes. Die systemimmanente Relation der Kategorien 'Literatur' und 'Realität'* (Stuttgart, Berlin, Cologne, and Mainz: Kohlhammer, 1975) 15–40, for a discussion of the hermeneutics of recontextualization through republishing lyric poems in the eighteenth century, as well as Karl Eibel's discussion of "Gelegenheit" and "Ensemble" as organizing categories for his Deutscher Klassiker Verlag edition of Goethe's poetry, which I feel is now the best available collection (FA, 1:729–40).

[28]I will cite "Die Metamorphose der Pflanzen" according to line numbers from the FA 1:639–41.

[29]Near the beginning of the poem, the poet defines his task with the verb "überliefern" (line 6).

Some thirty years after scripting his visit to the Homeric garden in Palermo as an enticement into the "Weltgarten" of botanical emergence, Goethe characterized the plant elegy as an attempt to mollify some female friends who had expressed discontent with his "abstract gardening." The original *Versuch* of 1790, their complaining had gone, was an impoverishment of botanical shape, color, and scent "zu einem gespensterhaften Schemen" (FA 24:420). In response to these complaints, Goethe continued, he had concocted an enticement of his own. He would try luring ("locken") his well-meaning friends back into his circle by reincorporating the botanical experiences of the schematic *Versuch* into the rhythms of poetry:[30]

> Da versuchte ich diese wohlwollenden Gemüter zur Teilnahme durch eine Elegie zu locken, der ein Platz hier gegönnt sein möge, wo sie, im Zusammenhang wissenschaftlicher Darstellung, verständlicher werden dürfte, als eingeschaltet in eine Folge zärtlicher und leidenschaftlicher Poesien.
> (FA 24:420)

After its initial emergence from the Italian *Urpflanze* and the botanical treatise, then, Goethe's plant elegy had "fatefully" migrated by the year 1817 from Schiller's *Musen-Almanach*, through the ensemble "Elegien II" in his various collected works, to the first issue of *Hefte zur Morphologie*, from where it would finally land (twice!) in the authoritative 1827 collection of his poems. All told, "Die Metamorphose der Pflanzen" appeared six times through the course of the poet's life with only a few minor revisions. And four times during this drama of repeated publication, it found itself transplanted into new text ensembles, which in turn revised the meaning of its almost identical words.

The first contextualization of Goethe's plant poem was comprised by the series of "sentimental" poems that he mentioned in "Schicksal der Druckschrift" in 1817. In addition to "Die Metamorphose der Pflanzen," this ensemble of thirteen contributions from his pen included, most prominently, the elegy "Euphrosyne," which the poet would send to his friend Knebel in the "snow-covered season" of January, 1799, as "eine freudliche Natur- und Kunstblume" (WA IV, 14:6) in the hope of illuminating the darkest months of the new year.[31] The defining event of his sister poem to the plant elegy, of course, was

---

[30]Interesting in this regard is the semantic range of the words *versuchen* and *Versuch*, which suggest treatise, inquiry, test, and seduction. Cf. in this connection Goethe's characterization of the distracting spirits in Palermo (HA 13:266).

[31]Goethe published two sets of poems in Schiller's *Musen-Almanach für das Jahr 1799* (Tubingen: J.G. Cottaische Buchhandlung, 1799). "Die Musageten" (19), "Sängerwürde" (91), and "An meine Lieder" (231) all appear under the pseudonym Justus Amman (which contains the interlocuted palindrome *amma*, or mother!). The last of these three poems, which asserts that works of art, like all living things, grow old and disappear, was published here, ironically, for a second time. The following poems appeared under Goethe's own name: "Euphrosyne. Elegie (Zum Andenken einer jun-

the conversation atop a Swiss mountain with the ghost of the Weimar theater ingenue Christiane Becker-Neumann, the news of whose premature death had reached Goethe in the Hades-like region of the Gotthard during his journey to Switzerland in the fall of 1797.[32] So from the glass-entombed plants of the pre-Italian winters in Germany, through the *Urpflanze* of the Sicilian "Weltgarten," to the post-Italian schema of the phantasmal *Versuch* of 1790 and its rhythmical rebirth as a poem in distichs in 1798–99, "Die Metamorphose der Pflanzen" was always curiously marked by its ghost-like insistence on transition, migration, and reincarnation. Within Schiller's *Musen-Almanach* and calendar, moreover, where the poem saw the first light of day, it became part of a body of classical poetry that was framed, on one side, by Goethe's elegiac monument for Becker-Neumann and, on the other, by Schiller's prologue to *Wallenstein*, which had been recited a few months earlier at the dedication of the renovated theater in Weimar in October, 1798.

Notably, Schiller's own New Year's calendar-greeting to the German public, "an des Jahrhunderts ernstem Ende" (NA 8:4),[33] celebrated the same theatrical arts and their refurbished "Schattenbühne" (NA 8:4) in Weimar that Goethe's ghost elegy had memorialized in its meditative ascent of a mountain. In other words, the elusive experience (or idea) of the "model plant" that had "caught" Goethe in Palermo was itself again "caught,"[34] when it landed between two haunted stages on the platform of the 1799 *Musen-Almanach*. A new, classical age of aesthetic reconstruction, according to Schiller, "die der Kunst Thaliens/Auf dieser Bühne heut beginnt," had emboldened him to displace

---

gen, talentvollen, für das Theater zu früh verstorbenen, Schauspielerin in Weimar, Madame Becker, gebohrene Neumann" (1), "Die Metamorphose der Pflanzen" (17), "Am 1. Oktober 97" (61), "Das Blümlein Wunderschön" (69), "Der Edelknabe und die Müllerin. Alt-englisch" (102), "Der Junggesell und der Mühlbach. Alt-deutsch" (107), "Der Müllerin Verrath. Altfranzösisch" (116), "Die Reue. Altspanisch" (129), "Amyntas. Elegie" (145), and "Stanzen" (204). I cannot provide a detailed discussion of the many important interconnections between these poems, which might also include a look at the cycle of mill poems in terms of Herder's notion of folk poetry and Goethean *Weltliteratur*.

[32] For Goethe's trips to Switzerland, cf. Wolfgang Binder, *Das Ungeheure und das Geordnete: Die Schweiz in Goethe Werk* (Zurich and Munich: Artemis, 1979); Barbara Schnyder-Seidel, *Goethes letzte Schweizer Reise* (Frankfurt am Main: Insel, 1980); and Barbara Schnyder-Seidel, *Goethe in der Schweiz: anders zu lesen. Von der Wahrheit in der Dichtung letztem Teil* (Bern and Stuttgart: Francke, 1989).

[33] Schiller's works will be cited according to the following edition by volume and page number. NA=*Schillers Werke. Nationalausgabe*, in 43 vols., eds. Julius Petersen et al. (Weimar: Hermann Böhlaus Nachfolger, 1943ff.).

[34] In a letter to Jacobi, as cited in the *Italiensche Reise*, Goethe used the word "erhaschen" in this sense (HA 13:565).

("versetzen") his audience "auf einen höhern Schauplatz," from where art would soar, "[s]oll nicht des Lebens Bühne sie beschämen" (NA 8:5). Accordingly, a classically educated German audience,

> der rührbar jedem Zauberschlag der Kunst,
> Mit leisbeweglichem Gefühl den Geist
> In seiner flüchtigsten Erscheinung hascht
>
> (NA 8:3)

would henceforth learn to think from the dynamic vantage point upon the renovated Weimar stage, where the theater's transformative magic productively links old and new beliefs, or real and imagined worlds, by acknowledging the temporal sitedness of all cultural experience, including both science and art.

The refurbished theater in Weimar emerged during the next decade as a *locus classicus* of German classicism precisely in the terms celebrated by the *Almanach* prologue to Schiller's historical play. Furthermore, as Theodore Ziolkowski has argued, "the classical German elegy" also emerged during these years as a similar site of historical and philosophical reflection. By displacing the individual subject onto the higher perceptual plane of the elegy's complex temporal structuring, we are told, the poet-reader learns through the course of these poems (which paradigmatically trace meandering walks up mountains) to recompose the ephemeral realities of life, or the fleeting events of times past, into integrating moments of illumination.[35] And in this regard, Goethe's "Die Metamorphose der Pflanzen," which similarly discovers an elevated vantage point onto the living world by tracing the climb of plant metamorphosis,[36] seems to me—despite its exclusion from *The Classical German Elegy*—to belong to the very family of texts that Ziolkowski's precise readings first ingeniously described for me in his graduate seminar almost twenty-five years ago.[37]

---

[35] Theodore Ziolkowski, *The Classical German Elegy, 1795–1950* (Princeton: Princeton UP, 1980). Ziolkowski's discussion of the topical mountain climb in Schiller's "Der Spaziergang" (3–26), as well as his historical account of this *topos* (27–54), provide important contexts for reading about other elevated sites from this period, as "einen höhern Schauplatz" (NA 8:4).

[36] The poet ends the elegy by enjoining his beloved to partake in the harmonious contemplation of "die höhere Welt" (line 80). Cf. also in this connection "Die Absicht wird eingeleitet" (FA 24:395).

[37] Cf. Ziolkowski's summary of the form that follows his readings of "Der Spaziergang" and "Euphrosyne": "On the basis of the two model poems the classical German elegy would seem to be an extended poem in elegiac distichs, organized as a first-person framework embracing a central meditative core and moving from thematic tension toward resolution" (99). Ziolkowski further defines this tension as an "outgrowth of the traditional mixed sensations" that arise from "a contrast within the meditative core between two ostensible opposites: the real and the ideal, present and past, freedom and necessity, society and nature, temporality and timelessness..." (99). The argument

When Goethe published his edifying poem about botanical *Bildung* for the fifth time (within a third body of texts) as part of several short, historical introductions to the serialized *Hefte zur Morphologie*,[38] he explicitly lamented the tendency in the dominant science of his day to suppress its origin in the fundamental experience of nature as art.[39] In other words, some thirty years after displacing Linnaean nomenclatures with the *Urpflanze*, and some twenty years after publishing "Die Metamorphose der Pflanzen" in a volume that had placed it on a trajectory between "Euphrosyne" and Schiller's *Wallenstein* prologue, Goethe republished his plant poem as part of an essay ("Schicksal der Druckschrift") that noted once again how the complex organizing structures within nature, art, and society could not be caught just by tabulating visible features within exhaustive systems of universal commensurability. Another kind of thinking would, in fact, turn things around one day, according to Goethe's retrospective reflections, and properly return science, "auf höherer Stelle" (FA 24:420), to its original conversation with art.

Along these lines, we can now imagine that in constructing his lyrical monument for Becker-Neumann in 1798, Goethe was also preparing some higher ground, like the Weimar "Schattenbühne," on which the obsolescent *Lehr-*

---

concludes by suggesting that when "the poetic persona reappears in the concluding part of the framework, it has been elevated through meditation, whose intensity produces a timeless state of entrancement, to a higher level of consciousness..." (99–100). The terms of Ziolkowski's analysis, I believe, also work—with some variation—when reading Goethe's plant elegy.

[38]The essay ensemble that Goethe used to introduce *Hefte zur Morphologie* in 1817 included "Das Unternehmen wird entschuldigt," "Die Absicht eingeleitet" (FA 24: 389–95), as well as "Der Inhalt bevorwortet," "Geschichte meines botanischen Studiums," "Entstehen des Aufsatzes über Metamorphose der Pflanzen," "Schicksal der Handschrift," "Schicksal der Druckschrift," "Entdeckung eines trefflichen Vorarbeiters," "Caspar Friedrich Wolff über Pflanzenbildung," "Wenige Bemerkungen," and "Glückliches Ereignis" (FA 24: 399–438). The continuation of the first volume three years later included the "Urworte. Orphisch" cycle of poems and the results of his Kant studies in 1817: "Einwirkung der neueren Philosophie," "Anschauende Urteilskraft," "Bedenken und Ergebung," and "Bildungstrieb" (FA 24:439–52).

[39]Cf. "Schicksal der Druckschrift:" "Von andern Seiten her, vernahm ich ähnliche Klänge, nirgends wollte man zugeben, daß Wissenschaft und Poesie vereinbar seien. Man vergaß daß Wissenschaft sich aus Poesie entwickelt habe, man bedachte nicht daß, nach einem Umschwung von Zeiten, beide sich wieder freundlich, zu beiderseitigem Vorteil, auf höherer Stelle, gar wohl wieder begegnen könnten" (FA 24:420). This is also an issue that Peters treats in detail throughout the second section of his book, which is entitled "Enträtselung des Weltgartens durch Wissenschaft und Poesie" (163–241).

gedicht would awaken from its winter sleep and be reborn.[40] The versified botany of "Die Metamorphose der Pflanzen," after all, took shape as a love poem and an elegy, just as the tender elegy "Euphrosyne" would one day be read, conversely, as an implied poetics. In fact, when read as reciprocally illuminating texts, these sister poems from the 1799 *Almanach*, along with the *Wallenstein* prologue, appear to restore the lost dialogue that Goethe would invoke between (imaginative) learning and (edifying) art in 1817 by assigning to poetry the role of inducing wonder in our experiences of both nature and art.[41]

Michael Oakeshott has called this function "poetic" and has linked it to "contemplative imagining," which like Goethe's *anschauende Urteilskraft*, enables us to see relationships among and between the things of the world by resituating them into unfamiliar patterns.[42] As Goethe reminded us in one of his three short essays from *Hefte zur Morphologie* on the botanist Caspar Friedrich Wolff,[43] if we see not only with the body's eyes, but with "Geistes-Augen" (FA 24:432) as well, we will not feel epistemologically compelled to ground the "reality" of things in some universal, or fixed, "truth." Or in Oakeshott's words, as poets, we detach the images of our thinking from the facts and causes of the mechanical world in order to compose them "into larger patterns which are themselves only more complex images and not conclusions."[44]

To the degree that Goethe ventured beyond the bounded world of the familiar, then, in order to reexperience the organization of life as wonder and open it, in turn, to interpretation, his thinking was hermeneutical and not epistemological. And like all hermeneutic programs, it was also haunted, in the sense that it was driven by the desire to capture new meanings out of old experiences within border regions of emergence. That is, Goethe staged all life, poetically, as a drama of change and survival that is constituted by a series of entrances and exits, or scenes of momentary embodiments.[45] Furthermore, by

---

[40] For a discussion of anachronism in didactic poetry cf. Leif Ludwig Albertsen, "Spiel und Gespenst: Bemerkungen zu einigen vom klassischen Goethe aufgegriffenen Irrationalismen," *Goethe-Jahrbuch* 91 (1974): 78–91. Cf. also Bennett, *Goethe's Theory of Poetry*, for a discussion of Goethe's imitation in *Faust* of the playful approach that he attributed to all poetry, from Homer through Manzoni, toward old beliefs (143–44).

[41] Peters mentions "Erstaunen" in the context of the plant elegy's final publication with the poems of "Gott und Welt" (228).

[42] Michael Oakeshott, "The Voice of Poetry in the Conversation of Mankind," in *Rationality in Politics and Other Essays* (New York: Basic Books, 1962) 197–247.

[43] FA 24:426–31.

[44] Oakeshott 224.

[45] Cf. in this regard the "Klassische Walpurgisnacht" in *Faust II*, where Homunculus traipses through a landscape saturated with time in search of embodiment. The act, which has many of the marks of an allegorical *Festspiel*, is comprised of three such meandering walks. Each of these, in turn, involves an entrance and exit. Here Faust also

perpetually reconstructing the old as something new, his art and science mimicked nature's stage, which—with its ever changing sequence of memorable events—was also for him a stage of history. In this regard, the transformative magic of his ghost poem "Euphrosyne," where the nameless shadows "in Persefoneias Reiche" (line 123) are given new life by the muse as they join the chorus (line 126) of tragic song, recalls "das wunderlichste Geschöpf von der Welt" (HA 11:324), the phantom *Urpflanze* in his 1787 letter to Herder. Similarly, it also anticipates the "Wundergebild" (line 40) of botanical florescence in the 1798 plant elegy, or the "Erstaunen" of the poem "Parabase" (FA 2:495) in "Gott und Welt" (FA 2:489–512), where "Die Metamorphose der Pflanzen" was cited one last time in 1827. In order to appreciate how this final site of citation captured the spirit of Goethe's remarkable poem as the poetic quality of hermeneutic wonder, however, we must follow the meandering path of its haunting, forty-year emergence still further.

When he composed his elegy by the middle of the summer in 1798, Goethe had been contemplating ghosts of various kinds for almost a year. Thus, on June 22, 1797, shortly before completing "Euphrosyne" as a personal monument to Becker-Neumann,[46] he reported in rather ill-humor to Schiller that he had at last been moved by his friend's proddings to reestablish contact with the "dream-world"[47] of his dormant *Faust*. He would now recollect and redeploy the

---

finds his way to Persephone's underworld, while Mephistopheles is out looking for the ancient Phorkyiads.

[46] Cf. Goethe's letter to Meyer of March 23, 1798, where he connects his elegy with his own and Meyer's plans for a traditional stone monument honoring the dead actress: "Denken Sie doch auch gelegentlich an das Monument für die Beckern, ich will indessen die Elegie die ich ihr gelobt habe auch auszuarbeiten suchen" (WA IV, 13:101). Goethe pursues the same connection, again in a letter to Meyer, on June 15, 1798: "Meine Elegie auf die Beckern ist fertig und darf sich, hoff' ich, unter ihren Geschwistern sehen lassen. Schiller meint, man solle vor den Almanach etwas auf sie bezügliches setzen. Wie wäre es, wenn Sie das skizzierte Monument ins Reine zeichneten, es hat mir immer sehr wohl gefallen. Es schadet nichts wenn wir Psyche auch vor übers Jahr vorräthig behalten da doch mit dem Kupferstecher immer eine solche Not ist" (WA IV, 13:178). In his letter to Böttiger of October 25, 1797, Goethe had already spoken about Becker-Neumann's death and his plan to write something "zu ihrem Andenken" (WA IV,12:345). An "Euphrosyne" monument was erected for her in Weimar in 1799. The proposed drawing for the frontispiece to Schiller's *Musen-Almanach* remained unrealized. In its place we find the engraving of Psyche that Goethe had mentioned to Meyer. I feel that its implicit connection with "Euphrosyne," as an episode about rebirth from Ovid's *Metamorphoses*, as well as with Goethe's poem about plant metamorphosis, is noteworthy.

[47] Cf. Goethe's letter to Schiller of June 22, 1797, where he requests his friend to think about Faust on a sleepless night, "und so mir meine eignen Träume, als ein wahrer Prophet, zu erzählen und zu deuten" (WA IV, 12:167).

"Luftphantome" (WA IV, 12:179) from the published fragment for eventual dispersion throughout the body of his massive text, "indem ich das, was gedruckt ist, wieder auflöse und mit dem, was schon fertig oder erfunden ist, in grosse Massen disponiere, und so die Ausführung des Plans, der eigentlich nur eine Idee ist, näher vorbereite" (WA IV, 12:167). After releasing the "barbaric composition" (WA IV, 12:169), together with years of notes and sketches, from the packet where he had interred them eight years before, Goethe next prepared "ein ausführliches Schema"[48] on June 23, as a kind of phantom promise of future value, although he still opined several days later that *Faust* would never be anything more than a fragment.[49] By June 24, however, he had already commemorated the text's eventful resurrection in the dedicatory poem, "Zueignung," which would introduce all subsequent publications, significantly, with the return of shadows from his past: "Ihr naht euch wieder, schwankende Gestalten,/Die früh sich einst dem trüben Blick gezeigt" (HA 3:9).[50]

As many of Goethe's letters during these months suggest, the significance of the "Zueignung" and its ghostly legion was not limited to his commitment to return to *Faust*. Hence the frequent mention—also in terms of return—of travel plans as well, and their ultimate connection—so typical for Goethe—to his own intellectual resurrection. Already toward the end of April, 1797, he had written to his friend Meyer, the art historian, about touring among the ruins and collections of Rome, which he would revisit for the third time in his life—by two further descents into his personal past—via Frankfurt and Switzerland. And while concerns over an unsettled political climate and Meyer's ill health ultimately moved Goethe to change his itinerary and abandon the segment of his trip to the "eternal city," he ironically announced on July 21, 1797 that his clothes, as well as his disembodied mind, were now drifting toward Meyer by way of his hometown, where his mother would be awaiting them. The rest of Goethe, or his body, the letter concluded, would soon follow:

> Hier ist, mein werter Freund, die dritte wöchentliche Sendung, mit der ich Ihnen zugleich ankündigen kann: daß mein Koffer mit dem Postwagen heute früh nach Frankfurt abgegangen und daß also schon ein Teil von mir nach Ihnen zu in Bewegung ist; der Körper wird nun auch wohl bald dem Geiste und den Kleidern nachfolgen. (AA 12:78–79)

---

[48] As cited in *Goethe ueber seine Dichtungen: Versuch einer Sammlung aller Aeusserungen des Dichters ueber seine poetischen Werke*, II, 2, ed. Hans Gerhard Gräf (Frankfurt am Main: Literarische Anstalt Rütten & Loening, 1904) 62. For more on Goethe's recourse to this schema, cf. his letter to Schiller of May 5, 1798 (WA IV, 13:136–37).

[49] To Schiller on June 27, 1797 (WA IV, 12:170).

[50] Cf. Ilse Graham, *Goethe: Portrait of the Artist* (Berlin and New York: Walter de Gruyter, 1977) 357, who relates "schwankende Gestalten" to the force of "wieder" in Goethe, as well as to his "haunting *Urpflanze*."

By equipping his spiritual part with clothes, Goethe could enjoy the transformative power of textiles and make his way through the uncertain world protected and preserved. As "a man of cloth(es)," moreover, he had also prepared himself to endure the hardships of travel properly "vested," and so his vulnerable, material part could trudge behind as an afterthought.

Interestingly, just three days later—and only one day after committing himself to the future redemption of *Faust* by investing its unruly "idea" and its unstable materials in the preparatory medium of the "Schema"—Goethe wrote a last will and testament for the first time in his life. He thereby evoked in the disengaged diction of a legal text both his own and his mother's deaths. Furthermore, by planning for the final disposition of the Goethe *corpus* in its entirety, he established for himself a kind of ghostly afterlife as well. "[D]as aus einer vollständigen Ausgabe meiner Werke allenfalls zu erlösende Kapital" (AA 12:768), the will provides, would be vested with his son and only heir, August. Dr. Goethe's literary remains, that is, would be preserved for the future by properly preparing them for dissemination through the uncertain world—like *Faust*, or the poet's botanical experiences, or his "Geist" and vestments just sent on ahead of his body by the post coach—as a kind of intellectual capital.

How Goethe understood both his own "survival in script" and the related process of "textually" preparing his literary remains for capitalization may be gleaned from the personal account of his subsequent activities in the city of his birth, which Eckermann edited after his death as part of the Goethean *Nachlaß* and then published in 1833 as *Reise in die Schweiz 1797*. Goethe's record of his return home that summer, however, reveals no trace of conventional sentimentality.[51] That is, it offers neither the melancholy glance toward lost innocence that might be expected of an aging writer reflecting on his formative years, nor the tender reflections of a famous son who was seeing his mother after a long separation, or visiting the family house on the former *Hirschgraben*, which had since been sold.[52] Instead, the detached eye of the scientific observer catches the ephemera of a once familiar world, in "Schemata" (AA 12:92) again, for storage

---

[51] Cf. Goethe's crucial letter to Schiller of August 16, 1797, where he attempts to explain the "sentimental" and its relationship to his increasingly self-conscious "poetic mood" (WA IV, 12:243–47).

[52] In the first chapter of *Dichtung und Wahrheit* Goethe recalls that the street where he grew up had formerly lain outside the city and served as a kind of wildlife refuge at its edge. The city fathers had protected the preserve as a source of deer for a yearly celebration, which had become a tradition. Interestingly, Goethe has located himself during his own formative years on a spot that was both wild and cultured, outside as well as inside (HA 9:12). Cf., in this connection, my discussions on the theater in Ludwigsburg, the cemetery in Stuttgart, and the falls at Schaffhausen in the second section of my essay, as well as my treatment of interlocution and the margin as a site of emergence in the third section.

and later use.⁵³ As Goethe dispassionately recorded on August 9, 1797, he wanted to catch the objects ("Gegenstände") around him in the immediacy of their emergence so that he could later take stock of the material ("das Vorrätige") as the stuff ("Stoff") of more refined consideration (AA 12:81). Apparently, he would construct his Frankfurt sojourn as an experimental way station, or stage, for the kind of schematic method to which he had turned upon reopening the spooky *Faust* materials almost two months earlier and to which he would return throughout the rest of his journey to and across Switzerland.⁵⁴

On August 15 Goethe offered a detailed description of this method in anticipation of eventually publishing an account of his travels with Meyer's assistance. Typically, his reflections begin, tourists judge the objects of their immediate experiences prematurely. However lively ("lebhaft") their first, crude ("roh")⁵⁵ impressions are, however, they inevitably remain one-sided, unless certain corrective steps are undertaken. Accordingly, Goethe has now adopted the practice of supplementing his initial, private observations while traveling with documents of a more public nature ("Akten") in order to establish a historical basis for any future attempts at refining them:

> Ich habe mir daher Akten gemacht, worin ich alle Arten von öffentlichen Papieren, die mir jetzt begegnen: Zeitungen, Wochenblätter, Predigtauszüge, Verordnungen, Komödienzettel, Preiskurrente einheften lasse und sodann auch sowohl das, was ich sehe und bemerke, als auch mein augenblickliches Urteil einschalte. Ich spreche nachher von diesen Dingen in Gesellschaft und bringe meine Meinung vor, da ich denn bald sehe, inwiefern ich gut unterrichtet bin, und inwiefern mein Urteil mit dem Urteil wohlunterrichteter Menschen übereintrifft. Sodann nehme ich die neue Erfahrung und Belehrung wieder zu den Akten, und so gibt es Materialien, die mir künftig als Geschichte des Äußern und Innern interessant genug bleiben müssen. Wenn ich bei meinen Vorkenntnissen und meiner Geistesgeübtheit Lust behalte, dieses

---

⁵³One of these sketches, which Goethe eventually published in 1823 in *Über Kunst und Alterthum*, provides an outline of the writer's intellectual constitution and life that would become the basis of many subsequent autobiographical reconstructions. Additional schemata were written during these months for an epic poem, *Die Jagd* (which became *Novelle*), as well as for the dramatic trilogy, *Die Natürliche Tochter*, which Goethe published as a fragment at the turn of 1804. For more on Goethean schemata, ghosts, and commemoration, cf. Helmut Schanze, *Goethes Dramatik: Theater der Erinnerung* (Tubingen: Max Niemeyer Verlag, 1989) 123–41.

⁵⁴Cf. Goethe's letter to Schiller of August 9, 1797 (WA IV, 12:217–18).

⁵⁵Cf. Goethe's letter to Schiller of August 15, 1797 as cited in his *Reise in die Schweiz 1797* (AA 12:92).

Handwerk eine Weile fortzusetzen, so kann ich eine große Masse zusammenbringen. (AA 12:92)[56]

Significantly, Goethe wanted to amass and control the random flow of his incidental travel souvenirs so as to connect the isolated and ephemeral objects of the world and his experiences of them within a dynamic textual body of public conversation and historical accounting. The resulting reconstruction, in turn, which promised to hold his attention once these objects had passed from view, would be comprised as an "organic" totality—by which Goethe understood the complex organization of any self-sustaining process of composition.[57]

In order to collect and prepare his empirical observations within the dynamic field of such a process, and thereby capitalize on all that was familiar to him, Goethe decided to conduct a kind of experiment during the first stop of his trip home. As reported in a seminal letter to Schiller on August 16, 1797, he planned on using the stay in Frankfurt to test his new theory of symbolic seeing: "Ich will es erst noch hier versuchen, was ich symbolisches bemerken kann, besonders aber an fremden Orten, die ich zum erstenmal sehe, mich üben" (WA IV, 12:246). That is, he would, as was his habit now, suppress all conventional sentimentality by conducting himself like a stranger within the field of objects from both his personal and collective past. He would thereby also parallel the procedures of the *Faust* schema of a few months before, where he had similarly "fixed" old materials for later use by confronting the once familiar ephemera of his (creative) past, likewise grown ghostly and strange, and then disposing of them "in große Massen" (WA IV, 12:167). In both cases, that is, Goethe intended rescuing the past from dissolution by undoing and then reweaving its loose threads into a new text(ile), which would lend the wavering forms of accumulated experience a fullness, or mass, and therefore, also, an organized complexity that they currently lacked.

In this spirit, he had already reported to Schiller before leaving for Frankfurt that he wanted to have a new *Faust* manuscript prepared. The portions of the text that had been published as the resurrected *Fragment* in 1790 were to be transcribed by a copyist, "da denn das neue desto besser mit dem alten zusammen wachsen kann" (WA IV, 12:179). Goethe's grafting operation, which is also a technical device for making the old (here the printed text) look new (here

---

[56] Goethe's letter to Schiller on August 22, 1797 is almost identical (WA IV, 12:260–61).

[57] According to Stuart Atkins, "Goethe used 'organic' not—as did some younger German contemporaries of Coleridge—to mean 'coming into being by a primarily unconscious growth process,' but to express what Aristotle and other critics have understood by the term: constituting a complex integrated whole." Cf. "On Goethe's Classicism," in *Goethe Proceedings: Essays Commemorating the Goethe Sesquicentennial at the University of California, Davis*, eds. Clifford A. Bernd et al. (Columbia, SC: Camden House, 1984) 13.

the transcribed, or manuscript text) anticipated the technique of his symbolic seeing, which would soon confront him with the old and once familiar world of Frankfurt as though he were experiencing it for the first time. But almost ten years earlier, while working on the Göschen edition of his works in Rome, Goethe had already looked at the *Faust* materials through the estranging lens of time and expressed the same hopeful belief, "den Faden wiedergefunden zu haben."[58] Only then it had been a freshly composed scene, intended for publication in the forthcoming edition, that was new and the yellowed and tattered *Urfaust* manuscript that was old:

> Das alte Manuskript macht mir manchmal zu denken, wenn ich es vor mir sehe. Es ist noch das erste, ja in den Hauptscenen gleich so ohne Concept hingeschrieben; nun ist es so gelb von der Zeit, so vergriffen (die Lagen waren nie geheftet), so mürbe und an den Rändern zerstoßen, daß es wirklich, wie das Fragment eines alten Codex aussieht, so daß ich, wie ich damals in eine frühere Welt mich mit Sinnen und Ahnen versetzte, mich jetzt in eine selbstgelebte Vorzeit wieder versetzten muß.[59]

Here Goethe has linked the structure of his *Faust* work to the same kind of historically informed, or symbolic, seeing that had already structured the Nightscene and that for the next decade or so would characterize his penchant for ghosts as a metaphorical indicator of the defining experience of temporal estrangement. The point, then, is not so much an ability to determine which medium is old and which is new—the handwritten draft or the text intended for the printer—as it is to understand time in terms of the reciprocal relationship between the modes of past, present, and future. When Goethe melded the old into the new, or vice versa, the remains of a uniquely constituted past resurfaced in the living parts of an irreversible present, which he in turn could experience as something more than everyday, or ephemeral, only after recognizing that every present has always been haunted, or inhabited, by the past. To have a future and thereby appear "eternal," the Goethean moment, or *Augenblick*,[60] typically acknowledges a destiny of perpetual transition, reincarnation, and belatedness. Thus, in Goethe's 1788 comment on *Faust*, he considered deceptively aging the paper of his more recent work on the play, so as to create, in the reconstructed mass of the forthcoming *Fragment*, the same kind of labyrinthine confusion of old and new that he would mention to Schiller in 1797 before departing for Frankfurt: "Ich habe schon eine neue Scene ausgeführt, und wenn ich das Papier räuchere, so dächt' ich, sollte sie mir niemand aus den alten herausfinden."[61]

[58] Gräf, II, 2:42.

[59] Gräf, II, 2:43–44.

[60] Cf. Andreas Anglet, *Der 'ewige' Augenblick: Studien zur Struktur und Funktion eines Denkbildes bei Goethe* (Cologne, Weimar, and Vienna: Böhlau, 1991).

[61] Gräf, II, 2:42–43.

Interestingly, Goethe's aesthetic discussion in his letter of August 16 provides a theoretical framework for linking his literary and scientific activities of 1797–98 to the language of capitalization from his last will and testament and to his representation of ghosts as the estrangement of time. His comments begin by displacing the suppressed sentimentality of the empirical subject onto the experience of observing otherwise quotidian objects ("Gegenständen"). As he reminds Schiller toward the end of the letter, he had always felt ill-at-ease in front of the raw stuff of experience and would have preferred going directly home, "um, aus meinem Innersten, Phantome jeder Art hervorzuarbeiten, als daß ich mich noch einmal, wie sonst (da mir das Aufzählen eines Einzelnen nun einmal nicht gegeben ist) mit der millionfachen Hydra der Empirie herumgeschlagen hätte" (WA IV, 12:247). But Goethe did not retire to his writer's study in Weimar with its more tempting ghosts of his own creation, because—unlike Hercules, who supposedly survived by strangling the serpent Hydra—he had found a liberating alternative in the ghosts of the world around him. Rather than destroying the monsters of touristic seeing, which threatened to overwhelm his eyes by repeatedly forcing him to shift his focus from one thing to another, he had learned to incorporate his travel souvenirs "in der ganzen Masse meiner Kenntnisse" as symbolic reconstructions. Accordingly, they had become pleasant for him after all ("nicht unangenehm"), or aesthetically charged, and their productive value ("Capital") had increased (WA IV, 12:243).

The effect that enabled Goethe to transform incidental objects and their accumulated memories into symbolic "Gegenstände" (WA IV, 12:244) was not pure, however. Thus, after locating the source of a kind of "Sentimentalität" (WA IV, 12:243) within them and then further describing them as "nicht ganz poetisch" (WA IV, 12:243), he linked the experience of such objects to a transitional moment, or "Mittelzustand" (WA IV, 12:244), that recalled the etiology of the "sentimental" in Schiller's *Über naive und sentimentalische Dichtung*.[62] The 1795–96 *Horen* essay of Goethe's most important aesthetic interlocutor[63] had already analyzed the modern poet's "mixed" pleasure in certain unassuming, natural objects—"eine unscheinbare Blume" (NA 20:414), for example—as the estrangement of time.[64] Such objects attract the attentions of modern sensibilities, according to Schiller, because upon observation, they appear—much like Goethe's haunting spirits—to be inhabited by the displaced desire for "das stille, schaffende Leben" (NA 20:414) that we lack within ourselves:

[62] As Goethe himself pointed out in his letter of August 16: "Ich berufe mich auf das, was Sie selbst so schön entwickelt haben, auf das was zwischen uns Sprachgebrauch ist..." (WA IV, 12:245).

[63] At the time, Schiller himself was struggling with the massive historical materials surrounding the Thirty Years' War, which he would stage, over the next few years and with Goethe's assistance, as the tragedy *Wallenstein*.

[64] Ziolkowski links this to his theory of the classical German elegy, 82 ff.

> Sie sind, was wir waren; sie sind, was wir wieder werden sollen. Wir waren Natur, wie sie, und unsere Kultur soll uns, auf dem Wege der Vernunft und der Freyheit, zur Natur zurückführen. Sie sind also zugleich Darstellung unserer verlornen Kindheit, die uns ewig das theuerste bleibt; daher sie uns mit einer gewissen Wehmuth erfüllen. Zugleich sind sie Darstellungen unserer höchsten Vollendung im Ideale, daher sie uns in eine erhabene Ruhe versetzen. (NA 20:414)

Now, according to Goethe's very similar line of thought, objects emerge "symbolically" from the crowded field of casual observation, when the poetically attuned observer intuitively sees, or reconstructs, them as part of a larger, complex totality that is also temporally determined. The process in question, he asserted, which makes unassuming, even hauntingly oppressive, objects into liberating ones, involves

> eminente Fälle, die in einer charakteristischen Mannigfaltigkeit, als Repräsentanten von vielen andern dastehen, und eine gewisse Totalität in sich schließen, eine gewisse Reihe fordern, ähnliches und fremdes in meinem Geiste aufregen und so von außen wie von innen an eine gewisse Einheit und Allheit Anspruch machen. Sie sind also, was ein glückliches Sujet dem Dichter ist, glückliche Gegenstände für den Menschen . . . (WA IV, 12:244)

Two such "felicitous" objects had already presented themselves in Frankfurt, Goethe continued, and it is significant that he understood both spatially—as places that had emerged through time and were therefore positioned to direct his attention, hermeneutically, "auf's bedeutende" (WA IV, 12:246). The first of these *topoi*, or localities, Goethe identified, with little elaboration, as "den Platz, auf dem ich wohne, der in Absicht seiner Lage und alles dessen was darauf vorgeht, in einem jeden Momente symbolisch ist" (WA IV, 12:245). He constructed his second example, however—"den Raum meines großväterlichen Hauses, Hofes und Gartens" (WA IV, 12:245)—as a defamiliarized place that had dynamically comprised the social, political, and cultural field of his own emergence into public prominence. Here was another "lofty" vantage point, he implied, from where he could observe the creative and destructive interventions of historical events in the random flow of time. In other words, Goethe had finally discovered in the ghost-like presence of the symbolic *topos* and its sequential emergences a new and complex organizing structure, which was also charged with redemptive potential. From the "summit" of his grandfather's former residence, he was able to "see" the surrounding world, with "Geistes-Augen," as the eventful stage of historical transformation. The present of his return home had become a site of perpetual renovation for him—a place, as he put it,

> der aus dem beschränktesten, patriarchalischen Zustande, in welchem ein alter Schultheiß von Frankfurt lebte, durch klug unternehmende Menschen zum nützlichsten Waaren- und Marktplatz verändert wurde. Die Anstalt ging

durch sonderbare Zufälle bei dem Bombardement zugrunde und ist jetzt, größtentheils als Schutthaufen, noch immer das Doppelte dessen werth, was vor 11 Jahren von den gegenwärtigen Besitzern an die Meinigen bezahlt worden. In so fern sich nun denken läßt daß das Ganze wieder von einem neuen Unternehmer gekauft und hergestellt werde, so sehn Sie leicht daß es, in mehr als Einem Sinne, als Symbol vieler tausend andern Fälle, in dieser gewerbreichen Stadt, besonders vor meinem Anschauen, dastehen muß (WA IV, 12:245–46).

Like the creative subject of his 1771 commemorative essay on Shakespeare's historical stage,[65] the successive proprietors of Goethe's alienated (maternal!) "patrimony" had exemplified a Promethean urge to shape and inhabit huts of their own making. By renewing the ancient, free-imperial city of Frankfurt, moreover, these builders had also responded to its challenge as a fragment or ruin. Joined in a collective struggle against the corrosive effects of temporality, each of them had, in his individual presumption of freedom, confronted a shared human destiny and thus answered the introductory call of Goethe's youthful Shakespeare encomium, "auch dann zu bleiben, wenn das Schicksal uns zur allgemeinen Nonexistenz zurückgeführt zu haben scheint" (HA 12:224). Through the vantage point of the grandson's experience of symbolic seeing, that is, the grandfather—whom Goethe's autobiography would portray as a latter-day Alcinous[66]—had collectively emerged with his successors from a grave of ghostly oblivion by confronting the unstoppable passage of time. The site of their ephemeral projects of renovation, moreover, had become a stage on which the entire history of the city could be viewed still playing itself out. Accordingly, as the spectator Goethe looked on, the partially capitalized property of the venerable *Schultheiß*—which the recent wars had transformed into a valuable ruin—was expanding beyond its first, confining borders. Indeed, it had already merged, in Goethe's final, symbolic, view of the place, with the pulsating totality of the complex urban bustle that surrounded it. In other words, the "Weltgarten" Frankfurt had finally emerged on this ancient spot—where the old could no longer be distinguished from the new—as a frontier region of future commerce and growth.[67]

---

[65]"Zum Shakespeares-Tag" (HA 12:224–27). For a discussion of Goethe's Shakespeare as *Denkmal* cf. Clark Muenzer, "Ihr ältesten, würdigsten Denkmäler der Zeit: Goethe's *Über den Granit* and his Aesthetics of Monuments," in *Ethik und Ästhetik: Werke und Werte in der deutschen Literatur vom 18. bis zum 20. Jahrhundert. Festschrift für Wolfgang Wittkowski zum 70. Geburtstag*, ed. Richard Fisher (Frankfurt am Main: Peter Lang, 1995) 183–84.

[66]Cf. Book 1 (HA 9:39), as well as Peters 163–75.

[67]Goethe's dynamic representation of urban growth appears to anticipate Robert Venturi's architecture of "complexity and contradiction." Cf. his *Complexity and Contradiction in Architecture* (New York: The Museum of Modern Art, 1966) 101.

Such, then, were some of the more prominent personal and intellectual circumstances of Goethe's life as he left Frankfurt for Meyer and Switzerland on August 25, 1797. Journeys, finances, and wills; outstanding writing projects, schemata, and literary remains; epic hexameters and elegiac distichs; collected works, editorial collaborations, and travel souvenirs; art objects and natural specimens; aesthetic and scientific methodologies; rocks and bones; history and war; urban organization and renewal were all on his mind as he traced the labyrinthine route to his 1798 poem about plants. Yet these individual concerns, many of which found expression in Goethe's reflections as haunting ideas in search of worlds to inhabit, were not simply competing for his undivided attention, but rather aligning themselves in reciprocal relationships. No single strand of his thought during these years can be followed without taking up other threads as well. When viewed together, moreover, the totality of strands constitutes a textual web, or symbolic place of sorts, which I have imagined as the porous intellectual field of Goethe's emergence as a mature writer and thinker. Much like his grandfather's property—which had become productively entangled with the city that surrounded it—the unsettled and distracted impresario on the stage of his nation's cultural rebirth was poised in the summer of 1797 to become an increasingly complex symbolic *topos* himself.[68]

The Plant as Poem and as Monument

The route followed by Goethe from Frankfurt to Switzerland during the late summer and early fall months of 1797 included stops in Heidelberg and along the fertile Neckar valley, now alive with the sensations of harvest. Many of his visits, moreover, engaged him in observations that sustained his thinking about symbolic seeing in terms of local topics and their histories. Various monuments, in particular, served as points of orientation across the region and came to occupy pivotal places in the posthumously published travel account. Two prominently placed statues of the Great Elector and Minerva, for instance, adorned either side of the bridge by which he had made his entrance into historic Heidelberg, and he further situated the city by referring to the natural and artificial

---

[68]In this sense, Goethe was always involved in his own reconstruction. His autobiographical works, in particular, along with his constant work on successive Goethe editions, including the *Ausgabe letzter Hand*, reproduced him as a kind of Goethean *Denkmal*. Accordingly, that part of Goethe canonized as *Genie*, or "authoring" instance, cannot be disentangled from the complex totality of contexts that have sustained him as the difficult challenge of his own protean and migratory culture (*Goethezeit*). Cf. in these connections the "Selbstschilderung" of 1797 (HA 10: 530–31). Cf. also Gerhart von Graevenitz, *Das Ich am Rande: Zur Topik der Selbstdarstellung bei Dürer, Montaigne und Goethe* (Constance: Universitätsverlag Konstanz, 1989), for a similar approach to the structure of *Dichtung und Wahrheit*.

formations of granite that had framed his view both when arriving and departing (AA 12:108–112). Similarly, in Heilbronn, certain architectural monuments encircling the town had caught his attention, including the ancient towers and the famous walled-in graves, which he noted as "ein wichtiges Denkmal der vorigen Zeit" (AA 12:115).[69]

Future readers of the posthumously published *Reise* would feel inclined to view Goethe, the chronicler, as an actor on the historical stage of his own travels—right along with the cast of characters that his script brings to life. Hence his frequent references to what was old or curious or vestigial in setting the scene of a new locality *en route*, which he typically approached and left in his account through the wings. Beyond such gestures of entrance and exit, however, Goethe often conflated his roles as observer or chronicler, on the one hand, and historical actor, on the other. Once he found himself within a particular field of monumentality, that is—which he liked picturing in theatrical terms—the border between spectator and stage tended to blur or dissolve. While on his next stop in Ludwigsburg, for example, he thoroughly inspected—both from within and without—the grand wooden opera house, where he had taken detailed and precise measurements of the stage and proscenium, as well as the orchestra and galleries, in order to configure the interior as a reciprocal arrangement of spectator space and stage. His initial description of the house as "ein merkwürdiges Gebäude, aus Holz und leichten Brettern zusammengeschlagen" (AA 12:122), moreover, had already linked it to the hastily constructed world on boards that it contained, thereby underlining the conflation of world and spectacle, outer and inner in his thought. When pictured as a monument and situated within a historical community—Goethe's thinking seems to go—a theater cannot be thought apart from the transformative magic of the acting that takes place inside it. Like all hermeneutically charged *topoi*, "das große Operntheater" in Ludwigsburg presented him with a complex organization of interrelated parts that had emerged as a totality through the gradual process of his own methodical reconstructions. After observing the stage on which history is played out as a succession of scenic events (i.e., entrances and exits), then, the Goethean spectator finds himself gradually entering its arena as a historical subject in his own right. Furthermore, because his creative interventions finally change the context of his initial observations, they also transform the original sequence of scenes. Ultimately, the properly attuned spectator merges with the actors on the stage of history, where as in the "Vorspiel auf dem Theater" of *Faust*, a composite voice speaks the parts of poet, impresario, and player all at once.

Stuttgart was the next city on Goethe's itinerary, and significantly, he viewed it during the early morning hours of his first day there against a backdrop of graves again, which the industrious local inhabitants had "used" and

---

[69] An almost identical phrase occurs in *Die Wahlverwandtschaften* to describe the renovated gothic chapel where Ottilie and Eduard are interred (HA 6:366).

"transformed" over the years back into "Weinberge und Gartenpflanzungen" (AA 12:123–24). Their noteworthy work, which Goethe captured with the single word "verwandelt," also implies that the recreative activity of the community had eliminated the terrifying border between the dead and the living by folding old burial grounds—which had once set the city's limit—back into its web of daily concerns. It should not be surprising, therefore, that Goethe should note a resemblance between the center of Swabian cultural life and parts of the old-city Frankfurt, which he had recently construed, symbolically, as a place saturated with time. Along these lines, he also noted with interest that Stuttgart officials had begun construction again on a portion of the ducal castle, which had caught fire after some recent renovations (AA 12:125). In short, he had discovered yet another place—like his grandfather's Frankfurt property, or the public gardens in Palermo and its *Urpflanze*—where the old had merged with the new and where perpetual projects of renovation would enable him to see through time's foliations by productively returning the past to the future.[70]

As Goethe's sojourn in Stuttgart continued, the city became the stage of several eventful encounters with eminent local personalities, whose work further captured for him the symbolic significance of his entire trip within the field of cultural production. Thus, we see the traveler in the studio of the sculptor Dannecker, where an array of props, including an alabaster vase, several unfinished marble statues, an astonishing plaster bust of Schiller, and numerous other studies first stimulated his thinking about the care that artists should exert in choosing the proper subject matter (topics) and materials to incorporate their ideas (AA 12:124–25). Or, in Professor Scheffauer's "Werkstatt," we find him similarly considering a marble statue of a sleeping Venus and Amor, several ancient *bas reliefs*, and the plaster model of a monument for an obelisk to commemorate the ruling duke's recovery from a serious illness.

The narrative of Goethe's hectic schedule from in and around Stuttgart continues schematically for several more pages and, as might be expected, his

---

[70]Cf. Goethe's letter to Herder on May 17, 1787, as cited in the *Italienische Reise*: "Vorwärts und rückwärts ist die Pflanze immer nur Blatt" (HA 11:375). In his seminal essay on Goethe, "The *Bildungsroman* and Its Significance in the History of Realism (Toward a Historical Typology of the Novel)," in *Speech Genre and Other Essays*, ed. Caryl Emerson and Michael Holquist, transl. Vern W. McGee (Austin: University of Texas Press, 1986) 34, M. Bakhtin notes that in the Goethean vision of historical time "the past itself must be *creative*. It must have its *effect* in the present (even if this effect is negative or one Goethe considers undesirable). Such a creatively effective past determining the present, produces in conjunction with the present a particular direction for the future, and, to a certain degree, predetermines the future. Thus, one achieves the fullness of time, and it is a graphic, visible completeness." Cf. also in this connection his "Forms of Time and the Chronotope in the Novel," in *The Dialogic Imagination: Four Essays*, ed. Michael Holquist, transl. Caryl Emerson and Michael Holquist (Austin: University of Texas Press, 1981) 84–258.

observations frame a large number of disparate topics. Portraits, historical paintings, and landscapes; collections of drawings and copper engravings; a library with its own displays of antiquities and natural specimens; theater visits, stage props, and scenery; war devastation and renewal; meetings with a well-known architect to review plans for rebuilding the charred remains of the ducal palace in Weimar; exotic plants, including a blooming amaryllis and a giant aloe about to bloom after transplanting; stucco wall and ceiling decorations with exquisite botanical motifs; a neo-gothic chapel with some notable stained glass; an invitation from Cotta, the future publisher of the *Ausgabe letzter Hand*, to use his Tübingen home as a refuge from uncomfortable inns; a cantata based on the writer's youthful *Ossian* translations; camel jaws, ox skulls, and fossilized mammoth bones; a human fetus preserved in alcohol and half a deformed human jaw—all of these curiosities and topics attracted Goethe's attention while in Stuttgart during the last two days of August and the first week of September, 1797, and each exemplified, in its own manner, the dynamics of cultural production as adumbrated in his Frankfurt letter to Schiller on symbolic seeing.

If, along these lines, culture (*Bildung*) is the complex site where communities emerge and define themselves by staging the meaningful reciprocity of the old and the new, then the hurried and twisting account of Goethe's travel ephemera itself makes sense as part of the foliating life of Weimar classicism and its ongoing project of hermeneutic recovery. Goethe's meandering route from Weimar to Switzerland and back, which became an important segment of the serpentine path to his plant elegy, turned back and forth through the hidden axis of time, in the same manner that the 1798 distichs would wend their way through the dynamic Goethe *corpus* for some thirty more years, or for that matter, in the same way that the migrating and protean leaf of annual plants spirals, according to Goethean thinking, through the pulsating body of the *Urpflanze*. Let me therefore continue unraveling the creative network, or "schaffendes Gewebe" (FA 24:395), of his exemplary *Bildungsreise* near the end of 1797 by noting his own pronounced inclination to view the things he encountered within the larger context of their emergence in a pulsating temporal environment. As Goethe came to understand them, the self-sustaining structures of natural, cultural, and scientific formation all stage life by making visible those junctures of signification where (new) meanings are produced from (old) things as they reappear in changing shapes and configurations. Botanically speaking, he chose the "topics" of his symbolic attention by seeing in them a hidden purposiveness that extends backward and forward through time and beyond the boundaries of any single, or closed, field of conclusive knowledge.[71]

---

[71] Cf. §120 of *Versuch die Metamorphose der Pflanzen zu erklären*: "[G]egenwärtig müssen wir uns damit begnügen, daß wir uns gewöhnen die Erscheinungen vorwärts und rückwärts gegen einander zu halten. Denn wir können eben so gut sagen: ein Staubwerkzeug sei ein zusammengezogenes Blumenblatt, als wir von dem Blumen-

Richard Rorty's account of the journey of western philosophy offers a useful paradigm for situating Goethe's *Bildungsreise* toward the metamorphosis elegy, and toward Weimar classicism, by contrasting two "ideal opposites," which he calls epistemology and hermeneutics.[72] The "foundational" discourse of epistemological thinking, according to Rorty's framework, is sited within worlds that are known to the community according to objective and timeless standards, while the "edifying" discourse of hermeneutical thinking breaks paths through uncharted worlds, where we find "new, better, more interesting, more fruitful ways of speaking."[73] Whereas the former is satisfied in "discovering truth," Rorty summarizes, the latter "aims at continuing a conversation."[74]

When Goethe returned to Weimar after his edifying journey of 1797, then, he contemplated a kind of work for himself that resembled the work of generations of industrious Stuttgarters, who had productively reincorporated the outlying graves of their ancestors into the gardens and vineyards now sustaining the city. In fact, according to his account, Goethe had begun his mental reconstruction of Stuttgart as a meaningful place of cultural emergence by taking an early morning tour in full view of these transformed burial sites, which traditionally had marked the city limits. The implication therefore arises that Stuttgart had also emerged in his own field of view as a living monument to the struggle within all cultural life against time. Here was a place—again like the grandfather's home and garden—where an urban center had emerged and survived the vicissitudes of time, because its inhabitants had transgressively invited the ghosts of their dead back into their midst. Like the exemplary builders of Frankfurt, Stuttgart's historical community of artists, scientists, and artisans had collectively erected one of those felicitous places of Goethean experience upon the debris of the past. And even though Goethe feared that the best fruits ("Früchte") of their composite culture of art, natural science, and the crafts might not be harvested in Württemberg itself, he still hoped that a portion of its bounty could be transplanted, and profitably take root, "an andern Orten" (AA 12:157).

Such had already been the case with his own *Ossian* translations, he discovered, which he found grafted during his Stuttgart sojourn onto the musical culture of the city:

> Abends bei Herrn Kapellmeister Zumsteeg, wo ich verschiedene gute Musik hörte. Er hat die Colma, nach meiner Übersetzung, als Kantate, doch nur mit Begleitung des Klaviers übersetzt, sie tut sehr gute Wirkung und wird viel-

---

blatte sagen können: es sei ein Staubgefäß im Zustande der Ausdehnung" (FA 24:150).

[72]Rorty 318.

[73]Rorty 360.

[74]Rorty 373.

leicht auf das Theater zu arrangieren sein, worüber ich nach meiner Rückkunft denken muß. (AA 12:138)

Ironically, a quarter-of-a-century earlier, Goethe had dragged this monument of Celtic song[75] back home to Germany and *Werther*, from where it would subsequently reemerge in Kapellmeister Zumsteeg's apartment. And now he imagined transplanting it back home again, to the Weimar stage, as a full-fledged theatrical production. Like the phantom *Urpflanze*, which he had constructed for Herder as the model of all possible plants, his *Ossian* reconstruction thus became the organizing ground of its own endless life in translation. First we have the forger MacPherson, who gave body to an entire world of ghostly voices by claiming to have uncovered the remains of bardic culture and recirculating them—as fraudulent citation—in his translations from *The Poems of Ossian*. Next, Goethe reinvented Ossianic culture by prominently situating it—as Werther's own translation work—in his fledgling novel. In other words, like MacPherson, Goethe gave (textual) body to a (second) ghostly voice by a double act of translation and, in the process, he produced the stunningly effective youth culture of his memorialized hero. Clearly, however, the original, or "characteristic," voice of the translator Werther, an authentic *Kraftgenie*, had itself been overlain with the voice of the forger *qua* translator, MacPherson-Ossian. And had Goethe's plans for an *Ossian* performance in the court theater materialized, Werther's ghost might well have risen from his novel upon the stage of Weimar classicism—just as Helena would emerge on the stage of *Faust II*[76]—to wonder at his curious survival as a rhetorical topic of praise and derision. All projects of transmission and translation, it seems, when part of some larger hermeneutical program, must eventually acknowledge their life in the estrangement of time. They are haunted from the start by the power of return, which also is fundamentally disorienting.

The actual "goal" and farthest reach of Goethe's wending journey of 1797 was Switzerland, where he "wandered" from the falls at Schaffhausen, via Zurich and its lake, all the way through to the terrifying and oftimes "formless"[77]

---

[75] For more on the connections between Goethe's essay "Von deutscher Baukunst" and Herder's *Ossian* essay, cf. Clark Muenzer, "Herders *Von deutscher Art und Kunst*: Der Sturm und Drang deutscher Selbst-Legitimierung. Ostern 1773," in *Zwischen Traum und Trauma: Die Nation*, ed. Claudia Meyer-Iswandi (Tübingen: Stauffenberg, 1994) 39–57.

[76] Cf. Clark Muenzer, "Goethe's Gothic Classicism: Antecedents to the Architecture of History in *Faust II*, Act III," in *Faust Today*, ed. C. Hamlin and Jane Brown (Columbia, SC: Camden House, 1994) 187–206.

[77] Cf. Goethe's letter to Böttiger of October 25, 1797, where he reports that news of Becker-Neumann's death reached him "in den formlosen Gebirgen" (WA IV, 12: 345). In "Euphrosyne" this landscape is further connected with the underworld: "Denn

terrain of the Gotthard, before "turning back" to Weimar. Since his first Swiss excursion in 1775, in fact, the Gotthard summit had become a point of spiritual return for Goethe, as well as a kind of turning point through which he would typically emerge from a personal crisis by making some crucial creative decision.[78] And so, too, in 1797, he assaulted the dangerous summit one last time, where less than a year hence he would imagine the conversation between himself and the ghost of the young actress. But certainly in imagining his ascent, Goethe was also descending—like Faust in search of "the Mothers"—into the dizzying nether world of the monument and cultural production.[79] In this connection, moreover, his poetological conversation with the ghost "Euphrosyne," as well as the plant elegy of a short time later, seem to me to reveal significantly more about the dynamic nature of vantage point and vision in his thinking than any picturesque view he might have enjoyed, once he completed his trek up the side of the mountain. The view from the Gotthard, that is, and the secret of its "summit" for Goethe, lay precisely in the difficult "totality" of the twisting path up (or down) its slope and its granite terrain. As he had once suggested in his 1784 rhapsody "Über den Granit," the primeval formations of the "Urgestein" offer themselves as monumental figures of complex temporal layering, baffling endurance and change, challenging largeness, and stubborn resistance to facile systems of classification.[80] By climbing the Gotthard, therefore, Goethe situated himself within the protean, migratory, and transgressive region of "ancient monuments of time." Their ascent could be achieved, but it would certainly become a disorienting experience.

When on several occasions Goethe mounted wooden viewing platforms for tourists near the Rhine Falls in Schaffhausen, he was already thinking about the difficulty of natural monuments and their complex temporal structure, as well as their refusal to fix inside or outside in any conclusive way. In each of these instances, he had first occupied a spot *within* a powerful "Naturszene" (AA 12:174), as he called it, from where he physically experienced the force of the water's mass and motion and observed its incommensurabilty. Yet he also enjoyed their aquatic displays of overwhelming natural power from the relative safety of a spectator's station. Accordingly, Goethe's first (preliminary) experience "vom hölzernen Vorbau" (AA 12:174) was sensual, and largely fleeting, he

---

gestaltlos schweben umher in Persefoneias/Reiche, massenweis, Schatten vom Namen getrennt" (FA 1:638).

[78] Cf. Rosmarie Haas, "Goethes Elegie 'Euphrosyne,'" *Jahrbuch des freien deutschen Hochstifts* (1994): 27ff.

[79] As Mephistopheles commands Faust: "Versinke denn! Ich könnt' auch sagen: steige!/'s ist einerlei. Entfliehe dem Enstandnen/In der Gebilde losgebundne Reiche!" (lines 6275–77) (HA 3:193).

[80] Cf. Muenzer, "Ihr ältesten, würdigsten Denkmäler der Zeit."

reported. The water was all dizzying movement, or "siedende Strudel" (AA 12:174), but it was also "sinnliche Erscheinung" (AA 12:174), or a spectacle for the eyes. Consequently the vortex did not immediately swallow him up. The otherwise unfathomable waves of the cascade were momentarily fixed in colors, we learn, just as the streams flowed away. As Goethe further reflected, however, the ground of the "Erscheinung" before him was also paradoxically constituted in a perpetual "Fortfließen" (AA 12:174), or disappearance. Like the inexorable flow of time in his "Rede zum Shakespeares-Tag," the inexorable fall of the water threatened to obliterate everything in its path: "Es wallet und siedet und brauset und zischt" (AA 12:174).[81] In other words, so long as he thought about them only as an accelerating succession of fading moments and ceaseless change, the falls would continue reminding him of his own insignificance and fallen condition. By further venturing into the field of the falls, however, and mounting nature's stage, he was able to confront the power of this "underworld" in a creative act of rapprochement.

That is, Goethe finally reconstructed the cascading water by positioning himself to understand its significance—and his own—in terms of the purposive survival that defines all self-organizing life. In order to see beyond the falls as mere flux, he approached them several more times from a wooden viewing platform again, which he configured first as a stage, or "Bühne,"[82] and finally as a small grandstand, or "Gerüste" (AA 12:179). And on both occasions, the platform—which, properly speaking, was neither exclusively within nor outside the spectacle—became a vantage point for viewing the amazing play of colors in a rainbow. Amidst all the furious movement, then, Goethe had observed something lasting, which had in turn also anchored him in an otherwise unbearable scene of devastation. What one day would become the astonishing image of "Dauerwechsel" in *Faust*, he first read at Schaffhausen, in this refreshing drama, or "Schauspiel" (AA 12:178), of dynamically organized color as the paradigmatic scene of rebirth and regeneration. "Der Regenbogen," he summarized, with its glorious "Farbenspiel" (AA 12:178),

> stand mit seinem ruhigen Fuß in dem ungeheuern Gischt und Schaum, der, indem er ihn gewaltsam zu zerstören droht, ihn jeden Augenblick neu hervorbringen muß. (AA 12:176)

In other words, Goethe saw within the complex reciprocity of sunlight and moving water a hidden point of emergence, or origin, through which the wonderful arc of color would perpetually reproduce itself (and, therefore, also each moment) as a covenant with some higher power. As with all life, including the plant's, the world at Schaffhausen was organized to rise perpetually out of its own ruins:

---

[81]The lines are from Schiller's ballad "Der Taucher."

[82]"Ich trat wieder auf die Bühne an den Sturz heran" (AA 12:176).

In dem ungeheuren Gewühle war das Farbenspiel herrlich. Von dem großen überströmten Felsen schien sich der Regenbogen immerfort herabzuwälzen, indem er in dem Dunst des herunterstürzenden Schaumes entstand. Die untergehende Sonne färbt einen Teil der beweglichen Massen gelb, die tiefen Strömungen erschienen grün und aller Schaum und Dunst war licht und purpur gefärbt; auf allen Tiefen und Höhen erwartete man die Entwicklung eines neuen Regenbogens (AA 12:179–80).

The Flowers of Interlocution

Toward the middle of November Goethe arrived back home in Weimar again, where he began vigorously transforming his travel experiences into the cultural capital of German classicism. Thus, during the next twelve months alone, we find him completing ballads and elegies; revising and extending *Faust* and organizing a schema for the entire play; making plans and sketches for an epic poem about Achilles's death and its aftermath; resuming plans for a philosophical nature poem in the manner of *De rerum natura*; reading Homer, Euripides, Aristophanes, Herodotus, Virgil, Thucydides, Lucretius, Pliny, Voltaire, Diderot, Friedrich Schlegel, and Schelling; supervising the reorganization of the ducal library and nature cabinets; pursuing studies in classical philology, including theories of epic and tragic poetry and the debates about Homer; continuing experimental work in optics and color theory, magnetism, astronomy, and osteology; resuming discussions with Schiller on scientific method; publishing aesthetic essays and satirical epigrams in literary and scientific journals; editing *Die Propyläen*; assisting in the renovations of the Weimar theater, producing its gala reopening, and assuming it directorship; developing horticultural plans for the country estate "Oberroßla" in the textile district of Apolda; and continuing his epistolary conversation with Schiller, where the two friends exchanged a number of ideas about the forthcoming *Musen-Almanache*.

Together with some ballads and elegies, including both "Euphrosyne" and "Die Metamorphose der Pflanzen," Goethe proposed appending several epigrammatic quatrains to the 1799 edition of Schiller's anthology.[83] In the spirit of his suggestion, I have attached one of these "Weissagungen" to my essay, although Goethe did not actually publish his garland of "riddles in distichs" until 1800. Among other things, this small flower poem talks about progress in terms of detours and retrospective recovery, and so it seems appropriate to me that I should cast a glance back toward it now, as I take a last detour in my spiraling approach toward the plant elegy of the same year:

---

[83] Cf. Goethe's letter to Schiller on January 27, 1798, where he obliquely suggests including some poems like the "Xenien" and "Venezianischen Epigramme" as an "Anhang" for the 1799 *Almanach*. According to Gräf, Goethe is probably referring to his "Weissagungen des Bakis" (Gräf, III, 1:308).

> Lang und schmal ist ein Weg. Sobald du ihn gehest, so wird er
> Breiter; aber du ziehst Schlangengewinde dir nach.
> Bist du an's Ende gekommen, so werde der schreckliche Knoten
> Dir zur Blume, und du gib sie dem Ganzen dahin (FA 2:230).

If, as I have suggested, Goethean hermeneutics is about pathfinding, then, according to this construction, we can track paths through life by construing them either narrowly or broadly. When narrowly construed, a temporal path becomes no more than a fruitless chronology. That is, if we only look statically at the world in front of us, through a single focal point, we will never pass through it drawing anything more than a timeline. By contrast, if we abandon the ideology of chronological narrowness by moving radially outward from a single grounding center (and so back and forth across its linear extension), we will—more appropriately in our fallen state—constitute both ourselves and our world, retrospectively, as a spiraling web of reciprocally related moments of emergence. According to this process of reconstruction, moreover, the simple before's and after's of bare chronology are replaced in our thinking by events that occur on the margins of the familiar. Like the plant, or for that matter, like all living things, we survive by growing at nodes, where the threads of old patterns unravel to be rewoven, in turn, into new patterns of relations.

As far as texts are concerned, all this suggests that as readers, we must similarly contrast the narrow and the wide approach. If we read Goethe's poem "Die Metamorphose der Pflanzen" simply as a versified restatement of his conclusive scientific observations, then we will never leave the familiar ground of botanical metamorphosis as it is described in the 1790 *Versuch*. But Goethe's botanical essay does not, in fact, supply a conclusive key to all the problems in his poem, which I have tried to situate more broadly within a Goethean inspired program of hermeneutical inquiry. In other words, rather than viewing the poem as a straightforward reflection of the treatise's authoritative text,[84] we can—more fruitfully, I believe—view it as a creative interruption in Goethe's presumably exhaustive explication there of plant metamorphosis. In a sense, Goethe inserted the plant elegy as a citational moment within the plant treatise in order to open the *Versuch* for further review by resituating it, in turn, as the sustaining context of the rhythmical interlocution. By directing the reader's attention onto his new poem, he had also refocused his old metamorphosis discourse through a complex of "marginal notes" about it that he had scribbled in distichs to himself in the fall of 1798.[85]

---

[84] As in Overbeck.

[85] Two recent studies provide valuable insights into the complexities of reading as they define Goethean hermeneutics. Cf. Benjamin Bennett, *Beyond Theory: Eighteenth-Century German Literature and the Poetics of Irony* (Ithaca and London: Cornell UP, 1994), especially the section on romance reading, 20ff., and von Graevenitz's discus-

But to read Goethean *Metamorphose* through the poem also requires situating its "meaning" at the margins. Wherever the elegy would land over the years, it would find itself surrounded by additional "texts" that, together with it, comprised the grounding context of a spiraling process of signification. In other words, "Die Metamorphose der Pflanzen" appears to have been constructed as an interlocution in order to interrupt its own reading as an authoritative, or timeless, text. As pure intervention,[86] it blocks its own ideal comprehension, so that the meaning of metamorphosis can reemerge "in-between" the lines of the poem and in reciprocal relationship with the multiple contexts at its edge. I suggested earlier that Goethe revised his botanical elegy through its thirty-year history of publication—changing only a few words—by transplanting it four times into different ensembles of texts. Now I can complete my thought by further proposing that, as a reading strategy (or "Lesart"), the poem survived through its connection to other, similarly structured readings in the garlanded *topos* ("Gewinde") of Goethean *Metamorphose*.[87]

Along these lines, the many stops in Goethe's twisting and turning itinerary in 1797 are neither as narrow, or insignificant, or random, as their chronological listing might make them appear at first glance. Within the context of spiraling memories, according to the young ghost in "Euphrosyne," even the most incidental and fleeting moments of prior experiences become enlarged:

> Laß mich der Tage gedenken, da du das Kind mich dem Spiele
> Jener täuschenden Kunst reizender Musen geweiht.
> Laß mich der Stunde gedenken und jedes kleineren Umstands.
> Ach! wer ruft nicht so gerne unwiderbringliches an.
> Klein erscheinet es nun, doch ach! nicht kleinlich dem Herzen;
> Macht die Liebe, die Kunst jegliches Kleine doch groß.
> (lines 35–42)

When reciprocally staged through the lens of time-past and time-future, that is, the chronologically ordered days, or moments, of calendar time are interrupted. They no longer extend as the monotonous line of a here and now, but like all living things, including works of art and love, circumvent death through the

---

sion of the relationship between narration and self in terms of texts and their margins 20–37.

[86]Helena reads herself in this manner, an an "Idole," in the third act of *Faust II*, which Goethe initially conceived as a phantsmagorical "Zwischenspiel" to his epic play. Cf. WA, IV 41:202–3.

[87]In "Schicksal der Druckschrift" Goethe connects his idea of metamorphosis with the botanical decorations that entwine themselves around classical and neo-classical pilasters (FA 24:419). Cf. also von Graevenitz's reading of the decorative, botanical marginalia as presented in the "Venezianischen Epigramme" of the same period, 20ff.

self-transforming process of *Metamorphose*. They reach beyond their borders and survive as "monuments of time."[88]

All this should help us understand how a putative didactic poem about plant growth can also become a love poem or a "classical German elegy." We need only remind ourselves that, according to Goethean thinking, the paths of natural, social, and cultural formation are all hermeneutical in the sense that the *Bakis* quatrain about serpentine movement and garlands and flowers suggests. It should come as little surprise, then, that "Die Metamorphose der Pflanzen" similarly stages the growth of a plant upon the festival stage of life and love, where the emerging flower with its supporting apparatus (i.e., pedicle, calyx, and corolla)—"ein Wundergebild"—intervenes to interrupt the process of stem and leaf growth by displaying its crowning colors—"über dem schlanken Gerüst wechselnder Blätter"—in the stunning spectacle of botanical inflorescence:

> Doch hier hält die Natur, mit mächtigen Händen, die Bildung
>   An, und lenket sie sanft in das Vollkommnere hin.
> Mäßiger leitet sie nun den Saft, verengt die Gefäße
>   Und gleich zeigt die Gestalt zärtere Wirkungen an.
> Stille zieht sich der Trieb der strebenden Ränder zurücke,
>   Und die Rippe des Stiels bildet sich völliger aus.
> Blattlos aber und schnell erhebt sich der zärtere Stengel
>   Und ein Wundergebild zieht den Betrachtenden an.
> Rings im Kreise stellet sich nun, gezählet und ohne
>   Zahl, das kleinere Blatt neben dem ähnlichem hin.
> Um die Achse bildet sich so der bergende Kelch aus,
>   Der zur höchsten Gestalt farbige Kronen entläßt. (lines 33–44)

From this summit of vegetative growth and reproduction, then, the poet-botanist next teasingly instructs his beloved in the mysteries of sexuality and species survival. His valedictory words to her, moreover, which end with the same "gedenke" (l. 71)[89] that the tutelary ghost Euphrosyne pronounced, explain "das Geheimnis der Fortpflanzung" (FA 24:393) in terms that recapitulate the ser-

---

[88] Cf. the following "Xenien," which were published in Schiller's 1797 *Musen-Almanach*: "Immer war mir das Feld und der Wald und der Fels und die Gärten/Nur ein Raum, und du machst sie, Geliebte, zum Ort;" or "Raum und Zeit, ich empfinde es, sind bloße Formen des Denkens/Da das Eckchen mit dir, Liebchen, unendlich mir scheint"; or finally "Leben muß man und lieben! Es endet Leben und Liebe!/Schnittest du, Parze, doch nur beide die Fäden zugleich" (FA 1:609, 613).

[89] Cf. in this regard the poet's use of the imperative "gedenke" in his transition near the end of the poem from the idea of metamorphosis to its instructive application in his relationship with his beloved. This gesture links Goethe's reconstruction of botanical thinking as hermeneutics to the field of monuments and commemoration, as well as to his "Natur- und Kunstblume," the elegy "Euphrosyne." Cf. also Peters 183–89.

pentine path of hermeneutical *Verpflanzung*.⁹⁰ Looking retrospectively through the corolla, he thus first commemorates the sleeping seed, which once buried in the earth "nur halb geformt und farblos"(line 17), eventually rose like an apparition "aus der umgebenden Nacht" (line 21). But the poet also gazes prospectively from the same place, and for a second time, at nature's germinal force, which will soon reappear encapsulated, or "gehüllt" (line 58)⁹¹ within the womb of the plant's protective fruit. Seed, flower, and fruit, therefore—all interconnected stages within the self-perpetuating life of the plant—describe the path of the elegy, which, according to Goethe, is also the path of any living thing.⁹²

As both the *Versuch* and the poem additionally instruct, the self-organizing plant works its transformative magic through "immer *dieselbigen Organe*, welche in vielfältigen Bestimmungen und unter oft veränderten Gestalten die Vorschrift der Natur erfüllen" (FA 24:149). In other words, the protean leaf, which insistently emerges in different configurations as it climbs through a succession of nodal points from the *Samenblätter* through the *Laubblätter* to the *Blumenblatt* with its various *Kelchblätter* and *Kronenblätter*, is the botanical *after*-effect of the mysteriously *pre*-scribed purposiveness within all living things. And it displays its effectiveness in the towering "Wunderbau" (FA 24:395)⁹³ that it constitutes by passing from earth (where the roots descend from the buried seed) to the heavens (toward which stem and flower strive):⁹⁴

> Gleich darauf ein folgender Trieb, sich erhebend, erneuet
>   Knoten auf Knoten getürmt, immer das erste Gebild,
> Zwar nicht immer das gleiche, denn mannigfaltig erzeugt sich
>   Ausgebildet, du siehsts, immer das folgende Blatt,
> Ausgedehnter, gekerbter, getrennter in Spitzen und Teile
>   Die verwachsen vorher ruhten im untern Organ.

⁹⁰I am imagining the structures of botanical inflorescence as the summit region in "Euphrosyne," where, according to Ziolkowski, the encapsulated reflections of the poem occur in the conversation between the poet and the actress's ghost.

⁹¹Goethe analyzes such "Hüllen" as a protective medium against decomposition and decay ("Verwesung") in "Die Absicht wird eingeleitet" (FA 24:395).

⁹²Cf. *Metamorphose der Pflanzen. Zweiter Versuch*, where Goethe states that "alle Geschöpfe welche wir lebendig nennen darin überein kommen, daß sie die Kraft haben ihres gleichen hervorzubringen . . ." (FA 24:152).

⁹³Cf. in this connection my "Von Deutscher Art und Kunst," 52–57, where I examine Goethe's treatment of gothic architecture in similar terms.

⁹⁴Cf. "Die Absicht wird eingeleitet": "Indem wir den vegetativen Typus betrachten, so stellt sich uns bei demselben sogleich ein Unten und Oben dar. Die untere Stelle nimmt die Wurzel ein, deren Wirkung nach der Erde hingeht, der Feuchtigkeit und der Finsternis angehört, da in gerade entgegengesetzter Richtung der Stengel, der Stamm, oder was dessen Stelle bezeichnet, gegen den Himmel, das Licht und die Luft emporstrebt" (FA 24:395).

> Und so erreicht es zuerst die höchst bestimmte Vollendung,
>   Die bei manchem Geschlecht dich zum Erstaunen bewegt.
>   (lines 23–30)

The architecture of plant life, according to Goethe's rhythmic reconstruction, reveals a towering complex of spiraling nodes, or border regions, of transition. Here growth and generation are caught in the self-reflexive leaf as it works at renewing itself through a progression of embodiments that together define all meaningful moments, or "epochs,"[95] in the course of botanical life. Old leaf forms pass away at such sites, but they also rise there to pass on their incomplete work to successor generations of leaves, until the most ephemeral and eventful emergence is attained in this play of the old and the new. The moment of inflorescence arrives, and it is followed, in turn, by fertilization and the subsequent encapsulation of the germinating seed.

In this regard, the transitions of botanical life, which the plant elegy preserves in its encapsulated reflection of the 1790 *Versuch*, imply a hermeneutic program within nature that is captured in the relationship between the encapsulated botanical lesson, on the one hand, and the evolving love story of the frame, on the other. As that lesson ends and passes into the frame, the poet has offered a kind of parable to describe the culminating moment of fertilization and germination:

> Aber die Herrlichkeit wird des neuen Schaffens Verkündung.
>   Ja, das farbige Blatt fühlet die göttliche Hands,
> Und zusammen zieht es sich schnell, die zärtesten Formen
>   Wickeln sich zwiefach hervor, sich zu vereinen bestimmt.
> Traulich stehen sie nun, die holden Paare, beisammen,
>   Zahlreich reihen sie sich um den geweihten Altar,
> Hymen schwebet herbei und herrliche Düfte, gewaltig,
>   Strömen süßen Geruch alles belebend umher. (lines 49–56)

By evoking the marriage altar here in order to escort his beloved into a more elevated world as the poem ends, the poet also helps frame his reconstruction of the plant as a site similarly tensed toward the future—where new connections arise out of old ones, thereby keeping the species alive. Every plant, according to this way of thinking, signals laws, which like the yellowed and tattered Codex of the *Urfaust* manuscript, creatively permit the old and the new "to grow together" upon the altar of metamorphosis:

---

[95]"Epoche" is a word that Goethe used to indicate a moment of historical proportions. Cf. Gabrielle Bersier in "Der Fall der deutschen Bastille: Goethe und die Epochenschwelle von 1806," *Récherches Germaniques* 20 (1990): 49–78. The word occurs several times in the *Versuch* to mark the place of metamorphosis as a site where the plant's entire constellation shifts.

Jede Pflanze winket dir nun die ewgen Gesetze,
   Jede Blume sie spricht lauter und lauter mit dir.
Aber entzifferst du hier der Göttin heilige Lettern,
   Überall siehst du sie dann, auch im verändertem Zug. (lines 65–68)

For years, critics have noted that "das lösende Wort" (line 8) of Goethe's sacred garden riddle is *Metamorphose*. But this straightforward solution is also too simple, I believe. More recently, Günter Peters has properly cautioned in his thorough and insightful reading of the elegy that

> zur Lösung des Rätsels... sich das Wort seinerseits "löst": verflüssigt, entwickelt, verlebendigt. Das lösende Wort muß Erzählung, Erinnerung, Gleichnisrede, Gespräch oder wissenschaftliche Abhandlung werden, um die Einheit, die in der Mannigfaltigkeit der Erscheinungen als Gesetz anwesend und verborgen ist, darstellen zu können.[96]

Along these lines, I would like to conclude my remarks by emphasizing that, like other Goethean *topoi*, or monuments, *Metamorphose* marks a temporally layered site of some complexity. We must therefore read it, as we have learned to read plants and love and even classical poems about plants, through the interlocuted marginalia of other readings. Astonishingly, the word *Metamorphose* itself is comprised in part by the *interlocuted* words *amor* (when read forward) and *Roma* (when read backward).[97] In other words, the solution to Goethe's poem about plant metamorphosis lay in his program of hermeneutical thinking—as it emerged in the discourses of nature (*Metamorphose*, or the plant), society (*amor*, or the family), and culture (*Roma*, or history as both science and art).

Central to Goethe's program, which was also the program of German classicism, was the belief that "the voice of poetry" must enter and form "the conversation of mankind." Not just a conclusive scientific term that exhaustively explained organic life, Goethean *Metamorphose*, we can now see, also underlay the path of this classicism, which, in Rorty's sense of "edifying" discourse, became a search for

> finding new, better, more interesting, more fruitful ways of speaking. The attempt to edify (ourselves or others) may consist in the hermeneutic activity of making connections between our own culture and some exotic culture or historical period, or between our own discipline and another discipline which seems to pursue incommensurable aims in an incommensurable vocabulary. But it may instead consist in the "poetic" activity of thinking up such new aims, new words, or new disciplines, followed by, so to speak, the inverse of hermeneutics: the attempt to reinterpret our familiar surroundings in the unfamiliar terms of our new inventions.... Edifying discourse is supposed to be

[96] Peters 202.

[97] Peters 202.

abnormal, to take us out of our old selves by the power of strangeness, to aid us in becoming new beings.[98]

According to this approach, it seems useful to me to view Goethe's reintroduction of the "Metamorphose der Pflanzen" six times, and in four different contexts, into a range of "ensembled" publications with only a few minor changes as a *topos* of cultural production.[99] Every time that he let the plant elegy speak, it reorganized itself to speak otherwise, or to make its point about *Metamorphose* somewhat differently. As a leaf in the *Musen-Almanach*, for example, where it lived within a family of aesthetically self-conscious texts, it initially addressed the role of art, poetry, and theater within a society that, like the poet in "Euphrosyne," was learning to understand its historical mission as a conversation with the dead. In addition to art, however, love, according to the actress's ghost, also elevates, refines, or extends "jegliches Kleine" (line 42), by which Goethe meant anything that could comfortably be contained within the narrow borders of the familiar. So the love theme continued to unfold, appropriately, within the cycle of Müllerin poems and "Amyntas," where "eros" became an eruptive, even creatively disruptive, power that can precipitously intrude into texts from without to open them up.[100] With "Elegien II," of course, the new conversation of Weimar classicism was well under way, and so we find the earlier aesthetic themes deployed within explicitly social and historical fields. Interlocuted conversations thus play structurally significant roles in many of these poems, where they often emerge in the reflexive core, as encapsulated citations.[101] In order for these conversations to pass from the core of the familiar to the frame of discovery, however, yet another site had to be constructed—like the "höhere Welt" (line 80) of "gleicher Gesinnungen" (line 77) in "Die Metamorphose der Pflanzen," for example, which also rose progressively out of familiarity, we are told, or "dem Keim der Bekanntschaft" (line 71), through "holde Gewohnheit" (line 72) and "Freundschaft" (line 73) to achieve a new (sexual) unity and, hence, also the start of a new family.

Goethe called this site "Gott-Natur," and he first located it, between 1817 and 1820, in his morphological publications, which portrayed science and poetry hermeneutically, as both method and history. Ten years later, however, after

---

[98] Rorty 360.

[99] Cf. von Graevenitz for a discussion of topics and topology in the sense that I have developed here and in my analysis of the Goethean symbol, 7–13.

[100] Cf. Bennett, *Goethe's Theory of Poetry*, 316, where the "Bergschluchten" sequence at the end of *Faust II* is analyzed in these terms. Cf. also in this connection the poem entitled "Eros" in the *Urworte. Orphisch* cycle, which Goethe published, like the plant elegy, both in his *Hefte zur Morphologie* (1820) and in "Gott und Welt" (1827).

[101] Cf. in this connection "Euphrosyne" again, as well as "Alexis und Dora," "Der neue Pausias und sein Blumenmädchen," "Das Wiedersehen," and "Amyntas."

finally abandoning lifelong plans to write a "Roman über das Weltall,"[102] he relocated his project in the testamentary *Ausgabe letzter Hand*, where he again considered the historical reconstruction of knowledge in the lyrical ensemble "Gott und Welt."[103] And it was here that "Die Metamorphose der Pflanzen" appeared—astonishingly—one last time, and as a citation of itself. I would like to end my discussion, therefore, by citing one of its many "sister poems" in the ensemble, "Parabase," which was also enjoying a return performance from *Hefte zur Morphologie*:

> Freudig war, vor vielen Jahren,
> Eifrig so der Geist bestrebt,
> Zu erforschen, zu erfahren,
> Wie Natur im Schaffen lebt.
> Und es ist das ewig Eine,
> Das sich vielfach offenbart;
> Klein das Große, groß das Kleine,
> Alles nach der eignen Art.
> Immer wechselnd, fest sich haltend.
> Nah und fern und fern und nah;
> So gestaltend umgestaltend—
> Zum Erstaunen bin ich da. (FA 2:495)

Edifying philosophers, according to Rorty, "want to keep space open for the sense of wonder which poets can sometimes cause—wonder that there is something new under the sun, something which is *not* an accurate representation of what was already there, something which (at least for the moment) cannot be explained and can barely be described."[104]

---

[102] Cf. von Thadden 49ff.

[103] Cf. Leif Ludwig Albertsen, "'Gott und Welt,'" *Text und Kontext* 15 (1987): 70–96.

[104] Rorty 370.

HILDBURG HERBST

Unterhaltungen deutscher Ausgewanderten, Political and Otherwise

Goethe and Politics—this is a topic remarkably absent from Goethe-scholarship. The German politologist Ekkehart Krippendorff points out that a bibliography "Goethe und..." would fill tomes, whereas "Goethe und Politik" would produce extremely meager results.[1] He comes to the conclusion: "Goethe und die Politik: das scheint eher ein Un-Thema, fast eine Peinlichkeit zu sein, ein dunkler Punkt an der sonst so strahlenden Gestalt des bewunderten Mannes."[2] A recent electronic library search covering the years 1981–1994 generated 2599 entries under the headword "Goethe;" 7614 under the headword "Politics;" but only a single one for the combination "Goethe and Politics."[3] The reasons for this strange lacuna seem to be manifold. Though Goethe spent about eleven years of his life as the chief advisor of Herzog Karl August of Weimar and was thus actively involved in politics, political concerns as the major subject of his literary work are rare. Those pieces which do deal with current issues like the plays *Der Groß-Cophta, Der Bürgergeneral, Die Aufgeregten,* or the narrative cycle *Unterhaltungen deutscher Ausgewanderten,* all written in quick succession shortly after the French Revolution, are considered to be of minor artistic merit and therefore generate only minor scholarly interest. The problem is confounded by the fact that various fictional characters express quite different views and that Goethe's *personal* view, if voiced at all, is scattered over a truly vast œuvre. Another problem is intimated by Krippendorff when he mentions

---

[1] Ekkehart Krippendorff, *"Wie die Großen mit den Menschen spielen:" Versuch über Goethes Politik,* edition suhrkamp 1486, Neue Folge, vol. 486 (Frankfurt: Suhrkamp, 1988) 7.

[2] Krippendorff 13.

[3] "Goethe and the French Revolution" showed 36 entries for this time span, mostly around the bicentennial of the French Revolution; only one of these studies deals with Goethe's *Unterhaltungen.* The most comprehensive work in this field ist still Dieter Borchmeyer, *Höfische Gesellschaft und französische Revolution bei Goethe: Adliges und bürgerliches Wertesystem im Urteil der Weimarer Klassik* (Kronberg: Athenäum, 1977). It does, however, not take a closer look at the two political adversaries in the framework, Karl and the Geheimerat.

that the topic "Goethe and Politics" tends to cause a certain embarrassment. It seems that Goethe, this poetic genius, simply failed to create an image of "political correctness" for himself—though, admittedly, "political correctness" may mean something quite different to different people at different times.

The purpose of this article is to take a very small bite out of the very large and elusive *Un-Thema* "Goethe and Politics" by examining the political problems discussed in the framework of the *Unterhaltungen deutscher Ausgewanderten*. This frame has been scrutinized thoroughly by many scholars.[4] But they mostly focus on its importance for the genesis of the German novella or on its marked improvement over Boccaccio, and usually discuss political aspects only in a sentence or two. Concentrating on political aspects, this article will show that Goethe does not simply lace the frame with some conservative political sentiment, but that he deftly outlines and juxtaposes the two major political positions in Germany which were provoked by the French Revolution. It will be shown that through the debate between Karl and the Geheimerat, which has nothing to do with generic concerns, Goethe proves to have been keenly and accurately aware of current political trends and their roots. The frame of the *Unterhaltungen*, the last work in the cluster of pieces dealing overtly with the French Revolution, reflects the political climate at the end of the eighteenth century more soberly than the preceding comedies, yet indirectly it also delivers the message that a poet should concentrate on *de*scription, not *pre*scription. Thus—despite the spirited political debate—the reader will look in vain for any partisan guidance or a call for political action.

Before proceeding to close scrutiny of the political debate in the *Unterhaltungen*, two things must be clarified: What do we mean by the term "politics" and what is the main thrust of the critics' assessment of Goethe's position in this respect, even if they should mention this matter only in passing?

The American Heritage Dictonary defines "politics" as follows:

> 1. The art or science of political government. 2. The policies, goals, or affairs of a government or the groups or parties within it. 3a. The conducting of or engaging in political affairs. 3b. The business, activities, or profession of a person so involved. 4. The methods or tactics involved in managing a state or government. 5. Partisan or factional intrigue within a given group. 6. Opinions or principles dealing with political subjects.[5]

In principle, these definitions were as true for Goethe's times as they are for ours; this is borne out in the correspondence between Schiller and Goethe, concerning the *Unterhaltungen* and in Schiller's *Horen* which opened with the

---

[4] The frame is almost invariably part of generic discussions of the German novella; special consideration is given to it in Jane K. Brown, *Goethe's Cyclical Narratives*: Die Unterhaltungen deutscher Ausgewanderten *and* Wilhelm Meisters Wanderjahre (Chapel Hill: University of North Carolina Press, 1975).

[5] "Politics," *The American Heritage Dictionary of the English Language*, 1973 ed. 1015.

*Unterhaltungen.*⁶ "The methods or tactics involved in managing a state" interested Goethe most (as will be seen in more detail below); "partisan or factional intrigue," only too prevalent during the late phase of absolutism, was the aspect which he abhorred. His realistic assessment of Weimar politics is reflected in a typically "Storm and Stress" letter to his old friend Merck: "Übrigens ist eine tolle Companie von Volk hier beysammen, auf so einem kleinen Fleck; wie in Einer Familie findet sich's nicht wieder so."⁷ But Goethe also stressed that he was "mehr als jemals am Platz . . ., das durchaus Scheisige [sic] dieser zeitlichen Herrlichkeit zu erkennen."⁸ The fact that he did not immerse himself in Weimar politics again after returning from Italy is probably a sign of his general disillusionment but also of his conclusion that writing—not painting, not politics—was his true calling.

If critics address the topic of "Goethe and Politics" at all, the majority of their findings tends to gravitate toward one of three categories: 1. Goethe's attitude was *anti*-political; 2. Goethe's attitude was *a*-political; 3. Goethe was a "Fürstendiener." It is true, in "Auerbachs Keller" one of the students exclaims: "Ein garstig Lied! Pfui! ein politisch Lied,"⁹ and this remark of a half-drunken figure in a play is often enough interpreted as *the* political credo of the author, supporting the preconception that he had nothing but contempt for politics. More well-meaning critics try to explain Goethe's abstinence from politics over long periods of time by stressing that his strong leaning toward the natural sciences destined him to be an *a*-political man, by nature handicapped in grasping political concepts and obligations. The epithet coined by Börne branding Goethe a "Fürstendiener" has been invoked by later critics innumerable times. What is often registered with concern is the fact that Goethe did, indeed, dedicate his first eleven years in Weimar to serving Herzog Karl August and his small duchy. What is overlooked is Goethe's impetus to do so, vividly described in *Dichtung und Wahrheit*. When Goethe—after all, a celebrated poet at the age of twenty-six—met the eighteen-year old Herzog for the first time, the two did *not* discuss literature, but a political treatise, Justus Möser's *Patriotische Phantasien*. The limitations which the duchy of Weimar shared with Möser's city-state of Osnabrück and the desire of the young prince, "an seiner Stelle entschieden

---

⁶Einladung zur Mitarbeit. Friedrich Schiller, *Sämtliche Werke*, Jost Perpfahl, ed., vol. 5 (Munich: Winkler, 1975) 837–40. From now on quoted as "SW." Also: Ankündigung, SW 840–44 und Gekürzte Ankündigung, SW 844–45 and the Schiller/Goethe letters from late 1794 and 1795, Johann Wolfgang Goethe, *Gedenkausgabe der Werke, Briefe und Gespräche*, Ernst Beutler, ed., 2nd. ed., vol. 20 (Zurich: Artemis, 1965). From now on quoted as "GA."

⁷Letter to Johann Heinrich Merck of November 22, 1776. GA 18, 354.

⁸Letter to Johann Heinrich Merck of January 22, 1776. GA 18, 304.

⁹*Faust*, GA 5, 205.

Gutes zu wirken,"[10] seemed to offer Goethe a unique chance to transform some political ideas which he embraced into concrete reality. Dieter Borchmeyer points out that Goethe went to Weimar "nicht vornehmlich als Dichter..., sondern um sich im Bereich politischer Praxis 'nützlich' zu machen."[11] "Praxis" and "sich nützlich machen" seem to describe Goethe's kind of political engagement—while it lasted—more appropriately than "Fürstendiener," which smacks of vainglory and servility.

As is well known, Goethe wrote the *Unterhaltungen deutscher Ausgewanderten* as a favor to Schiller, who was extremely interested in having Goethe participate in his newly founded *Horen*. It was Schiller who originally requested a nonpolitical tone in his call for contributions: "vorzüglich aber und unbedingt wird sie [i.e., die Monatsschrift] sich alles verbieten, was sich auf Staatsreligion und politische Verfassung bezieht."[12] He reiterates his nonpolitical program in the advance notice for the general public:

> Je mehr die allgemeine Aufmerksamkeit durch die lebhafteste Teilnahme an den politischen Begebenheiten des Tages, und den Kampf entgegengesetzter Meinungen und Parteien, jetzt auf die Gegenwart gerichtet ist; desto dringender wird das Bedürfnis, die dadurch eingeengten Gemüter durch ein allgemeineres und höheres Interesse an allem, was rein menschlich... ist, wiederum in Freiheit zu setzen.[13]

Planning an intellectually stimulating journal which should simultaneously be a commercial success, Schiller had to tread gingerly and expected the same from his collaborators. Yet Goethe ignored the guidelines; he did not ban "Teilnahme an den Begebenheiten des Tages, und den Kampf entgegengesetzter Meinung" from the frame of his *Unterhaltungen deutscher Ausgewanderten*. Schiller, tactfully, withheld criticism and took to the controversy between the Geheimerat and Karl; but, referring to the promises made in his advance notice, Schiller suggested Goethe should tone down the political debate somewhat.[14] Goethe was pleased with this first constructive criticism, something which would continue on a mutual basis until the end of Schiller's life. "Ich freue mich, Ihre Anmerkungen sogleich zu nutzen und dadurch neues Leben in diese Komposition zu bringen,"[15] Goethe wrote and promised, "ich will... dem Geheimen Rat... Sordinen auflegen und Karlen vielleicht noch ein Forte geben,

---

[10]*Dichtung und Wahrheit*, GA 10, 703.

[11]Dieter Borchmeyer, *Die Weimarer Klassik: Eine Einführung*, vol.1 (Königstein: Athenäum, 1980) 124.

[12]Einladung zur Mitarbeit, SW 5, 837–40.

[13]Ankündigung, SW 5, 844.

[14]Letter to Goethe of November 29, 1794. GA 20, 41–42.

[15]Letter to Schiller of December 2, 1794. GA 20, 43.

so wird's ja wohl ins gleiche kommen."[16] Christine Träger suggests that in creating this "Werkchen," Goethe used commonly known subject matter, "das er mit Hilfe einer Rahmenerzählung ... gefällig und zeitgemäß moderierte."[17] But the correspondence between Schiller and Goethe suggests that both were interested in more than simply arranging existing texts pleasantly. It seems, after once they had agreed on going beyond the original program, they wanted the political issues balanced as fairly as possible. It is obvious that for Goethe the political debate was important in its own right. One character is introduced solely to facilitate the clash of political opinions; the Geheimerat's function is strictly limited to the political, not the generic strand of the framework. When Schiller suggested, "daß Sie ihn doch durch den hitzigen Karl, wenn er sein Unrecht eingesehen, möchten zurückholen und in unserer Gesellschaft bleiben lassen,"[18] Goethe did not oblige. As soon as the Geheimerat had fullfilled his function to represent the conservative section of German society, he could safely be dismissed, never to return.

Since in most of the critical discussions of the *Unterhaltungen deutscher Ausgewanderten* the frame is seen as having an ancillary role, either holding a number of disparate stories together, or providing a forum for discussing the rather new and untested genre of the novella, its role in pulling the French Revolution into this narrative is often underestimated. Josef Kunz's remark is typical for the widespread vague generalization concerning the revolutionary backdrop: "Vor allem [die] Erfahrung der Ungesichertheit ist es, die die Rahmenhandlung des Novellenzyklus bestimmt."[19] Theodore Ziolkowski pinpoints the intentions of the author more precisely when he claims: "the framework interested [Goethe] at least as much as the individual tales,"[20] and when he stresses: "[he] reveals the terror of the French Revolution ... through the effect that it exercises upon various characters."[21]

Goethe wrote the *Unterhaltungen deutscher Ausgewanderten* in 1794–95. By that time the enthusiasm for the French Revolution had gone sour for many German intellectuals. In January 1793 the unimaginable had happened, the French king had been beheaded on the guillotine. Schiller's reaction seems to have been typical; shortly after the execution he wrote to his close friend Körner:

[16] Letter to Schiller of December 2, 1794. GA 20, 43.

[17] Christine Träger, "Goethes 'Unterhaltungen deutscher Ausgewanderten' als Ausdruck eines novellistischen Zielbewußtseins," *Goethejahrbuch* 107 (1990): 145.

[18] Letter to Goethe of November 29, 1794. GA 20, 42.

[19] Josef Kunz, *Die deutsche Novelle zwischen Klassik und Romantik*, 2nd ed. (Berlin: Erich Schmidt, 1972) 16.

[20] Theodore Ziolkowski, "Goethe's 'Unterhaltungen deutscher Ausgewanderten': A Reappraisal," *Monatshefte* 50. 2 (1958): 59–60.

[21] Ziolkowski 60.

"Ich kann seit 14 Tagen keine franz. Zeitung mehr lesen, so ekeln diese elenden Schindersknechte mich an."²² Also, revolutionary France had begun to pose a military threat to Germany. Goethe had a chance to get a close look at the upheavals in the wake of the Revolution when he accompanied Herzog Karl August in the French campaign of 1792 and watched the siege of Mainz in 1793. Never an enthusiast for the Revolution in the first place, his own experience as an observer made him even more critical and has, no doubt, found its way into the *Unterhaltungen*.

It is most likely that Goethe's *personal* sentiments are reflected in the narrator's opening comments. The war that provides the backdrop for the "Unterhaltungen" which take place means hardship, pain, and fear for those affected. The very first words set the tone: "In jenen unglücklichen Tagen. . ."(279);²³ and though the reader meets only a small group of aristocrats and their friends, the sweeping statement is made that these days had the saddest consequences "für Deutschland, für Europa, ja für die übrige Welt" (279). Goethe's choice of words supports the feeling of turmoil and uncertainty. We hear of the French army which "in unser Vaterland einbrach," of "Bedrängnisse," "Flucht," "Furcht," "Schrecken," "Sorge," and "allgemeine Zerrüttung" (279–280); this puts the responsibility on the invaders. But the other side bears some responsibility for the existing chaos, too; their flight was "übereilt," their fear "falsch" or "unzeitig" (279), and the French marched into Germany "durch eine übelverwahrte Lücke" (279). Subtly Goethe intimates that human flaws are evenly spread among the oppressors and the oppressed. Pathos or sentimentality are kept at bay when further reports are tinged with irony: "der schöne Genuß dieser reizenden Gegend [wurde] oft durch den Donner der Kanonen gestört" (285), or "ungern hatte, wie man leicht denken kann, die ganze Gesellschaft ihre Wohnungen verlassen" (281); also, one learns that the estate which Karl is supposed to inherit is in the hands of the enemy, "der nicht zum besten darauf hauste" (281). Goethe chose a young woman—by gender and age least responsible for political and military conflict—as the one in this group most deeply affected by the war. Since her fiancé is fighting the French with the allied troops, her wedding had to be postponed and, should the young man be killed in action, may never take place. This is a sad situation, but sentimental pity is prevented by calling her "ein lebhaftes, heftiges und in guten Tagen herrisches Frauenzimmer" (280). It is a clearly discernible strategy of Goethe to infuse his contemporary subject matter with a dose of realism; victimization does not eradicate human foibles and flaws.

---

²²Letter to Christian Gottfried Körner of February 8, 1793. Friedrich Schiller, *Briefe*, Reinhard Buchwald, ed. (Leipzig: Inselverlag, n.y.) 318.

²³*Unterhaltungen deutscher Ausgewanderten*. GA 9. 279–402. Pages in ( ) within the text.

Wilhelm Raimund Beyer compares Goethe's and Brecht's "Flüchtlingsgespräche"[24] and is stridently critical of the limited social range provided by Goethe. Even during his lifetime, Goethe experienced such criticism; his reaction, as related by Eckermann, is disarming: "Ich habe in meiner Poesie nie affektiert. Was ich nicht lebte ... habe ich auch nicht gedichtet."[25] To anchor his framework correctly in his own time, he had to establish the story in a realm that was familiar to him, i.e., in a socially privileged circle at the fringes of this revolution. Goethe does not lead his readers into battle; they do not see any blood or gore; they do not observe the socially disadvantaged dealing with the revolution and its aftermath; but with a few strokes he shows how the shock waves of this war—any war—throw these people—any people —off balance, off guard, create fear, a sense of panic, and misguided aggression.

Jane K. Brown calls Goethe's little group "a microcosm of the society around it."[26] The stress is on "around it" because, as Beyer points out, "'Die im Dunkeln'—die kommen im Goethe-Text nicht vor."[27] However, if we ignore the social range, which is, indeed, quite narrow in the *Unterhaltungen*, and focus instead on the political range, Brown is correct in stating:

> The whole spectrum of political opinions is represented from Karl, the radical aristocrat passionately and mindlessly devoted to the democratic position, through the Hofmeister, who agrees with Karl in silence, and the Abbé, who disagrees with Karl in silence, to the Geheimrat von S., who is as passionate and rigid as Karl ... in defending the opposite point of view.[28]

It is a historical fact that far from the epicenter of the French Revolution in late eighteenth-century Germany the ideological battle was not waged in the streets, but in the salons, in journals and newspapers, among educated members of the bourgeoisie and lower aristocracy. It is, of course, also true that the socially disadvantaged would experience emigration quite differently,[29] as Beyer asserts. But to stay within the historical context of the late eighteenth century, it is justifiable to ask: how many members of the lower classes could afford to flee from the oc-

---

[24]Wilhelm Raimund Beyer, "Goethe im Themenfeld von Flüchtlingsgesprächen," *Goethejahrbuch* 98 (1981): 156–78.

[25]*Gespräche mit Eckermann*.GA 24, 733.

[26]Jane K. Brown, *Goethe's Cyclical Narratives:* Die Unterhaltungen deutscher Ausgewanderten *and* Wilhelm Meisters Wanderjahre (Chapel Hill: University of North Carolina Press, 1975) 9.

[27]Beyer 167.

[28]Brown 9–10.

[29]Beyer 167.

cupied territories?[30] and how many of them in the rest of Germany were sufficiently educated and had the time to follow the political debates surrounding the French Revolution? It would have been quite contrived if Goethe had chosen a man from the lower classes to take on the conservative aristocratic Geheimerat. It is in keeping with real-life situations that Goethe made Karl and the Geheimerat members of the same social class, yet representatives of diametrically opposed political positions. Both men are clearly meant to be typical of their respective group: the pragmatic, conservative political realist versus the ideologically motivated, progressive political idealist; yet at the same time they are individualized enough to be more than mouthpieces for certain ideas or trends. The part containing the political debate is more tightly knit than the rest of the frame; the paragraphs dealing with Karl's background and ideas and those dealing with the Geheimerat's background and ideas are neatly dovetailed into a compact narrative that escalates from factual information to heated arguments and finally to a sensational clash, all in less than seven pages. According to Goethe, the front between German supporters and detractors of the French Revolution was less defined by social class than by age; generally speaking, those opposed to the Revolution were older people, more experienced in actual life and convinced that they followed reason; those in favor of the Revolution were of the younger generation, still rather inexperienced, and fiercely determined to follow their hearts.

The Geheimerat represents the conservative camp. He is described as a man of discipline and strictness: "Er hielt sich streng an Grundsätze und hatte über manche Dinge seine eigene Denkweise. Er war genau im Reden und Handeln.... Ein konsequentes Betragen schien ihm die höchste Tugend" (284). He is a man, "der das Zutrauen seines Fürsten verdiente und besaß" (284). But Goethe expands this aristocrat's life beyond the typical when he presents him as a man "dem die Geschäfte von Jugend auf zum Bedürfnis geworden waren" (284). Even if we do not learn anything about the nature of his "Geschäfte," he obviously possesses competence in a field that is considered to be more bourgeois than aristocratic. Therefore, one may be led to believe that a person of this background would also have acquired a healthy flexibility in other matters. This is, of course, not true, as the reader finds out quickly; and other shortcomings are hinted at by the laconic remark: "daß er manches mit hypochondrischem Gemüte betrachtete und mit Leidenschaft beurteilte" (284).

It is important to notice that the Geheimerat is an enemy of the French Revolution not simply as a matter of principle, but also for concrete reasons: "Sein Fürst, das Land, er selbst hatten viel durch den Einfall der Franzosen gelitten" (284). He is also disillusioned by the discrepancies between words and

---

[30] In *Hermann und Dorothea* the flight of a group of peasants plays an important role; but the actual information that spawned this epos did not refer to refugees fleeing the French Revolution, but to a group of farmers who left Salzburg for religious reasons.

deeds of the revolutionaries: "er hatte die Willkür der Nation, die nur vom Gesetz sprach, kennen gelernt und den Unterdrückungsgeist derer, die das Wort Freiheit immer im Munde führten" (284). There is then—quite important for Goethe—substantiation for this character's political position drawn from his own experience. Addressing the reader directly, the narrator suggests: "Man kann leicht denken, daß der Geheimerat diejenige Partei anführte, welche dem alten System zugetan war" (285). Since he has found a comfortable niche in the old system—appreciated by his prince, pursuing his own business, obviously being healthy and wealthy, a husband and a father—he personally has no interest in change; and the well-being of others is of little concern to him.

The feelings of others seem to be of equally little concern to him. Though Karl's empathy for the revolutionaries and sympathy for the clubbists is well known in this group, the Geheimerat does not spare him "wenn er den Verstand dieser Leute angriff und sie einer völligen Unkenntnis der Welt und ihrer selbst beschuldigte" (286), or when he calls them "verblendet" (286) and "Werkzeuge" (286) of those in power. He predicts that France will use foreign collaborators for a while and then discard them. "Und glaubt ihr denn," he asks sarcastically, "daß die große Nation nach dem Glücke, das sie bisher begünstigt, weniger stolz und übermütig sein werde, als irgend ein anderer königlicher Sieger?" (286). He cannot be reined in by the Baronesse or his wife, once he has embarked on his campaign, "treffende Pfeile auf Jugend und Unerfahrenheit loszudrücken, und über die besondere Neigung der Kinder mit dem Feuer zu spielen, das sie noch nicht regieren könnten, zu spotten" (288).

During his long and active life the Geheimerat had a chance to learn much about people in general, their flaws, their shortcomings; he looks at politics from an entirely pragmatic point of view. His claim that he did not see any fundamental changes in human behavior along with fundamental changes in politics rings true. But he himself is not ready to change either; he remains inflexible, almost ossified in his adherence to (what he thinks to be) the tried and true throughout the agitated debate. There is no willingness on his part to ask for reasons that led to the French Revolution; there is no tolerance for deviant viewpoints; there is no capacity for compromise. The chances of *evolution* instead of *revolution*—a concept so dear to Goethe's heart—were marred by sticklers for their own principles, like the one Goethe has brought to life so vividly and critically in the frame of the *Unterhaltungen deutscher Ausgewanderten*.

While the Geheimerat is one of the ultraconservatives, Karl is a follower of the revolutionaries. Goethe stresses the division by age ironically: "Der Hofmeister gab [Karl] im stillen recht, der Geistliche im stillen unrecht" (282). Karl fullfills all the prerequisites of a dashing young "Storm and Stress" hero: "Jugend," "gute Gestalt," "leidenschaftliche Natur" (all 282). The Baronesse calls him "ein edler guter Mensch" (289). But like his opponent, he is not without flaws; he reacts with "Heftigkeit" (281, 286), he lavishes "unmäßiges Lob" (282) on the French, he expresses "lautes Vergnügen" (282) about their military progress, and is one "der sich im Zorn nicht mehr kannte" (288). The Geheimerat's passion is paired with hypochondria, Karl's is paired with a wanton lack of moderation. For both—in quite different ways—it is their unbridled emotionality which mars their impact on the other.

To dispel all suspicions that Karl's spirited defense of the Revolution may have personal reasons, his material independence is emphasized: "Er glaubte um so freier sich diesen Gesinnungen ergeben zu können, als er selbst ein Edelmann war, und ... ein ansehnliches Vermögen zu erwarten hatte" (281). As single-mindedly as the Geheimerat is interested in maintaining the status quo, Karl is interested in the changes promised by the French Revolution. He does not care if the French troops are currently ruining his future estate; he does not care if he is alienating parents, relatives and friends. Goethe chooses a fitting metaphor for his political infatuation: Karl is in hot pursuit of his one and only love, the Revolution. The servant girls would gladly add some concrete meaning to it: "Die Kammermädchen ... hörten ihn gerne reden, weil sie sich durch seine Gesinnung berechtigt glaubten, ihre zärtlichen Augen, die sie bisher vor ihm bescheiden niedergeschlagen hatten, nunmehr in Ehren zu ihm aufzuheben" (282). But he cannot dally with a person of real flesh and blood at a time when his less material love, the Revolution, has taken total possession of his heart.

What Karl expects from the Revolution is nothing less than "Heilung und Belebung des alten kranken Zustandes" (285). Different from the old Geheimerat, he has less experience of life, and more importantly, he has no firsthand experience in the political arena; he must rely on what he hears or reads about the French Revolution, and since he is "ein edler guter Mensch" (288) he chooses to believe in the goodness of others, too: "Karl [konnte] einer Nation nicht feind werden, die der Welt so viele Vorteile versprach, und deren Gesinnungen er nach öffentlichen Reden und Äußerungen einiger Mitglieder beurteilte." (281) Compared with the Geheimerat's disillusioned pragmatism, Karl's arguments do sound somewhat naive when he claims:

> daß er von der französischen Nation überzeugt sei, sie werde die edlen Deutschen, die sich für sie erklärt, zu schätzen wissen, als die Ihrigen ansehn und behandeln, und nicht etwa aufopfern oder ihrem Schicksale überlassen, sondern sie mit Ehren, Gütern und Zutrauen überhäufen (288).

What has long been a well functioning, time-honored political system for the Geheimerat, is slavery for Karl, and he states boldly, "daß er jeden Deutschen auffordere, der alten Sklaverei ein Ende zu machen" (288).

W. Daniel Wilson says: "Goethe shows a consistent and politically motivated tendency to portray revolutionaries as selfish demagogues who are motivated by the most elemental physical drives, which contrast crassly with their profession of high-minded ideals and vision."[31] The *Unterhaltungen* are not included in his study; but it is fair to say that Karl would be the exception to this proclaimed rule. The ironic vignette with the enchanted maids to whom Karl does *not* respond serves as proof for Karl's lack of ulterior motives; he is hardly a selfish demagogue; his drive is of a naively idealistic nature. He does, indeed, suffer from a certain amount of "Unkenntnis der Welt" (286) and "Unerfahrenheit" as the Geheimerat superciliously ascertains (288).

Borchmeyer points out that Goethe's own keen observations have found their way into the *Unterhaltungen*: "Schicksal und Verhalten der Emigranten hat Goethe selbst genau beobachtet."[32] Keeping in mind that this is the late eighteenth, not the late nineteenth century, the "realism" in the frame of this narrative cycle is remarkable. The escalating battle of words, the loss of self-discipline and noble restraint, the insults and ridicule hurled at each other—all of this rings very true, given the stressfully uncertain atmosphere established as a backdrop for these "Unterhaltungen." Borrowing a term from *Wahlverwandtschaften*, Brown feels we are watching "society in a test tube."[33] The circumstances are clearly defined by the age of the French Revolution, but the psychological precision of the escalating political debate makes this a timeless piece. Beyer claims: "Das Flüchtlingsgespräch reift nicht zum Disput, der Diskurs rangiert als 'Unterhaltung,'"[34] but for the exchange between the two political antagonists this is not true; this is no longer a polite conversation; here, opinions clash. However, when the Geheimerat expresses the hope that eventually all collaborators with the French would be hanged, and Karl outdoes him in a tactless, tasteless way, shouting: "er hoffe, daß die Guillotine auch in Deutschland eine gesegnete Ernte finden und kein schuldiges Haupt verfehlen werde" (288), this is neither a dispute nor a conversation, but an insult to the concept of civilized discourse, that, unfortunately, seems to occur in political arenas of all times.

After the debate in the *Unterhaltungen deutscher Ausgewanderten* has run its emotional course, the Geheimerat is not needed any longer; he leaves for good, dutifully followed by his wife and daughters. But Karl, who at the end disqualifies himself as much as the older man by gleefully calling for the physical extermination of political opponents, is retained. Goethe does not endorse either of the positions explicated so carefully. He who once characterized himself "der ich keine kriegerische Natur bin und keinen kriegerischen Sinn habe..."[35] found hanging or beheading as a political measure totally distasteful and disgraceful.

---

[31]W. Daniel Wilson, "Hunger/Artist: Goethe's Revolutionary Agitators in *Götz, Satyros, Egmont,* and *Der Bürgergeneral.*" *Monatshefte* 86. 1 (1994):80.

[32]Borchmeyer, *Höfische Gesellschaft,* 224.

[33]Brown 10.

[34]Beyer 163.

[35]*Gespräche mit Eckermann*, GA 24, 733.

Therefore, something else must have redeemed Karl in the eyes of his creator. Though opposed to the French Revolution on principle, Goethe understood what had caused it and earlier in the debate had made Karl a passionate spokesman for the underprivileged, who had just begun to shake off their shackles:

> Wie kann man diese Menschen so geradezu verdammen? Freilich haben sie nicht ihre Jugend und ihr Leben zugebracht, in der hergebrachten Form sich und andern begünstigten Menschen zu nützen. Freilich haben sie nicht die wenigen wohnbaren Zimmer des alten Gebäudes besessen und sich darinne gepflegt; vielmehr haben sie die Unbequemlichkeit der vernachlässigten Teile eures Staatspalastes mehr empfunden, weil sie selbst ihre Tage kümmerlich und gedrückt darin zubringen mußten: sie haben nicht, durch eine mechanisch erleichterte Geschäftigkeit bestochen, dasjenige für gut angesehen, was sie einmal zu tun gewohnt waren; freilich haben sie nur im stillen der Einseitigkeit, der Unordnung, der Lässigkeit, der Ungeschicklichkeit zusehen können, womit eure Staatsleute sich noch Ehrfurcht zu erwerben glauben; freilich haben sie nur heimlich wünschen können, daß Mühe und Genuß gleicher ausgeteilt sein möchten! Und wer wird leugnen, daß unter ihnen nicht wenigstens einige wohldenkende und tüchtige Männer sich befinden... (286–87).

This remarkably bold assessment of life under absolute rule proves Goethe's independence as a thinker. Even as a staunch opponent of this revolution—any revolution—he allows his youthful protagonist to solicit sympathy for the *cause*. Wilson refers to the fact that Goethe shows more empathy for the plight of the poor in private letters than in published works and proves that he even edited out partisan sentiments between the first and the final version of *Götz von Berlichingen*.[36] In the *Unterhaltungen* this is not the case; on the contrary, Goethe may even have "edited in" additional critical insight and empathy, after having promised Schiller: "Ich will ... Karlen vielleicht noch ein Forte geben."[37] The correspondence with Schiller and the tight structure of the political debate within the otherwise rather loose framework of the *Unterhaltungen* suggest that Karl's emotional plea is placed there quite intentionally. It may be paradoxical, as Borchmeyer points out,[38] that Karl, the privileged aristocrat, speaks for those in distress and despair; but looking in from the outside adds a measure of objectivity to his voice. He addresses the fact that the original revolutionaries did *not* belong to the privileged part of society. Comparing their lives to life in a large state palace is appropriate; those who eventually took to revolution did *not* grow up in the few pleasant rooms available, could *not* pamper themselves and had to

---

[36] Wilson 81, 83, 85.

[37] Letter to Schiller of December 2, 1794. GA 20, 43. It would be interesting to compare the original with the final version, but no first draft of the *Unterhaltungen* has ever surfaced.

[38] Borchmeyer, *Höfische Gesellschaft*, 224.

make do with the uncomfortable and neglected quarters of the building. Their lives were wretched and depressed; and yet, only in secrecy could they register partiality, disorder, carelessness, and poor management of those in power; and only in secrecy could they wish that hardship and pleasure would be handed out more equally. It is, of course, impossible to fashion Goethe into a proto-socialist; but tucked away in a frame that is scrutinized almost exclusively for literary/aesthetic reasons is a statement that is amazing in its political/ethical progressiveness, especially coming at this time from this corner.

In his response from the head, his disdain for terror and usurpation of power, Goethe's own position seems to have been closer to that of the Geheimerat; in his response from the heart, his desire for fairness, justice, and harmony, his own position seems to have been closer to Karl's. Pitching these two against each other not only reflects the political discourse of the day, but also hints at the difficulty of balancing the head and the heart in politics. With jovial bitterness, the Geheimerat attributes Karl's account to youthful idealization, whereas Karl maintains that those are to blame "welche nur nach alten Formen denken könnten" (287). Being strongly opposed to violence as an integral part of revolution does not necessarily mean being opposed to change, gradual, organically developed change. In a talk with Eckermann more than thirty years later, Goethe returns to this problem:

> Da aber neben vielem Guten zugleich viel Schlechtes, Ungerechtes und Unvollkommenes besteht, so heißt ein Freund des Bestehenden oft nicht viel weniger als ein Freund des Veralteten und Schlechten. Die Zeit aber ist in ewigem Fortschreiten begriffen und die menschlichen Dinge haben alle fünfzig Jahre eine andere Gestalt.[39]

Not only is Karl an advocate of change (though admittedly of violent change), but he also puts the blame squarely on the privileged few in power. That, too, is an aspect to which Goethe returns in the same conversation with Eckermann:

> Auch war ich vollkommen überzeugt, daß irgendeine große Revolution nie Schuld des Volkes ist, sondern der Regierung. Revolutionen sind ganz unmöglich, sobald die Regierungen fortwährend gerecht und fortwährend wach sind, so daß sie ihnen durch zeitgemäße Verbesserungen entgegenkommen und sich nicht so lange sträuben, bis das Notwendige von unten erzwungen wird.[40]

The frame of the *Unterhaltungen deutscher Ausgewanderten* allows Goethe to describe a problem, its causes, but not necessarily its cure. In his lovingly irreverent talk "Goethes Anziehungskraft," delivered as an acceptance speech for his honorary doctorate from the University of Constance, Martin Walser suggests:

---

[39] *Gespräche mit Eckermann*, GA 24, 550.

[40] *Gespräche mit Eckermann*, GA 24, 550.

"Vielleicht war er voller Lösungen, für die er dann Konflikte suchte."[41] The *Unterhaltungen* are different in this respect. Here, Goethe works with a conflict of overpowering magnitude that was a historical given and thus could not be adjusted to a preconceived solution. The "solution" contained in the *Unterhaltungen*, is shifted from the public to the private sphere. This shift is what many critics find so disappointing about Goethe; they feel he was shunning responsibilities as a figure so prominently in the public's eye. Occasionally, one remark of the Geistliche is interpreted as a personal statement of the author: "Zur Übersicht der großen Geschichte fühl' ich weder Kraft noch Mut, und die einzelnen Weltbegebenheiten verwirren mich" (298). Goethe was, of course, not the only one who was bewildered by the monstrous happenings in France; but the skillfully crafted ideological battle between Karl and the Geheimerat does not at all betray a lack of political insight; and in some of its aspects the "Ferdinand-Novelle" in the *Unterhaltungen* shows an equally keen grasp of economic-political trends. As Albert Soboul points out in his *Kurze Geschichte der Französischen Revolution*, the Revolution destroyed the old feudal system for good and marks the transition to capitalism.[42] Goethe works this development into his novella by having the young merchant Ferdinand familiarize himself "mit einer entfernten Fabrikanstalt... in einer Gegend, wo die ersten Bedürfnisse und die Handarbeit sehr wohlfeil waren" (354), and where the young man is supposed "durch Geld und Kredit die Anstalt ins Große zu treiben" (354). This example of nascent capitalism in one of the novellas of the *Unterhaltungen* further supports the idea that Goethe lacked neither "Kraft" nor "Mut" to observe and to evaluate current political or economic-political trends intelligently. What he obviously lacked was the desire to take a partisan position in the political strife of his day.

The Baronesse, who tells none of the stories, has two functions within the frame: through her, Goethe clarifies generic aspects of the novella and through her he intimates how civilized members of society might react in times of political unrest. The Baronesse is described as a graceful pragmatist; she is "entschlossen und tätig," a woman "[von] durchdringendem Geiste," and "eine gute Hausmutter" (all 279). After the political debate has ended in an irreconcilable clash, she admits: "Es wäre töricht, wenn ich das Interesse abzulenken gedächte, daß jedermann an den großen Weltbegebenheiten nimmt" (292); and yet, she asks not to make a public spectacle of it; she proposes to seek instead privacy for political discussions. There, she suggests, "man genieße recht lebhaft die Freude einer leidenschaftlichen Überzeugung" (292). She makes this request "nicht im Namen der Tugend, sondern im Namen der gemeinsten Höflichkeit" (292).

[41]Martin Walser, *Goethes Anziehungskraft*. Konstanzer Universitätsreden (Constance: Universitätsverlag, 1983) 30.

[42]Albert Soboul, *Kurze Geschichte der Französischen Revolution* (Berlin: Wagenbach, 1988) 7–8.

For her, this is as much a matter of tact as of tactics: people as social beings have to live with each other. Borchmeyer claims: "Goethe [sucht] bestimmte aristokratische Haltungen, welche durch die Revolution ihre Funktion eingebüßt zu haben scheinen, wenigstens in den Bereich der ästhetischen Bildung hinüberzuretten."[43] This (one may add) not because of an unwavering infatuation with aristocracy, but because *certain* aristocratic values help achieve a measure of harmony and balance in human society.

To restore harmony within this group of émigrés Goethe lets them move from debate to storytelling, from political to aesthetic concerns. The *Unterhaltungen* offer the most serious discussion of political issues in all of the Revolution pieces, but they also show a shift back from the political to the poetic. This is even reflected in the structure of the cycle. Excluding the "Märchen" which is added under its own caption, the *Unterhaltungen* are divided into two parts of almost equal length: general introduction plus the first day of discussions and storytelling; the second day of discussions and storytelling. The length of each story on the first day shows a fivefold *in*crease on the second day; the volume of the frame on the first day shows a *de*crease to approximately one fifth on the second day.

Writing various installments of the *Unterhaltungen* was a slow process; during this time Goethe's understanding seems to have grown that as a poet he should address the *Mensch*, perhaps the *Bürger*, but not the *citoyen*. Despite the wide range of duties and interests he pursued in his long life, he also felt: "Das Vernünftigste ist immer, daß jeder sein Metier treibe, wozu er geboren ist und was er gelernt hat, und daß er den andern nicht hindere, das Seine zu tun."[44] His "Metier" was writing, and he dealt as a *writer* with the enormous impact of the French Revolution on German thought and conduct. After he had done his part, he felt it was up to his reader "das Seine zu tun" and to draw his *own* conclusions. Friedrich Förster, a historian who as a young man had been dismissed from his position for supposedly subversive activities, relates a charmingly diplomatic remark by Goethe who felt annoyed by the constant demand for partisan commitment: "Die Leute wollen immer, ich soll auch Partei nehmen; nun gut, ich steh' auf meiner Seite."[45] But not always could he muster such good humor; up to the end of his life he grappled with the vexing problem of not having achieved (in the eyes of some) a happier marriage between literature and politics:

> Ich weiß recht gut, daß ... all mein Wirken in den Augen gewisser Leute für nichts geachtet wird, eben weil ich verschmäht habe, mich in politische Parteiungen zu mengen. Um diesen Leuten recht zu sein, hätte ich müssen

---

[43] Borchmeyer, *Höfische Gesellschaft*, 224.

[44] *Gespräche mit Eckermann*, GA 24, 91.

[45] Visit by Förster on August 4, 1831. GA 23, 761.

Mitglied eines Jakobinerklubs werden und Mord und Blutvergießen predigen."[46]

If Goethe "preached" in the *Unterhaltungen*, his sermon was about avoiding, not committing "Mord und Blutvergießen," no matter if it comes in progressive or conservative guise.

Close scrutiny of the frame of the *Unterhaltungen deutscher Ausgewanderten* reveals that Goethe's examination of the French Revolution was more systematic, more serious, and even more sympathetic than generally maintained. The author does not present himself as a "Fürstendiener"; on the contrary, he has a young aristocrat criticize those in power most severely. He does not present himself as *a*-political; on the contrary, he shows an amazingly accurate grasp of the complex political problems raised by the French Revolution. He is *anti*-political in the sense that he follows Schiller's suggestion to concentrate on "ein allgemeineres und höheres Interesse an allem, was rein menschlich ... ist."[47] Though recognizing the relevance of the frame's subject matter, and dealing with it, he eventually leads his readers *beyond* it. The conviction that his political responsibility is not partisanship, but improvement of his readers as human beings, is reflected in his question: "Wenn ein Dichter lebenslänglich bemüht war, schädliche Vorurteile zu bekämpfen, engherzige Ansichten zu beseitigen, den Geist des Volkes aufzuklären ... und dessen Gesinnungs- und Denkweise zu veredeln, was soll er da Besseres tun?"[48]

In his very last conversation with Eckermann, Goethe once again turned to the issue of how well literature and politics could coexist in the work of one and the same person. He cited the politically active poet Ludwig Uhland and said: "Geben Sie acht, ... der Politiker wird den Poeten aufzehren."[49] Obviously, Goethe decided early enough that the poet in himself should not be consumed by the politician. From our vantage point this seems to have been an infinitely wise decision.

---

[46] *Gespräche mit Eckermann*, GA 24, 510.

[47] See footnote 13; SW 5, 844.

[48] *Gespräche mit Eckermann*, GA 24, 509.

[49] *Gespräche mit Eckermann*, GA 24, 510.

PAOLA MAYER

Friedrich Schlegel's *Theorie der Entstehung der Welt:* A Romantic Cosmogony[1]

In his *Rede über die Mythologie* (*Gespräch über die Poesie*, KA 2, 311ff.),[2] Friedrich Schlegel pleads for the creation of a new mythology, arguing that Romantic literature needs to find a focal point in a Romantic mythology in order to be able to rival, or indeed surpass, classical literature. Like its predecessors, this new mythology would be a symbolic account of the creation and organization of the natural world. At the same time, it would represent a radical departure from earlier forms of mythology in that it would derive, not from naive imagination, but from sophisticated intellect, in particular, from modern idealistic philosophy. In fact—the *Rede* implies without actually saying so—this new mythology would be the means of achieving Romanticism's most prized goal: the harmonious fusion of *Poesie*, philosophy, religion and natural science. It would provide each of the last three with what they most lacked, to wit, the symbolic form of expression which alone is appropriate to the highest truths, and, through this, integrate them into the realm of *Poesie*.

Schlegel's preoccupation with creating his own original contribution to this new mythology underlies a large proportion of the entries in the philosophical and literary notebooks. Remarks on the possibility of synthesizing Fichte with Spinoza (who was recommended in the *Rede* as model and source for future mythologs), plans for romanticizing Böhme in a new *Aurora* or *Kosmogonie*, the assembling of materials for a mystical-mythological theory of nature—all these, and indeed many other topics, bear directly or indirectly on the question of the new mythology. The notes relating to the physical sciences (especially the sections of notebook III entitled *Zur Physik* and *Materialienklasse*) are particularly revealing of Schlegel's intentions, since they are the raw materials out of which Schlegelian mythology was to be constructed. The theory of nature that

[1] I would like to thank my colleague Steven Taubeneck for his detailed and helpful comments on an earlier draft of this essay.

[2] All references to Schlegel's works are to: *Kritische Friedrich-Schlegel-Ausgabe*, eds. E. Behler et al. (Paderborn: Schöningh, 1958-).

Schlegel was contemplating was to serve as anchor point for the fusion of the higher disciplines, in as much as it would draw on all of them: natural science would provide its content, Neoplatonic mysticism its imagery and overall conceptual scheme, contemporary idealism its basic philosophical premises. The ultimate result would be *Poesie*, since such a theory could only find expression through the medium of allegory.

Not surprisingly, this rather staggeringly ambitious theory of nature remained unrealized, with the sole exception of one text. Only in 1805 (nearly seven years after the idea was first formulated) did Schlegel write a full-fledged cosmogonic myth. Whether this can be regarded as the fulfillment of his earlier plans remains somewhat questionable. By 1805, the Jena circle had long disintegrated and Friedrich Schlegel, now increasingly drawn to Christianity, was engaged in a radical revision of his former philosophy. Oddly enough, this development only adds to the interest of the myth, which displays a Janus-like character: it looks backwards to the Jena period insofar as it represents the culmination of Schlegel's plans for a new mythology, and forward to the Catholic period insofar as it attempts to pave the way for a reconciliation of idealism and Christianity. Moreover, the context in which this myth is embedded affords a highly revealing glimpse into Schlegel's approach to creativity and to reading, since Schlegel not only employs, but also openly defends, the idiosyncratic method of combining (or attempting to combine) heterogeneous sources in unexpected ways, which had always been the source of his originality.

Schlegel's cosmogonic myth, *Theorie der Entstehung der Welt*, forms the centerpiece of the third book in a cycle of lectures which purport to present the history of philosophy: *Zur Entwicklung der Philosophie in zwölf Büchern*. In actual fact, only the first of the twelve books is directly concerned with the history of philosophy, while the other eleven present Schlegel's own attempt at constructing an idealistic system. The first book, however, retains a key position, in that the theories which follow constantly borrow from, argue with or respond to, the philosophies critiqued in the historical overview. Conversely, a close look at the history presented in the first book soon uncovers its highly selective and tendentious character: whenever convenient, Schlegel skims over, or even ignores, schools, philosophers or aspects of philosophies, and concentrates on those that are relevant to his own system. His treatment of these is polemical, not only in its selection of topics for discussion, but also because he does not hesitate to overstate or misrepresent ideas that he wishes to attack. Seen in this light, the title of the lectures is revealed as the first instance of a rhetorical strategy at work throughout: Schlegel is presenting his own thought as the fulfillment and logical culmination of the entire development of philosophy, the ultimate system toward which the discipline had all along been moving.

In support of this strategy, or perhaps making a virtue of his necessity, Schlegel prefaces his historical overview with an apology of his combinatory method, presenting it as the sole means by which philosophy could perfect itself. A new philosophical system, a passage early in the first book claims, must begin with a historical overview of the discipline, just as Schlegel's lectures do. This is necessary because every philosophy is inescapably grounded in all preceding ones, so that failure to acknowledge the relationship betrays either dishonesty or self-delusion. True ignorance of history entails the risk of repeating past errors rather than learning from them. The historical overview must therefore identify advances towards truth and deviations from it, and uncover the sources of both, in order to enable the new system to build on the gains and avoid the errors. With this, the methodology and intentions of Book one have been outlined. Schlegel's survey proceeds in two phases: a critical typology of philosophical approaches is followed by a chronological account of Western philosophy. Both claim to isolate the contributions to the discipline's ultimate development, and to anatomize the aspects which prevented all past philosophers from reaching the truth. From this analysis, Schlegel draws the conclusion that all errors can be laid at the door of the concept of substance. Implied is the contention that any system that succeeds in avoiding this concept will be the true, the ultimate idealism.

This introduction is an advance justification of the highly derivative character of Schlegel's system: if his premises are accepted, it follows that failure to adopt any true theories already in existence, or to address errors to be rectified, is necessarily misguided. For interpreters of the lectures, this apology should act as a warning that the following books must be read in the light of the first. That is to say, Schlegel's attempt at constructing his own idealistic system is the direct outcome of his relationship to past philosophers, and can only be understood in this context. This bond is strengthened by the fact that the extreme selectivity of Schlegel's historical survey causes it to beg the question (he concentrates on those thinkers or texts that addressed the issues he himself wished to raise, in ways that were either complementary or a foil to his own).

The cosmogonic myth in Book three is important for an understanding of Schlegel's thought in three respects. It is a key document for his concept of mythology's role in fusing *Poesie*, philosophy and religion, since it is an attempt to actualize this plan; it reveals how Schlegel conceived idealism during a major transition in his intellectual journey; finally, when the treatment of its sources is examined, it becomes an important means of grasping Schlegel's approach to philosophical creativity. I therefore propose to address two main issues in my reading of this myth: its role in Schlegelian idealism (to which end the premises established in the preceding book, the theory of consciousness, must first be considered), and its relationship to the five philosophies which most obviously contributed to it, to wit, Plato, Böhme, Kant, Fichte, and the tradition which Schlegel termed ancient emanation theory.[3]

---

[3] By emanation theory, Schlegel means the belief that the universe results from the overflowing of a perfect, all-encompassing first principle, entailing a progressive de-

Before proceeding to a discussion of Schlegel's views on these five philosophies, a first tentative description of their respective roles can be put forward. By far the most important was Kant's critical philosophy: not only are Schlegel's terminology and many of his concepts Kantian, but, most importantly, the cosmogony is structured around a theory of time and space to rebut and replace Kant's. In the same way, Schlegel's deduction of a first principle in the theory of consciousness both relies on and reacts against those of Kant and Fichte. Plato provoked Schlegel's attempt to provide new—to him more satisfactory— theories of recollection and of love. Schlegel's attitude toward emanation theory was equally contentious. He planned to adopt its view of perfection, but to reverse its interpretation of the process of emanation. Towards Böhme alone was Schlegel largely uncritical, yet his discussion of the mystic is also the most general. Böhme's contribution is therefore arguably the smallest (or perhaps least specifiable); in essence, Böhme provided an example of the approach by which the other philosophers could be modified or refuted, and so brought into line with Schlegelian idealism.

Schlegel's Critique of Philosophy

Of all the philosophers discussed in Book one, Plato received the longest treatment. Schlegel had always had a very high opinion of him, and described him here as one of the greatest philosophers of all time.[4] Nevertheless, by 1805, Schlegel disagrees fundamentally with Plato's doctrine, claiming that it contains a basic misconception which prevented him from reaching the truth. Schlegel classifies Plato as an intellectual dualist (the type of philosopher who posits two eternal principles, spirit and matter, but subordinates the latter to the former [KA 12, 136]).

The form of Plato's oeuvre accords well with Schlegel's views on mythology, and is consequently praised for its classical beauty and suitability for the subject matter. As it emerged from the *Rede über die Mythologie* and from the philosophical notebooks of the Jena period, it was Schlegel's belief that the highest truths can only be expressed allegorically, and that, consequently, it was the task of mythology to fuse religion, philosophy and natural science by giving allegoric expression to their contents. Seen in this light, Plato's use of myth and allegory is clearly significant to Schlegel's choice of the mythic mode for his theory of the

---

cline. He saw this philosophy exemplified primarily in ancient Indian religion, but also to some degree in Plato, and to a greater extent in Hellenistic and Near Eastern philosophies, particularly Plotinian Neoplatonism.

[4]Very much the same discussion of Plato, in many passages expressed in exactly the same words, is found in Schlegel's lectures on literature from the same period. See KA 11, 118–25.

world's origin. It is, presumably, to this end that he—approvingly and utterly inaccurately—attributes to Plato the belief that the highest is inexpressible and can only be negatively known: "Nach Plato gibt es von der Natur nur ein wandelbares, kein strenges, bleibendes Wissen,—von der Gottheit zwar eine reine, aber nur negative Erkenntnis" (KA 12, 208–209). Since Plato unquestionably believed that the philosopher could attain true knowledge of the Good through contemplation,[5] Schlegel must be romanticizing Plato by reading him in the light of later Neoplatonic (and Augustinian) mysticism. This supposition is borne out by a subsequent remark which universalizes Plato's occasional use of allegory: "Von dem Verhältnis der Gottheit zu der Natur gibt es nur eine bildliche allegorische Erkenntnis" (KA 12, 209).[6]

What Schlegel found especially praiseworthy in Plato's philosophy is that it attempted to deduce the entire universe from one first principle and—to Schlegel a truly 'idealistic' trait—that he sought to derive the finite consciousness from the infinite one (KA 12, 219). Unfortunately, Schlegel claims, Plato could not fulfill his lofty aims, because he failed to subordinate matter to spirit, and therefore in the last analysis fell back into materialism. Schlegel locates the cause of this failure in the definition of the first principle implied by the theory of ideas (KA 12, 215ff.; also 139ff.). A highest intelligence which shapes the world out of preexisting matter according to the blueprint provided by its own perfect and eternal ideas, is like a human artist who fashions its artifacts out of preexisting material, and is therefore bound by its limitations. This view, Schlegel objects, in fact accords primacy to matter, since it existed before spirit brought order to it (indeed Schlegel at one point claims, before spirit itself existed),[7] and since its imperfections prevent the divine intelligence from creating a perfect copy of its ideas, thus subjecting it to a higher necessity.

Such a fall into materialism, Schlegel argues, is inevitable as long as intelligence is posited as first principle, for intellect, unlike will, cannot produce matter. It is in this respect, he continues, that Böhme came far closer to true ideal-

---

[5] See, for instance, books VI and VII of *The Republic*.

[6] For a general characterization of Schlegel's Plato-reception (and of its influence on later ones), see Hans Krämer, "Fichte, Schlegel und der Infinitismus in der Platondeutung," *DVjS* 62 (1988): 583–621.

[7] In his preliminary discussion of Plato (found in the typology of philosophies) Schlegel states: "... der Geist wird durch die Materie bedingt und ihr gar untergeordnet, die Materie als das erste und älteste angesehen — denn insofern sie der Gottheit ewige Schranken und Grenzen setzt, ist sie über den Geist, hat dann indirekt den Vorrang" (KA 12, 140). In the longer discussion of Plato, Schlegel does not repeat this erroneous claim, limiting himself to the more accurate view that Plato's system is dualistic in that it posits two coeternal principles. The earlier account was nevertheless worth mentioning as an unresolved inconsistency, and as an example of Schlegel's practice of polemical overstatement.

ism, since his first principle, love, is a truly creative force (KA 12, 217–18, 225). Schlegel regards Plato's theories of recollection and of love as the most idealistic elements of his philosophy, since they are presented as man's link with his divine origin, and therefore as the only sources of true knowledge (KA 12, 218ff.).[8] These would have led Plato to true idealism, had he not subordinated them to the intellect: "Plato dachte sich das Ideal des Bewußtseins als Verstand und bezieht also auch hierauf die Erinnerung; aus dieser leitet er denn auch die *Liebe* her, sie ist ihm die vollkommne Erkenntnis der *ewigen Schönheit*. Es ist die Frage, ob er nicht einen bessern Weg eingeschlagen hätte, die Erinnerung auf die Liebe zu beziehen, als einzig auf das Wissen und Erkennen?" (KA 12, 219, Schlegel's italics).

From this discussion of Plato, certain basic considerations that shaped Schlegel's own speculative thought can be isolated. Schlegel particularly approved of all ideas that stress the link between the infinite consciousness and its product and expression, the finite one. Beyond this, he aimed to establish the supremacy of the volitional over the intellectual faculties, and to identify the infinite consciousness with love. As will become clearer, these intentions are the first sign of Schlegel's emergent desire for a marriage of idealism with traditional Christianity.

Unlike Plato, Böhme is unequivocally and enthusiastically praised (KA 12, 256ff.), because Schlegel saw in him a first embodiment of certain tendencies that he himself planned to develop. This led him to state that, of all past philosophers, Böhme came closest to true idealism. Böhme's writing, imaginative and figurative, could be described as allegoric,[9] his whole endeavor (explaining God and the created world) as a first harmonious combination of theosophy, philosophy and *Poesie*: "In kurzem läßt sich die Philosophie des Böhme am besten also charakterisieren: die Form derselben ist religiös, der Inhalt philosophisch, der Geist poetisch" (KA 12, 260). Further, he was preferable to other philosophers because he accorded with Schlegel's growing interest in traditional Christianity. Böhme was a Christian who claimed to draw his insights from revelation, and who derived his whole system from a personal God of love. At this time, Schlegel was disposed to identify the highest truth with just such a God, and therefore to regard Böhme's theosophy as philosophy in the highest

---

[8]Schlegel here refers to the Platonic doctrine of anamnesis (found in several dialogues, but presented most fully in the *Phaedrus*, 245ff.) according to which knowledge is the reawakening in the soul of the truths it saw in a previous life, before it was weighted down by a body, while love is the emotion the soul feels for that which reminds it of eternal beauty.

[9]KA 12, 260. The importance accorded to allegory is based on the Romantic conviction that the highest truths are inexpressible and can only be portrayed indirectly, that is, by means of symbol and allegory. See, for instance, KA 18, V, 315; KA 19, VIII, 227 or, with reference to Böhme, KA 19, X, 457.

sense: "die *höchste Philosophie* kann nichts anders sein als *Wissenschaft* von der *höchsten Realität*, d.h. von der Gottheit, ihrer Natur und ihren Verhältnissen;— diese ist aber eben Theosophie und *nicht ohne Bezug auf die Offenbarung möglich*" (KA 12, 258, Schlegel's italics), and so, "wenn auch Böhmes Form nicht mit der philosophischen Lehrmethode übereinstimmt, so ist doch der Inhalt seiner Lehre eine erhabene Philosophie und von ganz idealem Charakter, sie ist im hohen Sinne das, was er selbst davon aussagt: *Wissenschaft von Gott*" (KA 12, 259, Schlegel's italics).

Despite this panegyric, the content of Böhme's thought is discussed only along general lines. Whereas, in the case of Plato, Schlegel evaluated specific theories or even specific dialogues, here he merely draws attention to two main principles extrapolated from Böhme's thought as a whole. Böhme, Schlegel states, is a true idealist because he resolves everything into life and activity: his first principle is a God who is Himself involved in an eternal process of becoming, and even matter, which results from the interplay of elemental forces, is not solid and permanent.[10] In praising Böhme for positing love as productive first principle from which everything is derived, Schlegel is giving a free interpretation of the mystic's thought. It is true that love plays a key role in the constituting of Böhme's personal God, but it is only one of several elements whose interaction make up the life of the divinity. Also, Böhme's teaching on both love and the nature of God is often obscure and contradictory, as well as changing from work to work. Once again, Schlegel's remarks reveal more about his own aspirations than they do about Böhme. Specifically, his précis of Böhme signals his wish to reconcile idealism and Christianity by identifying the divinity with a first principle conceived as pure activity, and by positing love as first impulse to creation.

Schlegel presents not only Böhme, but also Kant, as a precursor of his own brand of idealism. In this section of the lectures, Kant is described as the father of modern idealism, who was himself too timorous to carry through what he had begun, namely, the founding of a philosophy which would eliminate the concept of substance and replace being with becoming. In this section it first becomes apparent that Schlegel's cosmogony will take the form of a theory of time and space. Out of Kant's vast oeuvre, Schlegel chooses to discuss only the first Critique and, within it, he deals almost exclusively with two topics: the question of human cognition and the nature of time and space.

Schlegel approved of Kant's belief that reason cannot lead to cognition of the infinite, and indeed espoused it himself. However, he could not be satisfied with (in his eyes) so negative a stance, and criticized Kant for not seeking an alternative: "Er verwarf... die Vernunft als ein unvollkommenes Werkzeug, als

---

[10]Although this claim involves a radical simplification of a highly complex thought, it is true that the concept of a divinity involved in an eternal cycle of becoming is Böhme's most original idea.

nicht tauglich zur positiven Erkenntnisquelle, ohne andere aufzusuchen, die andere Philosophen angenommen hatten ... man dürfte zwar zugeben, daß die natürliche Vernunft nicht die höchste, sondern eine bloß negative Erkenntnisquelle sei, daraus folgt aber nicht notwendig das Rückkehren zum Empirismus" (KA 12, 287–8). In his own system, Schlegel will attempt to rectify this omission. Further, he objected to Kant's theory that cognition results from the interaction of external stimuli with the categories of the mind. External objects and the activity of the mind—Schlegel argued—are utterly heterogeneous, and it is therefore impossible to see how they could affect each other (KA 12, 289). Finally, he found Kant's failure to eliminate the concept of substance inconsistent: "er unterordnet die Dinge den Formen und Gesetzen des Geistes so sehr, daß man nicht einsieht, warum er sie nicht eben auch zu Produkten des Geistes macht" (KA 12, 289).

The subject that most concerned Schlegel is Kant's theory of time and space. He states that, for Kant, time and space are forms of intuition (that is, inherent in the human mind). He then proceeds to criticize this notion, claiming that it raises several unanswerable questions: "man kann sich ja nicht erklären, wie und woher die Anschauung zu solchen Formen komme, warum gerade zu diesen, warum in diesem Verhältnis und dieser Zahl, warum sind der Formen nicht mehr" (KA 12, 287). Furthermore, Schlegel maintains, since Kant's theory accords them only subjective ideality, it is not clear whether time and space also have objective reality (KA 12, 287). As the tone of these remarks suggests, Schlegel's criticism is prompted by polemical considerations rather than by a genuine effort to understand the theory on its own terms. Kant, after all, makes it clear that he singled out time and space because he saw them as the only forms which necessarily accompany all intuitions, and states even more unequivocally that time and space have only subjective, ideal, definitely not objective reality.[11] Having pinpointed the areas in which he disagrees with Kant, Schlegel then proceeds to appropriate the philosopher for his own cause, by means of a rather enigmatic remark: "Bei Kant liegt schon, so sehr er dies auch versteckt, stillschweigend eine Voraussetzung übersinnlicher Anschauungen zugrunde, insofern er nämlich Raum und Zeit als *ursprüngliche* Formen der Anschauung annimmt, die auch noch andere haben kann" (KA 12, 287, Schlegel's italics). It should be noted that the last part of this sentence is not Kant, but the consequence which Schlegel drew from his own questions to Kant, strategically intermingled with factual reporting. From this analysis, Schlegel concludes that Kant's theories of time and space, and of the innate concepts of the understanding, contain the seeds of true idealism. The coupling of these two theories

---

[11] See *Transzendentale Ästhetik*, B33/A19 ff., for instance B52/A35, 36, Immanuel Kant, *Kritik der reinen Vernunft*. Schlegel must have been aware that he was misrepresenting Kant, since, at the end of the section (KA 12, 290), he contradicts his earlier statement and correctly reports Kant's thought.

gives us some clue as to what might be meant. By placing time and space, as well as the categories of the understanding, in the human mind, Kant has made it possible for a later, idealistic philosopher (Friedrich Schlegel himself), to reach a true theory of cognition. This can be done by, first, deriving the external world from mind as the creation of its categories, and, secondly, presenting these as functions governing the activity of a universal consciousness.

If Schlegel is to be successful in presenting himself as the thinker who will complete what Kant began, Fichte's claim to that role must somehow be disposed of. Accordingly, Schlegel's attitude to Fichte is as polemical as that to Kant, and the entire cycle of lectures engages more or less overtly in a constant disputation with both. Because he responds to Fichte throughout, Schlegel explains, very little space need be devoted to him in the historical overview. Here, he is content with a brief sketch of Fichte's failure to achieve perfect idealism. Fichte's first *Wissenschaftslehre* (1794), Schlegel states, carried Kant's thought to its logical conclusions, and was the most complete idealistic system to date. Later versions of it, however, fell back into the empirical idealism of his predecessor. Here, the remark is allowed to stand unexplained, but an earlier passage, found in the typology of philosophical approaches, attributes Fichte's failure to two basic shortcomings. Fichte's later philosophy reintroduced the concept of substance: "In der weiteren Ausführung seines Systems hat er indessen das *Ding an sich* als *ein Etwas* wieder in seine Philosophie eingeführt, als ein Etwas, das dem Ich zu den Vorstellungen den ersten äußern Anstoß geben muß..." (KA 12, 147, Schlegel's italics). Furthermore, he subordinated the activity of the ego to the laws (a form of limitation, and hence of permanence) which it gives itself. Fichte, in short, came no closer to eliminating substance than Kant did, so that the task outlined earlier has yet to be performed: it will be Schlegel himself, the rhetoric of the lectures suggests, who will be Kant's true heir, that is to say, who will develop the seeds of true idealism sown by Kant into a full-fledged system.

This reading of Schlegel's attitude to Kant and Fichte is confirmed by the remarks which conclude the historical overview. The concept of substance (identified with permanence) alone, Schlegel insists, is responsible for all philosophical errors, so that a truly idealistic system must be based on a first principle which is itself constantly active and developing. Accordingly, in Book two (the theory of consciousness), Schlegel sets out to construct such a first principle, which he then uses as a premise for the cosmogony.

Schlegel's Theory of Consciousness

Schlegel opens his philosophical system with a theory of consciousness on the grounds that the intuition of self (*Selbstanschauung*) is the only immediately evident fact. Like Fichte, he aims to construct an absolute and all-encompassing entity (which he will later identify with God), and like Fichte, he begins with the proposition a = a. Unlike Fichte, however, he does not first construct an absolute ego and then derive a finite one from it, but rather constructs the finite individual consciousness first and infers from it the existence of an infinite one. He therefore does not take the principle of identity as analogous to the proposition that the ego is identical with itself, but rather focuses on the act of intuition necessary to recognize the evidence of the axiom, and derives from it the basic faculties of consciousness: sensation, reason and will (*Sinn, Vernunft, Wille*). Three aspects of the theory which he then proceeds to build are important for the theory of nature. In the first place, Schlegel argues from the fact of consciousness to the primacy of will, and to its expression, love, as an original creative force. Second, he presents eternal becoming and its laws as a necessary concomitant to the life of the absolute. Last, he bases cognition on the three faculties which will play a central role in the cosmogony: memory, love and presentiment (*Ahnung*).

Schlegel begins his deduction of consciousness (KA 12, 324ff.) by stating that, in order to perceive anything (such as the axiom a = a), the ego must have the ability to perceive itself as distinct from its object (otherwise it would be lost in the object and no act of intuition could take place). This ability does not differ significantly from what Kant termed pure apperception: "Das: Ich denke, muß alle meine Vorstellungen begleiten können; denn sonst würde etwas in mir vorgestellt werden, was gar nicht gedacht werden könnte, welches eben so viel heißt, als die Vorstellung würde entweder unmöglich, oder wenigstens für mich nicht sein."[12] Schlegel, however, calls it reason (*Vernunft*), with the clear intention of drastically reducing its range and importance as compared to Kant's concept of reason. For intuition to occur, the passive capability of being affected by an object is also needed. This, for Schlegel as well as for Kant, is sense or sensation (*Sinn*). Schlegel then adds a third element, to which he plans to assign primacy, namely the will (*Wille*). Will is needed to stop what would otherwise be the infinite regression of self-intuition, and to direct attention to a given object to be intuited.

At this point, Schlegel emphasizes that, while it is possible to doubt the existence of external objects, the ego is immediately and absolutely certain of its own existence, which therefore need not and cannot be proved. In this way, he responds to the attempted demonstration of the ego with which Fichte begins his system. The ego's unshakable and absolutely certain belief in itself is of central importance to Schlegel, since it forms the basis of his theory of knowledge and, indirectly, of the notion of eternal becoming: "Jene willkürliche Überzeugung in Rücksicht auf uns selbst nannten wir den ursprünglichen, einzig wahren *Glauben*, aus welchem aller andere Glaube ... abgeleitet werden muß.

---

[12]Kant, *Kritik der reinen Vernunft*, B132, 133. See also the rest of section 16 for a more detailed discussion.

Dieser Glaube an uns selbst und der Zweifel am Ding sind die beiden ersten Grundfäden der Philosophie" (KA 12, 333, Schlegel's italics).

Schlegel grounds his theory of knowledge on will by claiming that cognition begins with the ego's desire to know itself (*Wißbegierde*, a function of will), which is in turn triggered by its belief in itself (KA 12, 331). Before he develops this theory, however, Schlegel turns to establishing the necessity for the concept of becoming by means of what he terms the antinomy of perception (*Empfindung*) (KA 12, 333ff.). The ego, he says, cannot truly intuit itself (it infinitely eludes its own grasp), but only think itself.[13] When it does this, it thinks of itself as infinite, yet, in active life, it feels itself as all too finite. This antinomy—that we perceive ourselves as both finite and infinite—is only solvable by means of the concept of becoming, by whose agency finitude and infinity are different not in kind, but only in degree. That is to say, the ego is finite in extension but, insofar as it is involved in an eternal process of becoming, it is infinite in potentiality. This, it may be said in passing, is offered as an alternative to the notion of the self-limiting activity of the ego by which Fichte addressed the same paradox.

The antinomy of perception also enables Schlegel to proceed from the individual to the infinite consciousness: "Wenn wir uns beim Nachdenken nicht leugnen können, daß *alles in uns ist*, so können wir uns das Gefühl der Beschränktheit, das uns im Leben beständig begleitet, nicht anders erklären, als indem wir annehmen, *daß wir nur ein Stück von uns selbst sind*" (KA 12, 337, Schlegel's italics). From this belief, Schlegel derives an *Ur-Ich*, an *Ich* and a *Gegen-Ich* or *Du*, all alive and active, intended as an alternative to Fichte's absolute ego, finite ego and non-ego. The *Ur-Ich* is Schlegel's version of the absolute: it encompasses everything, and is, in all its parts, alive and eternally becoming. With this, Schlegel has arrived at the basic premise on which he will ground the cosmogony: Since nothing is outside the ego, and the ego is eternally becoming, it follows that the world is "ein unendliches Ich im Werden," which is identified with "eine werdende Gottheit" (KA 12, 339). This "werdende Gottheit" is a key example of how Schlegel achieves originality by idiosyncratic combinations of heterogeneous sources. His concept of infinity is unique because it amalgamates Fichte's absolute ego, Böhme's eternally developing divinity, and the all-encompassing perfection which is the first stage in theories of emanation, while yet going beyond each insofar as it adds the other two to it.

Before this claim can be illustrated by a reading of the cosmogony, Schlegel's theory of cognition must still be explained, since it provides the remaining elements taken up by the theory of nature. Schlegel terms the three

---

[13] It is hard to see how this statement can be reconciled with the theory's initial premise that only self-intuition is evident. If a different kind of perceiving is intended, Schlegel does not say so, but uses the term *Anschauung* in both instances.

higher faculties of consciousness memory, understanding and love. He derives the first from the antinomy of perception, defining it as the continuous thread of consciousness which links the infinite ego with the derived one and enables it to return into itself. Memory, in other words, is the reawakening of the infinite ego in the finite one, and therefore the highest source of cognition. Understanding is free active thought (as opposed to the passive activity of reason). Love is an integral part of the act of intuition, or, more precisely, of the new kind of intuition which Schlegel introduces, calling it "geistige Anschauung."[14] Since the world of objects is composed not of non-ego but of live, ensouled anti-ego, understanding objects means allowing one's spirit to unite with theirs. This occurs by means of feeling (*Gefühl* [KA 12, 355ff.]) and is made possible by love.[15]

There can be no doubt that this theory is intended as a response to Plato's. As mentioned earlier, Schlegel endorsed Plato's view of memory and love as instruments of cognition, but criticized their subordination to intellect. Accordingly, his own theory of cognition presents all three as equal and independent. However, as was also indicated by his critique of Plato, Schlegel intended to go a great deal further and posit love as first creative principle. He achieves this by means of the concept of longing (KA 12, 371ff.). The beginning of consciousness, he states, cannot be located in an intellectual activity, because this presupposes consciousness; it must, therefore, lie in a volitive activity. Since nothing exists as yet, it must be a kind of striving (*Streben*) which is utterly undetermined, unlimited and without goal. This is longing (*Sehnsucht*), which is a form of love. The beginning of consciousness, both finite and infinite, and of the latter's world-producing activity, is therefore found in love, expressing itself as longing. In this way, the achievement for which Böhme was praised (in the comparison with Plato) has been incorporated into Schlegel's system. It must be remembered, however, that, though longing plays a central role in the thought of both thinkers, its meaning is not the same. For Böhme, the longing which functioned as mainspring of the life of the divinity was the desire for self-manifestation, and its relationship with love was not one of identity.

---

[14]"Insofern das Gefühl, die unmittelbare Wahrnehmung des innern Sinnes, doch immer an Anschauung gebunden ist, . . . so kann man es auch wohl geistige Anschauung nennen, *frei von dem Vorurteile des Dings*" (KA 12, 356), Schlegel's italics.

[15]"Unsere geistige Anschauung beruht, wie gesagt, auf Berührung, Vermischung des Ichs mit dem Du in dem Gegenstande, und wir nennen dies gewiß mit Recht Liebe, denn es läßt sich nicht denken, daß ohne Hinstreben und Anneigen des Anschauenden zu dem Angeschauten die Berührung beider zustande käme" (KA 12, 356).

Time and Space

Now that the concept of a "werdende Gottheit" has been introduced and its faculties deduced, the premises needed for the *Theorie der Entstehung der Welt* (the centerpiece of the theory of nature) have been established. It is preceded by two introductory sections, the first of which goes a long way toward confirming the thesis that the cosmogony was intended as a reverse emanation process built around a counter-Kantian theory of time and space.[16] Schlegel opens the theory of nature with a statement of its goals. He then turns immediately, and for the second time in the lectures, to a discussion of space and time. He attempts to secure objective reality for space and time by linking them with the concept of the infinite: "Sie werden nie ohne das Unendliche gedacht, sind daher für diejenigen, die sich noch nicht... als unendlich ergriffen haben, das Medium, wodurch sie unfehlbar den Begriff des Unendlichen erhalten; und insofern sind sie ganz objektiv" (KA 12, 411–12).

Despite their unquestionable reality, Schlegel continues, time and space have always proved the worst stumbling block for philosophy. In illustrating this, he concentrates on Kant's *Kritik der reinen Vernunft*, which he saw as a major turning point. Before Kant, Schlegel tells us, time and space were regarded as concepts, whereas Kant defined them as subjective intuitions ("subjektive Anschauungen" [KA 12, 412]).[17] Schlegel rejects Kant's thesis. To him, time and space are far beyond common intuition (*gemeine Anschauung*), indeed confound this, because they are inextricably connected with the infinite. Because they partake of several faculties (memory, intuition, prophecy), they cannot be subordinated to any one, unless this be "die Einbildungskraft..., als welche in der Mitte liegt, wo alle Formen des Bewußtseins wieder zusammenfließen" (KA 12, 412).[18] By means of this connection, Schlegel is able to propose a pre-

---

[16] The second half of this thesis was discussed by Manfred Frank, albeit only in passing. Frank also provides supporting evidence by citing entries in the philosophical notebooks which announced Schlegel's intention of revising Kant's theory of time and space. See Manfred Frank, *Das Problem 'Zeit' in der deutschen Romantik: Zeitbewußtsein und Bewußtsein von Zeitlichkeit in der frühromantischen Philosophie und in Tiecks Dichtung* (Munich: Winkler, 1972), the chapter on Schlegel, p. 22ff., especially p. 83.

[17] The formulation is somewhat misleading, as Kant, while calling time and space pure a priori intuitions, defines them as the forms and necessary conditions of intuition (see *Kritik der reinen Vernunft*, B37/A22, 23ff).

[18] In the theory of consciousness, Schlegel defined imagination as the faculty for free, independent thought. Understanding, which had at first been assigned this role, is now subordinated to imagination as one of its two poles: "Beiden, sowohl der *Dichtungskraft*, als dem Vermögen, die Welt zu einer unendlichen Mannigfaltigkeit und Fülle zu entwickeln und auszubilden, wie dem *Verstande*, als dem Vermögen, die Fülle und Mannigfaltigkeit der Welt zur Einheit zusammenzudrängen und zusammenzufassen, beiden ist *Einbildungskraft* nötig" (KA 12, 361: Schlegel's italics).

liminary definition of time and space: "Raum und Zeit sind eigentlich Einbildungen zu nennen, in jenem Leben der Einbildungskraft, als dem Vermögen des Ein- und Ausatmens der Welt, ist die Zeit das Leben selbst, der Raum aber die Nahrung dieses Lebens..." (KA 12, 412). Since he earlier defined *Einbildungen* as "innere Vorstellungen" (KA 12, 358), Schlegel's time and space differ from Kant's in two respects only: they are objectively, rather than merely subjectively, real, because they inhere in the infinite consciousness rather than the individual human mind; and they are the product of free thought, which is higher than and independent of common intuition.

Schlegel then proceeds to a more detailed discussion of each, together with a refutation of previous definitions. The question of time, he asserts, has so far been approached in one of two ways. Mysticism has always held to the concept of eternity, while dismissing finite time as illusion; whereas Kant maintained that finite time alone is real and denied eternity any form of reality.[19] Since it is the avowed intention of Schlegel's idealism (and indeed of Jena Romanticism as a whole) to establish the absolute supremacy of spirit without renouncing the beauty and richness of the corporeal world, it is clear that he cannot accept either of these solutions. Accordingly, he attempts to reconcile the two by means of the concept of becoming. Just as finitude and infinity do not differ absolutely but only in degree (insofar as one is forever approaching the other), so too there is no absolute opposition of finite time and eternity, but only a relative (and infinitely diminishing) one of "vollendete" and "unvollendete Zeit" (KA 12, 414). With his campaign against the concept of substance in mind, Schlegel departs from past theories of time in one more respect. Thus far, he claims, eternity had been conceived as "Zeitleere," an infinite present without future or past, and therefore unchanging and immobile. By contrast, he proposes to define his "vollendete Zeit" as "Zeitfülle," composed of the intermingling of past and future (excluding the present, which is equated with permanence) and therefore infinitely alive and active (KA 12, 414ff.).

Space receives similar, if far briefer, treatment. It has always been thought of as more or less material, that is, as the receptacle for matter.[20] Schlegel finds such a concept nonsensical, since an empty receptacle is in fact nothing. Space,

---

[19] "... die ... Mystiker ... nahmen bloß die Ewigkeit als reell an, und da sie nur einen negativen Begriff des Unendlichen hatten, mußten sie alles Zeitliche, wo es nicht ganz geleugnet werden kann, als Schein erklären;—Kant dagegen gab der Zeit nur für das Endliche formelle Realität, für das Unendliche war sie ihm bloß ein subjektiver Schein..." (KA 12, 413).

[20] KA 12, 415. It is typical of Schlegel's arbitrary treatment of his sources that, unlike the discussion of time, that of space does not include Kant, whose theory could not be so easily dismissed. Kant himself rejected the notion of space as an empty receptacle, defining it instead, as Schlegel very well knew, as one of the two pure forms of intuition innate to human consciousness.

he proposes, is not corporeal but spiritual. He concludes the discussion of time and space by reiterating his contention that they are objectively real because they are essential components of the World-Ego, time being its life and space the food of this life: "Der Raum ist sowohl als die Zeit etwas ganz Geistiges, er ist ein geistiges, in sich *vollendetes* Wesen. Die Zeit ist *unvollendet wie die Welt selbst*, sie ist das Leben, der Raum ist die Nahrung der Welt; dies ist die Ansicht des Idealismus über Raum und Zeit. . ." (KA 12, 416, Schlegel's italics).

The introductory section of the theory of nature contains not only the discussion of time and space but also that of the concept of becoming (*Werden*) (KA 12, 417ff.). Schlegel outlines the laws governing becoming, but stresses that freedom, which constitutes the beginning and end of the universe's development, is above and beyond all laws. He concludes this section by comparing his version of idealism to what he terms older mysticism—in particular, to ancient emanation systems. Emanation theory, Schlegel explains, had a true concept of the absolute (as all-encompassing perfection which combines the infinite multiplicity of life with infinite unity). Its error, however, was to place this ultimate state at the beginning of the cycle instead of at the end. As a result, it portrayed creation as a gradual decline and falling away from perfection—a tragedy mitigated solely by the hope of eventual return into the one (KA 12, 419). From these prefatory remarks, the overall design of Schlegel's own cosmogony can be predicted: it will take over the concept of infinite perfection found in emanation theory, but will reverse the direction of the cycle, positing a gradual ascent towards infinite perfection rather than a descent from it, and it will portray this development as spatio-temporally determined.

The Cosmogony

The section entitled *Theorie der Entstehung der Welt* presents a mythico-philosophical account of the development of the World-Ego (*Welt-Ich*). It attempts to identify the World-Ego, the idealistic construct derived from the theory of consciousness, with a mystical divinity. By these means, Schlegel hoped to bridge the gap between idealistic philosophy and religion (the seventh book of the lectures, *Theorie der Gottheit*, will then try to give this idealistic divinity a truly Christian aspect).

The first stage of the World-Ego is infinite unity. As the comments on emanation theory led us to expect, this unity is not one of perfection but of unrealized potentiality, or complete absence of differentiation.[21] The first stirring

---

[21] Parallels to this concept can be found among Schlegel's favorite philosophers: undifferentiated oneness characterizes Fichte's ego before it achieves consciousness by positing limitations within itself, as well as Böhme's divinity in its inception as infinite brightness without oppositions or self-awareness. Whether Schlegel intentionally fol-

of life within this unity is occasioned by a presentiment of—and therefore a longing for—the infinite multiplicity in which it will eventually fulfill its destiny: "Das Welt-Ich kann sich dieser Einheit (Einfachheit), nicht bewußt sein, ohne eine unendliche *Sehnsucht* zu fühlen, diese ursprüngliche *Leerheit* durch Mannigfaltigkeit und Fülle zu bereichern. Die Ahnung der unendlichen Fülle gibt der Tätigkeit des Welt-Ichs den ersten Anstoß" (KA 12, 429, Schlegel's italics).[22] This longing necessarily expresses itself as indefinite (and infinite) expansion in all directions, resulting in the creation of space. As he had indicated earlier, Schlegel is now seeking to secure reality for space (and subsequently time) by presenting its relationship to the World-Ego as one of mutual interdependence. Space is the first product of the World-Ego, yet one which the latter must needs bring forth if it is to achieve true existence. The two being thus inextricably bound, the implication is that, if the World-Ego is real, so too is space.

Schlegel makes the transition to the second stage by means of one of the laws of becoming that he had set forth in the introductory section of this book: a movement that reaches its goal must then proceed circularly back to its beginning. Accordingly, longing, having achieved its first objective (the creation of space), must now return to its origin. However, its nature has been changed by its activity. The birth of space has increased emptiness, and therefore only intensified longing.[23] Because it is more intense, faster moving and less tranquil, longing has now become striving, or, more precisely, that "unruhiges, heftiges Streben" which is better called desire (*Begierde* [KA 12, 432ff.]).[24] The return of

---

lowed these models, or merely took the only logical course to reversing the cycle of emanation, is impossible to determine.

[22]It will be remembered that Schlegel defined true idealism as the philosophy that would eliminate the concept of substance, and criticized Fichte for allowing substance to reenter his system in the guise of the "something" that prompts the activity of the ego (see above, p. 17). By assigning this function to an emotion, Schlegel hopes to resolve the difficulty and achieve what he described as the ultimate philosophy.

[23]Here, Schlegel is once again guilty of self-contradiction. He unconcernedly adopts a position which he had condemned as nonsensical in his critique of theories of time and space: his space too—it would appear—is an empty receptacle.

[24]The choice of "Begierde," a term which plays an important role in Böhme's thought, is probably not accidental, yet its nature and the function it assumes in the two systems are entirely different. Böhme associates it above all with the first quality, that is to say, it is the desire of contraction to draw everything into itself; though in the *Aurora* it is also the desire of the first and third qualities (sharp and bitter) for the second (sweetness or water). What the two systems have in common is primarily the fact that they operate on the level of mythological, rather than discursive, logic. J.J. Anstett expressed a similar view: "Trotz der scheinbar logischen Parallelisierung der Kräfte des Bewußtseins und der Elemente und Momente der Welt hat die Darstellung einen eher dich-

this desire to the point of origin results in an excess of activity, and at the same time in the need to be free of it. Through the conflict of these two opposite tendencies, unity becomes duality (*Zwiespalt*).

At this point Schlegel introduces a new aspect to his theory, one that illustrates both his (deliberate) proximity to Böhme's mode of presentation[25] and the wide gulf that separates him from Böhme's way of thinking. Both Böhme and Schlegel follow the lead of medieval and Renaissance science in deriving the world from the interaction of the elements, yet both deviate from the traditional scientific view by defining the elements as dynamic forces rather than—in the words of both—as grossly (*grob*) corporeal entities. This willful archaism on Schlegel's part places his cosmogony yet more firmly in the realm of mythology, but it also reveals a deeper difference from Böhme. For Böhme, the seven elemental forces were literally and truly the raw material of the divinity and of the world it created. While Schlegel apparently presents a similar account, for him the elements are incidental, as the argument is actually determined and carried by the interaction of the abstract concepts which the elements symbolize. His reason for introducing elemental imagery is that, as the first product of longing was space, the following creations must also take a spatial form. In more general terms, this somewhat uneasy marriage of archaic science and abstract idealism is intended to contribute to the Romantic fusion of physics, mythology or *Poesie*, and philosophy, which is the goal of the entire project.

The element assigned to *Begierde* is fire, the most appropriate symbol for its essence. From the struggle of this fire with the original quiet motion of longing, Schlegel rather shakily derives the birth of time (KA 12, 434ff.). According to the laws of becoming, once the raging torment of fire has reached its peak, it must bring about a reversion to its opposite, which was peace and unity (the first stage). With renewed awareness of the initial peace come pain and remorse over

---

terischen Ton und Gang, der unverkennbar auf Einwirkungen J. Böhmes zurückzuführen ist..." (KA 13, 448, note 15). Though essentially correct, this claim appears to me exaggerated insofar as it presents Böhme as sole inspiration for Schlegel's mythic form: as mentioned earlier, Schlegel's praise of Plato suggests that he was an equally influential model.

[25] It is reasonable to suppose that the figurative, mythological style of this cosmogony is intentionally modeled after Böhme, since Schlegel repeatedly praised the mystic for giving poetic expression to philosophical (Christian) truths. See, for instance, KA 18, V, 848; KA 16, IX, 734; KA 18, VI, 270; KA 3, 7; and in the lectures in question here, KA 12, 260 (quoted above, pp. 11–12). Of especial interest is a note from the year 1804, which suggests what Schlegel found desirable in Böhme's presentation, and how he was planning to improve on it: "Im Böhme ist lauter geistige Anschauung ohne alle Logik; daher die fragmentarische Form nicht bloß aus Nachahmung der Bibel sondern nothwendig. Für die φσ[Philosophie] selbst wäre dieß das Höchste, nur fehlt es an Gliederung oder Constr.[uktion] des Ganzen..." (KA 19, X, 440).

its loss. This new stage marks the birth of memory, defined as the harking back to the beginning, in full awareness that it was a beginning. With memory, time comes into being, because future (toward which longing looks) and past (to which memory is directed) have now come together. Since the intent of memory is to allay struggle and restore the original unity, its element is water, and from the interaction of fire and water all else comes to be. On the symbolic level, the created world results from the interaction of fire and water; yet, if we remember that fire is the elemental expression of desire impelled by a presentiment of future perfection, and water is the elemental expression of the recollection of past unity, we realize that physical nature is in fact the product of the interaction of future and past. In other words, Schlegel is suggesting that the created world results from the gradual unfolding of time in space (culminating, as we shall see, in the dissolution of space into motion).

This elemental conflict can have one of three outcomes. If it is informed by love, it becomes playful and free, bringing forth light and, by its agency, the infinite multiplicity of life (KA 12, 437ff.).[26] If it does not become playful, the struggle of fire and water can lead to destruction. Should the elements suddenly realize that their enmity can cause their death, they become rigid with fright (*Schrecken*) and freeze into immobility, becoming solid, corporeal matter (KA 12, 438ff.). Because it entails permanence, substance is associated with present time. Schlegel identifies this outcome of the elemental conflict with destruction, on the grounds that, to a true idealist, loss of freedom and mobility is tantamount to death. Nevertheless, he stresses that this state is a reversible one: the body marks the imprisonment, not the death of spirit. Spirit, then, will eventually be freed from matter by the influence of light and by its own striving.

Furthermore, present time and the material world are not merely an evil to be overcome. Light, Schlegel explains, is simple, so that it could not, by itself, produce the infinite variety which is the ultimate goal of the World-Ego (KA 12, 443). To this end, light must work in and through the earthly element, which thus represents a necessary stage in the development of the infinite. By assigning this positive function to the material world, Schlegel differs from the thinkers who contributed to his cosmogony: Plato, Böhme and emanation theory all associated matter with some form of fall,[27] while Fichte termed it non-

---

[26] The description of light is another contact point which illustrates both Schlegel's affinity to and fundamental difference from Böhme. Both thinkers portray light as the expression of divine love and therefore the life-giving principle; yet, as will be discussed later, Schlegel also lends it an idealistic dimension in accordance with the scope of his theory.

[27] As already mentioned, Schlegel drew attention to emanation theory's view of matter as decline from the original perfection, and to Plato's attribution of all imperfections to its agency. Though Schlegel does not mention it, Böhme also saw matter as a result of a fall, or more precisely, of two falls, first Lucifer's and then man's.

ego, and accorded it the purely negative role of foil or barrier with reference to which the ego defines itself.[28]

The third possible outcome of the struggle of fire and water is the evil principle (KA 12, 444ff.). It comes into being if fire withdraws into itself, becoming self-destructive. Such a withdrawal is caused by egoism and self-will (*Willkür*). The explicitly Christian terminology with which Schlegel describes evil is the first overt indication of his intention to reconcile his version of idealism with an established religion: "Dies ist Luzifer, der aus Hochmut und egoistischer Freiheitssucht sich gegen Gott empört, sich der Herrschaft der Liebe entzieht und aus dem Reiche des Lichts in das des ewigen Feuers herabgestoßen wird" (KA 12, 446). The form of consciousness assigned to this principle is *Grimm*. This too is a Böhmist term, but once again the apparent similarity only highlights the underlying fundamental differences. For Böhme, *Grimm* (or *Zorn*) belonged to the first principle, the dark core of the divinity, and was therefore the source of life. Schlegel, by contrast, identifies it solely with evil and assigns it no function in the development of the World-Ego. In fact, the role of evil marks the greatest difference between the two writers. For Böhme, evil springs from the very core of the divinity, and plays an essential part in the unfolding of God and his creation (if there were no evil, good could not be manifest). In Schlegel's cosmogony, the evil principle is contingent, irrelevant to the development of the World-Ego, and will eventually self-destruct (KA 12, 446ff.). The jarring note struck by the inclusion of an account of evil which is unmotivated and irrelevant to the system as a whole is a symptom of the impossibility of what Schlegel was attempting: a Christian cosmogony must include Lucifer, but an idealistic cosmogony must derive everything from an absolute principle of pure activity, and therefore allows no room for an active evil.

Schlegel's final remarks about light lead back to the all-important theory of time and space. As mentioned before, all matter is endowed with spirit and therefore potentially alive. Inherent in this imprisoned spirit is the longing to be free of body. This goal cannot be achieved without the aid of light. Light is the expression of perfect love, and the force which shapes, develops, and ultimately dissolves body. It is the agency by which everything, including space itself, is transformed into activity, and hence into freedom: "Das Licht ist das raumerfüllende Prinzip, durch die unermeßliche, überall sich verbreitende Tätigkeit des Lichts wird der Raum selbst aufgelöst, und in ein Meer von Bewegung, Tätigkeit, Freiheit verwandelt" (KA 12, 479). Having thus come full circle,

---

[28] Almost from the first, Schlegel objected to Fichte's characterization of the non-ego, proposing instead a live "you:" "Nicht Ich ein leeres Wort; es sollte *Etwas* heißen. *Ich* ist sehr gut, weil es das sich selbst Constituiren so schön bezeichnet.—Die σθ [Synthese] wäre dann ein *Du*" (KA 18, IV, 1253, Schlegel's italics); see also the concept of the object as live, ensouled "Du," as put forward in the book of consciousness of the 1805 lectures (discussed earlier in this essay).

Schlegel concludes the cosmogony by reiterating his thesis that space and time are "reelle, lebendige, geistige Wesen und Kräfte" (KA 12, 480), because they are essential components of the infinite World-Ego, and that this is the principal tenet of idealism.

If, having reached the end of the theory of nature, one looks back to the introductory book of the lectures, Schlegel's claim that any new philosophy should be prefaced by a critical history of the discipline is recognized as a self-fulfilling prophecy. Schlegel's own system did indeed grow out of his analysis of what he saw as errors committed by other philosophers, but the relationship does not function only in the one direction to which Schlegel drew attention. Rather, the reverse is also true: Schlegel's analysis of previous systems is slanted towards those areas in which he wished to propose new theories; nor does he hesitate to ignore theories which do not suit his purpose, or to misrepresent others which only partially do so. The case of Kant provides the most striking example. As we have seen, out of the entire critical philosophy, Schlegel selects only two ideas, both drawn from the *Kritik der reinen Vernunft*, and these he distorts (either by overstating the case, or by reporting only part of Kant's reasoning). The much-vaunted critical history with which the lectures open is in effect a polemical history, intended to show the need for a new idealistic system, and to lay claim to this role for the theories that follow.

Underlying this strategy is the highly personal quest which had motivated, and continued to motivate, all of Schlegel's philosophical endeavors: the search for a worldview that would satisfy—and reconcile—his various emotional and intellectual needs. His efforts in this direction failed here, as they had always done, because of their overreaching universality, and because his needs, and therefore the systems by which he sought to satisfy these, were ultimately irreconcilable. Just as, during the Jena years, Fichte and Spinoza had proved impossible to fuse, the same happened in 1805 with idealism and Christianity: even by doing violence to both, as these lectures undoubtedly do, Schlegel could only achieve a highly precarious union.

ELLIS FINGER

The Poetry of Friedrich Rückert in the Songs of Schubert, Schumann, and Mahler

In his 1920 essay, *Tradition and the Individual Talent*, T.S. Eliot admonished the modernist generation not to forsake the foundations of past learning that defined the legacy of creative discourse among men: "Tradition ... cannot be inherited, and if you want it you must obtain it by great labor. It involves, in the first place, the historical sense, which we may call nearly indispensable to anyone who would continue to be a poet beyond his twenty-fifth year; and the historical sense involves a perception, not only of the pastness of the past, but of its presence; the historical sense compels a man to write not merely with his own generation in mind, but with a feeling that the whole of literature ... has a simultaneous existence and composes a simultaneous order."[1] His admonition came at a time when radical revisions of form were being tested in literature, the visual arts, and music. Joyce, Proust, Pirandello, Kafka, and Eliot himself were stretching the boundaries of literary possibility, and Picasso, Kandinsky, Schönberg, Stravinsky, and Bartok were challenging the same traditions in painting and in music. Eliot's words of caution were clearly not intended to proscribe further venture by artists; his own poem, *The Waste Land* (two years from publication), was testimony that extraordinary creative advancements could be made from within the foundation of one's literary ancestry.

The modernist generation included many examples of seminal creative minds reassessing the past even as they were charting new territory, to validate the sense of "simultaneous order" of past and present: Picasso's reworkings of Velázquez in the *Meninas* series, Stravinsky's homage to Pergolesi in *Pulcinella*, and Joyce's return to Homer's *Odyssey* in *Ulysses*. Equally important to the historians of culture are those important instances of composers, painters, and writers who recovered past influences from other disciplines, giving new life to artistic antecedents whose creations enabled artists of this century to further their own creative ambitions. Alban Berg's authoritative recasting of Georg Büchner's *Wozzeck* as a pioneering twelve-tone opera accentuated the proto-

---
[1] *The Sacred Wood. Essays on Poetry and Criticism* (London: Methuen, reprinted in University Paperbacks, 1970) 49.

modern aspects of Büchner's imagination and redefined the work as an exemplary expressionist creation. As a fictional parallel, Thomas Mann's conception of Adrian Leverkühn in *Doktor Faustus* included significant periods of experimentation by this composer with the dramas of Shakespeare and the poems of Brentano.[2] This essay will examine one such legacy in the resurgence of interest in the poetry of Friedrich Rückert (1788–1866) through the music of Gustav Mahler (1860–1911).

II

Friedrich Rückert's standing in German literature remains somewhat clouded and unresolved. In her Rückert monograph of 1987, Annemarie Schimmel mused that the bicentennial of the poet's birth was not likely to alter substantially the common view of Rückert, among both scholars and laity, "als reimfroher Sänger ansprechender gemütvoller Liebeslieder und weitverbreiteter Stammbuchverse."[3] Despite early acclaim for a volume of patriotic songs written during the wars of liberation (*Geharnischte Sonetten*) and the popularity of his collection of lyrical poems entitled *Liebesfrühling*, Rückert chose alternative directions for his creative gifts by embarking in 1823 on studies in near-Eastern languages in Vienna under Hammer-Purgstall, whose German translations of Persian poetry had inspired Goethe's *Westöstlicher Divan*. Although his academic career as an Orientalist, first in Erlangen and later in Berlin, never fully eclipsed his work as a poet, the corpus of his writings failed to achieve broad public recognition, and the best of his work was too often compromised by the large number of inconsequential poems that also appeared under his name. The late-Romantic tone of his writings, more evocative of a waning past than focused on sensibilites of a new era, has resulted in the kind of characterization which Benno von Wiese gave him (and others in his circle) in his anthology of nineteenth century German literature, "Das Epigonentum als bewahrtes Erbe."[4] Many of his finest po-

---

[2] The fictional parallel between Leverkühn's Brentano songs and Mahler's attachment to the poems of Rückert is treated by Gunilla Bergsten in her study, *Thomas Mann's Doctor Faustus. The Sources and Structure of the Novel*. Despite the direct involvement of Brentano's influence in the many poems which Mahler adapted from *Des Knaben Wunderhorn*, the musical examples of Leverkühn's Brentano Songs are closer in technique to Schoenberg's twelve-tone compositions than to the more lyrically diatonic songs by Mahler. The more accurate connection between Leverkühn and Mahler is thought to lie in stylistic parallels between Leverkühn's *Lamentation* and Mahler's *Das Lied von der Erde*. Bergsten, tr. Krishna Winston, Chicago: University of Chicago Press, 1969, pp. 88, 90, 112, 200.

[3] *Friedrich Rückert. Lebensbild und Einführung in sein Werk* (Freiburg: Herder Press, 1987) 7.

[4] *Das 19. Jahrhundert.* Texte und Dokumente (Munich: Beck'sche Verlag, 1965) 38.

ems, from the collection known today as the *Kindertotenlieder* (including the five texts which Mahler chose for his song cycle of the same name), went unpublished during his lifetime, serving primarily as private meditations commemorating the deaths of two of his children in 1833 and 1834.

What rises above the flawed image of Rückert's attainments as a poet is the unanimous acclaim for his skills with language. Schimmel cites Theodor Benfey's 1869 appraisal of Rückert's "höchst eigentümliches Sprachgenie" (70), and she extols his "unerhörte Leistung poetischer Übertragungen" (8), a judgment as much based on his virtuosic skills with meter, rhyme, assonance, and phrasing as on his scholarly learning. He was a master of the *craft* of poetry, and his consummate grasp of how language functioned in poetic utterance endowed his verse with a deep innate musicality that exerted special appeal to composers.[5] After a long period of neglect following his death in 1911, Mahler's music slowly began to receive major acclaim, first through the influence of his early disciples Bruno Walter and Wilhelm Mengelberg in the 1930s, and later in the inspired advocacy of Leonard Bernstein and many others. Today his symphonies rank among the most frequently performed and recorded works of this century, and his songs enjoy equal popularity, both in the recital hall and in symphonic programs.

Mahler's music, perfectly positioned at the threshold of our century, moved our musical history forward, as he ventured into new areas of orchestration and formal invention. He also helped to reclaim areas of previous accomplishment, particularly in the poetic texts which served such crucial purposes in his music, from his groundbreaking entree into the symphonic arena with his Symphony No. 1, *The Titan* (inspired by Jean Paul's novel of the same name) and the ensuing Wunderhorn symphonies (Nos. 2, 3, and 4), extending to his use of Goethe's *Faust II* texts in his Symphony No. 8 and Hans Bethge's translations of Chinese poems in his valedictory work, *Das Lied von der Erde*.

This essay will deal with the reception of Friedrich Rückert's poetry by Mahler and by two of his predecessors, Franz Schubert and Robert Schumann. In observing changes in Rückert's presence within the body of Lieder which each composer produced, we will also gain insight into the changing relationship of this late-Romantic poet to various periods of German history, extending from the time around 1822 when Rückert texts first began to appear in Lieder by Schubert to the mid-nineteenth century when further gestation is observed in Rückert's impact on musicians, through the stylistic advancements made by Schumann. We conclude with the neo-Romantic Rückert settings by Mahler, where the fin-de-siècle melancholy that defined so much of Mahler's music

---

[5]Goethe was among the first to recognize the musical underpinnings of Rückert's poetry and translations. In writing about the 1821 volume of Rückert's translations from the Arabic, *Östliche Rosen*, Goethe wrote, "[diese Gedichte] kann ich *allen Musikern* empfehlen" (emphasis mine). Quoted in Schimmel 28.

found its fitting textual partner in the personal writings of Rückert, creating one of our culture's great cross-generational collaborations in poetry and music.

III

Even the most casual knowledge of Mahler's music includes some understanding of how deeply indebted the composer was to the traditions of German poetry, particularly to the folk songs of the Romantic period. The early poems of his own creation (*Lieder aus der Jugendzeit* and *Lieder eines fahrenden Gesellen*) exude the spirit, the thematic language, and the emotional timbres of the Romantic period. As he turned from his own writings to other source books in the 1890s, the Arnim-Brentano *Wunderhorn* texts—already influential as models for his "Jugendzeit" poems—became an enduring source of inspiration, both for the textual interpolations for his Second, Third, and Fourth Symphonies (often referred to as the Wunderhorn Symphonies) and for the monumental set of *Wunderhorn Lieder*, with orchestral accompaniment, completed in the 1890s. His turn to Rückert's poetry as a specific body of writings for which he felt special kinship came to fruition between 1901 and 1904, with the cycle of songs, *Kindertotenlieder*, and the five individual compositions which are now routinely grouped together as the *Rückert Songs*.

To value properly the spiritual kinship between Mahler and Rückert, let us look at the first of the five Rückert songs, entitled "Ich atmet' einen linden Duft."

> Ich atmet' einen linden Duft.
> Im Zimmer stand ein Zweig der Linde,
> Ein Angebinde von lieber Hand.
> Wie lieblich war der Lindenduft!
>
> Wie lieblich ist der Lindenduft,
> Das Lindenreis brachst du gelinde!
> Ich atme leis im Duft der Linde,
> Der Liebe linden Duft.

A first reading of the poem makes it seem like an odd textual choice for a composer whose music helped redefine the foundations of modern music.[6] The sim-

---

[6]The pejorative judgment of Rückert as a poet of the second order also extends to biographers of Mahler. Henry-Louis de la Grange makes the odd claim that Mahler held such high regard for the great writings of Goethe and the true pantheon of German poetry that he chose the lesser work of such writers as Rückert for his music, out of concern that he would violate the acknowledged masterworks by using them in his compositions. ". . . unlike Schumann, Mahler almost never used for his compositions the poems he admired the most . . . The lyrics of Mahler's songs were taken either from Friedrich Rückert, a minor romantic poet, or from *Des Knaben Wunderhorn*, a

plicity of its themes and the narrow range of phrasing and imagery have little in common with the modernist upheavals in language, formal structure, and intellectual quest that defined Viennese artistic life at the turn-of-the-century. The premise of receiving a blossom of lime from one's lover and delighting in its sweet fragrance betokens an innocence and an almost anachronistic dislocation from the composer's own historic moment. Rather than embracing the literary advancements of his contemporaries, he seems to be looking backwards to the defining styles of an earlier age, when folk ballads and simple songs of affection were more the norm. Moreover, the large epic scale of Mahler's symphonic music, with its sweeping landscapes of sound and its heroic statements of grandeur, seems out of balance with the delicate intimacy of Rückert's poem, with its inner filigree of echoing phrase and variation of wording. In its rounded boundaries and enclosed vistas, the poem is really a miniature world of inner reflection. Such is the "at first glance" appearance.

In fact, the kinship between Mahler and Rückert is far deeper and more organic than historic circumstances would suggest. The very qualities which appear to compromise and foreshorten the thematic scope of the poem—its dependency on repetitions and rephrasings and its rather meager inventory of expressive ideas—endeared the text to Mahler's musical ear, as he detected inner resonances of affection, sentiment, and emotional bearing which suited perfectly the pointillistic and expressive properties of his music. The very simplicity of the statements opened for Mahler a vast tapestry of sound by which he articulated symphonically the aura of pleasure and the very perfume of the lime blossom gift, as a sensuous unfolding of the heartfelt text.[7]

---

folklore anthology. He was too receptive to poetry not to understand that the most beautiful, the most perfect poems are complete in themselves and that, in consequence, the greatest poets are always betrayed by composers." *Mahler* (Garden City: Doubleday & Co, 1973) 104. This biographer's judgment is undercut by the views of Bruno Walter and of Mahler, himself: Citing Mahler's "rare understanding of poetry," Walter gave highest praise to "Ich atmet' einen linden Duft" as "a melodic and poetic jewel" (*Gustav Mahler* (New York: Knopf, 1958)) 102, 109), and Mahler's letter to Alma, dated April 2, 1903, makes clear his great esteem for Rückert, whom he regarded as a poet poorly understood and inadequately valued by the public. "How few know anything of those two [Rückert and Fechner]!" Alma Mahler, *Gustav Mahler. Memories and Letters*, ed. Donald Mitchell, transl. Basil Creighton, (New York: Viking Press, 1969) 226.

[7] Donald Mitchell, the authoritative scholar of Mahler's music, sees in the opening bars of this song the foundations of new musical advancements by Mahler, all of which are needed to communicate the extraordinary mood and atmosphere which the composer found in Rückert's song. "[Mahler] creates an intimate world of whispers, of nuances, of timbres and colour persuaded from a handful of instruments playing mostly the same note." *Gustav Mahler. Songs and Symphonies of Life and Death* (Berkeley: University of California Press, 1985) 69.

In part the musicality of setting is already inspired by subtle details of Rückert's poem, particularly the refinements of rhyme and assonance which extend beyond the formal strophic ordering of lines, extending into careful interlinear variations of sound and wording. Each line of the poem is infused with the core phrase, "Linde," and the unfolding of the word's sensuous perfume is furthered by the many other liquid consonants within the poem—"Liebe, lieblich, leis, gelinde." There are also secondary rhymes within several of the lines which enhance the musical "hearing" of the text: the crossing rhymes of "stand" and "Hand" and "Linde" and "Angebinde" in lines 2–3, for example, and "Lindenreis" and "leis" in lines 6–7. Also, the small change in wording between "Wie lieblich war der Lindenduft" (line 4) to the present tense "Wie lieblich ist der Lindenduft" (l. 5) is a significant modulation for Mahler, the musician, in ways that verbal dexterity cannot accomplish in quite the same way.

Mahler's setting of the poem is an extraordinary evocation of sensuous delight. The singer is assigned a slow, measured tempo and a muted dynamic, and the statements of gratitude and love are conveyed in the most tender intimacy. Mahler's orchestration respects the intimate nature of the song; the larger dynamic forces that his music often favors are withheld in this extremely tender setting. The power of the song's emotional impact lies in the gentle undulations of strings and winds which underlie the whole of the song, as a rhythmic "blossoming" of sound which pulses through every measure of the music, mirroring the suffusion of the lime blossom's aroma through the "room" of the protagonist and through the musical "hallways" which Mahler creates to inhale the sweet aroma of the flowery gift.

IV

As we go back in time to trace the earliest evidence of Rückert's influence on composers, the obvious starting point is Franz Schubert, the most prolific and enduring composer of Lieder. Schubert's brief life (1797–1828) barely intersected with public recognition of Rückert's poems. Even without confirming Rückert's publication dates in relation to the flourishing of Schubert's songwriting, the meager presence of Rückert texts within the vast oeuvre of Schubert's song literature attests to the fleeting contact that this composer must have had with our poet. *Grove's* entry on Schubert lists 960 songs, the majority of which are based on poets' work who still rank within the canon of German poetry from the late eighteenth and early nineteenth centuries: Goethe, Schiller, the Schlegels, Stolberg, Hölty, Körner, Matthisson, Müller (the poet of *Die schöne Müllerin* and *Die Winterreise*), even Ossian. Yet in comparison to the 14 poems of Hölty and 39 of Matthisson which Schubert immortalized through music, only six Rückert poems were set, all in the 1822–23 period, a full four years before Schubert's early death at the age of 31.[8]

One might read from this brief and passing interest a lack of sympathy for the language, strophic qualities, or musicality of the poet's work. However, the six poems which did merit Schubert's attention all exhibit special care with phrasing, mood, and metric pulse, and three of the six—"Du bist die Ruh," "Lachen und Weinen," and "Sei mir gegrüßt"—endure as songs of extraordinary beauty and impact.

We will examine the first two of these settings, both of which are short strophic compositions. The two stanzas of "Lachen und Weinen" follow a common rhyme scheme of aabccb. Presented as a five-stanza poem, "Du bist die Ruh" appears to be the more ambitiously conceived of the two. The short metrical unit chosen by Rückert—two beats per line—gives the poem an integral conciseness and coherence, further tightened by the abab rhyme scheme maintained throughout the five stanzas. In each poem Rückert interweaves delicate verbal threads within the body of the text which yield a grander artistic structure than would be suggested by the simplicity of the rhyme scheme.

A full reading of "Du bist die Ruh" immediately conveys the distinctive blending of simplicity and inner richness that must certainly have impressed Schubert in his choice of text:

>Du bist die Ruh',
>Der Friede mild,
>Die Sehnsucht du,
>Und was sie stillt.
>
>Ich weihe dir
>Voll Lust und Schmerz
>Zur Wohnung hier
>Mein Aug' und Herz.
>
>Kehr ein bei mir
>Und schliesse du
>Still hinter dir
>Die Pforten zu.
>
>Treib andern Schmerz
>Aus deiner Brust!
>Voll sei dies Herz
>Von deiner Lust.

---

[8] *The New Grove Encyclopedia of Music and Musicians*, 20 vols., ed. Stanley Sadie (London: Macmillan, 1980). Schubert entry by Maurice J.E. Brown, vol. 16, pp. 788–810.

> Dies Augenzelt,
> Von deinem Glanz
> Allein erhellt,
> O füll es ganz!

The opening lines establish a hushed sense of intimacy between two lovers—the "ich" and "du" of the poem. Invocations of repose, peace, and solace dominate the thematic landscape of the appeal, but not without eliminating completely a disquieting element of yearning which unsettles the poem's emotional balance. The exquisite pairing of contrary thoughts—"die Sehnsucht du/und was sie stillt"—places in momentary turmoil the poignant ache of longing and its very cessation when a lover's absence is ended. In the lovely flowering of intimacy, union, and joy that this poem conveys, Rückert never allows the foreboding of pain ("Schmerz") to vanish completely, even by reopening the theme in stanza four as something to be banished.

Dominant imagery throughout the poem centers on enclosures, sequestrations, places of refuge. Doors are closed and locked, the exterior world sealed off, and unusual containments are created, such as the "the eye's canopy" ("Augenzelt," as a deft variation on the more familiar "Augenweide" favored for centuries by German poets). Regions of the body, both actual and figurative, are by turns filled and emptied, as pain is driven from the breast, pleasure enters the heart, the glow of happiness fills one's gaze, and the entire poem concludes with the command, "o fill it completely." Enclosures of home and hospice ("zur Wohnung hier" and "kehr ein bei mir") and figurative recesses of the soul are interwoven to yield an ineffable pleasure of cohabitation and shelter.

It is fascinating to speculate on how Schubert heard the inner musical language of Rückert's text and settled on the tone, the rhythmic pulse, and harmonic language he would use to set the words to music. The process of recomposing an existing poem, by which the artistic resources of music are added to the formal completeness of a verbal text, is one of the most rewarding areas of inquiry in German letters. Two Schubert song settings of familiar Goethe texts provide revealing examples of the transforming powers of music, which elevate an already "perfect" text into another dimension of artistry. The first example is Gretchen's spinning song from *Faust*, where Schubert conceives of a gently undulating ostinado which the piano accompaniment maintains throughout the song, to replicate the turning of the spinning wheel, as a brilliant rhythmic underpinning to Gretchen's song of remorse. The second is the dramatic ballad, "Der Erlkönig," where Schubert made it possible for the singer to inhabit the three voices of Goethe's poem—the father's rational mind, the son's sense of terror, and the words of the erlking himself. The narrator's overview of the drama's unfolding and the pianist's replication of the horse's galloping hoof beats complete the musical animation which Schubert added to this already vibrant poem.

Hearing Schubert's setting of "Du bist die Ruh" reveals a similar sense of genial "recomposition" of a poem already finished and self-sufficient in itself. First, Schubert succeeds beautifully in capturing the mood of privacy and repose, as if he were providing musical "language" for the most intimate of songs to be exchanged between lovers. The tempo is spaciously laid out, but with an underlying pulse of forward movement which balances expertly the sense of time's cessation and the lovers' eagerness for their rendezvous. The five verse units given by Rückert are reduced to three by Schubert, as he collapses verses 1 and 2 and verses 3 and 4 into two coherent 8-line strophes which share a single melody and harmonic texture.

Schubert's musical emphasis lies squarely on the final verse: with the words "Dies Augenzelt allein erhellt von deinem Glanz," he elevates the melodic line in a dramatic way, to underscore the sudden glow of warmth and light from the lovers' eyes, and he then repeats the quatrain for final emphasis, with additional harmonic modulation which gives the setting, through pure musical effect, an exquisite burnished glow of fervor and delight. The song is a refined augmentation of what was already a beautiful poem, as writer and composer have joined in a shared process of creating a lyrical treasure greater than the sum of its parts.

The second poem, "Lachen und Weinen," is briefer, with only two 6-line stanzas. But the longer metrical units used in each line give it a feeling of scope that the earlier poem lacked. In comparison to "Du bist die Ruh," "Lachen und Weinen" is more formulaic, with almost contrived structural parallels between the two stanzas:

> Lachen und Weinen zu jeglicher Stunde
> Ruht bei der Lieb' auf so mancherlei Gründe.
> Morgens lacht' ich vor Lust;
> Und warum ich nun weine
> Bei des Abendes Scheine,
> Ist mir selb' nicht bewusst.
>
> Weinen und Lachen zu jeglicher Stunde
> Ruht bei der Lieb' auf so mancherlei Gründe.
> Abends weint' ich vor Schmerz;
> Und warum du erwachen
> Kannst am Morgen mit Lachen,
> Muss ich dich fragen, o Herz.

The opening opposition between laughter and tears, as symmetrically laid out as the familiar two masks of comedy and tragedy, is developed by Rückert as a formula for observing mood changes between happiness and melancholy. Unlike the other poem, the emotional world centers only on the central persona, with no identifiable "other." The basic structure of the two verses is formal and thorough. The "Lachen/Weinen" inversion, coupled with related reversals of theme ("Abend/Morgen" "Lust/Schmerz") leads to the common ending of each stanza, as an unresolved question to oneself ("mir selbst nicht bewusst" "Muss ich dich fragen"). "Lachen und Weinen" is basically a one-dimensional poem, lacking the thematic richness and resonance of imagery we found in the earlier work.

Schubert's setting of the poem confirms this sense of uncomplicated strategy. The themes of happiness and sadness are alternated in regular shifts from major key to minor key. The tempo of the song is more briskly paced, as if both poet and composer were content with surface contemplation of the changes in one's temperament, rather than probing the depths of melancholy or chronic joy and despondency. Rückert's poem resides on the exteriors of life's changeablilty, never venturing into personal grief or anguish, and Schubert takes the suggested discourse at face value, giving the musical setting a surface sheen that delights the ear, without submerging the mind more profoundly in weightier themes.

V

As we turn now from the songs of Franz Schubert to those of Robert Schumann, we move a full generation forward in gauging the interests of German readership in poetry, both from the early Classic-Romantic decades of 1790–1810 and from the more recent publications by poets whose accomplishments became recognized in the years following 1830. Twenty-three years Schubert's junior, Schumann enjoyed great early success as a composer, with significant works for the piano in the decade following Schubert's death in 1828. His fascination with Lieder, however, did not blossom until 1840, not by coincidence the same year that marked the beginnings of his relationship with Clara Wieck. Of the 330 songs by Schumann that are catalogued in *Grove's Encyclopedia*, over one-third were composed in this immensely productive year. Included in this body of work are the twelve songs published as Opus 37 (three of the nine are credited to Clara, nine to Robert).[9]

The meager presence of Rückert's poems in Schubert's compositions contrasts sharply with the significant role that this poet played in Schumann's choices of texts for his songs. Thirty-two of Schumann's songs are based on

---

[9] Rückert acknowledged Schumann's musical tributes to his poetry with a bittersweet poem of dedication which he sent to Robert and Clara in 1856, shortly before Robert's death. In it he recognized how powerfully Schumann's music had enhanced the stature of his poetry, while also reiterating his sense of regret over the meager recognition which the world had accorded him as a poet: "Meine Lieder / Singt ihr wieder, / Mein Empfinden / Klingt ihr wieder, / Mein Gefühl / Beschwingt ihr wieder, / Mich, wie schön / Verjüngt ihr wieder: / Nehmt meinen Dank, wenn auch die Welt, / Wie mir einst, ihren vorbehält." Quoted in Eduard Hanslick's 1899 article, "Robert Schumann in Endenrich," reprinted in Susan Gillespie's translation in *Schumann and his World*, ed. Larry Todd, (Princeton: Princeton UP, 1994) 279.

Rückert poems, including all 12 of the Opus 37 songs, the collaborative project between Robert and Clara which underlay the blossoming of their relationship. If we include the large number of choral songs which Schumann wrote for mixed voices and for men's and women's chorus, an additional 16 Rückert texts become part of the total body of work from Schumann's hand. Looking beyond personal tastes and curiosities which Schumann may have felt for individual poets, the substantial growth of Rückert's profile from the 1822–23 period in Schubert's music to the Schumanns' work around 1840 marks a major advancement in the visibility of this poet's writings within the general readership in Germany.

The three Schumann settings of Rückert poems chosen for this study are all duets. My choice of duets is guided in part by the musical accomplishment of the three settings, all of which are exceptionally beautiful and unusually well established in the performance repertory of vocalists. The focus on duets also presents us with the opportunity to explore certain writings of Rückert which either presume the presence of two personas or benefit from having the texts articulated by a male-female duo, rather than lying solely in the voice of a single speaker.

The two Schubert songs we examined straddled the dividing line between a single character's experience and an emotional world clearly rooted in a love relationship between two people: "Lachen und Weinen" held vague intimations of a love partner, but the fluctuations between joy and sorrow remain fairly narrowly situated within the solo persona. "Du bist die Ruh," although written for a single voice, obviously presumes the partner's participation in the sharing of statements, as listener or recipient of the accolades.

The three Schumann songs straddle this same dividing line, but with the major difference that all three are conceived as duets, with equality of involvement by the soprano and baritone, either to dramatize fully the actual voice assignments which exist within the original poem or to enlarge upon call-and-response situations which lie latent within the text. We will see that the composer is even capable of establishing an additional dramatic dimension for a second singer which Rückert may not himself have intended: the linear limitations of a verbal text, with a single phrase moving forward through the poem, can be surmounted in music by the composer's ability to interweave two voices simultaneously in counterpoint with each other.

The first poem we will treat is the seventh of the 12 Opus 37 songs, "Schön ist das Fest des Lenzes." It is a simple poem in two four-line stanzas, with a delicate *abab* rhyme scheme that extends through both stanzas.

> Schön ist das Fest des Lenzes,
> Doch währt es nur der Tage drei.
> Hast du ein Lieb', bekränz es
> Mit Rosen, eh' sie gehn vorbei!

> Hast du ein Glas, kredenz' es,
> O Schenk, und singe mir dabei:
> Schön ist das Fest des Lenzes,
> Doch währt es nur der Tage drei.

Rückert draws upon several poetic traditions in the poem's design. The specific setting of springtime revels marks it as an occasional song, common both within the folk traditions and the favored tropes of "Kunstdichtung." As a drinking song, with its invitation to raise a toast and to honor the season of year, it bears broad kinship to countless similar invocations which flourished in popular festivals of the nineteenth century. There is a specific lineage with the Anacreon tradition, with the custom of presenting wreaths of roses, offering a cup of wine, and invoking the carpe diem theme of grasping for permanence within the fleeting moment, "nur der Tage drei."

The interesting feature of the poem, as chosen by Schumann for a lovers' duet, is the rather public nature of the setting. Such toasting songs were generally intended for group enjoyment, and notwithstanding the reference to "a loved one" ("hast du ein Lieb..."), Rückert's poem lies within the very public world of groups of revelers, rather than within the private domain of two lovers. Schumann's setting for soprano and baritone does not violate the public nature of the poem, per se. But it certainly particularizes the exchanges of affection and situates the offering of roses and wine within the more private world of two lovers.

Schumann's attraction to the poem as material for a more personalized love song may well result from the several touches of special poetic craft by which Rückert elevated what first appears to be a fairly routine drinking song into a composition of cunning architecture. The simplicity of the phrasing, as in many of Rückert's poems, is deceptively artful. The poem opens with a stock invocation of spring's short duration, and the repetition of this opening couplet as the closing phrase of a poem only eight lines long leaves precious little room for creative expression. Yet within this limited structure, Rückert succeeds in creating a tightness and muscularity of poetic fabric by use of the parallel phrasing of "Hast du ein Lieb... Hast du ein Glas," by the subtle rhyming sonority of "bekränz es... kredenz es," and by reformulating the opening couplet, first sounded as a rather vague and clichéd phrase, as a personalized song of celebration shared between comrades or lovers. The result is an absolute gem, tightly woven, skillfully shaped, and brilliantly articulated.

Schumann's song mirrors this sense of inner cohesion. He chooses a brisk and animated tempo, appropriate to the energetic spirit of the season, and carves out integrity for each of the singer's voices by structuring the song as a canonic round, with the soprano mirroring the baritone's lead delivery of the text, in sequence two measures delayed. Schumann blurs the strophic interval and shapes the entire eight-line text as a unit. The critical musical moment occurs between line 6 and line 7, when the composer causes the baritone to pause briefly, eliminating the distance between the two voices, and together the singers, in unison for one line only, resoundingly sing "Schön ist das Fest des Lenzes." In the final line Schumann creates a new and altogether fresh impression of the "seize the day" theme, as the soprano, now the leading voice, resumes the canon, and the baritone answers, plaintively, inwardly, and with unprecedented personal intimacy. The piano echoes their final phrase, as a closing seal to their toast to each other. Taken together, the final two lines unite the public, communal spirit of the toast, with the extroverted unison phrasing, and the inner world of privacy and seclusion that lovers would celebrate in honoring each other's company.

The twelfth and final of Schumann's Opus 37 songs is Rückert's "So wahr die Sonne scheinet," a poem similar in structure to "Schön ist das Fest des Lenzes," but more immediately conceived as a love song appropriate for duet setting.

> So wahr die Sonne scheinet,
> So wahr die Wolke weinet,
> So wahr die Flamme sprüht,
> So wahr der Frühling blüht;
> So wahr hab' ich empfunden,
> Wie ich dich halt' umwunden:
> Du liebst mich, wie ich dich,
> Dich lieb' ich, wie du mich.
>
> Die Sonne mag verscheinen,
> Die Wolke nicht mehr weinen,
> Die Flamme mag versprühn,
> Der Frühling nicht mehr blühn!
> Wir wollen uns umwinden
> Und immer so empfinden;
> Du liebst mich, wie ich dich,
> Dich lieb' ich, wie du mich.

This poem, too, is in simple strophic form, but twice the length of "Schön ist das Fest des Lenzes." In both poems repetitions of cadence-like couplets are used to develop the musicality of the wording; the couplet refrain used in the first poem as a framing devise, at beginning and end of poem, functions differently in "So wahr die Sonne scheinet," as the repeated figure is used to conclude each of the stanzas. And within the couplet itself there is a graceful play of wording that entwines the two personas of the poet and his reader ("Du and mich . . . ich and dich") and, in music, the voices of the two singers.

This second poem is no less the product of careful poetic craft by Rückert, especially given the methodical "So wahr" sequence that dominates the first strophe. Litanies of this type teeter on the verge of collapsing into monotony.

But Rückert salvages the rhetorical value of the recurring verbal pattern, first by choosing several strokes of original imagery and, second, by fully transforming the "So wahr" sequence of invocations in a beautifully conceived rewording of the six original lines, with reordering of tenses from present and present perfect in verse one to the future tense and "infinitive" in verse two.

The imagery is important to value, for Rückert once again treads precariously close to hackneyed and overworked material, with invocations of "die Sonne scheint" and "der Frühling blüht." His originality, however, works to good effect with the inner images of a weeping cloud and a spewing flame, both of which function as subtle manifestations of love's ardor and sorrows. The beauty of Rückert's rephrasings in verse two lies in his retaining the image and verb structure of each of the leading thought patterns, carefully shifting each verb from its finite form (the present tense "scheinet, weinet, sprüht, blüht" and the participles "empfunden, umwunden") to future tense infinitives. The effect is subtle and complex: in some cases the change in verb form signals the extinguishing of life forces—sun, flames, springtime—but in the two critical areas of the lovers' abiding embrace, the infinitives "umwinden" and "empfinden" are set free from their past tense form in verse one to a true "infinity" of future love.

Schumann's setting centers on the concept of the embrace. He chooses a slower tempo than was used in the first song, to encourage a more reflective and introverted mood to establish itself. Instead of working in canonic round as before, the two voices move as one, and each phrase unfolds naturally as if spoken by the partnership of the two singers. In verse one the soprano is given the melody, while the baritone encircles the melodic line, sometimes in lower register and sometimes, in falsetto, rising above his partner. In verse two the roles are reversed: the baritone is given the melody, and the soprano, dropping to mezzo range, provides underpinning, occasionally moving into her higher register to complete the encirclement of voices which Schumann creates as his core musical idea for the song. The effect of an enduring embrace—literally "umwunden"—is accomplished both in text and in music, as the partnership between poet and composer culminates in the final line of the poem, which is repeated at the very end with a subtle reversal of vocal lines between the two singers.

The third Rückert poem we will examine in a Schumann setting comes from a later period in the composer's career. His 1849 Opus 101 songs mark a return both to the Lieder genre and specifically to the poems of Rückert. Like the twelve songs of Opus 37, the eight songs of Opus 101 are all settings of Rückert poems. The one we will examine, "Ich bin dein Baum," is especially interesting, once again, in its relative brevity, and in its direct folklike imagery.

> Ich bin dein Baum: o Gärtner, dessen Treue
> Mich hält in Liebespfleg' und süsser Zucht,

> Komm, dass ich in den Schoss dir dankbar streue
> Die reife dir allein gewachsne Frucht.
>
> Ich bin dein Gärtner, o du Baum der Treue!
> Auf andres Glück fühl' ich nicht Eifersucht:
> Die holden Äste find' ich stets aufs neue
> Geschmückt mit Frucht, wo ich gepflückt die Frucht.

The poem's appeal to Schumann is clear in one regard, for the two verses very clearly belong to separate voices, and the appropriateness of the text for duet setting is obvious. The fact, however, that so rustic a text, rather simplistic in its basic premise, should result in a musical setting of extraordinary resonance and architectural richness is a surprise.

The basic concept of envisioning love through the analogy of cultivation, grooming, and bearing of fruit is a simple one, often used by poets as passing reenforcement of themes, but rarely as such an end in itself as in this poem. The specific themes of "Zucht" and "Eifersucht," connected through deep rhyming patterns that extend across strophes, cite a familiar theme often connected with love, as inclinations of jealousy are balanced by the restraint of discipline. A second deep rhyme between the strophes ("streue" and "aufs neue," linking the third line of each verse) and a thematic arch connecting the final lines of the two verses ("Die reife dir allein gewachsene Frucht" and "Geschmückt mit Frucht... gepflückt die Frucht") further strengthens the inner foundations of language that drew Schumann to the poem. The latter connection between "fruit that has been ripened just for you" and "the fruit I have picked" secures the dramatic framework that served the composer's intentions for writing a duet. And in these several linkages of themes and verbal motifs we begin to discover resonances that Schumann was able to develop in sophisticated musical ways that added a more satisfying artistic impact than the poem may have possessed on its own.

Schumann's song begins with a basic decision to entrust the first verse to the soprano, allowing for an elegant rephrasing of the fourth line of her stanza, and to have the baritone begin the second verse also as a solo. But midway through the first line of this second verse the soprano begins a full repetition of her text, with the two voices moving forward in canonic form, as a musical structure similar to that used in "Schön ist das Fest des Lenzes." Thus begins an extended interweaving of the two voices, each articulating its own assigned text and the two converging, in beautifully appointed music, on the rhyming words of "Zucht" and "Eifersucht" and "streue" and "aufs neue." The melodic phrasing laid out in the soprano solo evolves into a deeply satisfying web of musical and verbal counterpoint, as threads of melodic texture tighten the exchanges of wording between the two lovers. Symbolically, the final form of Schumann's song creates an exquisite "ripening" of artistry, accomplished through cultivation of musical forms and the organic powers of counterpoint.

VI

The advancements in formal structure noted in Schumann's three duets and the expanded representation of Rückert's writings in the body of Schumann's Lieder return us to the privileged place which Rückert occupied in the music of Gustav Mahler. Almost as if to set a lasting monument to this poet's stature, Mahler devoted two of his most enduring compositional labors to poems by Rückert: the *Kindertotenlieder* and the five *Rückert Songs*.

The first of these was completed by Mahler between 1901 and 1904, at a time that his relationship with Alma Schindler was in its earliest years (they married in the winter of 1902). It consists of five poems taken from an extensive set of poems also entitled *Kindertotenlieder* which Rückert composed in a therapeutic attempt to assuage the grief of his daughter's death in December, 1833, and that of his two-year-old son some six weeks later. The morbid dimension of Mahler's attraction to these poems during the months just preceding his marriage to Alma is heightened by the tragic coincidence of a death by scarlet fever of Mahler's own daughter, Maria, in 1907, some five years after the songs' completion.[10] As interesting as these compositions are, both musically and in cross-generational kinship between Mahler and Rückert, we will turn our attention instead to the set of five *Rückert Songs*, two of which will be viewed in detail.

Composed by Mahler in the productive summer of 1901 as individual works rather than as a cycle, these songs are almost always grouped together, either on recital programs or recording projects, and over time they have come to be regarded as a coherent set of songs, simply called the *Rückert Songs*. The five poems vary greatly. As we saw at the outset of this study, the first of the five is a brief and tightly centered poem about a lover's pleasure over receiving a blossom from a lime tree. Another, entitled "Liebst du um Schönheit," poses the question of various motives and satisfactions for sustaining a love relationship. Still another, "Blicke mir nicht in die Lieder," develops from the clever premise that one's partner should not peer into the creative process of writing

---

[10]Kurt Blaukopf discourages us from drawing connections between these two accidental turns of fate. He argues that Mahler undertook his work with Rückert's poems to work through his lingering emotional struggles with the childhood death of his brother, Ernst, with whom he was very close, and the deaths, in infancy, of four younger brothers within the Mahler family. *Gustav Mahler*, transl. Inge Goodwin, (New York: Praeger, 1973) 198. Alma's abiding discomfort over the songs, however, dominated her personal memoirs of this period of her troubled relationship with her husband. As Egon Gartenberg reports, "So strong was her resentment of the songs that even her critical judgment of the artistic validity was clouded and she could not bring herself to acknowledge their greatness . . . Alma felt chilled as he spoke about the [Sixth] Symphony, because she felt that the work, together with the *Kindertotenlieder*, was a true mirror of his life and fate—a withdrawal into gloom, darkness, and tragedy." *Mahler. The Man and His Music* (New York: Schirmer, 1978) 126.

poetry or composing songs, just as bees cannot abide having an outsider observe them while they are hard at work shaping the honeyed cells of their hive. Rückert chose the term "Lieder" for his own poetic writings, begging privacy from outside observers, and the songwriter Mahler, still very much divided in his career between conducting and composing, no doubt felt a real personal sense of identification with Rückert's entreaty.

Our work will center on the two most ambitious *Rückert Songs,* "Um Mitternacht" and "Ich bin der Welt abhanden gekommen," both of which tower above their three partner songs, in regards to thematic depth and musical scope. As conceived by Rückert, these two poems have a common foundation. Each is composed from the vantage point of a single persona, and the world that this persona inhabits is marked by silence, isolation, solitude, loneliness. In each, the protagonist is situated within a vast emptiness—in one case the darkened heavens of a midnight sky and in the other, the external world of day-to-day occupations, the "Weltgetümmel," from which the speaker has sought refuge.

Each poem carries undeniable markings of the late romantic period, as exemplary products of the mid-nineteenth-century imagination. "Um Mitternacht" fits nicely within the pictorial landscapes favored by Caspar David Friedrich, with the solitary individual profiled against the vastness of an open landscape. And "Ich bin der Welt abhanden gekommen" manifests one of the dominant themes of romantic poetry, that of the individual summoning the courage of an inner life of the imagination to compensate for an insufficient exterior world.

Both poems, moreover, speak to the intellectual landscape of the modernist age, as if themes originally laid out by Rückert in the early nineteenth century, appropriate to his own era and life experience, evolved as prophetic voicings of metaphysical struggle and psychological perception that could as easily have been articulated by contemporaries of Mahler. The heightened sense of solitude, the dwarfing of human experience in face of a cosmic void, the collapse of communication between poet and world, the anguished introspection of personal quests, and the subcurrent of melancholy and despair that lurks just beneath the surface of the text—these are all qualities which defined the modernist experience that Mahler inhabited and which his music exemplifies.

As we have summarized certain common threads which unite the two poems, we should also allow each poem its own thematic integrity and note certain obvious differences between their separate emotional worlds. "Um Mitternacht" is the longer of the two, and it extends well beyond the rather enclosed poetic worlds encountered earlier, reaching into more ambitious areas of statement and theme:

> Um Mitternacht hab' ich gewacht
> Und aufgeblickt zum Himmel;

> Kein Stern vom Sterngewimmel
> Hat mir gelacht um Mitternacht.
>
> Um Mitternacht hab' ich gedacht
> Hinaus in dunkle Schranken,
> Es hat kein Lichtgedanken
> Mir Trost gebracht um Mitternacht.
>
> Um Mitternacht nahm ich in acht
> Die Schläge meines Herzens;
> Ein einz'ger Puls des Schmerzens
> War angefacht um Mitternacht.
>
> Um Mitternacht kämpft ich die Schlacht,
> O Menschheit, deiner Leiden;
> Nicht konnt' ich sie entscheiden
> Mit meiner Macht um Mitternacht.
>
> Um Mitternacht hab' ich die Macht
> In Deine Hand gegeben;
> Herr über Tod und Leben,
> Du hältst die Wacht um Mitternacht!

Its five quatrains carry many of the stylistic markings we have observed in earlier poems: a steady abba, acca, adda rhyme scheme and the use of a recurring phrase, "um Mitternacht," as a consistent framing device for each verse, together with an internal rhyming pattern ("gewacht," "gelacht," "gedacht," "gebracht," "acht," "angefacht," "Schlacht," "Macht," and "Wacht") to enrich the texture of the poetic fabric. There are also some features we have not encountered before, including the irregular metrical patterns of alternating lengths among the lines, with a shorter rhymed couplet lodged between each of the longer exterior "Mitternacht" lines.

The poem builds its emotional world step by step, moving from the opening statement of solitude and cosmic silence to the final invocations of existential triumph ("kämpft ich die Schlacht") and consolation in God ("hab ich die Macht/in Deine Hand gegeben"). The first three verses detail the experience of anguish, personalized in the isolated world, void of solace ("[kein] Trost") and of heightened awareness of one's own "pulse of torment" ("Puls des Schmerzens"). Even with the eventual turn toward triumph and transcendence, the poem never fully surmounts the dire sense of anxiety of inhabiting a world void of human community. The graceful and celebratory songs of love that Schumann drew from Rückert's inspiration, and even the charmed world of Mahler's own "Ich atmet einen linden Duft," seem fully eclipsed by the desolate world of silence portrayed here.

Mahler's setting of this poem moves through similar stages of development. The opening stanzas, both in the vocal line and in the orchestration, are tinged with melancholy. The text is delivered as an inner entreaty, as the singer responds with stringent dejection to the darkness of the heavens and the utter absence of communication. The rhyming word, "gelacht," carries special ironic impact.

Mahler builds his musical forces to a more heroic mood in verse four, as the vocal line is endowed with greater dramatic urgency, and the orchestration reflects the sense of metaphysical struggle. Brass and tympany augment the forces of strings and winds, to bring the composition to a resounding close, as the singer pleads an ultimate faith in transcendent powers in verse five.

The final poem we will examine is "Ich bin der Welt abhanden gekommen." It is at once the most despondent of Rückert's poems, with its utter sense of dislocation and abandonment from the world, and the most poignant statement of self-reliance, at peace with the resources of one's own imagination and inner life—appropriately symbolized, for both Rückert and Mahler, by the concept of the song ("in meinem Lied"). Of the ten poems we have examined, it is also the most idiomatic and unbridled in its phrasing, free and improvisational in meter and less overtly concerned with virtuosic rhyming effects (the poet contents himself with a basic abab, cdcd, efef structure) than with conveying content of great personal consequence.

So direct is the wording and so secondary are the poetic structures that elsewhere have tended to announce themselves in rhetorical ways that this particular composition has almost the character of a soliloquy or dramatic monologue. However, the highly reflective and brooding qualities of the wording make this a poem of extraordinary lyrical import, squarely focused on the confessional nature of one's most private thoughts, fears, and sources of resolve.

> Ich bin der Welt abhanden gekommen,
> Mit der ich sonst viele Zeit verdorben;
> Sie hat so lange nichts von mir vernommen,
> Sie mag wohl glauben, ich sei gestorben.
>
> Es ist mir auch gar nichts daran gelegen,
> Ob sie mich für gestorben hält;
> Ich kann auch gar nichts sagen dagegen,
> Denn wirklich bin ich gestorben der Welt.
>
> Ich bin gestorben dem Weltgetümmel,
> Und ruh' in einem stillen Gebiet;
> Ich leb' allein in meinem Himmel,
> In meinem Lieben, in meinem Lied.

The sympathetic appeal of this text to Mahler is clear: the inner landscape that unfolds, verse by verse, depicts a world that we have come to associate with Mahler's work as a composer, in summer Alpine retreats far removed from the frenetic demands of his professional services in Vienna. Moreover, the elements of loneliness, reclusiveness from the world, and isolation within one's own inner thoughts and feelings bring to mind so many passages in Mahler's symphonies where the boisterous, extroverted music of which he was capable surrenders its might to the pure lyricism and tender inner dialogue such as the "Ruhevoll" movement of Symphony No. 4 and the Adagietto movement of Symphony No. 5.

In its slow evolution and the unusual spaciousness of Mahler's shaping of the orchestral texture this song approaches the scope of a symphonic interlude. Its duration and scope are far greater than the twelve lines of text would ever suggest to the eye, and the emotional journey which Mahler accomplishes in moving through the three verses is enormous.

I close my essay with this song for several reasons. First, it demonstrates more clearly than any other available example the transforming powers of a composer to bring a poem forward from its nineteenth-century origins to a modernist world of radically different intellectual bent, whereby the musical setting elicits new dimensions of meaning and emotional power. Second, it brings to a fitting closure several earlier themes we encountered with Schubert and Schumann.

This song by Mahler has a close spiritual and musical connection with the Schubert song we examined earlier, "Du bist die Ruh." Both songs have as their musical character a quietude and a hushed sense of inner privacy that border on extraordinary intimacy. The melodic life of each poem is poignantly tender, and the gradually evolving tempo is perfectly appropriate to the privileged depiction of a sanctified inner world. The greatest difference between the two songs is this: Schubert's song celebrates the happiness of a love relationship between two people, for whom the exterior world has been shuttered, so that the bright glow within their "eye canopy" can flourish in utter peacefulness. Mahler's song is of another era, as the singer's world of solace is also a world of solitude. A sustaining love is mentioned ("in meinem Lieben, in meinem Lied"), but the frames of reference are to a single spirit, and the final image one has at the song's quiet ending is one of utter loneliness.

There is an important compositional element in Mahler's song which also serves to connect this work with the three Schumann duets, all of which exploit poetic opportunities posed by Rückert to "hear" two voices together in song. Mahler placed within his conceptual framing of this song the plaintive melody of an English horn which moves throughout the orchestral texture of setting, as a kind of vocal partner to the singer. This instrumental "voice," of deep melancholy and longing, functions as a second melodic solo during the orchestral passages, echoing the voice of the singer. The song ends with a brief orchestral passage which follows the conclusion of the text, "in meinem Lied," and the English horn brings to closure the melodic and the thematic flow of the song, as the echoing completion of an elegant duet between the individual poet/singer and the "Lied."

The closure of the Rückert period in Mahler's career is viewed by Donald Mitchell as also being the foundation of the final phase of his music. Following three symphonies in which poetic texts were not used as creative structural elements, the Fifth, Sixth, and Seventh Symphonies, Mahler returned to two heroic text-based compositions in his final years, the Eighth Symphony and *Das Lied von der Erde*, which join with the Ninth and unfinished Tenth Symphony as the final testament of his life and music.

Mitchell illuminates the indirect connections which lead from Mahler's five-year preoccupation with Rückert's poetry to the penetration revelations which define the emotional parameters of *Das Lied von der Erde*—in Mitchell's estimation, the very summit of Mahler's creative genius. He correctly cites the appeal of the intrinsic Oriental qualities of Rückert's writings—both his prodigious translations from Arabic, Persian, Indian, and Chinese sources *and* his original poetry—to Mahler's spiritual journey and to his music. The publication of Hans Bethge's *Die Chinesische Flöte* in 1907, quickly seized upon by Mahler as the perfect poetic source book for his orchestral song cycle, is regarded by Mitchell as the appropriate closure to a pervasive influence which Rückert's life and work exerted on Mahler's music. "There can be no doubt at all that Mahler would have been aware of this [Chinese] dimension to Rückert's interests, and it seems to me to be equally beyond doubt that when . . . Bethge's slim volume fell into Mahler's hands, in 1907, his enthusiastic response to it had already been conditioned—preconditioned—by his intimate association with Rückert. So from this point of view too (literary and philosophical), the Rückert songs . . . can be seen as decisive, albeit unconscious, preparation for the great undertaking that was still to come."[11]

---

[11] Mitchell 128.

KATHRYN SHAILER HANSON

The Transitory Individual: Tieck's *Der Runenberg* and Handke's *Die Wiederholung* as Allegories of Aging

When Peter Handke stated in a 1972 essay by the same title, "die Literatur ist romantisch," he was echoing the sentiment of his poetic forebear, Ludwig Tieck, who had explained nearly a century and a half earlier, "Ich weiß zwischen poetisch und romantisch überhaupt keinen Unterschied zu machen," and affirming Friedrich Schlegel's earlier conclusion to his famous Athenaeum Fragment 116, "... in einem gewissen Sinn ist oder soll alle Poesie romantisch sein."[1] Similarities between romantic and late modern/postmodern literature, from their common subjectivity, self-reflexivity, and metaphysical concerns, to their shared predilection for crossing, ignoring, and erasing borders—physical, literary, temporal—have been noted in numerous articles and books, prompting Theodore Ziolkowski's recent comment that the late 1970s and 1980s "have seen an almost obsessive return to Romanticism not only in scholarship but by many novelists as well."[2] Nevertheless, the common ground of such obviously kindred spirits as Tieck and Handke has yet to be explored. Both gifted and ar-

[1]Peter Handke, "Die Literatur ist romantisch," in *Ich bin ein Bewohner des Elfenbeinturms*, (Frankfurt: Suhrkamp, 1972) 35–50; Rudolf Köpke, *Ludwig Tieck*, Zweiter Teil, (Leipzig, 1855) 173; Friedrich Schlegel, "Athenaeum Fragmente," *Kritische-Friedrich-Schlegel-Ausgabe*, vol. 2 (Paderborn: Schöningh, 1967) 183.

[2]Theodore Ziolkowski, *German Romanticism and Its Institutions*, (Princeton: Princeton UP, 1989) 383. Cf. also Ziolkowski's earlier essay, "Das Nachleben der Romantik in der modernen deutschen Literatur: Methodologische Überlegungen," in *Das Nachleben der Romantik in der modernen deutschen Literatur*, ed. Wolfgang Paulsen (Heidelberg: Stiehm, 1969) 15–31; Per Øhrgaard, "Die Romantik als Bezugspunkt in der deutschen Gegenwartsliteratur," in *Aspekte der Romantik*, ed. Sven-Aage Jørgensen, Per Øhrgaard, and Friedrich Schmøe (Copenhagen-Munich: Fink, 1983); Paul Michael Lützeler, "Von der Spätmoderne zur Postmoderne," in *Spätmoderne und Postmoderne: Beiträge zur deutschsprachigen Gegenwartsliteratur* (Frankfurt: Fischer, 1991) 11–22; and Claus Sommerhage, *Romantische Aporien: Zur Kontinuität des Romantischen bei Novalis, Eichendorff, Hofmannsthal und Handke* (Paderborn-Munich-Vienna-Zurich: Schöningh, 1993).

rogant experimenters, beginning with the theater and extending to other literary modes, they also share a compulsive need to test the power and limitations of literary language to define and represent the self and the world. Indeed, once one begins to read Handke's texts with an eye to Tieck's and vice versa, the points of comparison become too numerous to elucidate in the context of a short study. The focus here, therefore, will be confined primarily to the *naturphilosophische* images and themes as they are manipulated within the allegorical structures of two works, Tieck's *Der Runenberg* and Handke's *Die Wiederholung*.

Der Runenberg, a compact and enigmatic tale which Tieck wrote in a single night in 1802, probably numbers among the dozen or so most frequently and diversely interpreted stories in the German language.[3] It is therefore remarkable that little attention, if any, has been directed toward identifying and interpreting the ideas of Henrich Steffens contained in the piece,[4] despite common knowledge that the tale was inspired by his conversations with Tieck at Tharandt in 1801.[5] Undoubtedly the relative obscurity and inaccessibility of Steffens's early philosophic works account at least in part for this oversight, as well as for the general lack of recognition of his particular contribution to the further development of Schelling's *Naturphilosophie*. The natural scientist in Steffens sought to illustrate Schelling's system in terms of observable natural phenomena, and in so doing he succeeded far better than his mentor in achieving the desired effect of infusing philosophy with a mythology.

It is not difficult to imagine that Tieck must have found Steffens's mystical blend of physics and metaphysics more appealing and accessible than Schelling's and Fichte's systems. Indeed, one look at Steffens's early writings and one cannot help but be struck by the similarities between his main premises and the images and themes of *Der Runenberg*. An investigation of Steffens's ideas and analysis of Tieck's tale in light of those ideas is instructive with regard to the

---

[3]Among the numerous efforts to decipher the tale's enigmatic elements are those by Marianne Thalmann, Paul Gerhard Klussmann, W. J. Lillyman, Richard W. Kimpel, Wolfdietrich Rasch, Harry Vredeveld, Ralph W. Ewton, Jr., Maria M. Tatar, Norbert Mecklenburg, Victor Knight, William Crisman, Raleigh Whitinger, and Detlef Kremer. Although Ziolkowski never published a full interpretation of the work, he discusses it as an example of sexual imagery in the chapter, "The Mine: Image of the Soul," in *German Romanticism and Its Institutions*.

[4]Ernst Ribbat has dismissed Steffens's *Naturphilosophie* as having any direct influence on *Der Runenberg* merely on the basis of his reading of Steffens's later and much weaker work, *Grundzüge der philosophischen Naturwissenschaft* (Berlin, 1806); see *Ludwig Tieck. Studien zur Konzeption und Praxis romantischer Poesie* (Kronberg/Ts: Athenäum, 1978) 149.

[5]See H. Steffens, *Was ich erlebte*, vol. 3 (Breslau, 1841) 22–23; Köpke, vol. 1, 292; and Manfred Frank, "Kommentar," *Ludwig Tieck Schriften*, vol. 6: *Phantasus* (Deutscher Klassiker Verlag, 1985) 1282–83 (which includes excerpts from Steffens and Köpke).

central issue of the tale, for we discover that *Der Runenberg* is less concerned with sin or madness or alienation than with the crisis of aging and mortality. In turn, by reading Handke's extended allegory in light of Tieck's, we discover a similar coming to terms with mortality and the transitory nature of the individual.

The Scandinavian-born Steffens is probably best known to students of romanticism for the anecdotal portraits of German literary figures contained in his ten-volume memoirs, *Was ich erlebte*. With the aid of a grant from the Danish government, he studied in Germany from 1796 to 1801 with Fichte, A. G. Werner, and Schelling, through whom he came to know all the major figures of the Jena circle as well as Goethe and Schiller. In effect, he witnessed and peripherally participated in the rise and blossoming of "die neuere Schule," and in 1801 he published his own contribution to the movement, his *Beyträge zur innern Naturgeschichte der Erde*, a work that earned him considerable acclaim not only among his Jena colleagues,[6] but also in scientific and philosophic circles throughout Germany.[7]

Steffens drafted the *Beyträge* in 1800 during his period of study under the geologist A. G. Werner at the Bergakademie in Freiberg. Drawing on both his scientific training and the speculative philosophy of Fichte and Schelling, he developed a methodology which, according to Fritz Paul, "sucht nämlich durchaus eine Synthese zwischen empirischer Naturerfahrung und deren spekulativer Begründung auf erkenntnistheoretischer Basis zu vermitteln" (140). The work aspires to characterize the history of the earth as a succession of stages ("eine Stufenfolge") from the inorganic to the organic, and, within the organic, as a hierarchy of increasingly definitive individuation ("Individualität").[8] Although this idea of a unified nature with organic and inorganic separated only by degree, not by kind, was a common notion of the age,[9] Steffens viewed the productive force responsible for the process of differentiation as implicit in nature, as *naturimmanent*, and utilized such recent discoveries as galvanism and magnetism to describe it.

[6]With the notable exception of Friedrich Schlegel; cf. Fritz Paul, *Henrich Steffens. Naturphilosophie und Universalromantik* (Munich: Fink, 1973) 147ff.

[7]Cf. Paul 155.

[8]I have relied heavily on discussions of the *Beyträge* contained in Fritz Paul's book and in Else Huesmann's *Henrich Steffens in seinen Beziehungen zur deutschen Frühromantik unter besonderer Berücksichtigung seiner Naturphilosophie* (Kiel, 1929). However, the best explication of the work is contained in Steffens's own Copenhagen lectures of 1803: *Indledning til philosophiske Forelæsninger i Københavns 1803*, ed. B. T. Dahl (Copenhagen: Nordisk Forlag, 1905), and I have made extensive use of these lectures in this essay.

[9]Cf. Paul 145 and Huesmann 40 regarding parallels and differences between Herder's and Steffens's interpretations of this notion.

The basic premise of the book is that there exists a magnetic opposition of positive and negative forces which permeates nature, especially the geological formations, and which is in fact its true constituting principle ("Gestaltungsprinzip"). The polar tension created as magnetic forces engage in an ongoing process of attraction (unification) and repulsion (separation) leads to the segmentation and organic constitution ("Gestaltung") of the originally inanimate earth masses. In this way the organizing capability of nature reveals itself in the structure of the mountain ranges and the individuating tendency in crystallization (Huesmann 37–38).

A second principle, closely related to polarity, is that of continuous evolution or *Steigerung*: "Je höher die Stufe steigt desto individueller ist sie, und die Natur verwickelt sich immer tiefer in Widersprüche, je weiter sie in der Produktion fortschreitet."[10] At a certain point, inorganic matter develops *vegetative* and *animalisierende* tendencies, which then further develop into the plant and animal kingdoms, and so on with ever increasing individuation up the scale to man. Notwithstanding the stepladder evolution from inorganic to organic, Steffens clearly delineates animate from inanimate nature. The all-important individuating aspect of independent individuals, which is expressed through an egoistic tendency, is called life. Only organic nature has true individuals. In inorganic nature each separate object has meaning only in connection with the whole and has otherwise no independent existence.[11]

A universal polarity now emerges, for over and against the egoistic tendency that produces independent individuals, nature also possesses an endless tendency toward unity (*Einheitstrieb*). This polar tension manifests itself in an ongoing battle between organic and inorganic nature:

> All of inorganic nature is armed against organic life, and that is itself only a temporary victory. In this battle, the *species* survives as the victorious part; but individuals must without exception succumb. Life is but a transition to death; death is inorganic matter's triumph over life. Individuals come only to vanish, the one universal expression for their infinite multiplicity being unity, which without individuals is nothing and which alone continues unchanged. Generation is a means by which not individuals, but certainly the species is preserved.[12]

A corresponding microcosmic polarity exists at every rung of the evolutionary stepladder. At the human level, the *Einheitstrieb* manifests itself as morality and derives from human freedom:

---

[10] Steffens, *Beyträge zur innern Naturgeschichte der Erde* (Freiberg, 1801) 273.

[11] Cf. *Indledning* 72 and 3.

[12] *Indledning* 8 (my translation).

Man vacillates constantly between the egoistic *Glückseligkeitstrieb*,[13] which compels him to strive for his own, the individual's well-being, and the moral *Einheitstrieb*, which compels him to strive for the well-being of the whole. The endeavor to unite both we call wisdom.[14]

But man cannot be trusted always to choose the path to wisdom, so nature sometimes intervenes. Steffens is less than clear about the means and consequences of nature's intervention in man's life, but it is here that Tieck opens his story and proceeds to supply an answer.

The *Beyträge* were barely in print when Steffens and Tieck spent the summer of 1801 at Tharandt near Dresden. By all accounts, they saw each other almost daily, engaging in conversation about *Naturphilosophie*, geology, and nature mysticism.[15] Tieck drafted *Der Runenberg* in a single night about a year after his summer in Tharandt. Unlike most of his works dating from this period, it is not based on a medieval text and the story itself takes place in a fairly timeless setting. Nevertheless, the title and central images around which Tieck organized the story hark back to the Scandinavian *Urzeit*: the mandrake root (*Alrunenwurzel*),[16] the runic tablet, the Runenberg itself. Indeed, the rune image effectively evokes an atmosphere of mystery, mysticism, and the medieval past.

The story opens in an idyllic mountain setting ("im innersten Gebürge") where a young man, Christian, is sitting alone pondering his movements and decisions of the past few months. The first thing he contemplates is his age: "Er bedachte sein Schicksal, wie er so jung sei. . . ."[17] Despite his apparent youthfulness, his thoughts drift back to his earlier childhood: ". . .es fielen ihm die Szenen seiner Kindheit ein, die Spiele mit der Jugend des Dorfes, seine Bekanntschaften unter den Kindern . . ." (185). We learn that he has recently left his family and friends "um sich aus dem Kreise der wiederkehrenden Gewöhnlichkeit zu entfernen" (184). By journeying far from his home village to the unfamiliar mountains, he had hoped to break free from the cyclical routine of his existence, but now, to his astonishment, he realizes "daß er sich nun in diesem Tale in dieser Beschäftigung wiederfand" (184). Routine, that invariable and unrelenting indication of advancing time, is something he cannot escape.

---

[13]In Danish, *Lyksaalighedsdrift*, which Paul defines as *Bildungstrieb*.

[14]*Indledning* 9.

[15]Huesmann 56–64; also Edwin Zeydel, *Ludwig Tieck: The German Romanticist*, (Princeton: Princeton UP, 1935) 159–60.

[16]Maria M. Tatar notes Tieck's deviation in his spelling of *Alrunenwurzel* from the orthographic norms of his age (= *Alraunwurzel*), "Deracination and Alienation in Ludwig Tieck's *Der Runenberg*," *The German Quarterly* 51. 3 (1978): 286.

[17]Ludwig Tieck, "Der Runenberg," *Schriften in zwölf Bänden*, vol. 6 *Phantasus*, ed. Manfred Frank (Frankfurt: Deutscher Klassiker Verlag, 1985) 184.

Contrasted with Christian's sense of forward-marching time and aging is the route of his journey, which relates to a reverse tour back through natural history. The home village he has left behind lies out of view of the mountains and is characterized by the near absence of trees, cultivated grain fields, and orderly gardens. Here is Steffens's individuation hierarchy at its height, with inorganic nature out of sight and the lower forms of organic nature fully tamed and controlled by man. Christian now finds himself in the primeval forest on the lower reaches of the mountains, where as a hunter, he assumes an integral role in the daily routine of this middle rung of the evolutionary stepladder.[18]

Christian's decision to journey to the mountains is first explained as "freiwillig" (185). But later when he relates his background to the stranger, he describes an uncontrollable inner urge as the reason for his leaving: "es hat mich wie mit fremder Gewalt aus dem Kreise meiner Eltern und Verwandten hinweg genommen, mein Geist war seiner selbst nicht mächtig..." (187). These two contradictory motivations closely correspond to Steffens's universal polar forces: the *Einheitstrieb*, which manifests itself in mankind as freedom and morality, and the egoistic *Glückseligkeitstrieb*, which inclines man to seek himself individually. Since Christian was driven to undertake his journey by both of these forces, his odyssey becomes an endeavor to unite them, which in Steffens's parlance places him squarely on the path to wisdom. However, Christian's inner urge, it must be noted, had an alien aspect: "wie mit fremder Gewalt" it took over his thoughts and actions, such that "meine Seele [war verstrickt] in seltsamen Vorstellungen und Wünschen" (187), implying, just as Steffens had suggested might happen, that universal nature has intervened in Christian's life.

As Christian sits in the gathering darkness wondering what he should do next, universal nature—assuming the form of the supernatural here and throughout the story—intervenes again. He absent-mindedly uproots a plant, the mandrake, which issues a wail that stirs him to the core: "Der Ton durchdrang sein innerstes Herz, er ergriff ihn, als wenn er unvermutet die Wunde berührt habe, an der der sterbende Leichnam der Natur in Schmerzen verscheiden wolle" (186). The image of nature's corpse is striking, not only in connection with the plant Christian has just killed, but also in relation to Steffens's notion of the ongoing battle between organic life and inorganic nature. Apart from the superstitions surrounding the mandrake,[19] which now race through the boy's mind, the death of the anthropomorphic root serves as a vivid reminder of Christian's own immanent death, of his mortality.

This episode immediately foreshadows the continuation of Christian's journey to the next descending rung of the evolutionary stepladder: the world of in-

---

[18] Cf. Tatar 295, where Christian's vocation as a hunter is described as a contributing factor to his alienation from nature. This sounds more like a late twentieth-century than early nineteenth-century view of the hunter.

[19] Cf. Tatar 286–89 for a detailed discussion of the history of the mandrake mythology.

organic nature. No sooner does the image of nature's corpse enter his mind than a stranger appears, leads him through "einen dunkeln Gang des Waldes" (189), and directs him to the barren peak of the Runenberg, which is composed of the most primitive substances of all.

This journey back to the primordial phase of the earth's history, which we have already noted as being motivated by the combined forces of unification and individuation, and as therefore being an odyssey toward wisdom, also represents a journey into the furthest reaches of the subconscious. In this nebulous generative realm of the Fichtean ego—which is retained in Schelling and Steffens's *Naturphilosophie* through the ultimate identity of nature and spirit, and which permeates Tieck's works from *William Lovell* through *Kaiser Octavianus*—the distinction between past, present, and future as elements of time becomes obscured. One of Friedrich Schlegel's formulations of the three elements of time seems particularly applicable to, if not derivative from, Tieck: "1) Hoffnung = Zukunft, 2) Wehmut = Vergangenheit, 3) Schrecken = Gegenwart."[20] If we take into account an additional aphorism of Schlegel's, "einst wird es nur Vergangenheit geben" (Fr. 664, 181), then the past becomes symbolic of an ideal state: a state in which the horror and pain of the present would conclusively be surmounted and the promise of the future rendered redundant. With the attainment of self-realization or self-knowledge or wisdom, however we wish to term it, eternal *Wehmut* would prevail.

As the stranger and Christian part company and the youth begins his ascent of the Runenberg, he expresses the hope of finding "noch manch Wunder aus der alten Zeit da oben" (190). The stranger agrees, "Es kann fast nicht fehlen... wer nur zu suchen versteht, wessen Herz recht *innerlich hingezogen* wird, der findet *uralte Freunde* dort und Herrlichkeiten, alles, was er am eifrigsten wünscht" (190, emphasis added).

At the peak of the Runenberg, Christian is now at the core of Steffens's "innre Naturgeschichte der Erde." Quite abruptly the path ends and he discovers himself looking through the window of a large hall, "wunderlich verziert von mancherlei Gesteinen und Kristallen" (191) and illuminated by a moving light. As the bearer of the light comes into view, he sees a strong, beautiful woman with flowing black hair and an unearthly countenance.[21] As Christian watches, she sings a haunting song, carefully disrobes, and after a while takes a gem-studded tablet from a golden cabinet and hands it to the startled youth: "Die

---

[20] *Kritische-Friedrich-Schlegel-Ausgabe*, vol. 18, Fragment 742 (Munich: Schöningh, 1963) 188. See also Manfred Frank, *Das Problem 'Zeit' in der deutschen Romantik* (Munich: Winkler, 1972) 73.

[21] The identity of the figure has been widely interpreted; some have suggested Venus or, more promisingly, Diana; some see her as the muse of romantic poetry. But in view of her later appearances as an old hag and the fact that she rules over the dead stones, Tieck may also have had in mind Hel, the Norse goddess of the underworld.

Tafel schien eine wunderlich unverständliche Figur mit ihren unterschiedlichen Farben und Linien zu bilden" (192). Immediately, his perceptions of the natural world dissolve into a shimmer of color and a rush of affective melodies: "er sah eine Welt von *Schmerz* und *Hoffnung* in sich aufgehen, mächtige Wunderfelsen von Vertrauen und trotzender Zuversicht, grosse Wasserströme, wie voll *Wehmut* fliessend" (192, emphasis added). The sight of the runic tablet results in the merging of present and future ("Schmerz und Hoffnung") into an all-embracing past ("Wehmut").

One critic has argued that Christian's vision on the Runenberg is of his own bodily rebirth, and that throughout the story Tieck utilizes the mineral world to represent the life of the body and the plant world its death.[22] A birth it is, but in the deepest realm of the subconscious, this birth is anything but bodily. Far more, it is an insight into the ultimate ground of creation, where nature and spirit are identical. Steffens described "die entfernteste Urzeit" metaphorically as "die Kindheit der Welt, die wie ein verschollener Gesang sei."[23] The crucial aspect of Christian's moment of insight is that it transcends his finite existence, indeed transcends the finite existence of all organic nature. Within the context of the story's theme of aging and mortality, Christian's insight not only opens the possibility of, but ensures his spiritual immortality.

When Christian awakens from his dream, or rather, when he reemerges from the depths of his subconscious experience to a state of consciousness, he does not retrace his steps, but descends the other side of the mountain into what seems remarkably like a reflection or mirror image of his previous world. Now the psychologically most unsettling aspects of his dilemma come into play, for despite his momentary glimpse of the absolute, Christian, the finite individual, still exists, and he must content himself with living out his mortal existence.

On the other side of the mountains, Christian reenters the routine of forward-marching time and creates for himself an apparently idyllic life consisting of all the elements he had previously sought to escape: gardening, marriage, family, church life. As a mortal individual, he engages in what Steffens had defined as organic nature's only means of self-preservation: generation and procreation, the continuing participation of the species in the unity of universal nature.

Christian's contentment, however, is fragile and it soon becomes apparent that his happy mortal existence is superficial at best. He again catches glimpses of the absolute, but now these take on increasingly discomforting overtones. The friendly stranger who initially directed him to the ruins on the Runenberg reappears in the guise of a wealthy traveler whose gold triggers Christian's withdrawal from the surrounding world; the beautiful goddess reappears in the form

---

[22] Ralph W. Ewton, Jr., "Life and Death of the Body in Tieck's *Der Runenberg*," *Germanic Review* 50 (1975): 22–23.

[23] Quoted from Paul 149.

of the horrid and aged *Waldweib*; and in his dreams, the figures of the traveler and the *Waldweib* seem to merge into one.

Gradually, as Christian withdraws more and more into himself and closer to this unsettling vision, he loses all feeling for organic nature. The flowers and trees seem like a desolate monument of "vormaliger herrlicher Steinwelten," his wife Elisabeth seems aged and no longer attractive. When he withdraws completely, his once idyllic creation goes rapidly to ruin (the productive farm turns to dust, his well-to-do family is reduced to poverty), and he himself becomes physically "entstellt." It is as if his subconscious, in some perverse Fichtean sense, were seeking to project an accelerated aging process onto not only his bodily self, but also everything associated with him, in an effort to speed him on his mortal journey to his ultimate destiny. Indeed, the fact that Elisabeth, the children, and the farm suffer physically as he does, suggests that they are a world of his making, a material positing of the childhood village and friends he longed for just prior to his epiphany on the Runenberg. But even at this point, where he totally dissociates himself from organic nature and fully embraces the immortal world of the stones, he still has not overcome his own finite existence.

The bitter irony of the tale is that Christian's obsessive anxiety about the transitoriness of his mortal existence overwhelmed him when he was very young, when the majority of his physical life still lay ahead of him. That he was too young to withstand the loneliness which necessarily preceded the final leg of his journey to the vision on the Runenberg was noted even by the stranger: "Ihr seid noch jung ... und könnt wohl die Strenge der Einsamkeit noch nicht ertragen" (186). Too early an epiphany, the glimpse of wisdom before one can handle it, seems to upset the balance between the moral *Einheitstrieb* and the egoistic *Glückseligkeitstrieb* or, even worse, split the dualistic human condition between both poles.

At the end of the tale, several years after Christian has disappeared and is presumed dead, he pays a visit to Elisabeth and his daughter, Leonore, as they are looking after the few remaining sheep. He is changed beyond recognition:

> Es war ein Mann in einem ganz zerrissenen Rocke, barfüßig, sein Gesicht schwarzbraun von der Sonne verbrannt, von einem langen, struppigen Bart noch mehr entstellt; er trug keine Bedeckung auf dem Kopf, hatte aber von grünen Laube einen Kranz durch sein Haar geflochten, welcher sein wildes Ansehn noch seltsamer und unbegreiflicher machte. Auf dem Rücken trug er in einem fest geschnürten Sack eine schwere Ladung, im Gehen stützte er sich auf eine junge Fichte. (206)

His tone is "wehmütig," indicative of his spiritual unity with an eternal past, while his aging body is still engaged in the flow of time toward the future. In a poignant final scene, he asks for a kiss from his daughter—the next generation of the species—and then departs, never to be seen again.

In contrast to *Der Runenberg*, Handke's *Die Wiederholung* is unabashedly autobiographical and incorporates nonfictional geographic locations, historical events, and anthropological history. As much as Tieck's tale is compact, Handke's is expansive. Novelistic in length, it is, however, first and foremost an *Erzählung*, for the telling of tales is central to its structure and meaning.[24] It also alludes to being a *Novelle* ("... keine Begebenheit so unerhört wie die mit meinem Doppelgänger"[25]) and repeatedly orients itself to the *Märchen* (e.g., "Das richtige Märchen fing aber erst an..." [153] and "nicht in dem Sinn eines 'Es war einmal'" [285]). Reduced to its allegorical core, *Die Wiederholung* demonstrates the same preoccupation with transitory existence, aging, and mortality as *Der Runenberg* and follows a similar thematic path, but it culminates in a decidedly different outcome and develops a more hopeful perspective on the theme.

Handke's first-person narrator, Filip Kobal, who is now 45, recounts his journey as a twenty-year-old from his home village in Austria, over the border to Slovenia, the home of his father's ancestors, in search of traces of his brother who had disappeared during the war. If the name Filip Kobal does not seem as typically allegorical as Tieck's Christian—representative of the Christian era's modern man, from the vantage point of the early nineteenth century—Handke corrects that impression by the second page of the story: "Kobal sei doch ein slawischer Name, 'Kobal' heiße der Raum zwischen den gegrätschten Beinen, der 'Schritt'; und so auch ein Mensch, der mit gespreitzten Beinen dastehe.... das zugehörige Tätigkeitswort bedeute 'klettern' oder 'reiten', so daß mein Vorname Filip, der Pferdeliebe, zu Kobal passe" (9–10). Much later in the novel, Filip recalls his father's explanation of the name: "'Sieh her, was unser Name bedeutet: nicht *der Breitbeiniger*, sondern *die Grenznatur*.... Eine Grenznatur, das ist eine Randexistenz, doch keine Randfigur!'" (235). Filip Kobal is a traveler, looking for a place to belong, looking for a way to center his life on the margins. He is every immigrant, every refugee the world over. Filip also learns from the border guard that his family name is the same as the great Slovenian freedom fighter, Gregor Kobal, who led a failed peasant uprising in 1713 and was executed for treason a year later—the namesake, he realizes, of his lost brother. Memory and experience of both brother and hero—evoked through

---

[24] Cf. Jürgen Egyptien, "Die Heilkraft der Sprache: Peter Handkes 'Die Wiederholung' im Kontext seiner Erzähltheorie," *Text + Kritik* 24 *Peter Handke* (November 1989): 42–58; and Les Caltvedt, "Handke's Grammatology: Structuralism, Poststructuralism, Reading and Writing in *Die Wiederholung*," *Seminar* 28.1 (February 1992): 46–54. Also Detlef Kremer, "Die Schrift des 'Runenbergs,'" *Jahrbuch der Jean-Paul-Gesellschaft* 24 (1989): 117–44. Kremer focuses on Tieck's use of language and interprets the story "als Allegorie auf den Vorgang romantischen Schreibens" (128).

[25] Peter Handke, *Die Wiederholung* (Frankfurt: Suhrkamp, 1986) 258. All further references to this edition will be given in parentheses in the text.

history lessons and his brother's letters, horticultural notebooks, and Slovenian-German dictionary—become the stuff of Filip's own experience as a 20-year-old and of his retelling of that experience a quarter century later:

> Und Erinnerung hieß nicht: Was gewesen war, kehrte wieder; sondern: Was gewesen war, zeigte, indem es wiederkehrte, seinen Platz. Wenn ich mich erinnerte, erfuhr ich: So war das Erlebnis, genau so! ... und deshalb ist mir die Erinnerung kein beliebiges Zurückdenken, sondern ein Am-Werk-Sein, und das Werk der Erinnerung schreibt dem Erlebten seinen Platz zu, in der es am Leben haltenden Folge, der Erzählung, die immer wieder übergehen kann ins offene Erzählen, ins größere Leben, in die Erfindung. (101–2)

Like Christian, Filip is vaguely discontented with his life mainly because he hasn't "found his place" yet; indeed, "seinen Platz finden" becomes a subtheme of his story and one means by which he measures everyone he encounters. It is in this frame of mind—and also, he tells us somewhat disingenuously, because he lacked the funds to join his schoolmates on a trip to Greece—that he sets off to stalk the trail of a dead man in the land of his ancestors.

From Filip's home village of Rinkenberg, the Karawanken Mountains, which form the border between Austria and Slovenia (Yugoslavia in the novel), lie "immer fern vor Augen" and, like Christian's, his father tends an orchard, though not professionally but in memory of the absent Gregor who had originally nurtured and pruned the trees and who had studied horticulture in Slovenia. Filip's initial traversing of mountains to the border town of Jesenice is not over but through them, via the tunnel built, he recalls his history teacher telling him, by prisoners of war and at the cost of many lives. From the moment he emerges from the tunnel, he begins his own journey into the past, a metaphoric temporal change signaled almost cinematically by the switch to gray in contrast with the color of the Carinthian land- and cityscape, and by his reaction to it: "Eigenartig wie das allgemeine Grau, das Grau der Häuser, der Straße, der Fahrzeuge, ganz im Gegensatz zu der Farbigkeit der Städte in Kärnten ... meinen Augen wohltat" (11). By consciously spending the night in the tunnel, he in effect enters a *Märchen* of his history teacher's making: "Der Schlaf eines, so der Lehrer, 'noch Unschuldigen' würde dazu beitragen, 'die Unrechtsstätte zu entsühnen', 'die bösen Geister zu vertreiben', und 'das Grauen wegzublasen'; er schreibe gerade an dem entsprechenden Märchen" (107). Indeed, for Handke the distinction between history and fairy tales is moot, and the "märchenschreibender Lehrer"—who gives up the *Märchenform* at the end of the novel, in a play on words, for counting (*[er]zählen*)—provides a running commentary in Filip's memory. In tandem with his brother's books, this *Märchen* guides him on his journey back in time to World War Two (the tunnel), to the prewar era (Gregor's school and garden), to the peasant uprising of the original Gregor which resulted in the expulsion of his descendants from the Isonzo Valley over the Karawanken to Carinthia, to the centuries old cow paths etched in the mountainside, to the ancient geological wonder of the Karst (a high limestone plateau with sinks, underground streams, and caverns), to (in his mind's eye) the ancient Mayan civilization and its situation on the inverted Karst ("dessen 'Umkehrform'") of the Yucatan Peninsula: "die einzige wahre Geschichtsschreibung habe immer zur gleichen Zeit Erdforschung zu betreiben" (268).

Although Filip travels on his own, he spends most of his time around other people, even if only one other person, as when the old woman on the Karst takes him in without question, to which he responds in kind, "als sei es so Märchengesetz" (265). But he does eventually, like Christian in the opening pages of *Der Runenberg*, become overwhelmed by loneliness and have to confront his own "Fremder." This occurs in connection with his second mountain crossing, which he determines to undertake alone and on foot, and which more closely resembles Christian's mountain experience. As Filip climbs up the mountain, he is reminded of his only other mountain-climbing experience, namely with his father on the Austrian-Yugoslav border when he was just a child. It was on that peak that his father, feet splayed on either side of the border, declared that "Kobal" meant "Grenznatur." As he continues his ascent, his thoughts turn to his brother and he imagines he is sharing the same physical tribulations as Gregor once did. So strong is his identification with Gregor that an apparent transference of persona ensues: As he approaches a ruin at the crest of the mountain, he is overtaken by a thunderstorm and immediately reminded of the previous evening's story "von einem Gewittertoten." Then the first-person narrative switches to third person and, in a moment of lost perspective or revelation, he experiences a premonition of his/Gregor's death:

> Was er von weitem für das steinerne Gipfelhaus gehalten hatte, erwies sich oben auf dem Kamm als die Überreste einer Kriegsfestung; die Fenster einer möglichen Unterkunft als deren Schießscharten. Immerhin gab ihm die Ruine ein Dach über den Kopf. Ein Ruck, und Gleichmut ergriff ihn: Seelenruhig betrachtete er ein fernes Grasfeld, das, als einziger Fleck im Umkreis, auf den es sonst nur regnete, weiß von Hagelschloßen war; so groß dabei die Erschöpfung, daß der Blick die Perspektive vergaß und in der weißen Stelle ein Leintuch auf einer Bleiche sah. Wie er da saß, sank er um, wie bewußtlos; "Schlaf ohne Willen" nennt in einem Brief, geschrieben nach einem Gewaltmarsch, der Bruder die Ohnmacht. (237)

Later, after he comes to, he decides to spend the night in the ruin, which offers him another Runenberg-type experience: "Plötzlich auf seinem Gesicht Fingerkuppen, eine Berührung, wie sie wärmer und wirklicher nicht sein konnte, und eine vertraute Stimme, die sagte: "Mein Lieber!" Doch als der im Finstern die Augen aufschlug, war um ihn niemand . . ." (238).

At first light, Filip heads out along the mountain crest, hoping to recapture that first childhood walk along the border crest with his father. But his plan fails for this mountain, at the edge of the Karst, is too unrelentingly elemental: "hier aber war gleich alles die Urwelt" (239), and his plan is overruled by forces beyond his control. He is also alone: "Es fehlte dazu das Hand-in-Hand mit dem anderen." So instead of reliving a happy childhood memory, "wiederholte er nun im Morgengrauen . . . das Sich-Schleppen des Soldatenbruders durch die Ödnis hin zu einer Schlacht, die schon im voraus verloren war" (239). The mystical nature of his experience on the mountain, however terrifying and miserable, is underscored by his feelings as he tries to leave: ". . . jammerte mich der Gedanke, mich mit jedem Schritt von dem Ort zu entfernen, welcher mein Ein und Alles war" (240), and by the whining "albinobleiche" rabbit that signifies to him "das Bild einer heillosen Flucht." There is no escaping his mortality.

When he reaches the valley at the foot of the mountain, Filip becomes overwhelmed by the "monstrosity" of aloneness: "Zuerst sprang die Bangigkeit über in einen Schreck, so als sei es nun soweit, und der Schreck in ein Grauen" (241). It is then that he becomes aware of the presence of a stranger, "wie er fremder nicht sein konnte, welchen Ich war. Es war Ich, und diesen Ich schrieb sich groß, weil es nicht irgendwer war, sondern riesenhaft und raumbeherrschend über ihm stand, ihm die Zunge und die Glieder löste und sein Schreibname war. . . . [So] war es doch bei dem Erscheinen des Ich, als würde man gerade erschaffen . . ." (241–42).

In retrospect, the 45-year-old narrator calls this revelation a "Stand der Gnade des Wahnsinns der Unschuld" (242), which reason now precludes from his life—a seemingly whimsical interjection, which in the telling in fact spares his protagonist from the permanent madness or imbalance of his Runenberg counterpart. Unlike Christian's epiphany, Filip's revelation does not rob him of his spiritual individuality, nor does it empower his "Ich" to reduce the world around him to a mere projection. To the contrary, it allows him to step outside himself and see the big picture, but just long enough to assuage his fear and grant him a powerful "Erlebnis."

Following Filip's mountain experience, he wanders through the Karst, his true ancestral homeland, and notes with greater understanding the extent to which geographic anomalies and human settlement can accommodate one another for the sake both of survival and aesthetic pleasure: "Gerade die Bora[26] rückte das Einzelne aneinander und ließ das Einssein erkennen von Wehrhaftigkeit und Schönheit" (277). His contemplation of the meaning of these finds explicitly contradicts, and at the same time lends meaning, to the enigmatic ending of *Der Runenberg*. When Christian makes his brief visit to wife and daughter, he brings with him a sack of common stones:

> "Es ist nur," fuhr er fort, "daß diese Juwelen noch nicht poliert und geschliffen sind, darum fehlt es ihnen noch an Auge und Blick; das äußerliche Feuer mit seinem Glanze ist noch zu sehr in ihren inwendigen Herzen begraben, aber man muß es nur herausschlagen . . . . (207)

---

[26] A wind from the Adriatic.

He strikes two stones together to create sparks, but the inner force and beauty with which Christian spiritually identifies have no meaning, no value in this context outside the Runenberg. Filip, on the other hand, through the eyes of his older self as narrator, recognizes the folly of removing such finds from their underground home:

> Aber gehörten die Funde nicht einer vergangenen Epoche an, waren es nicht die letzten Reste, Überbleibsel und Scherben von etwas, das unwiederbringlich verloren war und durch keine Kunst der Welt mehr zusammengefügt werden konnte, und dem nur der kindische Finder noch einen glanz andichtete? Verhielt es sich mit jenen vermeintlichen Elementarteilchen nicht ähnlich wie mit den Tropfsteinen, die, in ihrer Grotte, im Kerzenflackern, einen Schatz verheißen und dann, abgeschlagen, draußen im Tageslicht, in der Hand des Räubers nur noch steinerne gräuliche Kartoffeln sind, wertloser als jeder Plastikbecher? Nein. Denn was zu finden war, ließ sich nicht mitnehmen; es ging nicht um die Dinge, die man, in den vollgestopften Taschen, wegschleppte, vielmehr um ihre Modelle, die sich dem Entdecker, indem sie sich zu erkennen gaben, einprägten in sein Inneres, wo sie, im Gegensatz zu den Tropfsteinen, aufblühen und fruchtbar werden konnten, zu übertragen in gleichwelches Land, und am dauerhaftesten ins Land der Erzählung. Ja. (284–85)

The intrinsic brilliance of past epochs has lasting meaning only through storytelling, through "romantische Poesie," for only then can the relationship between inorganic and organic nature, between individual and community, be placed in proper perspective. That perspective, Handke has already told us, comes through the process of remembering: "das Werk der Erinnerung schreibt dem Erlebten seinen Platz zu." It is a process which cannot coincide with experience: "Was der Zwanzigjähriger erlebt hatte, war noch keine Erinnerung" (101). That is now supplied by the older and presumably wiser Filip. The terrible tragedy of Christian's youthful seduction by the immortal world of the stones is averted by Filip primarily through the structure of the narrative: His brush with mortality on the mountain top followed by his encounter with the immortal *Ich* are tempered by his further experience in the Karst where inorganic and organic nature reside in a tenuous, but viable balance, and where he can "find his place" among his ancestors and even perceive "das Modell für eine mögliche Zukunft" (285). At least that is the way 45-year-old Filip Kobal remembers it—and that's all that counts.

OTTO W. JOHNSTON

Chromatic Symbolism in Gottfried Keller's *Romeo und Julia auf dem Dorfe*

After an unhappy episode with an incompetent teacher, culminating in dismissal from industrial school in 1834,[1] fifteen-year-old Gottfried Keller told his mother of his deep desire to become a painter.[2] Prevailing upon her for support, he dabbled in art at school in Zurich for a few years, and in 1840 undertook more serious studies at the Art Academy in Munich. But in 1842 his hopes were shattered when his teachers told him he could never become a successful artist because he couldn't paint human forms adequately.[3] Depressed and dejected, he returned home to Zurich after one of literary history's more glorious failures. Four years later, he turned to writing. A small volume of poems brought him modest recognition in 1846. Yet his ambition to create masterpieces on canvas hardly subsided. In fact, Keller succumbed neither to the disappointments at art school nor to the lure of approval by his reading public; instead, as we shall see, he sublimated his urge to paint in literary production. It can be shown that the painter deep within Gottfried Keller, the internalized mixer of pigment and blender of tones, often guided the pen of the latter-day narrator. As Hermann Boeschenstein has observed, "Keller hat nicht leicht auf die Malerei verzichtet."[4]

---

[1] For a detailed account of Keller's confrontation with the teacher Egli and the headmaster Meyer, including a discussion of the subsequent artistic representation in his novel, *Der grüne Heinrich*, see Emil Ermatinger, *Gottfried Kellers Leben, Briefe und Tagebücher. Auf Grund der Biographie Jakob Baechtolds dargestellt*, 5th ed., vol. 1 (Stuttgart: Cotta, 1920) 31–37. See also Wolfgang Preisendanz, "Gottfried Keller," *Deutsche Dichter des 19. Jahrhunderts*, ed. Benno von Wiese (Berlin: E. Schmidt, 1960) 440–462.

[2] H. E. Berlepsch, *Gottfried Keller als Maler* (Zurich, 1895); Carl Brun, "Gottfried Keller als Maler," *Neujahrsblatt*, ed. by the Municipal Library (Zurich, 1894) 31 pp.

[3] For a discussion in English, see J. M. Lindsay, *Gottfried Keller: Life and Works* (London: Oswald Wolff, 1968) 22.

[4] Hermann Boeschenstein, *Gottfried Keller*. 2nd rev. ed. (Stuttgart: Metzler, 1978) 9

For the most part, scholarship has recognized Keller's "künstlerische Doppelbegabung."[5] In 1936 Paul Schaffner dubbed him a "Malerdichter,"[6] while Benno von Reifenberg in 1954 delineated those vague boundaries separating painting, writing, and dreaming in Keller's psyche.[7] In the 1970s, critical inquiry focused on "the painter" in specific works. Esther Straub-Fischer, for example, described how Keller used color images in the lengthier texts, as she sought to interpret the meaning behind several of his choices.[8] Unfortunately, her analysis of chromatic imagery in the more popular "Novellen" was confined to recurrent patterns of a few basic colors. *Romeo und Julia auf dem Dorfe* (1856) was examined in less than five pages,[9] which provide little more than a catalogue of the more obvious prismatic symbols. In 1982 Laurence Rickels emphasized the importance of "pictorial signs" in Keller's works. Comparing his use of specific images with that of Lessing and Kafka, he argued that each possessed an "iconic imagination" dependent upon colors and their symbolic associations.[10]

A more detailed analysis of hues, shades, and various tinctures in Keller's narrative technique within this tale will reveal a much deeper and richer dimension than hitherto recognized. By applying Straub-Fischer's conjectural framework more vigorously, it can be demonstrated that Keller's fictional world in *Romeo und Julia auf dem Dorfe* is color-coded: the chromatology produces leitmotifs through which the narrator not only introduces the characters but also illustrates graphically their changing inner sensations. Colors associated with specific emotions,[11] as specified in the theoretical debates over art current in Keller's day, externalize the disposition of a given character at key points in the plot. The chromatic code is both a visual aid in determining the emotional un-

---

[5]Cf. Herbert Günther, *Künstlerische Doppelbegabungen*. 2nd ed. (Munich: Heimeran, 1960); also Louis Wiesmann, *Gottfried Keller. Das Werk als Spiegel der Persönlichkeit* (Frauenfeld and Stuttgart: Huber, 1967) 7–50.

[6]Paul Schaffner, "Gottfried Keller als Malerdichter," *Fünfter Jahresbericht der Gottfried Keller Gesellschaft* (1936–37); see also by the same author, *Gottfried Keller als Maler* (Stuttgart: Cotta, 1923).

[7]Benno von Reifenberg, "Malen, Dichten, Träumen," *Lichte Schatten* (Frankfurt a.M.: Societäts-Verlag, 1953) 176–96.

[8]Esther Straub-Fischer, *Die Farben und ihre Bedeutung im dichterischen Werk Gottfried Kellers* (Bern and Munich: Francke, 1973).

[9]Straub-Fischer 35–40.

[10]Laurence Arthur Rickels, "The Iconic Imagination: Pictorial Signs in Lessing, Keller, and Kafka," *Dissertation Abstracts International* 41 (1981 March): 4050A.

[11]Many studies exist of "Farbensymbolik" in German literature; see, for example, Wilhelm Wackernagel, "Abhandlungen zur deutschen Altertumskunde und Kunstgeschichte: Die Farben- und Blumensprache des Mittelalters," *Kleine Schriften* (Leipzig: S. Hirzel, 1872) vol. 1.

folding of a character and the narrator's means of foreshadowing things to come.

Scholars investigating the relationship between painting and writing in Keller's imagination generally overlook the popularization of color symbolism and allegory which took place while Keller was an art student. Of primary importance in this respect was Pierre Paul Frédéric de Portal's *Des couleurs symboliques dans l'antiquité, le moyen-age et les temps modernes* published at Paris by Treuttel and Würtz in 1837. Portal's analysis of color symbolism was widely used in art schools all over Europe, while gaining considerable popularity in art circles in the German-speaking countries during the 1840s.[12] Instructing young artists in color symbolism as found in the literature and art work of three historical periods, Portal argued that color produces three degrees or levels of interpretation because it has been used in *langue divine* (the Bible), in *langue sacrée* (sacred writings of non-Christians) and in a *langue profane*. He focused on all three levels for *blanc, jaune, rouge, bleu, noir, vert*, while describing *rose, pourpre, l'hyacinthe, violet, l'orange, tanné, gris* only on the level of a *langue profane*. Keller's literary use of these colors with their symbolic connotations was most likely influenced by the first few pages of Portal's *Résumé* at the end of the book, where he summarizes the symbolic meaning of the basic colors in west European, Christian tradition. German encyclopedias generally follow Portal's lead in their discussion of "Farbensymbolik."[13]

This is not to suggest that Keller held rigidly to the link between each color and the primary emotion proposed by Portal. In most instances, he does; hence white=purity, red=love, black=evil. However, Portal showed that several colors were associated with multiple sentiments; Keller uses these to illustrate conflicting emotions within a character. Latter-day research demonstrated that Portal overlooked certain ties that may have been known to Keller. As Karl Borinski pointed out in 1918, the color brown, identified by Portal as tied symbolically to several emotions including the love of both good and evil (254f.), also denoted "Trauer."[14] Nevertheless, Portal's work is a starting point for examining Keller's chromatic symbolism, for it became the bridge between the art of painting to which he aspired and the craft of fiction in which he excelled. It is also a check on the "intentio lectoris": one cannot simply ascribe any meaning to a color because it fits a particular interpretive paradigm. On the contrary, understanding the "intentio auctoris" involves limiting a color's conceivable emo-

---

[12] Carry von Biema, *Farben und Formen als lebendige Kräfte* (Jena: Diederichs, 1930); Faber Birren, *History of Color in Painting* (New York: Reinhold, 1965).

[13] A "Color Chart" for quick reference, containing the allegorical meanings of the various colors both in Europe and in Christianity, is available under "Farbensymbolik" in *Der Große Brockhaus*, 15th ed. vol. 6 (Leipzig, 1930) 66.

[14] K. Borinski, "Braun als Trauerfarbe," *Sitzungen der Bayrischen Akademie zu München*. Jg. 1918, Hft. 3, Abh. 10.

tional links to those circumscribed by Portal and those who supplemented his work. Seen in this light, *Romeo und Julia auf dem Dorfe* may be described in terms of a progression of color-coded images, which, once deciphered, afford the reader an unusual insight into the creative process of Keller's productive imagination.

The story itself has claimed a special place in literary studies.[15] With its many-faceted structure, rich texture, and explicit "realism,"[16] this "Novelle" has fascinated literary analysts for more than a century.[17] The obvious relationship to Shakespeare's tragedy of love has drawn Anglo-American readers more closely to the text,[18] which contains, according to Lee B. Jennings, both a model of the "Self"[19] and a series of productive insights that Self experiences.[20] Both Helmut Rehder[21] and Reginald Phelps[22] have compared the story to Keller's source material. E.A. McCormick[23] scrutinized the idyllic mode of expression and discovered an ambivalent attitude in the words of the narrator. Hildegard Wichert

[15] See Arthur Henkel, "Beim Wiederlesen von Gottfried Kellers Erzählung 'Romeo und Julia auf dem Dorfe'," *Text & Kontext* 6 (1978) 187–99; Bernd Neumann, *Gottfried Keller: Eine Einführung in sein Werk* (Königstein: Athenaum, 1982); Hans Wysling, *Gottfried Keller: Elf Essays zu seinem Werk; Papers from the International Gottfried Keller Colloquium, July 13–14, 1990* (Munich: Fink, 1990).

[16] See Walter Silz, "Romeo und Julia auf dem Dorfe," *Realism and Reality* (Chapel Hill: U of North Carolina P, 1954) 79–93; also Olive Everett Newton, "The Male-Female Relationship in Keller's Novellen. With special reference to 'Die Leute von Seldwyla'" (Diss. Louisiana State University, 1964).

[17] Cf. Charles Zippermann, *Gottfried Keller Bibliographie 1844–1934* (Zurich: Rascher, 1935); also Wolfgang Preisendanz, "Die Keller-Forschung der Jahre 1934–1957," *GRM* 38 (1958) 144–78. More up-to-date bibliographical material is available in the revised edition of Hermann Boeschenstein's introduction to Keller [note 4] in Sammlung Metzler (M 84).

[18] For Shakespeare's influence in Switzerland, see Theodor Vetter, "Shakespeare und die deutsche Schweiz," *Jahrbuch der deutschen Shakespeare-Gesellschaft* 48 (Berlin: Langenscheidt, 1912): 21–36; also Gerhard Stebner, "Romeo and Juliet im Vergleich zu G. Kellers Novelle 'Romeo und Julia auf dem Dorfe'," *William Shakespeare: Didaktisches Handbuch*, ed. Rüdiger Ahrens, vol 1 (Munich: Fink; 1982) 801–827.

[19] Lee B. Jennings, "The Model of the Self in Gottfried Keller's Prose," *German Quarterly* 56 (1983) 196–230.

[20] "Keller's Epiphanies," *German Quarterly* 55 (1982) 316–23.

[21] Helmut Rehder, "Romeo und Julia auf dem Dorfe—an Analysis," *Monatshefte für deutschen Unterricht* 35 (1943): 416–34.

[22] Reginald H. Phelps, "Keller's Technique of Composition in 'Romeo und Julia auf dem Dorfe'," *Germanic Review* 24 (1949) 34–51.

[23] E. Allen McCormick, "The Idylls in Keller's 'Romeo und Julia': A Study in Ambivalence," *German Quarterly* 35 (1962) 265–79.

Fife analyzed the black fiddler as a symbol of evil,[24] while Walter Hahn focused attention on the motif of "play."[25] Erika Swales recognized the "poetics of skepticism" in the story,[26] as Waltraud Kolb[27] and Heinz Rolleke[28] detected numerous connections to composers and music. Robert Holub studied the nature of desire in the tale,[29] which Gail K. Hart examined from its readers' point of view.[30] Both Hartmut Steinecke[31] and Martin Swales[32] investigated the role of the narrator, as G.A. Wales traced specific narrative techniques.[33] More recently, Günter Niggel surveyed the political environment in which Keller wrote the tale.[34] In this profusion of research, Keller's concern for color, except for Fife's identification of the black fiddler, has been neither evaluated nor pursued.

Yet whenever the narrator speaks of passion, his images abound in red; when he underscores innocence, he utilizes white. If he wishes to emphasize loyalty, his description favors blue, and so on. More complex psychic activity—mixed emotions or the evolution of a feeling—is expressed through images rich in color combinations. Since Keller also projects this color-code onto the landscape, his chromatics constitute a significant structural component. Throughout the narrative, Keller makes use of ten primary colors, which he occasionally

[24]Hildegard Wichert Fife, "Keller's Dark Fiddler in the Nineteenth Century Symbolism of Evil," *German Life and Letters* 16 (1962–63) 117–27.

[25]Walter Hahn, "The Motif of Play in Gottfried Keller's Novellen," *German Quarterly* 34 (1961) 50–57.

[26]Erika Swales, *The Poetics of Skepticism: Gottfried Keller and Die Leute von Seldwyla* (Oxford: Berg, 1994).

[27]Waltraud Kolb, "'Romeo und Julia auf dem Dorfe'—von der Novelle zur Oper," *Lenau-Forum 1993* 19 (1993) 57–71.

[28]Heinz Rolleke, "Keller, Mozart, Morike: Eine Anmerkung zu Hofmannsthals 'Unterhaltung über die Schriften von Gottfried Keller'," *Hofmannsthal Blätter* 35–36 (1987) 136–37.

[29]Robert C. Holub, "Realism, Repetition, Repression: The Nature of Desire in 'Romeo und Julia auf dem Dorfe'," *Modern Language Notes* 100 (1985) 461–97.

[30]Gail K. Hart, *Readers and Their Fictions in the Novels and Novellas of Gottfried Keller* (Chapel Hill: U of North Carolina P, 1989).

[31]Hartmut Steinecke, "Der Erzähler Gottfried Keller," *Zu Gottfried Keller*, ed. Hartmut Steinecke (Stuttgart: Klett, 1984) 8–17.

[32]Martin Swales, "Gottfried Kellers 'Romeo und Julia auf dem Dorfe'," *Zu Gottfried Keller* [note 31] 54–67.

[33]G. A.Wells, "Kellers Erzählkunst in 'Romeo und Julia auf dem Dorfe'," *Wirkendes Wort: Deutsche Sprache in Forschung und Lehre* 34 (1984 May-June) 169–81.

[34]Günter Niggel, "Gottfried Keller. Dichtung und Politik," *Ethik und Ästhetik. Werke und Werte in der Literatur vom 18. bis zum 20. Jahrhundert. Festschrift für Wolfgang Wittkowski*, ed. Richard Fisher (Frankfurt a.M.: Lang, 1995) 485–96.

combines in a double image (i.e., "grauschwarz," "blutrot"). Arranged in order of frequency these are: "rot," "schwarz," "weiß," "braun," "grün," "blau," "grau," "purpur," "silber," and "gold." He may mix two colors or simply add "dunkel," "tief," or "hell."

The frequency of the color red is a coefficient of the significance Keller ascribes to love and passion[35] as manifested in the romantic-physical yearning the offspring of Manz and Marti develop for each other. Compelling sexual desire is reflected by "rot" or a derivative (e.g., "errötend"). The color-image appears not only in the description of the characters themselves, when they experience desire, but also thirteen times in connection with objects in the story and in the landscape which surrounds them at a moment of passion. Keller employs "rot" eleven times in reference specifically to Vrenchen. Out of thirteen times that red is utilized in connection with the environment, she is present ten times. The first time "rot" is identified with Vrenchen, the narrator comments: "Als es [Vrenchen] sechzehn Jahre zählte, war es schon ein schlankgewachsenes, ziervolles Mädchen; seine dunkelbraunen Haare ringelten sich unablässig fast bis über die blitzenden braunen Augen, dunkelrotes Blut durchschimmerte die Wangen des bräunlichen Gesichtes und glänzte als tiefer Purpur auf den frischen Lippen..."[36] From this point on, Keller's narrator, through the use of color, portrays Vrenchen blooming into womanhood, maturing to that state in which she will be capable of experiencing lasting passion. "Dunkelrot" and "purpur" are used together to describe Vrenchen at a transitional point between "unreif" und "reif." "Purpur" is a secondary color consisting of red and blue; the color red is not a pure red in this passage, but rather a "dunkelrot;" thus her undeveloped passion is symbolized by the presence of a softer, more toned down red in both combinations. In order to show that Vrenchen has not yet become aware of her feelings, Keller skillfully employs two color combinations containing an understated "rot," thereby externalizing her evolving emotional make-up.

Vrenchen experiences a deeper passion when she again meets Sali after many years. He acts as the catalyst which brings about her recognition of womanhood. The first time the narrator indicates this unfolding, he uses the color "dunkelrot" by itself. As she and Sali hold hands, her tears begin to flow: "Tränen stürzten aus ihren Augen, während sie unter seinen Blicken vollends dunkelrot wurde..." (127). When next Vrenchen and Sali meet, she recognizes the passion within her, which the narrator now illustrates with a reference simply to her "roter Mund" (134). As young children, the two had played a game in which Sali counts Vrenchen's teeth, described at this point as "blendendweiß";

---

[35] For a brief discussion of the signification, see the article on "rot" in *Der Große Brockhaus*. 16th ed., vol. 10 (Wiesbaden, 1956) 98.

[36] *Gottfried Keller. Sämtliche Werke*, ed. Jonas Frankel, vol. 7 (Erlenbach-Zurich and Munich: Ernst Rentsch Verlag, 1927) VII: 105f. All quotes from this edition; page number indicated in parenthesis in the text.

her mouth was "purpur" (94). However, when they reenact the game years later, the color has changed as well as the emotion: "'Alle deine weißen Zähne hast du noch!' lachte er ... Sali wollte nun in seiner Einfalt jenes Spiel wieder erneuern und die glänzenden Zahnperlen zählen: aber Vrenchen verschloß plötzlich den roten Mund..."(134). When Vrenchen's emotional disposition ripens from a childish naiveté to a mature passion, the color changes from "purpur" to "rot."

The chronological development of "rot" in the *Novelle* corresponds directly to the unfolding of Vrenchen's sentiments. As Keller modulates the hue from "purpur" to "purpur und dunkelrot," then to "rot," Vrenchen's temperament evolves from innocent libidinal impulses to conscious desire and finally to unadulterated passion. When "purpur" (94) occurs by itself in the description of Vrenchen, she is a child playing with Sali in the fields of their fathers. Here Keller's narrative of their merriment reflects the childish creativity and innocence that children possess. Later, the combination of "purpur" and "dunkelrot" is employed to describe Vrenchen at sixteen (105), while "dunkelrot" appears when Sali and Vrenchen speak to each other for the first time about reestablishing their friendship. Finally, pure "rot" is used in the scene in which the two meet again in the fields where Sali takes Vrenchen's hand and physical contact is made.

The landscape also reflects this newly discovered passion. When Sali and Vrenchen play at the disputed edge of the two fields that once belonged to their fathers, the environment is described in the following terms: "Eine zahllose Menge von Mohnblumen oder Klatschrosen hatte sich darauf angesiedelt, weshalb der kleine Berg feuerrot aussah zur Zeit." With the next sentence this locale becomes "die rotbekleidete Steinmasse" (130), where the two lovers recognize their strong feelings for one another. The overriding presence of the color red in this passage—both the opium and the corn poppy are red—reflects symbolically the physical desire indicated by the combination of "Feuer" with "rot" in "feuerrot." Just as fire is an all consuming element, so are Sali's and Vrenchen's powerful sexual emotions. Moreover, as soon as the narrator uses red in its pure form to describe Vrenchen, he never reverts back to either "purpur" or to "dunkelrot" when alluding to her. This development in color images, culminating in Keller's use of only pure red in reference to Vrenchen, suggests that once she realizes the passion that Sali has awakened in her, she can no longer deny or suppress it.

At this point in the story, the two flee from the world and build a love nest "in den goldenen Ähren" (135), where they embrace and kiss until they no longer can. Their physical union has a spiritual dimension, we are told, because the kisses of two lovers live beyond the one or two minutes of actual contact and allow "die Vergänglichkeit alles Lebens mitten im Rausche der Blütezeit ahnen." The narrator skillfully foreshadows this physical-spiritual connection by using the color gold in his image of "goldene[n] Ähren." Portal explains that "l'or" in both "les langues divine et sacrée" designates spiritual union. At the same time, however, the color "represénte l'amour légitime et l'adultère charnel qui rompt les liens du mariage" (87) when found "dans la langue profane." Through the color Keller tells us that the lovers' sexuality exists on not only a physical but also a spiritual level and that their love breaks the bonds of marriage because their fathers have made the sanctification of their union impossible, and in so doing have consecrated their love not to life but to death. Thus the gold in nature and the gold of the lovers' devotion to each other is contrasted to the gold of the greed[37] consuming their fathers and permeating the world outside their would-be refuge. The narrator underscores this two-fold implication of "gold" by referring to the lovers' makeshift sanctuary as a prison ("einen engen Kerker"). Thus the color anticipates figuratively the lovers' tragic fate: their fathers' greed and jealousy of one another signified by gold will intrude into their idyllic, golden world and destroy them. Later, as we shall see in more detail, the narrator uses the same color to anticipate the demise of both fathers.

Goethe often applied the color in the same way. As Wilhelm Emrich has demonstrated, gold can often have a positive surface connotation in Goethe's works; yet behind the chromatic symbol frequently lurks some kind of "Verhängnis" for those associated with it.[38] Keller may well have acquired this particular usage from Goethe since *Romeo und Julia auf dem Dorfe* contains perhaps another example of Goethe's influence which we shall encounter in connection with the color black. On the other hand, both poets may have derived the symbolic meaning from the same source.

The passage quoted above also serves to introduce the most fascinating symbol in the story: the black fiddler. "Er mußte im Korn gelegen haben," (129) writes Keller, implying that the earthy fiddler arose from the golden grain. With the appearance of the fiddler, the colors in the paragraph are infused with yet another level of meaning. In a single 11-line sentence, containing two adverbs,

---

[37]According to *Der Große Brockhaus*. 15th ed. 7: 105, "Gelb" is part of the "Farbengruppe des Sonnenspektrums" with the symbolic meaning of "Neid und Haß." Since Keller does not use "gelb" in the story—"rotgelb" appears in connection with Vrenchen (126)—but employs "gold" frequently, we consulted *Meyers Lexikon*. 7th ed. 4 (Leipzig, 1926) 463, which contains an entry for *goldgelb*. Among other connotations is found "Symbol ... des Reichtums." Thus, it may be argued, Keller's literary utilization of "gold" suggests not only the richness of the idyll but also the envy and hatred associated with yellow as well as the desire for wealth (symbolized by gold), both of which bring about the conflict and eventual ruin of Manz and Marti.

[38]Cf. Wilhelm Emrich, *Die Symbolik von Faust II. Sinn und Vorformen*. 3rd ed. (Frankfurt and Bonn: Athenäum, 1964) 193; see also Gerhard Neumann, *Konfiguration, Studien zu Goethes Tasso* (Munich: W. Fink, 1965) 175. For a more comprehensive approach, see Peter Schmidt, *Goethes Farbensymbolik* (Berlin: Erich Schmidt, 1965); see also Marilyn K. Torbruegge, "Goethe's Theory of Color and Practicing Artists," *Germanic Review* 49 (1974) 189–99.

two adjectives and a participle denoting "black," the narrator emphasizes the fiddler's essential "darkness:"

> ... und sah übrigens schwarz genug aus; neben einem schwarzen Filzhütchen und einem schwarzen rußigen Kittel, den er trug, war auch sein Haar pechschwarz so wie der ungeschorene Bart, das Gesicht und die Hände ebenfalls geschwärzt. (129f.)

When this figure then jumps upon the "fire-red" hill, turns to the couple and declares prophetically that "ihr vor mir den Weg alles Fleisches geht" (130), he brings to mind almost at once the image of the devil, dancing on the fire and brimstone of hell. Yet there is more to this symbol than initially meets the eye.

In a penetrating study of "Keller's Dark Fiddler in Nineteenth Century Symbolism of Evil," Hildegard Wichert Fife concluded that "the fiddler does not suggest an indomitable evil."[39] Keller, she argued, combined in this figure three basic elements: "an embodiment of evil rooted in folklore, a social milieu, a didactic aim directed primarily toward a specific society despite its universal application." Fife, though not denying Keller "a creation of some originality," found the fiddler lacking "in stature and creative verve [compared] with the truly great examples of its age." Whereas the outstanding representatives of wickedness in nineteenth-century literature embody evil of vast proportions, Keller's black fiddler "is too neatly geared to a limited locale to take full possession of the reader." Fife asks whether Keller "underestimated the broader implications of local problems or lacked the power to create a symbol of truly great proportions."

Yet perhaps the dichotomy contained in the question limits the perspective unnecessarily. Our analysis of Keller's chromotology suggests an alternative to either "underestimated" or "lacked the power." The narrator's primary concern was creating an incarnation of black: not a representation of the devil himself, but rather a personification of that demonic social and ethical impulse described vividly in the greater part of Fife's study. However, Keller did not seek to portray "inscrutable natural forces," crushing "bourgeois stultification," nor "the degeneracy of whole nations grown heartless"—at least not as is suggested in Fife's comparisons. Instead, Keller retrieved from German folklore and from the social misery in the Switzerland of his day the essence of that black associated with the socially ostracized "Kohlenbrenner" and "Pechsieder in den Wäldern" (130). He needed black, for it connotes the impending death and social decay which Keller links to the estrangement experienced by these social outcasts soon to be joined by Vrenchen and Sali. Moreover, without that color, the portraits of Vrenchen and to a lesser extent Sali must, as we shall see, remain incomplete.

However, before examining black as an essential ingredient in the "final" portrait of the star-crossed lovers, we may pause to ask if, in fact, the dark fid-

---

[39] Hildegard Wichert Fife [note 24] 119. Subsequent quotes are found in the article, 119–22.

dler is to be understood exclusively as a Christian symbol. Fife regards him as "somewhat spiteful to be sure, but without active vengefulness." Is such a figure Keller's rendition of the Satan in the Old Testament, whose malevolence knows no bounds? As Fife points out, he is both "a man without a home, a proclaimer of the young people's imminent homelessness," and, in the scene at the inn, their old acquaintance, perhaps even their protector. Such a dual role coupled with that telltale blackness suggests a second literary source for the fiddler outside German folklore or Christian symbolism. Black is, after all, not a prerequisite for the devil's image in nineteenth-century conjurations: when Gotthelf, for example, personified a demon in *Die schwarze Spinne*, he colored him green. This is not to reject a Christian-folklorist interpretation completely. The fiddler himself corroborates the validity of such a reading when he, having pointed to his nose, puffed (*pustete*), squealed (*pfiff*), and hissed (*zischte*), much like the serpent in the Garden of Eden. Furthermore, Sali completes the catalogue of folkloristic requisites by calling to Vrenchen in the next scene: "O du Hexe" (132) and referring to her "Teufelskünste" (133).

At the same time, however, the black fiddler as an unpitying, inexorable, but not unjust personality, a terrible, but not totally evil antagonist, appropriates characteristics ascribed to figures in the mythology of classical antiquity. His features are reminiscent both of Pluto, the black god of shades, whose realm lies beyond the river of forgetfulness, and Charon who ferries Aeneas and the Sibyl across the rivers, passed Minos, the inflexible judge, and eventually to the Fields of Mourning, where unhappy lovers dwell, having been driven by their misery to kill themselves. In as much as he is their "acquaintance" and companion, the black fiddler escorts Sali and Vrenchen on the same fateful journey. Pluto was also called the God of Wealth, of the precious metals hidden in the earth; in Keller's story the greed of their fathers for the land provokes the tragic exploits of the children as they seek to escape. In Homer's epics, the underworld is a vague, shadowy place, in which nothing is real, not a place of everlasting torment.

The lovers' tragic death in the water (a symbol both of sexuality and release) suggests a final liberation in dark Hades, rather than fiery hell. "Black" denotes the gloom and finality of their fate in a social order which will not accept their status as lovers, just as it banishes the charcoal burners and pitch boilers to the forest; it does not imply the eternal burning of their souls in fire and brimstone. By his insistence on black as the leitmotif for the fiddler, Keller, with the skill of a master artist combining light and dark, blends the Judaic-Christian heritage of hellfire and damnation with those mythological elements of Stygian darkness and release common to the Hades of Greek mythology. With such a synthesis, Keller displays an indebtedness to Goethe and the tradition of Weimar as well as to that progression in Western thought which originates in the school of Alexandria in the middle of the third century. We shall return to "black" in yet another context, when we observe Keller completing his picture of Vrenchen. But first we must examine more closely her emotional disposition as expressed in the narrator's chromotology.

The color blue is used in connection with Vrenchen twice; both times it is in reference to her "wedding" dress: "ein einfaches Kleid ... von blaugefärbter Leinwand" (150). With this blue dress, she wears "ein schneeweißes Mousselinhalstuch" (150), and on her shoes are "rote wollene Schleifen" (151). The color combination here assumes symbolic significance with reference to Vrenchen and Sali's mutual attraction. Blue, the color of "Treue und Beständigkeit,"[40] reflects the quality and the durability of their strong affection, whereas the purity of their feelings is underscored by the "schneeweißes Halstuch." The touch of red on her shoes serves as a reminder of her natural progression to passion, which is a product both of her innate propensities and of the love situation which consumes her. In this description of Vrenchen's apparel we encounter blue, white, and red, which represent, in order of importance, those qualities Keller ascribes to their love: loyalty, innocence, and passion. Using such prismatic imagery, the narrator adds a concrete dimension to the character which prompts the reader's empathy. His color-images enable him to illustrate graphically the sincere, innocent sentiments of the lovers on the one hand, and the natural evolution to passion on the other.

Compelling physical desire is an important part of Vrenchen's character. However, innocence is also basic to her person. Early in the *Novelle*, we find the following description: "Die Sonne schien dem singenden Mädchen in den geöffneten Mund, beleuchtete dessen blendendweiße Zähnchen und durchschimmerte die runden Purpurlippen" (94). According to Portal's description of each color's significance, the combination generally sums up Vrenchen's character: white is a symbol for innocence[41]; whereas "purpur" is a secondary color consisting of red and blue, symbolizing passion and loyalty respectively.[42] In this passage, she has the innocence (white) characteristic of a young girl whose passion is not yet developed, indicated by a secondary color containing red. Because he is concerned primarily with the unfolding of passion in Vrenchen's personality, Keller uses red frequently; however, white also appears periodically in the story as a reminder of her basic innocence.[43]

Keller's use of brown illustrates the thematic variations which color undergoes in the story. As we have seen, red appears in different forms commensurate

---

[40] See the "Color Chart" under "Farbensymbolik" in *Der Große Brockhaus*, vol. 6, p. 66.

[41] *Der Große Brockhau*, vol. 6, p. 66.

[42] *Ibid.*

[43] "'Alle deine weißen Zähne hast du noch!'" (134). Here the narrator reminds us of Vrenchen's basic innocence. Another example is found at another key point in the plot: "Sie setzte sich wieder auf den Herd, zog den Rock etwas zurück und streifte den Schuh vom Fuße, der noch von der gestrigen Reise her mit einem weißen Strumpfe bekleidet war" (147).

with changes in Vrenchen's personality. Brown is linked with Vrenchen from the outset and thereafter consistently. In his initial description of her, the narrator tells of her "bräunliche Gesichtsfarbe" (88), and goes on to emphasize her "bräunliches Gesicht" (106), "braune Augen" (136) "braunes Auge" (167). At first glance, the brown of her hair, eyes and skin tones denotes the healthy, natural, vigorous characteristics of the "braune Dirnen" or "braunes Mädchen" found in such German folksongs as "Schwarzbraun ist die Hasselnuß" or "Dudeldei" ("Das schwarzbraune Bier / Das trink ich so gern / und schwarzbraune Mädel, / die küss' ich so gern"). At the same time, the depiction of her olive-toned complexion conjures images of the Mediterranean peoples, perhaps even of the people of Verona where the feud between the Montagues and the Capulets took place in Shakespeare's play. Her skin tone and brown eyes and hair constitute, in this instance, a clever allusion to the original story. Coupled to the name Sali, dark-complexioned Vrenchen becomes more concretely the Swiss version of Shakespeare's ill-fated couple. Yet, seen through Portal's eyes, Keller has also foreshadowed early on the tragic outcome of the story: in his scheme these various shades of brown represent "le symbole de l'amour infernal et de la trahison" (250). From its inception, Vrenchen's love possesses a demonic quality which will cause her to betray her father. By his choice of brown, Keller signals both the demonic, almost diabolical essence of their mutual love and her tragic destiny, which is to break her familial ties. Brown is a blend of red, yellow, and blue, which indicate symbolically the evolution of Vrenchen's character: her passion (red), though in tune with nature and hence potentially idyllic (gold), is undermined by the greed of her parents (gold). Emotionally, she is loyal to Sali and steadfast in her love (blue), yet forced to disloyalty (brown) by the actions of her father. If we now add the connotation "Trauer" insisted upon by Borinski, we see that Keller also uses brown to underscore the inevitable tragic conclusion to the lovers' relationship. The omnipresent brown symbolizes, in addition to infernal love and familial disaffection, the sad, inexorable fate awaiting the unfortunate pair.

With the skill of a master painter, Keller, the master storyteller, blends the passion of young love (red) with loyalty and steadfastness (blue), including all its serenely golden aspects, yet submerged in parental greed (also gold) to produce Vrenchen, whose demonic love compels her to disobey and thus betray her father. This sequence of events is prefigured by "her" color (red+blue+yellow = brown). She is also marked by white, which denotes her basic innocence as well as the initial innocence of the fathers, as we shall soon see. Yet the color white denotes more than unspoiled innocence: its use also adds a pessimistic tinge, especially when linked to "bleich" in describing Vrenchen as she leaves her home. At the end of the story, "zwei bleiche Gestalten" glide into the cold water, suggesting that the color white is meant to strike an ominous chord. The need for black now becomes apparent. When black is added to red, blue, and yellow, the result is a richer, fuller brown. By mixing in black in the person of death's dark fiddler, Keller enriches the brown as he completes Vrenchen's literary portrait.

Color occurs in connection with Sali in the visual image of his wedding clothes, which consist of: "ein großes schwarzes Mailander Halstuch mit rotem Rande" (149). While the white and blue in Vrenchen's dress reflect the innocence and consistency of their love, Sali's attire symbolizes both the way things might have been and the couple's doomed future. We have already traced the development of Vrenchen's passion through Keller's use of red; here, in Sali's shawl, we see the color once more, where it functions as a reminder of the lovers' overwhelming erotic feelings, impelling them toward union in their own symbolic marriage. They recognize, however, that the only way they can consummate their bond and hold on to their happiness is in death. Thus the large shawl with which Sali girds himself, having black as its dominant color, is at once the color of the suit in which the bridegroom customarily marries and, at the same time, a shroud, signifying the lovers' inescapable death, which now encircles Sali, just as it envelops their future.

The first color mentioned in the story is "weiß," used mainly in connection with Vrenchen, as we have already seen. However, it is initially employed in connection with Manz and Marti. Before the feud erupts, they wear "Zipfelkappen" which "wie zwei weiße Flammen gen Himmel züngelten" (87). The idyllic aspects of this opening scene are underscored by a reference to the "goldene Septembergegend." But, as we have seen, gold represents both the golden age of their farming idyll and their greed which brings about their jealousy, hate and eventual destruction. An ominous note is struck in the same sentence when the two plowmen are compared to "untergehende Gestirne." It is therefore not surprising that the color white will appear again, ironically, when Marti, having taken leave of his senses, is dressed at the asylum in a "weiße[s] Kittel" and "dauerhafte[s] Lederkäppchen," connoting his return to innocence in a state of mental deterioration. Within the complex of Keller's color scheme, white signifies that the two fathers are initially upright farmers unspoiled by greed, tending their bucolic fields. Once the two men are overcome with that jealousy and greed which produces an irrational hatred of one another, they are described as "ergraute Männer" (119). When they fight, the clouds become "grauschwarz." Since gray is made by simply adding white to black, we may recognize a symbol in this prismatic image of innocence turned by hate to that destructive behavior which consumes both men.

Later Marti wears a "schwarzwollene Zipfelmütze" (140), the color suggesting death. The image represents both a mental state (implied when Sali hits him on the head) and a moral condition (he faces financial ruin, while his upright reputation has been tainted). Marti's deep hatred brings about his eventual mental illness. Keller describes his ride to the asylum as a "Gang zu dem lebendigen Begräbnis." Tracing the colors used in reference to Manz and Marti, we see that the progression is correlated with the demise of the characters: initially dressed in "white," they are respected farmers; once gray delineates their attire or their beards, they have forfeited the respect of their neighbors and must struggle to support themselves; when black prevails, they have lost everything. Marti returns to a demented innocence symbolized by the white garb of the asylum.

Reginald Phelps divides *Romeo und Julia auf dem Dorfe* into two themes: the first is greed for the soil; the second he labels "the Romeo und Juliet motif."[44] Keller's use of colors substantiates this structural division in as much as the greed of Manz and Marti progresses achromatically from white to gray to black, and, for Marti, back to white again. At the same time, the Romeo und Juliet motif evolves chromatically through "braun," "weiß," "purpur," "dunkelrot," and "rot."

The symbolic significance of green helps us to understand numerous passages interlined by that color. When, as children, Vrenchen and Sali ride in their "grünbemaltes Kinderwägelchen," their lives are full of hope and joy. Portal records that green is foremost a symbol of hope, joy and youth: "le vert était la couleur de l'espérance dans ce monde ... il designait l'espérance, la joie et la jeunesse" (215). Green is also present in the green silken spencer Manz's wife wears in the tavern on which the two have pinned all their hopes for a new life. When she takes the green jacket off in the next paragraph, hope has vanished. When Sali secretly hopes to catch a glimpse of Vrenchen, he notices "das wilde grüne Gewächs" which has grown up chaotically around Marti's house. This green not only reflects Sali's hope but also foretells the impending madness of Vrenchen's father, for, as Portal observed, green can also mean "par opposition, la dégradation morale et la folie" (212). Once Vrenchen and Sali begin their last walk on the way to the dance, the narrator remarks: "Die Jugend hat keine Tugend, der Wald war grün ...," thus echoing the first part of Portal's comment. Still hoping for a way out of their dilemma, Vrenchen and Sali pass "an grüne Halden entlang" up to the heights where the best view is found. On walks through the woods, happy people break off green shoots, the narrator tells us, as Sali and Vrenchen, enjoying their time together as a couple, laugh at those walking with these green walking sticks in their hands. The green all about them echoes their joy. Throughout that evening, Sali's confused thoughts search "nach einem Ausweg," but he finds none. He has lost hope. At the same time, green vanishes from the narration. Finally, when they encounter the black fiddler who has prophesied their impending death, they notice "einen grünen Tannenbusch" on his hat. The green in the pine shrub branch signals the triumph of the black fiddler over the lovers' parents, whose sins are now visited upon their children. A secondary meaning for green, Portal observes is victory: "Le vert était le symbole de la victoire ..."(215). In each instance, Keller reiterates his narrative intention by painting the fictional landscape green which sig-

---

[44] Reginald H. Phelps [note 22] 36.

nifies hope, regeneration, victory, and in its negative connotations, degradation and madness.

Space will not permit an analysis of more complicated passages where Keller juxtaposes several colors in a single paragraph or even a single sentence. These include the grotesque fishing scene ("in einem langen braunen Bürgerrock... schwarze Füße"), the ring-buying scene, where the ring is "vergoldet" implying imitation of marriage, but the "Vergißmeinnicht" is golden, confirming the genuineness of their love and their intentions, and the dance scene ("ein schlankes hübsches Mädchen... ein schwarzseidenes Kleid... ein weißes Tuch... rote Streifen... veilchenblaue Augen... Kette von Vogelbeeren"). However, once the color-code is understood, the narrator's intention becomes clear. By interpreting these colors in accordance with Portal's description of their positive and negative symbolic meanings, we arrive at a better understanding of each passage and its function within the structure of the whole. Keller's choice of color reveals the emotion he seeks to describe. In those passages where a multitude of colors bombard the reader, an onslaught of corresponding emotions is also being elicited. We have but to sort them out by color to comprehend Keller's meaning.

Our analysis has demonstrated that Keller employed hues and shades to delineate the inner emotions of his characters. Colors are a distinct part of a particular character that identify and introduce him or her. Since color is also projected onto the landscape, this specific feature of Keller's technique permeates the structure of his composition. The chromotology represents a visual aid in determining the emotional unfolding of the character as well as a literary device for foreshadowing the course of events. Keller's world is color-coded. Through his use of color he allows us insights into his artistic workshop as well as into his archetypal thought patterns. What he was unable to do on canvas, he achieved admirably in his prose fiction. By utilizing in his creative prose the symbolism in the color combinations he learned as an art student, Keller infused into the structure of his tale a visual dimension which remains a unique aspect of his prose.

MARIA TATAR

"Das war ein Stück Arbeit!":
Jack the Ripper and Wedekind's Lulu Plays

Jack the Ripper may appear only briefly on stage at the end of Wedekind's *Büchse der Pandora*, but his role is central nonetheless. While most literary incarnations of the man who terrorized London's East End inspire fear or revulsion, Wedekind's Jack the Ripper becomes a kind of folk hero who puts an end to the disruptive reign of Lulu's transgressive sexuality by fulfilling her prophetic dreams about falling into the hands of a *Lustmörder*. That Wedekind intended to position the psychopathic murderer as a figure who is in some respects liberating becomes especially evident when we consider that the original "Monstretragödie" that comprised *Erdgeist* and *Büchse der Pandora* was prefaced with the dedication "Dem Rächer."[1]

Karl Kraus shared the suspicion that contemporary audiences were probably less horrified than relieved by the effect of Jack's grisly deed:

> So kommt bei diesem Werke schließlich auch der Sittenrichter auf seine Rechnung, der die Schrecknisse der Zuchtlosigkeit mit exemplarischer Deutlichkeit geschildert sieht und der in dem blutdampfenden Messer Jacks mehr die befreiende Tat erkennt als in Lulu das Opfer.[2]

In the real-life courtroom, Wedekind was not convicted on obscenity charges—in one instance at least—because Jack's murder was seen to represent a morally satisfying punishment for Lulu and avenged those on whom she had practiced

---

[1]David Midgley, "Wedekind's Lulu: From 'Schauertragödie' to Social Comedy," *German Life and Letters* 38 (1985) 205–32. Artur Kutscher also declares Jack the Ripper to be the inspiration for the play. See his *Wedekind: Leben und Werk* (Munich: List, 1964) 119–20. David Davidson ("From Virgin to Dynamo: The 'Amoral Woman' in European Cinema," *Cinema Journal* 21 (1981) 31–57 points out that Wedekind's Jack the Ripper incarnates a "higher justice" that conquers a "demon spirit by its antithetical demon spirit" (42). On the sexual murderer as mythical "folk-devil," see Deborah Cameron and Elizabeth Frazer, *The Lust to Kill* (Oxford: Polity Press, 1987) 35–68.

[2]Karl Kraus, *Literatur und Lüge* (Munich: Kosel, 1958) 9–21.

her seductions.³ "Du sollst gestraft werden—wo du gesündigt hast"—these are the words of the rogue Schigolch, in the manuscript version of the play, as he drives Lulu down into the streets.⁴ By presenting Lulu from one angle as a creature whose transgressive sexuality eventually finds its deserving punishment and its fulfillment in a *Lustmord*, Wedekind perpetuates the notion of female sexuality as sadistically destructive in its effect, yet ultimately masochistic in its desire.⁵

In a sense, Jack's deed can be seen as an exercise in social management, an expression of what Leon Trotsky—in direct contrast to Wedekind's avowed aims—saw as a "psychological need to institute a certain control, an extreme *censorship* over the elementary rhythms of life."⁶ Jack the Ripper restores the moral order by eliminating the subversive figure of Lulu—a woman who is perceived by Wedekind to be, like all women, a "Gegnerin der 'Sittlichkeit'— Opposition, Umstürzlerin, die unterminierende Gewalt."⁷

The second of the two Lulu plays names the real source of evil in a *double entendre* that refers both to the container for the troubles set free by a malevolent woman and to the sexual organ that "enslaves" men.⁸ The first published version

---

³Friedrich Karl Rothe, *Frank Wedekinds Dramen: Jugendstil und Lebensphilosophie* (Stuttgart: Metzler, 1968), p. 58.

⁴*Frank Wedekind: Die Büchse der Pandora. Eine Monstretragödie*, ed. Hartmut Vinçon (Darmstadt: Jürgen Häusser, 1990) 107.

⁵On the female principle as masochistic, see Audrone B. Willeke, "Frank Wedekind and the 'Frauenfrage'," *Monatshefte* 72 (1980) 26–38. Walter Sokel describes Lulu as straining toward Jack the Ripper "with her unconscious being... To be murdered in a sex crime is Lulu's dream." Sokel further documents the ways in which Wedekind linked female desire with sacrifice in a number of dramatic figures and finds Wedekind's construction of female sexual pathology particularly problematic in *Schloß Wetterstein*, which concludes with the suicide of the female protagonist while she is in the presence of a notorious *Lustmörder* ("The Changing Role of Eros in Wedekind's Drama," *German Quarterly* 39 [1966] 201–207).

⁶Trotsky, who was dismayed by Wedekind's popularity among members of the Russian intelligentsia, saw Lulu as an "evil earth spirit" who "infects old men and young men alike with the unconquerable frenzy of sex and designates her triumphal path with ruined lives and bodies." He finds that Wedekind's "aesthetic eroticism" turns into a kind of cold, mechanical violence against the body once it has exhausted itself in orgiastic pleasures. See "Frank Wedekind: Esthetics and Eroticism," trans. David Thorstad, *Boston University Journal* 23 (1975) 40–47.

⁷Cited by Willeke, "Wedekind and the *Frauenfrage*," 28. The statement appears in an unpublished sketch "Parthenon: Universalhandbuch der Frauenkunde."

⁸See David Midgley, "Wedekind's Lulu: From 'Schauertragödie' to Social Comedy," on the way in which the German *Büchse* has the same connotations as the English "box." H. R. Hays points out that interpretators early on turned the original jar in He-

of the play eliminated the gory reference in the original manuscript to that organ—the "prodigy" that Jack the Ripper secures from Lulu's body and carefully tucks into his breast pocket after wrapping it in a newspaper and washing his hands:

> I would never have thought of a thing like that.—That is a phenomenon, what would not happen every two hundred years.—I am a lucky dog, to find this curiosity. . . . When I am dead and my collection is put up to auction, the London Medical Club will pay a sum of three hundred pounds for that prodigy, I have conquered this night. The professors and the students will say: That is astonishing! [original in English][9]

Over the years, critics have been hard pressed to define Lulu's essence—what she represents in the social, erotic, and moral economy of the play. Artur Kutscher, Wedekind's confidante and earliest champion, openly set up the chain of associations (serpent in the Garden of Eden / sin / Eve / sexuality / nature / degradation / destruction) that have led several generations of critics to identify seductive femininity as a seditious principle:

> Die Schlange bedient sich der Eva beim Sündenfall, die Schlange ist in Eva, Sinnbild einer weiblichen Kraft. Der Geschlechtstrieb als solcher ist zerstörend. Lulu ist als stetiger Anreiz zu dieser Leidenschaft Prinzip der Zerstörung. . . . Sie ist . . . eine Naturgewalt, ein mystisches Wesen . . . Personifikation des weiblichen Geschlechtstriebes, der im Zentrum des Lebens steht, Geist der Erde, der herabzieht, ein vernichtender Dämon.[10]

Kutscher's associations, with their emphasis on the biblical intertext as the interpretive cue for understanding Lulu's role, is, to some extent, his own construction, but, as we shall see, it does not distort in any significant way the mystification of feminine evil that Wedekind put into his script.

Many readers and viewers of the plays have been quick to notice that Lulu is presented as something of a serial killer herself, a creature with no moral scruples whatsoever, who drives a schoolboy to suicide, kills her "benefactor" Dr. Schön, and is implicated in the deaths of two husbands. Schön calls Lulu a "Würgengel" to her face and asks whether she has taken note of the *"Schlachtopfer"* on her bed. Can it be coincidence that *Erdgeist* and *Büchse der Pandora* both reach their climax in murders? In the first of the two plays, Lulu shoots Schön, who dies with the word "Mörderin" on his lips; in the second, Jack the Ripper kills Lulu as she pleads for help and calls him a "Mörder."

---

siod's narrative into a box, while visual representations of Pandora's transgression situated the box precisely in the anatomical region where it would be turned into a sexual symbol. See *The Dangerous Sex: The Myth of Feminine Evil* (New York: Putnam, 1964) 85–86.

[9] Frank Wedekind: *Die Büchse der Pandora*, ed. Vinçon 132–33.

[10] Artur Kutscher, *Wedekind: Leben und Werk* 120–21.

The murder of Schön marked so decisive a moment in Wedekind's original manuscript that the playwright used it to mark the fissure dividing *Erdgeist* from *Büchse der Pandora*. While Lulu's transgressive sexuality is to some extent monitored and held in check by Schön throughout *Erdgeist*, it is released from all moral and social constraints in *Die Büchse der Pandora*. In the later work, Alwa succinctly formulates the way in which Lulu's body becomes the site of a subversive sexuality that incites men not only to riotous living but also to social rebellion: "Wer sich diesen blühenden, schwellenden Lippen, diesen großen unschuldsvollen Kinderaugen, diesem rosig-weißen strotzenden Körper gegenüber in seiner bürgerlichen Stellung sicher fühlt, der werfe den ersten Stein auf uns."[11] While "luxuriöse Prostitution" (I, 227), as Wedekind called it in "Über Erotik," can contain seditious behavior by serving as a form of licensed release, it ceaselessly threatens to break through social barriers to infect the general population with its transgressive spirit.

In the context of these observations, Alwa's agitated report of an uprising in France ("In Paris ist Revolution ausgebrochen." [*EG*, 594]) at the very moment when Schwarz is "beheading himself" (a horrified Escherich reports "Sich mit dem—Ra—Rasiermesser—den Ha—Hals abschneiden. . . ." [*BP*, 599]) begins to coalesce into a rhetoric of sexual politics with a consistent logic of its own. Small wonder that Lulu was referred to in one production as a "geißelschwingende Proletarierin."[12] *Frühlings Erwachen* had already starkly formulated the hazards of separating the carnal from the spiritual in its many references to beheaded figures and its climax in a graveyard scene that features a decapitated Moritz.[13] In the Lulu plays, unbridled female sexuality may have a liberating effect on men, but it is a short-lived release marked by the absence of reason and ending in destructive personal acts and social anarchy.

What is remarkable about the figure of Lulu, more than anything else, is the degree to which she is invested with a subversive power that threatens not only the ego boundaries of the masculine subject but also the stability of the entire social order. Woman becomes a disruptive figure of formidable energy. "In meiner 'Lulu' im 'Erdgeist,'" Wedekind observed, "suchte ich ein Prachtexemplar von Weib zu zeichnen, wie es entsteht, wenn ein von der Natur reich be-

---

[11]Frank Wedekind, *Werke in 2 Bänden*, ed. Erhard Weidl (Munich: Winkler, 1990), I, 708. Subsequent citations from *Erdgeist (EG)* and *Büchse der Pandora (BP)*—and from Wedekind's other works—are taken from this volume and indicated parenthetically in the text.

[12]See the observations on the first performance of *Erdgeist* in Leipzig in Erhard Weidl, "Philologische Spurensicherung zur Erschließung der 'Lulu'-Tragödie Frank Wedekinds," *Wirkendes Wort* 35 (1985) 99–119.

[13]For a full and astute discussion of the motif of headlessness, see Gordon Birrell, "The Wollen-Sollen Equation in Wedekind's *Frühlings Erwachen*," *Germanic Review* 57 (1982) 115–22.

gabtes Geschöpf, sei es auch aus der Hefe entsprungen, in einer Umgebung von Männern, denen es an Mutterwitz weit überlegen ist, zu schrankenloser Entfaltung gelangt."[14] In this theatrical empowerment of the feminine, it is difficult not to detect what Georges Balandier has identified as the "supreme ruse of power"—the tactic of allowing itself to be "contested *ritually* in order to consolidate itself more effectively."[15] By endowing the feminine with sexual power that shades into political subversion, Wedekind established a social rationale for controlling female sexuality and for preserving gender hierarchies rather than undermining them. Read in this context, it will quickly dawn on any reader of Wedekind's *Mine-Haha oder Über die Erziehung der jungen Mädchen* that the strict rearing and regimentation of girls in that text may be as close to a utopian model as it is to social critique.

In order to understand what brings Lulu to the East End to meet her death under Jack's knife, it will be important to understand how Lulu figures both as a product of Wedekind's own fantasies about female sexuality and as a construct based on "timeless" and "universal" cultural stories about women. Once Lulu deviates from the social script that dictates self-effacing compliance with the rigid codes and conventions governing femininity, she falls prey to a variety of strategies for mortification and containment, the most radical of which is put forth by Jack the Ripper, but all of which point to death.

* * *

Wedekind's contemporaries were unusually astute in recognizing the degree to which the playwright's female characters were constructed from fantasies rather than based on fact. Franz Blei declared that Wedekind's "Vaginismus"—rather than his "Moralität"—was what packed the theaters, and he insisted that "diese unersättlichen Mädchen mit den gespreizten Schenkeln" were nothing more than "wunschgenährte Erdenkungen Wedekinds, denen er seine Sinnlichkeit zu geben glaubt." Playing Lulu as Wedekind wanted her played would, he felt, re-

---

[14] Cited by Wilhelm Emrich, "Frank Wedekind—Die Lulu-Tragödie," in his *Protest und Verheißung: Studien zur klassischen und modernen Dichtung*, 3rd ed. (Frankfurt a.M.: Athenäum, 1968) 211. Emrich finds that Lulu, in all of her power struggles with men, remains "kraft ihrer Natur stets die Überlegene, Herrschende" (218). Artur Kutscher reports that Wedekind enjoyed taking walks in "idyllic" landscapes, but that he avoided the ocean and the mountains: "... die große elementare Natur, das Meer, das Hochgebirge war ihm unheimlich, er ging ihr aus dem Wege, er fühlte sich von ihr überwältigt, verschluckt" (*Frank Wedekind* [Bremen: Dorn, 1954] 22). In view of the cultural linkage between "Mother Nature" with the feminine, Wedekind's fear of women receives particularly pointed expression here.

[15] Georges Balandier, *Political Anthropology*, transl. A. M. Sheridan Smith (London: Allen Lane, 1970) 41.

quire an actress with nothing but dazzling good looks to recommend her—any stirrings of emotional vitality or intellectual activity, indeed anything that pointed beyond "sinnliche Animalität," would diminish the effect of the actress's performance. To the Dadaist Richard Huelsenbeck, Wedekind seemed obsessed with the notion of the *femme fatale*. But as Huelsenbeck noted in his diary, this *femme fatale* was an invention of the Victorian era and nothing more than a fantasmatic substitute for what Wedekind really feared: the economically independent woman, "die nicht mehr willens war, auf das männliche Kommando zu hören und sich vorbereitete, wenn nötig, ihre eigene Welt einzurichten."[16] Blei and Huelsenbeck together point to the way in which a figure like Lulu is constructed as a threat ("mit starkem Druck umringelt sie den Tiger" [*EG*, 553])—even when she has been declared to be tamed ("gebändigt durch das menschliche Genie" [*EG*, 551])—thus legitimizing strategies designed to control women and preserving for men the role of suffering victim.

Huelsenbeck hints that Lulu's identity is dictated as much by the social and cultural codes of the Wilhelmine era as by Wedekind's fantasies. But let us stop now to take the full measure of that identity, to see how Wedekind goes beyond the specificity of his time and place to create a figure that incarnates both a reinscription and a parody of "das Ewig-Weibliche." Wedekind is at pains to mark Lulu as a figure with no bourgeois social identity. For one thing, she lacks a genealogy: Schigolch may hint that he is Lulu's father, but in the end he denies it and asserts that she is fatherless. Schön's declaration that Lulu never knew a mother points to the effacing of a female progenitor as well. With no secure genealogical identity, Lulu lacks a patronymic to stabilize her social identity. She is defined almost exclusively by the men around her: Schigolch calls her Lulu; Schön refers to her as Mignon; Goll christens her Nelli; and Schwarz gives her the name of Eva.[17] One critic, who alludes to Lulu's lack of name and of date or place of birth, calls her "a bureaucrat's nightmare," thereby underscoring the way in which she resists integration into the social organization of bourgeois life.[18] This resistance is further emphasized in Schwarz's interrogation of Lulu after the death of Goll. The catechistic parody, with Lulu's litany ("Ich weiß es

---

[16] Franz Blei, *Über Wedekind, Sternheim und das Theater* (Leipzig: Kurt Wolff, 1915) 37–39. Huelsenbeck's observations on Wedekind appear in his *Reise bis ans Ende der Freiheit: Autobiographische Fragmente* (Heidelberg: Lambert Schneider, 1984) 80. Rolf Kieser discusses Wedekind's concept of "Das Weib" as a projection of male fantasies. See *Benjamin Franklin Wedekind: Biographie einer Jugend* (Zurich: Arche, 1990) 194.

[17] On the way in which Lulu's name can be linked to the bisyllabic words displaying vowel/consonant alteration first used by children (e.g. Mama, Dada), see Thomas Medicus, *"Die große Liebe:" Ökonomie und Konstruktion der Körper im Werk von Frank Wedekind* (Marburg/Lahn: Guttandin & Hoppe, 1982) 102–103.

[18] Peter Jelavich, *Munich and Theatrical Modernism: Politics, Playwriting, and Performance, 1890–1914* (Cambridge, MA: Harvard UP, 1985) 111–12.

nicht"), impresses itself upon the reader or audience as vivid evidence that Lulu is both an untutored spirit and a creature who will forever defy social regulation.

Lulu remains untouched by the socializing powers (such as they are) of the represented world in *Erdgeist*. A disruptive presence that stirs desire, undermines codes of social decorum, and fosters a spirit of exuberant excess, she remains supremely unruffled by the uproar she unleashes at virtually every turn. At the end of the first act, she retires to change her clothes while a distressed Schwarz holds a monologue over the corpse of the dead Goll; at the end of act two we see her—in a stunning inversion of the Lady Macbeth complex—assuring the agitated Schön that the blood of her husband, who has just committed suicide, will not leave stains; act three shows her coldly dictating a letter to a distraught Schön, who is forced to break off his engagement; even at the close of *Erdgeist*, when she takes the gun pointed at her and turns it on Schön ("Der einzige, den ich geliebt!" [*EG*, 634]), her survival instinct overrides any sense of guilt, shame, or remorse.

The pathological lack of affect in Lulu's behavior creates a sense of psychic vacuity that corresponds to the absence of social identity. In Pabst's cinematic representation of Lulu in *Die Büchse der Pandora*, Mary Ann Doane detects the same sense of a figure "totally devoid of thought," without any psychological depth whatsoever.[19] What, then, in the face of this social and psychic blank, defines Lulu? We can begin to answer this question by looking at the chain of signifiers, which in their very multiplicity reflect the inherent difficulty in naming the character we call Lulu. The title *Erdgeist*, with its transparent citation of the spirit conjured by Goethe's Faust and with its emphasis on both the earthy and the spiritual, is usually taken to refer to Lulu, though it could be nothing more than a way of articulating the thematics of integration enunciated in other works by Wedekind. Lulu has been seen as representing a kind of "undifferentiated primal nature," thus helping us to account for her indifference to others even as that label fails to demystify her consummate femininity.[20] The names Mignon and Nelli, with their nods in the direction of Goethe, seem somewhat less

---

[19] Doane finds, however, that in Wedekind's plays, Lulu "is at least given a veneer of intellectuality." See "The Erotic Barter: *Pandora's Box* (1929)," in *The Films of G. W. Pabst: An Extraterritorial Cinema*, ed. Eric Rentschler (New Brunswick: Rutgers UP, 1990) 62–79. Paul Coates also refers to the cinematic Lulu and her "lack of interiority." See *The Gorgon's Gaze: German Cinema, Expressionism, and the Image of Horror* (Cambridge: Cambridge UP, 1991) 59.

[20] The phrase is from Bram Dijkstra, *Idols of Perversity: Fantasies of Feminine Evil in Fin-de-Siècle Culture* (New York: Oxford UP, 1986) 151. Friedrich Karl Rothe (*Frank Wedekinds Dramen*, 38) takes issue with the (then) nearly unanimous view of critics that Lulu is a kind of primal natural force.

weighty than the names of Pandora and Eve, which, with their strong mythological and biblical resonances, merit closer investigation.[21]

That Lulu is presented as lacking a social and personal identity makes it all the easier to exhibit her as "pure" woman (*"das" Weib*). The prologue emphatically states the way in which Lulu will be (paradoxically) constructed as an essentialist vision of woman, a blend of cultural clichés about the essence of femininity. Lulu herself, dressed as Pierrot, never appears in the costume of the snake: it is the *Tierbändiger* who constitutes Lulu's identity by asserting that she is a snake and by mobilizing biblical diction to describe her:

> Sie ward geschaffen, Unheil anzustiften,
> Zu locken, zu verführen, zu vergiften -
> Zu morden, ohne daß es einer spürt. (*EG*, 553)

"Locken" and "verführen" both point to Lulu's physical allure, her ability to put others under her spell—a spell that is woven with cunning duplicity. That her murderous power manifests itself in the act of poisoning marks her as a creature of deception, one who works surreptitiously and with premeditation, without alerting her victims to danger.[22] The supreme danger of women lies in their ability to mask murderous intentions with a dazzlingly attractive appearance. It is to the revelation of this "true nature" that the appeals of the *Tierbändiger* are addressed:

> Mein süßes Tier, sei ja *nur nicht geziert!*
> *Nicht albern, nicht gekünstelt, nicht verschroben,*
> Auch wenn die Kritiker dich weniger loben.
> Du hast kein Recht, uns durch Miaun und Fauchen
> Die Urgestalt des Weibes zu verstauchen.
> Durch Faxenmachen uns und Fratzenschneiden
> Des Lasters Kindereinfalt zu verleiden!
> Du sollst—drum sprech' ich heute sehr ausführlich -
> *natürlich sprechen* und *nicht unnatürlich!* (*EG*, 553; my emphasis)

That Lulu, who may lack a social identity but who has received an extensive sexual education and who has taken cosmetic deception so far as to dye and curl the hair in her armpits, should be represented as "die Urgestalt des Weibes" and as a creature who—on command—can be "nicht geziert," "nicht gekünstelt,"

---

[21] On the significance of the various names given to Lulu and of the roles she is required to play, see Silvia Bovenschen, *Die imaginierte Weiblichkeit: Exemplarische Untersuchungen der kulturgeschichtlichen und literarischen Präsentationsformen des Weiblichen* (Frankfurt a.M.: Suhrkamp, 1979) 43–61.

[22] As Gräfin Orsina observes in Lessing's *Emilia Galotti*, when she hands Odoardo the weapon that will be plunged into Emilia's heart, "Gift ist nur für uns Weiber, nicht für Männer," and the number of literary "Giftmischerinnen" in German literary culture confirms her declaration.

and "nicht unnatürlich" is more than odd. Her years as waif and as kept woman seem to be erased in this declaration of her power to make the feminine transparent.

More important, this passage—with its male animal tamer who issues behavioral imperatives to a female "creature"—is a telling commentary on the way in which the principal woman of this drama is constructed by a male author. The *Tierbändiger* instructs Lulu to "act" according to her true nature even as *he* defines that true nature to be evil and duplicitous. This move on his part parallels that of the playwright Wedekind who insisted on an essentialist view of gender, yet who was at the same time perpetually writing scripts designed to define the women in his plays and in his life. Critics have wrestled repeatedly with the question of whether Lulu represents the spirit of naive carnality or of self-conscious evil and have staged a lively debate interrogating the degree to which the play takes a repressive or emancipatory ideological line when it comes to the question of female sexuality.[23] What they seem to forget is that Lulu can be both (the *Tierbändiger* identifies her from the start as the incarnation of "des Lasters Kindereinfalt") and that she must be both in order to accommodate the notion of "natural" (sexual) evil. More important, they fail to reflect on the degree to which the imposition of a cultural sentence on women—especially one that is declared to be "natural"—constitutes in and of itself a repressive strategy. Whether Lulu is represented as complying with that sentence by responding to male desire and fashioning herself as an object of exchange or whether she resists it through histrionic self-display exaggerated to the point of parody is the point that merits debate.

Though the prologue insists on an essentialist view of woman (all the while dictating to its female protagonist what woman's true nature is), the remainder of the play works hard to construct a Lulu determined by a number of cultural coordinates (most of which in turn insist on an essentialist view). To begin with, Lulu is affiliated with the biblical Eve and the mythical Pandora—two figures

---

[23]David Midgley has described the way in which Lulu's character shifts from "willful malice" to "naiveté" etc. What Gail Finney defines as Wedekind's "ambivalence" about women (he provides a critique of women's roles in society even as he reinforces the notion of their essentially masochistic nature), I see as a position that does not necessarily imply conflicting principles. Wedekind's critique of women's roles is, for example, driven to a great extent by the need to improve the physical and mental health of men. Thomas Elsaesser discusses the larger moral issue in Pabst's *Büchse der Pandora* and comes to the conclusion that Lulu is neither active nor passive, neither evil nor innocent: "Instead, it becomes a matter of presence of absence, of spectacle, of image and *mise en scène*.... The spectacle of her person, about which she controls nothing but the cadence and discontinuity of presence, is what gives rise to desire and fascination." See "Lulu and the Meter Man: Pabst's *Pandora's Box* (1929)," in *German Film and Literature: Adaptations and Transformations*, ed. Eric Rentschler (New York: Methuen, 1986) 40–59.

shouldered with the responsibility for the entrance of sin and evil into the world.[24] In looking at the evolution of Pandora and Eve, at the ways in which their "timeless" and "universal" stories actually inflect femininity in timebound and culturally specific ways, we can see the degree to which post-Enlightenment culture intensifies the combination of carnality and deceit that constitutes the beautiful evil that is woman.

Both Eve and Pandora operate through seduction. Although there are many ways of reading the account of Creation and the Fall in Genesis, traditional interpretations of recent centuries have transformed Eve into the snake in Paradise: she does not just succumb to temptation but doubles as a deadly agent of seduction. As Casti Piani declares in Wedekind's *Totentanz*, "In der Geschichte des Paradieses steht, daß der Himmel dem Weib die Macht der Verführung verlieh" (II, 307). Over the centuries, the cognitive knowledge that figures so importantly in Genesis has taken on a decidedly carnal coloring. Margaret Miles has convincingly demonstrated that the sixteenth century marked a turning point in our understanding of original sin—before that time, "there were few suggestions that the specific content of original sin was sexual desire."[25]

The story of Pandora, like the account of Eve in Genesis, has become a parable more concerned with the evils of female sexuality than with the ills of humanity.[26] As the Panofskys brilliantly demonstrate in their study of Pandora, the Fathers of the Church—"in an attempt to corroborate the doctrine of original sin by a classical parallel"—were chiefly responsible for the transformation of Pandora into a pagan precursor of Eve. The full effects of the transformation did not become evident until the sixteenth and seventeenth centuries, but they

---

[24] On the function of Pandora in Wedekind's play, see Jeannine Schuler-Will, "Wedekind's Lulu: Pandora and Pierrot, the Visual Experience of Myth," *German Studies Review* 7 (1984), 27–38. For a full discussion of the way in which the figure of Lulu resonates with cultural references, see J. L. Hibberd, "The Spirit of the Flesh: Wedekind's Lulu," *Modern Language Review* 79 (1984), 336–55. In this context, it is amusing to note Tilly Wedekind's outrage when she learned the implications of the titles *Erdgeist* and *Die Büchse der Pandora*: "Ich habe mir sagen lassen," she reported, "daß durch die Jahrtausende die verschiedensten Religionen der verschiedensten Völker darin übereinstimmen, daß alles Übel durch die Frau in die Welt kam. Ich finde das eigentlich unerhört!" See *Lulu: Die Rolle meines Lebens* (Munich: Rütten & Loening, 1969) 298.

[25] Margaret Miles, *Carnal Knowing: Female Nakedness and Religious Meaning in the Christian West* (Boston: Beacon Press, 1989) xiv.

[26] For some cultures, Pandora ("the all-gifted" or the "gift of all") came to be seen as the perfect blend of positive attributes; others stressed that she represented the fusion of blessing and curse; and still others saw her as a victim of ignorance, curiosity, or improvidence. Dora and Erwin Panofsky chart the course of Pandora's shifting fortunes in *Pandora's Box: The Changing Aspects of a Mythical Symbol*, 2nd ed. (New York: Pantheon, 1962).

persisted into the modern era. It was Paul Klee who, perhaps more frankly than any other artist, captured the essence of the modern myth of Pandora. His "Pandora's Box as a Still Life" (1920) turns the ominous container into an urn decorated with flowers and inscribed with what is unmistakably an image of the female genitals, from which dark vapors arise.[27]

That Lulu is fashioned from cultural citations becomes even more evident in the transparent references to Nietzsche's *Jenseits von Gut und Böse* in the prologue to *Erdgeist*. (It is worth noting that Wedekind stayed up until seven in the morning reading Nietzsche just ten days before he conceived the idea for the "Schauertragödie" that was to become the Lulu plays.) For Nietzsche, woman ("das Weib") has few redeeming features, but the one he singles out as worthy of admiration and fear is her *"Natur*, die 'natürlicher' ist als die des Mannes, seine echte raubtierhafte listige Geschmeidigkeit, seine Tigerkralle unter dem Handschuh, seine Naivität im Egoismus, seine Unerziehbarkeit und innerliche Wildheit, das Unfaßliche, Weite, Schweifende seiner Begierden und Tugenden."[28]

But just what does Nietzsche mean by woman's "nature"? What is it that makes his constructed version of her more "natural" than man? Woman's first and foremost duty is to bear robust children—thus woman, through her procreative powers, remains more closely linked to nature than man. Mocking efforts to "emancipate" women from their biological role, Nietzsche makes it clear that there is nothing more pathetic or perverse than a woman who devotes herself to the life of the mind. Yet for all his railing about woman's naiveté and absence of intellect—his orthodox alignment of women with the body and men with the mind—Nietzsche cannot resist insisting on woman's duplicity: "Nichts ist von Anbeginn an dem Weibe fremder, widriger, feindlicher als Wahrheit—seine große Kunst ist die Lüge, seine höchste Angelegenheit ist der Schein und die Schönheit."[29] Nietzsche's phrase about woman's "echte raubtierhafte listige Geschmeidigkeit" perfectly captures the supple double movement from artlessness to artfulness that constitutes the cultural identity of woman.

Beauty is repeatedly linked with duplicity in cultural constructions of female evil, but rarely is the connection between the two elaborated with the kind of frankness we find in *Jenseits von Gut und Böse*. Nietzsche's account makes it clear that the fear and admiration inspired by woman's affiliation with nature through the procreative powers of her body can lead to a frantic appropriation of the spiritual as a preserve of male superiority and to the exclusion of women from

---

[27]Dora and Erwin Panofsky, *Pandora's Box*, 113. I have not been able to establish whether Klee knew of Wedekind's play and had Schön's words about Lulu as a "still life" in mind when he executed this drawing.

[28]Frank Wedekind, *Die Tagebücher. Ein erotisches Leben*, ed. Gerhard Hay (Munich: dtv, 1990) 183.

[29]Friedrich Nietzsche, *Jenseits von Gut und Böse*, in *Werke*, ed. Karl Schlechta (Munich: Hanser, 1955), II, 703.

the "higher truths" of the mind. In this logic, woman's allegiance to the world of appearances is determined by her carnal orientation and fosters a form of self-conscious duplicity designed to cover up essences and "truths." Yet if we consider the degree to which Nietzsche valorized surfaces, appearances, and art in, say, *Die Geburt der Tragödie aus dem Geiste der Musik* or ponder just how sharply he resisted the cultural enshrinement of truth in *Von Wahrheit und Lüge im aussermoralischen Sinne*, then it becomes clear that the views elaborated in *Jenseits von Gut und Böse* are highly nuanced and complicated, even if the reception of those views is not.

Nietzsche's alignment of the feminine with nature and with duplicity could be made to dovetail all too neatly with many of the "eternal truths" about female evil elaborated in the stories of Eve and Pandora, and for that very reason, the Lulu plays, much as they may echo Nietzschean notions about gender roles, represent little more than the rewriting of a familiar cultural script. Yet there is another element to Nietzsche's account of the feminine that is absent from narratives about Eve and Pandora but markedly present in Wedekind's plays. As Sander Gilman has pointed out, contemporary audiences immediately identified references to the whip, and to Lulu's need for it, with Nietzsche's writings on women.[30] Again and again, Lulu's desire is linked with pain and self-destructive behavior, most pointedly when she tells Alwa about a recurrent dream in which she falls into the hands of a *Lustmörder*.[31] What is important for our context is the way in which Lulu's death is doubly determined, first by a masculine need to master brute, unruly, nomadic female sexuality, then by a feminine need to subject itself to that mastery. Nietzsche's whip, a sign of male pleasure in domination and female desire for pain, is the instrument that organizes the moral and social economy of heterosexual relationships in Wedekind's play.

Emptied of all personal, individualized passions and deprived of a social identity, Lulu becomes the site of multiple cultural citations conflated to fashion "ein Prachtexemplar von Weib." She figures both as an idealized vision of woman and as a showy realization of cultural fears and fantasies about women. That women can become active participants in their own objectification and that their self-display is also a form of self-effacement (or death) is a point not lost on Elisabeth Bronfen, who makes a case (in another literary context) for positioning the "speculated woman" as both agent and victim. Edith Wharton's

[30]Sander L. Gilman, "The Nietzsche Murder Case," *New Literary History* 14 (1983) 359–72.

[31]Audrone B. Willeke emphasizes that "Lulu is actually in search of a master, of a strong male who can tame her...." She interprets Lulu's dream about a sexual murderer as an expression of an "innermost desire" to be "mastered." See "Wedekind and the 'Frauenfrage,'" 28. That Lulu can satisfy both sadistic and masochistic desires is a point made by Annemarie Taeger, *Die Kunst, Medusa zu töten. Zum Bild der Frau in der Literatur der Jahrhundertwende* (Bielefeld: Aisthesis, 1987) 23–30.

Lily Bart in *The House of Mirth*, she argues, "'kills' herself before her time by turning herself into an artwork, and in so doing emerges as an accomplice to the culture that requires such reification of its feminine members." At the same time, Lily Bart's self-representation is also "her form of individual, creative self-expression":

> Given that in staking herself as 'speculated woman' she is inconsistent and incalculable, never clearly directed at one intended spectator and shifting between an affirmation of this position and its refusal, she demystifies such a reduction to the status of image. In doing so, she seems to disclose the mortifying tendencies of the very conventions she complies with, turning her feigned complicity as dissimulation into the hysteric's form of resistance.[32]

Lulu's adherence to the conventional script for the *femme fatale*, along with her deadpan parody of that script, reveals the deadly power of the aestheticizing strategies practiced by her many admirers. The script—followed straight—dictates endlessly mortifying postures; the parody of it ends in social exclusion and death. In a sense, Lulu gives us an overly compliant, excessive enactment of the role assigned to all women in a patriarchal order—the "schrankenlose Entfaltung" of the feminine to which Wedekind referred. Toril Moi aptly formulates how Luce Irigaray's theatrical staging of a mime aims to "*undo* the effects of phallocentric discourse by *overdoing* them," and Lulu can similarly be perceived as a subversive subject aping, and thereby exposing and defying, the mimicry required of women.

But even as Wedekind's plays can be read as parodying and mounting resistance to what is required of women in the bourgeois social order, they reinscribe the social differentiations and exclusionary sexual politics of that order. The prologue to *Erdgeist* introduces a sharp demarcation between the world of high culture ("Possen, Ibsen, Opern, Dramen"), with its soothing flow of comfortable babble, and the domain of low culture, the circus with its perilous and provocative amusements. It is the *Tierbändiger* who sets the terms for the social division between high and low, civilized and natural, tame and wild, polite and vulgar, and who also aligns Lulu, along with the play in which she figures, with the latter of the two terms. As many critics have pointed out (in other contexts), the kinds of differentiations mapped out by the *Tierbändiger* hinge on deeply ingrained notions about the corrupting power of "filth" in its literal and figurative meanings. The bourgeois subject, as Peter Stallybrass and Allon White have noted in a study that stands under the influence of Bakhtin, "continuously defined and redefined itself through the exclusion of what it marked out as 'low'— as dirty, repulsive, noisy, contaminating."[33] But in creating its identity through

---

[32] Elisabeth Bronfen, *Over Her Dead Body: Death, Femininity and the Aesthetic* (New York: Routledge, 1992) 275.

[33] Peter Stallybrass and Allon White, *The Politics and Poetics of Transgression* (Ithaca: Cornell UP, 1986) 191.

prohibitions and taboos (chiefly concerned with bodily functions), that same subject produced a powerful form of transgressive desire, one that ceaselessly undid the work of "civilization" and came to constitute the "imaginary repertoire" of the dominant culture. "What is *socially* peripheral is so frequently *symbolically* central," Stallybrass and White assert, pointing up the way in which the devaluation and denial of the "low" invested it with a heightened psychic, if not social or political, significance.[34]

Wedekind was unusually prescient in his understanding of the consequences of sexual repression—of the way in which the phobic exclusion of sexuality from "polite" culture leads to the degradation of bodily functions and urges, thereby only intensifying their hold on the psyche and producing a form of enslavement to the body. In the context of observations about "dirty" jokes ("Zoten"), he observed: "In der Verächtlichmachung und Beschimpfung liegt dann eine Art von ohnmächtiger Empörung, von Protest gegenüber einer tyrannischen Gewalt, gegen die es für diese Leute in Wirklichkeit kein Aufkommen gibt" (I, 228). The secretiveness permeating bodily needs and desires ensures that sexual traffic remains underground, creating a fugitive subterranean economy as corrupt as it is opulent. Stefan Zweig, in his autobiography, recalled the degree to which a conspiracy of silence surrounded sexuality and how an architecture of visible, "morally pure" façades was protected by an underground drainage system into which the "filth" of the sewers was poured:

> Wie die Städte unter den sauber gekehrten Straßen mit ihren schönen Luxusgeschäften und eleganten Promenaden unterirdische Kanalanlagen verbergen, in denen der Schmutz der Kloaken abgeleitet wird, sollte das ganze sexuelle Leben der Jugend sich unsichtbar unter der moralischen Oberfläche der "Gesellschaft" abspielen.[35]

Alain Corbin has written convincingly about the way in which the nineteenth century regarded prostitution as "an indispensable excremental phenomenon that protects the social body from disease."[36] As effectively as this drainage system may have worked, there was always the threat of contamination, hence the steady proliferation of programs for the social regulation of this subterranean culture. While some critics have argued that Lulu is less prostitute (she resists the idea of entering a bordello and is not oriented—until the end—toward pecuniary gain) than courtesan or hetaera, she becomes more and more firmly anchored in a moral and social culture that self-consciously sets itself

---

[34]Ibid., 5.

[35]Stefan Zweig, *Die Welt von Gestern* (Stockholm: Bermann-Fischer, 1942) 102.

[36]Alain Corbin, *Women for Hire: Prostitution and Sexuality in France after 1850*, transl. Alan Sheridan (Cambridge, MA.: Harvard UP, 1990) 4.

apart from the bourgeois sphere.[37] The extent to which Lulu becomes affiliated with the world of prostitution becomes evident in a scene from the first version of the play that shows Alwa reaching a sexual climax as he passionately expresses his devotion to Lulu's body. "Und dein warmes elastisches Fleisch unter der weichen Seide! Man fühlt kein Hemd... nur dich—wo man hingreift!—Du bist jetzt erst Weib!" When Lulu bids him to go to her bedroom, he responds with a verbal assault unparalleled elsewhere in the play in its aggressive rage: "Du Abzugskanal!—Du Reibeisen!—Du Kloake!—Du Spucknapf!—Du Rotzlappen!—Du Jaucheloch!—Du Schraubstock—Du Kothabfuhr—Du Misthöhle."[38] In Alwa's move from delirious adoration to abject disgust, we can see just how the failure to master sexual desire leads to the degradation of the feminine, which, in its affiliation with the carnal and "natural," becomes the target of a discourse linking immoral behavior, excremental waste, and infectious disease. As Schön puts it, Lulu is an "unheilbare Seuche"—she will forever remain a pestilential force, contaminating everything she touches.[39]

In a move unprecedented for the German theater, Wedekind placed the spotlight on a subject that was normally sealed off from the public arena, and especially from the realm of high art, the cultural space in which the Lulu plays came to be performed. Lulu, the heroine of the "Monstretragödie" tellingly called *Erdgeist* and *Büchse der Pandora*, literally takes center stage in a social formation that usually excludes her kind. But in centering Lulu, endowing her with almost irresistible sexual power, and by allying female sexuality with corruption, transgression, and disease, Wedekind effectively underwrote Western cultural myths and discursive practices about the feminine.[40] To be sure, Lulu is put on display in a markedly ambiguous way—one that stages her as the fulfillment of male desires and anxieties about seductive feminine beauty yet positions her as parodying this ideal through the excesses of her nomadic, volatile behavior (which in turn leads to her mortification and death). Still, the critique of male fantasies about femininity is so driven by a language invested in cultural

---

[37] Alfons Höger, *Hetärismus und bürgerliche Gesellschaft im Frühwerk Frank Wedekinds* (Munich: Fink, 1981) 132–36.

[38] *Frank Wedekind. Die Büchse der Pandora. Eine Monstretragödie*, ed. Vinçon, 65.

[39] In the original manuscript version of the plays, Alwa likens Lulu's power to that of disease: "Sie hat mich ausgefressen wie eine Pestbeule" and "Sie hat mich zu einem Versammlungslokal gemacht, in dem alle Gifte und Parasiten ihre babylonischen Orgien feiern" (*Frank Wedekind. Die Büchse der Pandora. Eine Monstretragödie*, ed. Vinçon, 118).

[40] Elizabeth Boa notes that Wedekind was "trapped in some of the more virulent sexist ideas of his time," but that the "theatrical effect of the major plays... undermines that very ideology." See *The Sexual Circus: Wedekind's Theatre of Subversion* (Oxford: Basil Blackwell, 1985) 25.

clichés about femininity that it risks reverting into an affirmation of those clichés.

* * *

It is through the figure of Alwa Schön that the reader becomes fully aware of the way in which the socially mobile courtesan is represented as a seditious force, destroying the bourgeois respectability of those whom she infects with the excesses of her irresistibly attractive carnality. In a tête-à-tête with Lulu shortly after the death of his father, Alwa describes the way in which Lulu's presence creates a challenge that can be mastered only through artistic or erotic channels: "So z.B. bleibt mir dir gegenüber nur die Wahl," he declares to Lulu, "dich künstlerisch zu gestalten oder dich zu lieben" (*EG*, 669). The manuscript version puts slightly different words into Alwa's mouth: "Ich muß meiner Schwärmerei Ausdruck geben, wenn sie mich nicht zum Lustmörder machen soll," setting up murder, rather than artistic expression, as an alternative to sexual release.[41] What is interesting here is the installation of art and murder as homologous strategies for managing sexual desire, with the one spiritualizing desire through aestheticization of the body, the other eliminating desire through the most radical possible form of physical degradation. The intermingling of sexual desire, artistic frenzy, and murderous passion becomes the signature of many figures in Wedekind's dramas, but in particular of painters who represent the female body. In *Frühlings Erwachen*, the artist Heinrich finds his model/mistress Ilse so beautiful that he wants to murder her, and in *Erdgeist*, Schwarz becomes so aroused by Lulu's breathing while she is modeling for him that he commands her to stop or to risk sexual assault.

"Zum Morden schön" (I, 515)—this phrase from *Frühlings Erwachen* captures the way in which sexual desire mingles with aesthetic admiration to produce anxieties so unsettling that they engender the need to silence, immobilize, and eliminate their source. We know that anxiety figures as a prominent feature of the effect of looking at the female body from the prologue to *Erdgeist*, which couples desire (*Wollust*) with fear (*Grauen*) as the response to the sight of Lulu and which rhymes *Frauen* with *Grauen*. Ironically, the very strategies designed to frame Lulu, to contain the desires and fears aroused by her body, serve only to intensify her power. I have tried to show how the playwright Wedekind made a point of erasing Lulu's genealogy in order to present a figure whose identity is based on textual citations and cultural stories. What I have not yet noted is the way in which Wedekind destabilizes and disperses Lulu's identity by creating multiple Lulus along with multiple simulacra of Lulu on the stage. There is the Lulu of the prologue—a snake dressed in the costume of Pierrot (who reappears

[41]*Frank Wedekind. Die Büchse der Pandora. Eine Monstretragödie*, ed. Harmut Vinçon, 60.

reflected in Schwarz's eyes); there is Schwarz's portrait of Lulu, which Gräfin Geschwitz so treasures and which survives the vagaries of Lulu's career; there are the images of Lulu reflected in the mirrors carefully installed in many of the play's scenes (Lulu even finds it possible to admire the image reflected to her from a gleaming dustpan); there is the dancer Lulu; and there is the heroine of Alwa's play *Erdgeist*.[42]

In this steady proliferation of images we can perceive a nervous series of unsuccessful efforts to contain Lulu through artistic representation, to construct art against nature. Again and again, Lulu's body performs what Charles Bernheimer has described as the function of the prostitute: to "stimulate artistic strategies to control and dispel her fantasmatic threat to male mastery."[43] Yet the production of images eventually reaches a point of such excess that Lulu's power accelerates rather than declines—in the end Jack the Ripper must be summoned to eliminate the model for the powerful images put into circulation. *Erdgeist* gives us a Lulu who remains to some extent the prisoner of aestheticizing strategies practiced by promoters of images, masquerades, transformations, and roles, yet it also shows how those strategies misfire by producing doubles that intensify Lulu's hold on others—one need only think of Gräfin Geschwitz and her ferocious attachment to Lulu's portrait.[44]

That Jack the Ripper's murder is driven in part by aesthetic appreciation of Lulu ("Ich habe noch keinen hübscheren Mund gesehen" [*BP*, 719]) and by the need to establish a reputation through the creation of a collector's item may seem to provide only the most tenuous link between his violent acts and the

---

[42] Hauke Stroszek makes the point that Lulu's fate mirrors that of art and that Lulu comes to stand as an allegorical representation of art in general and the theater in particular. See "'Ein Bild, vor dem die Kunst verzweifeln muß': Zur Gestaltung der Allegorie in Frank Wedekinds Lulu-Tragödie," in *Literatur und Theater im Wilhelminischen Zeitalter*, ed. Hans-Peter Bayerdörfer, Karl Otto Conrady and Helmut Schanze (Tübingen: Niemeyer, 1978) 217–37. On Lulu as Pierrot, see Naomi Ritter, "The Portrait of Lulu as Pierrot," in *Frank Wedekind Yearbook 1991*, ed. Rolf Kieser and Reinhold Grimm (Bern: Peter Lang, 1992) 127–40.

[43] Charles Bernheimer, *Figures of Ill Repute: Representing Prostitution in Nineteenth-Century France* (Cambridge, MA: Harvard UP, 1989) 2.

[44] That Lulu nevertheless undergoes something of a silencing cure as she is turned into a fetishistic spectacle for the male gaze is a point that has not been lost on feminist critics. She makes her first appearance as a snake, a creature that, for all its associations with wiliness, remains mute save for its sibilants. In a moment of self-deprecation, Lulu calls herself an animal and Schigolch consoles her by reminding her that she is "Ein feines Tier!—Ein elegantes Tier!—Ein Prachtstier!" (*EG*, 582). The painting of Lulu as Pierrot seems to further underscore the way in which women become silenced, immobilized, and contained through aesthetic idealization—Schön even encourages the artist Schwarz to treat Lulu as a "still life." As dancer on the stage, Lulu loses her voice as she turns into pure spectacle.

practices of artists. But if we pause for a moment to consider the ways in which the compulsion to repeat bedevils Jack the Ripper—each successive murder intensifies rather than diminishes the psychosis—we can see how sexual murder directed at women, like the artistic representation of seductive femininity, strengthens the very anxieties it seeks to alleviate.

Jack's murder of Lulu ("ein Stück Arbeit") is described in much the same terms as Schwarz's efforts to represent Lulu ("die Arbeit" is the noun used repeatedly to characterize his profession and its products). But Jack the Ripper is linked just as naturally with libertines—he takes bodily violation to an extreme—as with artists. The libertine, unlike the artist, allows carnal seduction to triumph over aesthetic production. He too establishes a reputation—one that implies a mastery of women similar to that practiced by the artist in transforming real-life models into fetishized constructs. But the libertine, rather than creating idealized images of women, does just the opposite by destroying women's reputations, turning them into creatures of ill repute and thus excluding them from the order on which they depend for their social identity. It is this destructive dimension, along with the compulsion to repeat, that marks the libertine a kindred spirit of Jack the Ripper, who destroys the bodies of the women he violates. Georges Bataille recognized this affinity when he wrote that "physical eroticism" signifies "a violation of the very being of its practitioners . . . a violation bordering on death, bordering on murder."[45] If, at last, we take into account De Quincey's "On Murder Considered as One of the Fine Arts"—which insists that murder can be appreciated as a work of art—the web of connections linking artistic practices with libertine conduct and murderous behavior becomes more tightly woven than ever.[46]

* * *

"Du hast dir einen Namen geschaffen," Schön asserts to Schwarz when he reveals that Lulu is responsible for his artistic success and that she has secured his reputation. Very early on, Frank Wedekind, the author of diaries subtitled *Ein erotisches Leben* and of plays centered on women, had built a reputation for himself in both the sexual and artistic arena. And this reputation was no doubt part of what Brecht was referring to when he declared of his literary antecedent: "Sein größtes Werk war seine Persönlichkeit."[47] Tilly Newes, Wedekind's wife, took a special interest in the playwright of *Erdgeist* because he had been described to her as "Der Autor mit dem interessanten Ruf." As we learn from the

---

[45] Georges Bataille, *Death and Sensuality: A Study of Eroticism and the Taboo*, transl. Mary Dalwood (New York: Walker & Co., 1962) 17.

[46] On De Quincey's essay, see especially Joel Black, *The Aesthetics of Murder: A Study in Romantic Literature and Contemporary Culture* (Baltimore: Johns Hopkins UP, 1991).

[47] Bertolt Brecht, *Gesammelte Werke* (Frankfurt a.M.: Suhrkamp, 1967), XV, 4.

actress's autobiography, her husband was "notorious" as much for his womanizing as for his writing—sexual conquest and artistic achievement seemed to figure as the twin coordinates for constituting an artistic identity and establishing a reputation.[48]

A look at Wedekind's diaries gives a clear picture of the degree to which women and work hardened into compulsions, with sexual performance and creative labors becoming deeply entangled with one another. It is through the diaries and plays of Wedekind, along with the autobiographical reminiscences of his wife Tilly Newes, that I hope to construct a picture of how the playwright and the man built his reputation on a series of moves that contained the threat of female sexuality by transforming women into (exhibitionist) works of art and that radically disempowered women through a kind of censorship and scripting of roles consonant with theatrical practices.

Let us pursue the issue of artistic expression as a sublimation of sexual drives and consider the way in which the boundary between creativity and sexual performance becomes porous in the artistic practices of Alwa, who figures in some ways as Wedekind's double.[49] Through his role as director, Alwa finds a way in which to stage Lulu, to appropriate the allure of the feminine by creating a fetishized figure that becomes the target of the collective male gaze. By staging or constructing simulacra of the women he desires, the male artist makes a name for himself, stabilizes his identity, and builds a clientele or following. Heterosexual desire is repressed as a narcissistic desire to be desired emerges.

Frank Wedekind fell in love with Tilly Newes when she was playing the role of Lulu—reciting lines from a script he had created. What makes the relationship between the playwright/husband and actress/wife particularly fascinating is that they frequently appeared together, reading scripts fashioned by the one for the two of them to act in. The roles in the plays—much as they may have been fabricated for the stage—could not but color the life offstage. Stephen Greenblatt has eloquently described a moment of resistance to role-playing in his own life—resistance motivated by the recognition that the words we speak, even when they are not our own, shape our identity. For Greenblatt, it becomes impossible to say the words "I want to die:" "I was aware ... of the extent to which my identity and the words I utter coincide, the extent to which I want to

---

[48]"Daß er als verrucht galt und als eine höchst interessante Erscheinung mit einem einigermaßen abenteuerlichen Vorleben, erfuhr ich erst nach und nach," Tilly Wedekind notes. See her autobiography, tellingly called *Lulu: Die Rolle meines Lebens* (Munich: Rütten + Loening, 1969) 33.

[49]We should not forget that the name of the one contains an allusion to the inventor of the light bulb, while the name of the other—Benjamin *Franklin* Wedekind—was meant as a tribute to a figure who conducted experiments with electricity.

form my own sentences or to choose for myself those moments in which I will recite someone else's."[50]

While Tilly Wedekind was to some extent free to choose the moments when she would recite lines written by her husband, her autobiography documents in an extraordinary way how her life became dominated by the scripts of Frank Wedekind. When, for example, she was to don the Pierrot costume for a performance as Lulu, she retreated to an artist's studio, where she was surprised by an amorous Wedekind in search of a kiss: "Plötzlich blieb er wie erstarrt stehen, faßte sich an die Stirn und rief: 'Aber das ist ja *Erdgeist*, erster Akt.'"[51] At the very moment of appropriation from the aesthetic realm, Wedekind preserves the distinction between art and life by acknowledging his debt to the former, yet the experience of impersonating characters created by the self could not but intensify the hold of the aesthetic realm on shaping the self and on shaping other selves. To be sure, that aesthetic realm was often itself constructed from real-life experiences. To his wife, Wedekind observed: "Das ist ja nicht mehr Theater, was wir hier spielen. Das ist ja unser Leben."[52] The boundaries between life and the stage become blurred, with the life being determined by events on stage and the plays feeding on the material of life.

In *Erdgeist* and *Die Büchse der Pandora*, Wedekind wrote the script for a Lulu who reflected his fantasies about women and who became the role/model for a real-life woman with whom he fell in love. Tilly Wedekind, who was destined to play the role of Lulu until her husband—in a touch of supreme irony—could bear her success no longer, wrote poignantly of the way in which Wedekind was pained by her theatrical triumphs. At one time, he made a point of adding *Rabbi Esra* to the repertoire, giving the silent role of Moses to Tilly and playing the title character who recites a monologue that takes up virtually the entire work. Years after the performance, Tilly Wedekind reported with undisguised astonishment:

> Aber ich hatte nichts zu sagen! Ich war nur schöne Staffage! Am Anfang sprach ich drei Sätze, und dann kam der Monolog, der von ein paar Sätzen unterbrochen wurde, die Frank für den Moses hineinschrieb, aber die waren wahrhaftig nicht wichtig; der Moses war offensichtlich nur hübsch, aber ein Einfaltspinsel.
>
> Da habe ich gestreikt! Ich erklärte Frank, ich sei kein Schaustück, ich sei Schauspielerin und stellte mich nur einer Rolle zur Verfügung, nicht einem stummen lebenden Bild![53]

---

[50]Stephen Greenblatt, *Renaissance Self-Fashioning: From More to Shakespeare* (Chicago: U of Chicago P, 1980) 256.

[51]Tilly Wedekind, *Lulu*, 48.

[52]Ibid., 182.

[53]Ibid., 85.

Though indignant about the way she had been silenced, Tilly Wedekind seemed still to pride herself on the dazzling effect of her physical appearance: in loving detail, with undisguised gratitude, and with little awareness of the way in which she has been turned into a fetishized object, she describes the splendid costume that her husband had made for her. Frank Wedekind found it hard to bear admiration for anything beyond Tilly Wedekind's physical beauty. When the *Züricher Post* responded with enthusiasm to Tilly Wedekind's interpretation of Lulu, Frank Wedekind deflated the praise with remarks like this one: "Ich gratuliere dir zu deinem Erfolg. Es hat jetzt keinen Sinn mehr, daß wir zusammen spielen. Ich kann ja keinen Konkurrenten mitnehmen."[54]

Time and again, Tilly Wedekind describes efforts to pacify her husband by cancelling engagements and declining offers to play leading roles. The attractions of building a theatrical and personal reputation on his wife's physical beauty were, for Wedekind, ceaselessly shadowed by the envy he felt for the success and satisfaction that came to be her due. That Tilly Wedekind's art might prevail over his—just as Tilly Wedekind was likely to survive her husband, given the difference in their ages—was a thought that haunted Wedekind.

Tilly's role in her husband's life is enacted with frightening candor in *Die Zensur*, a one-act play that has been acknowledged as the playwright's most frankly autobiographical work.[55] Wedekind himself wrote about the drama as an enactment of his own life:

> Hätte ich das Kind beim rechten Namen nennen wollen, dann hätte ich den Einakter 'Exhibitionismus' nennen müssen oder Selbstporträt. Die Kritik hatte mir vielfach den Vorwurf gemacht, daß sich meine Dramen mit meiner eigenen Person beschäftigen. Ich wollte dartun, daß es sich der Mühe lohnt, meine Person auf die Bühne zu bringen.[56]

What is of interest here, beyond the combination of flagrant arrogance and nervous vulnerability implied by Wedekind's statement, is the way in which the play becomes his offspring ("das Kind") and the way in which the production of drama takes an exhibitionistic turn, unabashedly placing the playwright at the center of the work and revealing the degree to which the exhibitionism of the female characters figures as a projection of the playwright's own desires.

Die Zensur offers clear evidence that Wedekind was not uncritical of the way in which masculine identities and artistic reputations are built upon the sacrifice

---

[54] Ibid., 179.

[55] The first version names the two principal characters "Ich" and "Tilly." The congruity between the characters and real-life figures is astonishing in its detail. For example, Wedekind begins the play with Buridan's plea for a fourteen-day leave-of-absence. In September 1907, within the time-frame for the composition of *Die Zensur*, Wedekind complains to his wife that he must have fourteen days away from her. See Frank Wedekind, *Gesammelte Briefe* (Munich: Georg Müller, 1924), II, 189.

[56] Frank Wedekind, *Gesammelte Werke*, IX, 435.

of women, yet the staging of the critique could rarely divorce itself from the very practices condemned. Just as *Mine-Haha* can be read as a searing attack on prurient male desire for pubescent girls, it also pandered to that very desire in its prodigal descriptions of the girls' bodies and their preparation for a life devoted to corporal discipline and pleasure. The playwright who provided chilling critiques of prostitution in *Das Opferlamm* and *Tod und Teufel* and who witnessed firsthand the diseases, emotional despair, and abject poverty of streetwalkers in Paris was also the man who took up with one prostitute after another in a market that decidedly favored the buyer.[57] Thus the candor of the self-revelations and the implicit self-critique in *Die Zensur* are, in a sense, of one piece with the playwright's real-life indulgence in sexual, artistic, and social practices that fortify masculine identities by silencing, degrading, or deadening women.

Buridan, the troubled dramatist of *Die Zensur*, finds himself faced with the double challenge of meeting the erotic and emotional demands of his artistic partner Kadidja and extracting permission from a Dr. Prantl to bring his banned plays to the stage. Kadidja's function is much like that of Tilly Newes: her beauty is put on display to enliven performances and to rivet the attention of audiences on Buridan's work.[58] While Buridan is pleading with Prantl, Kadidja enters, dressed in "ein beliebiges geschmackvolles Phantasiekostüm" (II, 408). Prantl, who interprets her appearance as a premeditated effort to persuade him to release Buridan's plays for production, adamantly resists her charms:

> "Da ist er ja schon—der Feind! der Versucher!—die Schlange des Paradieses! . . . Wir lassen uns nicht verführen. Am allerwenigsten aber sind wir durch zauberhafte Gaukelspielereien zu erschüttern, die Ihre mittelalterliche Menschenkenntnis offenbar ausgebrütet hat, um in den Bekämpfern Ihres verderblichen Treibens die niedrigsten Begierden wachzurufen. . . . Zu dieser Gegenüberstellung also locken Sie mich in Ihr Haus!" (II, 409)

The double meaning of this last line could scarcely have escaped the attention of the theatergoers who had been lured to see *Die Zensur* in part because of Wedekind's reputation for putting the female body on display.[59]

When Prantl fails to respond to Buridan's pleas to lift the ban on his plays, Buridan swiftly retaliates by shifting the site of his efforts to fashion others—the arena of his domestic life becomes a substitute for the social world of the theater. To Kadidja, he declares, in a statement that alludes to Genesis, that he will

---

[57] Elizabeth Boa tracks the literary and sexual exploitation of women in "The Murder of the Muse, or the Wound and the Pen: Figures of Inspiration in Wedekind's Diaries and Kafka's Letters to Felice," in *Frank Wedekind Yearbook 1991*, ed. Rolf Kieser and Reinhold Grimm (Bern: Peter Lang, 1992) 81–100.

[58] Best, "The Censor Censored," 283.

[59] On Buridan's notorious statement and its significance for Wedekind, see John Hibberd, "'Die Wiedervereinigung von Kirche und Freudenhaus': Wedekind's *Die Zensur* and His Ideas on Religion," *Colloquia Germanica* 19 (1986), 47–67.

function as her censor: "Ich habe dich nach meinem Belieben geschaffen, ich werde dich nach meinem Belieben umschaffen" (II, 413). Having been subjected to censorship of his artistic efforts, he proceeds to impose the same coercive strategies on Kadidja. The very repressive structures that enable Prantl's regime and secure his power to determine the shape of Buridan's career also facilitate Buridan's control over Kadidja, his power to drain her of her selfhood and to substitute his own desires for hers. But Buridan's tyranny in the domestic sphere was established long before the censor interfered with his artistic reputation. "Ich bin durch meine Nachgiebigkeit und meine Selbstlosigkeit ein ganz anderes Geschöpf geworden, als ich damals war, als du mich zu dir nahmst" (II, 386), Kadidja insists at the start of the play. The sexual politics of the domestic sphere are then doubled and refigured in the social politics of the public world.

Buridan, like Wedekind, endorses the emancipation of the flesh, yet his efforts to celebrate sexuality are predicated on the submission of women to a program of social control. It is Kadidja who recognizes that Buridan's emancipatory rhetoric is a sham, that it is deeply enmeshed with the repressive discourses from which it seeks to divorce itself. Buridan's efforts to legitimize sexual pleasure and to integrate it into public, institutional life (he speaks of a union of the church and brothel) turn out to be little more than self-serving efforts to master the threat of female sexuality through art and social control. "Wenn dich die natürlichsten Dinge mit Entsetzen erfüllen, dann gehörst du doch selbst zu der furchtsamen Menge deren blinde Furcht du immer verspottest" (II, 393)—Kadidja's words reveal the degree to which the playwright inside the work and outside of it was able to provide a critique of repressive social structures even as he remained a prisoner of the roles that he created to satirize those repressive structures.[60]

Wedekind's impersonation of Jack the Ripper in the Viennese production of *Büchse der Pandora* has a certain logic once we consider the ways in which both the playwright and the historical figure build their reputations on the sacrifice of women. Wedekind's theatrical empowerment of the feminine is, as we have seen, part strategy for containing the threat of female sexuality, part ruse for staging the self for an audience. The murder of Lulu by Jack the Ripper does little more than to cap the gradual mortification and effacement of Lulu engineered by the playwright Wedekind, who emerges triumphant to take a bow as both author and assassin on the Viennese stage. Pabst must have sensed the alliance between playwright and historical figure when he concluded his filmed version of the play with Jack and Alwa—the survivors—exchanging glances in the fog of London.

That the need to script the (self-)effacement of women was a vital part of Wedekind's real-life experience becomes evident as we read Tilly Wedekind's

---

[60] Note Tilly Wedekind's observation about her husband: "Er lebt nur mit und in seinen Geschöpfen" (*Lulu*, 188).

memoirs and realize how true to life the relationship represented in *Die Zensur* actually was. Tilly Wedekind's suicide attempt may have misfired (though it left her hovering near death for some weeks), but in other respects the details of what goes on between Buridan and Kadidja seem to correspond to what transpired in the marriage of Frank and Tilly Wedekind. Both Kadidja and Tilly were obliged to put rubber soles on their shoes at home—to be as if "nicht vorhanden" was the goal. Self-mortification and abject submission to the scripts written by the playwrights in their lives made suicide a logical conclusion to lives bereft of agency. "Das war ein Stück Arbeit!"—these words, spoken by Schön just before Schwarz cuts his own throat and by Jack just before he murders Lulu, reveal the way in which the effort invested in engineering a death or committing murder is repaid with a sense of triumphant accomplishment. Jack may be misguided in his belief that he has secured a collector's item, but Wedekind could congratulate himself on having produced a signal theatrical achievement over Lulu's dead body.

GEORGE C. TUNSTALL

Some Reflections on the Form and Motivic Structure of Hofmannsthal's "Die Beiden"

In his lecture entitled "Poesie und Leben" from 1896 Hugo von Hofmannsthal summarized the essence of a poem in these terms:

> Ich weiß nicht, ob Ihnen . . . nicht das Bewußtsein dafür abhanden gekommen ist, daß das Material der Poesie die Worte sind, daß ein Gedicht ein gewichtloses Gewebe aus Worten ist, die durch ihre Anordnung, ihren Klang und ihren Inhalt, indem sie die Erinnerung an Sichtbares und die Erinnerung an Hörbares mit dem Element der Bewegung verbinden, einen genau umschriebenen, traumhaft deutlichen, flüchtigen Seelenzustand hervorrufen, den wir Stimmung nennen. . . . Die Worte sind alles, die Worte, mit denen man Gesehenes und Gehörtes zu einem neuen Dasein hervorrufen und nach inspirierten Gesetzen als ein Bewegtes vorspiegeln kann.[1]

The text, which appeared in print the same year as the poem "Die Beiden," focuses on the words as the essential elements which by means of the ordering principle, the acoustical composition, and the content of the poem create a certain mood (Stimmung). But between the first and the second sentence of his analysis there seems to be a minor, but significant shift in emphasis. It consists in the difference between the expressions "die Erinnerung an Sichtbares und die Erinnerung an Hörbares mit dem Element der Bewegung verbinden" and "Gesehenes und Gehörtes zu einem neuen Dasein hervorrufen und nach inspirierten Gesetzen als ein Bewegtes vorspiegeln." Although in the first sentence Hofmannsthal maintains that in a poem visual and acoustical elements can be woven into an animated image, he seems to express himself more precisely in the second by indicating that in the creative process something specifically seen and something specifically heard can be transformed into the moving image that makes up the poem. In other words, the conceptual pairs of "Sichtbares / Hörbares" and "Gesehenes / Gehörtes" are not synonymous, but belong to two different semantic categories having to do with the visually and audibly perceptible

---

[1] Hugo von Hofmannsthal, *Gesammelte Werke in Einzelausgaben: Prosa I*, ed. Herbert Steiner (Frankfurt am Main: S. Fischer Verlag, 1950) 306–7.

and their reproduction in the lyrical work of art. The first pair belongs to a general category, the second pair to a more specific one.

This becomes clear if one tries to apply these categories to "Die Beiden." At first glance, for example, the visual or visible seems to predominate as the formative principle because the poem depicts a scene that occurs silently—at least the text does not explicitly indicate that either anything was said or that any sound was made: a young maiden wishes to hand a goblet of wine to a mounted horseman, but both of them are trembling so much that their hands fail to make contact and the wine is spilled on the ground. Upon closer inspection, however, it becomes clear that the audible or acoustical actually plays an important role in the expression of the visual image through abstract words. The mood is conjured up not only by means of the described action, but just as much through the sequence and sound quality of the words that depict the action. I will return to this aspect of the poem below.

What about the other conceptual pair: "Gesehenes/Gehörtes" (things seen / things heard)? This pair can be interpreted in more than one way. One could pose the question, for example, whether the pair refers to specific things observed or heard or to things in general that then become the material out of which a poem arises. The ambiguity in the statement also suggests another possibility, one that may at first seem positivistic and naive: on a different semantic level the pair could possibly refer to literary predecessors. When one considers, however, how freely Hofmannsthal dealt with literary forerunners in his poetry and dramas—as the secondary literature on him has pointed out in great detail—the question seems more legitimate and even relevant. This observation is the point of departure for the present study. I propose to approach Hofmannsthal's poem not just as a poem unto itself, but from the broader perspective of the poem as a symbolic configuration in which the poet responds to previously experienced literary phenomena by reshaping it into his own personal form. The two aspects I find most fascinating are the uncertainty concerning the lyrical genre to which the poem belongs and the motivic structure it manifests, both of which seem to point to previous literary forms and treatments—and yet the poem remains intrinsically modern and sui generis. In other words, I do not view the literary sources to which I point as direct influences, but more as possible creative stimuli or catalysts that may or may not have inspired Hofmannsthal in the composition of his poem "Die Beiden."

> Sie trug den Becher in der Hand
> —Ihr Kinn und Mund glich seinem Rand—
> So leicht und sicher war ihr Gang,
> Kein Tropfen aus dem Becher sprang.
> 5 So leicht und fest war seine Hand:
> Er ritt auf einem jungen Pferde

Und mit nachlässiger Geberde
Erzwang er, daß es zitternd stand.

Jedoch, wenn er aus ihrer Hand
10   Den leichten Becher nehmen sollte,
So war es Beiden allzuschwer:
Denn Beide bebten sie so sehr,
Daß keine Hand die and're fand,
Und dunkler Wein am Boden rollte.[2]

The poem's fourteen lines are divided into three stanzas: two quatrains and a sestet. The verses are consistently iambic with four beats per line. The rhyme scheme is, however, irregular: the first quatrain contains two rhymed couplets with consistently masculine rhymes; the second quatrain consists of the pattern typical for an Italian sonnet: an embracing rhyme (in this instance the first and fourth lines are masculine—like the entire first quatrain—while the embraced rhyme is feminine); the sestet contains a feminine rhyme pair in lines two and six. Thus the poem ends with the second member of the feminine rhyme pair: "sollte / rollte" that by means of the liquid consonants symbolizes acoustically the flowing of the spilled wine. The poem embodies therefore the curious rhyme scheme: aabb / acca / adeead.

    Let me turn now to the issue concerning the literary genre to which the poem belongs. In September of 1902 Rudolf Borchardt gave a lecture entitled "Rede über Hofmannsthal" in which he mentions the first collection of his friend's poetry—which included "Die Beiden"—that was to appear in print the next year. In this regard Borchardt notes: "Unter diesen Gedichten, die in sparsamer und vom Gefühl ungemeiner Verantwortung bestimmter Publikation vorgelegt sind, finden sich nicht zwei, die gleicher Art miteinander wären. Jedes ist für sich und enthält in sich eine ganze Gattung, deren einmaliges Muster es aufstellt."[3] One wonders, however, precisely for which lyrical genre "Die Beiden" is supposed to be a prime example. Although in the secondary literature the poem is usually considered to be a sonnet, a number of interpreters do not really seem completely satisfied or comfortable with this designation. Werner Kraft states, for example, "die größte Überraschung in diesem überraschenden Gedicht ist—: es ist ein Sonett. Daß Hofmannsthal die beiden Terzette zusammenzog, könnte darauf deuten, daß er diesen Tatbestand, von welchem er

---

[2]Hugo von Hofmannsthal, *Sämtliche Werke, I: Gedichte 1*, ed. Eugene Weber (Frankfurt am Main: S. Fischer Verlag, 1984) 50.

[3]Rudolf Borchardt, *Gesammelte Werke in Einzelbänden: Reden*, ed. Marie Luise Borchardt with R. A. Schröder and S. Rizzi (Stuttgart: Ernst Klett, n.d.) 73.

vielleicht selbst überrascht war, verheimlichen wollte."[4] Rolf Tarot refers to the poem in a similar vein as a "verkappte[s] Sonett."[5] What would seem to contradict designating the poem as a sonnet are, among other things, the rhyme scheme of the first stanza (aabb) and the four-beat iambic meter. In regard to this last point, it is worth mentioning that Hofmannsthal wrote sonnets in a number of different meters: "Sonett der Welt" and "Sonett der Seele" are, for example, both composed in a four-beat trochaic meter and "Erfahrung" is even in Alexandrines. The fact that "Die Beiden" depicts a brief dramatic scene also does not correspond to the conventional content of the sonnet.

Another issue perhaps more significant than these is Hofmannsthal's personal preference or dislike for the genre in general. Although the poet wrote a total of fifteen poems that could possibly qualify as sonnets, of these he selected only "Die Beiden" for publication in the first collection of his poetry. It is also noteworthy that the other sonnets were written between 1890 and 1891—five to six years earlier than this poem. In addition, Hofmannsthal is hardly mentioned in the voluminous literature on the sonnet.[6] One need only read through the fifteen poems in question to discover why this is so: most of them are simply not good poems. Werner Kraft may be correct when he maintains: "Er [Hofmannsthal] wollte [in "Die Beiden"] ein schönes Gedicht machen und kein Sonett, und nur weil ihm jenes gelungen ist, gelang ihm auch dieses, denn in seiner allerfrühesten Zeit hatte er Sonette gemacht, und sie waren schlecht und haben ihm vielleicht die Gattung verleidet" (*Der Chandos-Brief,* 57). Although we will never know for sure what the poet had in mind when he composed this poem, it is not likely he meant it strictly as a sonnet; there is just too much evidence against such a supposition.

Under what other literary category could one place the poem then? The two forms suggested most often in the secondary literature are the lied and the ballad. Max Kommerell comments, for example, in his *Antrittsvorlesung* from 1930: "Mit diesem seinem tiefsten Gedicht ['Weltgeheimnis'] nebst noch zweien 'Vorfrühling' und 'Die Beiden,' mit nur drei Liedern also, ist Hofmannsthal ein Erneuerer des echten Lieds,—einer seltenen und kostbaren Sa-

---

[4]"'Die Beiden': Zu einem Gedicht von Hofmannsthal," *Neue Zürcher Zeitung,* August 8, 1965: 4; rpt. in *Der Chandos-Brief und andere Aufsätze über Hofmannsthal,* Erato-Druck 16 (Darmstadt: Agora, 1977) 57.

[5] *Hugo von Hofmannsthal: Daseinsformen und dichterische Struktur* (Tübingen: Max Niemeyer, 1970) 197.

[6] Most recently and in the greatest detail in the Metzler *Realienbuch:* Hans-Jürgen Schlüter, *Sonett: Mit Beiträgen von Raimund Borgmeier und Heinz Willi Wittschier,* Sammlung Metzler 177 (Stuttgart: J.B. Metzlersche Verlagsbuchhandlung, 1979) 120–21.

che nach dem Bänkelgesang des ausgehenden Jahrhunderts!"[7] Several years later Walter Perl writes in his study of Hofmannsthal's poetry: "Eine Abwandlung der liedhaften Form zur knappen prägnanten Ballade wird in dem Gedicht 'Die Beiden' vorgenommen."[8] The balladic quality of the poem is also emphasized by Wilhelm Schneider in his sensitive interpretation of the work. After indicating in a footnote: "Das Gedicht läßt sich als ein Sonett auffassen" (footnote 1, p. 366), he broaches the genre issue in these terms:

> Zum Schluß noch eine Frage,... die Frage nach der Dichtungsgattung. Keines von allen Gedichten, die zu erfassen wir uns bisher bemüht haben, ist so ausschließlich auf die Schilderung eines äußeren Geschehens beschränkt, in keinem wird so "erzählt" wie in diesem von Hofmannsthal. In keinem ... sind Gedanke und Gefühl des Dichters so versteckt.... Man ist geneigt, "Die Beiden" in die epische Dichtung einzuordnen und in die Nähe der Ballade zu rücken. Man wird darin bestärkt durch den Gebrauch der Zeitform der Vergangenheit, die eben über Vergangenes berichtet.[9]

Schneider goes on to modify his statement by pointing out the poem does not contain an action of the same type one finds in the conventional ballad or verse narrative; he concludes in this way: "Es ist vielmehr eine Szene, ein Bild, und zwar ein Sinnbild für die Macht und den Zauber der Liebe bei der ersten Begegnung" (277). It is clear he is not completely satisfied with either the designation of sonnet or of ballad. Despite the four-beat iambic meter, the narrative tone, and the use of the imperfect that are popular in both genres, somehow neither explanation is sufficient to settle the question once and for all; and indeed it may simply be an unsolvable riddle, perhaps even the very intention of the poet.

Another suggestion may strike the reader as one that seems to be as plausible as the others. I believe one can come to a somewhat different interpretation of the form of the poem if one uses Schneider's conclusion concerning the content of the poem as a point of departure and approaches the poem from the viewpoint of what it depicts. Along these lines one might summarize then: the poem deals on the surface with an encounter between two people, a maiden and a horseman; on a deeper level, however, it is about love, although the word does not occur in the text. In this regard Walter Berendsohn remarked already in 1920: "Daß manches völlig Unausgesprochene in ihm [in Hofmannsthals Werk

---

[7]Cited according to *Hofmannsthal im Urteil seiner Kritiker: Dokumente zur Wirkungsgeschichte Hugo von Hofmannsthals in Deutschland*, ed. Gotthart Wunberg, Wirkung der Literatur: Deutsche Autoren im Urteil ihrer Kritiker. Karl Robert Mandelkow, vol. 4 (Frankfurt am Main: Athenäum, 1972) 395.

[8]Walter Perl, *Das lyrische Jugendwerk Hugo von Hofmannsthals*, Germanische Studien 173 (Berlin, 1930; rpt. Nendeln, Liechtenstein: Kraus Reprint Limited, 1967) 38.

[9]Wilhelm Schneider, *Liebe zum deutschen Gedicht: Ein Begleiter für alle Freunde der Lyrik*, 5th ed. (Freiburg, Basel, Vienna: Herder, 1963) 277.

im allgemeinen] ist, beweist das Gedicht 'Die Beiden,' das scheu davor zurückweicht, das Gefühl zu benennen. Es ist nicht Scham, was ihn hemmt. Er und Leute seiner Art scheuen nichts mehr, als sich gemein zu machen, sei es auch nur in Worten, mit der Masse."[10] "Die Beiden" is then a love poem and indeed one of especially noble character.

If one then considers in which of the many different types of love poetry a similar situation could occur, one might think of the *pastourelle* from Provençal poetry of the French Middle Ages in which a knight encounters a shepherdess and asks for a drink. The shepherdess, after whom this medieval verse is named, is, however, usually a simple being and more often than not ends up getting seduced by the knight. This situation is the opposite of the one in Hofmannsthal's poem, in which the sensual is transfigured into something sublimely noble.

Another type of love poetry, however, related to the *pastourelle* through its origin in Provençal poetry fits better into the framework of the poem under consideration, not only from the point of view of content, but also in regard to the lyrical form. The canzone played an extremely important role in the love poetry of the Middle Ages in general, but especially in the Minnesang of the High Middles Ages in Germany, in which love was treated in a highly stylized and idealized way. There is also—theoretically at least—a possible link between the sonnet and the canzone that would explain certain formalistic similarities in both types. Jörg-Ulrich Fechner writes, for example, in the introduction to his book on the sonnet:

> Die sizilianischen Dichter waren mit der provenzalischen Canzone vertraut und bildeten sie gelegentlich nach; warum also sollte das Aufkommen des Sonetts nicht im Zusammenhang mit dieser Form betrachtet werden? Die Canzone besteht aus Strophen, deren eine Möglichkeit aus zwei Stollen und einem Abgesang gebildet ist. Dabei war auch der Abgesang in sich zwiegeteilt und wurde kürzer als beide Stollen zusammen gefordert. All dies trifft auf die äußere Beschreibung des Sonetts zu, das so eine zahlenmäßig festgelegte Sonderform der Canzonenstrophe sein könnte.[11]

It is my intention to interpret in the opposite direction: that Hofmannsthal's "Die Beiden" is meant as an allusion to the earlier canzone form, or more precisely as a symbolic reflection of it.

If we accept for the moment the proposition that the canzone form of the Middle Ages could possibly have served as the inspiration for the form of "Die Beiden," then we need to look more closely at the text itself in order to determine if there might be some explicit or implicit indication of a medieval framework. Upon inspection, however, one discovers that Hofmannsthal's text is de-

---

[10] Walter A. Berendsohn, *Der Impressionismus Hofmannsthals als Zeiterscheinung: Eine stilkritische Studie* (Hamburg: Wissenschaftlicher Verlag W. Gente, 1920) 22.

[11] Jörg-Ulrich Fechner, *Das deutsche Sonett: Dichtungen, Galtungspoetik, Dokumente* (Munich: Wilhelm Fink Verlag, 1969) 21.

void of any explicit time and space references and hence there are no direct indications as to a possible period in history in which the encounter might have taken place. This temporal and spatial uncertainty in the poem is probably intentional on the part of the poet. One can attempt to flesh out the picture, so to speak, but I find that a rather precarious undertaking. A case in point is Nikolas Benckiser's commentary on the scene depicted in the poem:

> Das Gedicht läßt eine Szene vor dem Auge auftauchen: auf einem Burghof vielleicht; der junge Reiter blickt von dem nervös tänzelnden Rappen herab, gewiß mit einem Lederwams angetan, geschlitzte Ärmel, den Federhut keck auf dem Kopfe; sie tritt hinzu im Mieder, gefälteten Rock, ein Band vielleicht im Haar, Kostüme und Dekor in gedämpften Farben und im Stile "deutsche Renaissance." Zwar könnte man es sich zur Not auch im modernen Kostüm vorstellen; indes, man ist ja im ausgehenden neunzehnten Jahrhundert ....[12]

An interpretation along these lines threatens to destroy completely the magical atmosphere the poem succeeds in creating.

The timelessness and the lack of spatial references, combined with the configuration of horseman / maiden / goblet / wine, seems to suggest the Middle Ages more than any other epoch. Only one place in all the secondary literature on this poem mentions a similar sentiment—the interpretation by Julienne Bourgier for the Goethe Institute, in which she observes: "So einfach in der Sprache, wie dieses [das echte Volkslied] zu sein pflegt, rückt es [das Gedicht 'Die Beiden'] das Ausgesagte außerhalb der historischen Zeit und der nationalen Räumlichkeit; kaum ahnt man, daß die Beiden aus einem zeitlosen Mittelalter hervorgehen."[13] Unfortunately she does not discuss this matter. Curiously, Heribert Rück does not go into the possible medieval background to Hofmannsthal's poem in his detailed comparison of it with Walther's "Unter der linden, an der heide." He is interested in other features manifested by the two poems, such as the presence and perspective of the poetological ego.[14]

Let me pursue now the possibility that the canzone form may have served as a model for Hofmannsthal's poem. The first step will be to look more closely at this medieval form to determine if there are any cogent points of comparison between it and "Die Beiden." When this thought first occurred to me some years ago, it seemed plausible that the form of the present poem might have been arrived at by simply doubling the seven-line canzone stanza that was

---

[12]Nikolas Benckiser, "Hugo von Hofmannthal, 'Die Beiden': Dunkler Wein," *Frankfurter Anthologie: Gedichte und Intepretationen*, ed. Marcel Reich-Ranicki (Frankfurt am Main: Insel Verlag, 1976) 69–72; 70.

[13]Julienne Bourgier, "'Die Beiden' von Hugo von Hofmannsthal," *Beiträge zu den Sommerkursen des Goethe-Instituts 1967*, 101–104; 103.

[14]Heribert Rück, "Gedichte von Walther von der Vogelweide und Hugo von Hofmannsthal: Ein Vergleich," *Der Deutschunterricht* 14. 3 (1963) 5–19. The comparison between Walther's poem and "Die Beiden" is found on pp. 14–18.

popular in the Minnesang as well as in later periods. It usually consisted of the rhyme scheme ababcxc. In their book on German metrics Otto Paul and Ingeborg Glier cite as an example of this simple canzone form the beautiful one-stanza lied by Hartmann von Aue from *Minnesangs Frühling*:

> Swelch frouwe sendet lieben man
> mit rehtem muote ûf dise vart,
> diu koufet halben lôn daran,
> ob si sich heime alsô bewart
> daz si verdienet kiuschiu wort.
> sî bete für sî beide hie,
> sô vert er für sî beide dort.[15]

In this lied lines 1 and 2 and then 3 and 4 make up the two *Stollen*, which are joined by alternating rhyme (abab) and together make up the *Aufgesang*. The *Abgesang* consists of the orphan tercet cxc. In Hartmann's poem the rhyme scheme and the syntactical units do not correspond to each other, as one might expect of this form. In Hofmannsthal's poem, on the other, the syntactical units correspond precisely to the metrical units: if one overlooks for the moment the fact that the rhyme schemes in the first and second quatrains are not the same, then the two quatrains form the *Aufgesang* and the third strophe consisting of six lines forms the *Abgesang*. The general rule for the relative proportions of the *Aufgesang* and *Abgesang* to each other is that the *Abgesang* is usually longer than the single *Stollen*, but shorter than both together. That Hofmannsthal chose to print the two tercets together would also correspond to the canzone form.

What in Hartmann's lied also reminds of "Die Beiden" are—besides the simple story it tells—the four-beat iambic meter and the exclusively masculine rhyme words, as in the first stanza of Hofmannsthal's poem. Hartmann's text is also a love poem, not one of incipient love, but of abiding love. It is probably pure chance that the word "beide" appears twice in Hartmann's canzone. But it is nevertheless worth mentioning. Whether Hofmannsthal was familiar with this poem by Hartmann is also not known.

Although my speculation that Hofmannsthal might have arrived at his form in "Die Beiden" by extending the seven-line canzone stanza to fourteen lines is still possible, the secondary literature on the sonnet tells a different story in regard to the origin of the sonnet. In 1857 Karl Bartsch attempted to prove that the sonnet had indeed developed out of a doubling of the seven-line canzone. In his words:

---

[15] Otto Paul and Ingeborg Glier, *Deutsche Metrik*, 5th ed. (Munich: Max Hueber Verlag, 1964) 86. Hartmann's poem begins MF 211, 20. In my edition of *MF*, the 33rd without notes (Stuttgart: S. Hirzel Verlag, 1962), the *frouwe* appears as *vrowe* (297).

Ich denke mir das Sonett durch Verdoppelung aus der siebenzeiligen Strophe hervorgegangen, die ja die eigentliche Grundlage der ausgebildeten Kunstlyrik ist, in der Form

a b b a c c c,

oder im Abgesange irgend welche andre Stellung der Reime, die ja in den Terzinen des Sonettes auch keine bindende Stellung und Ordnung haben. Diese siebenzeilige Strophenform ist bei den romanischen Dichtern sehr häufig.[16]

Heinrich Welti disproved Bartsch's theory in his history of the sonnet published in 1884.[17] Subsequent theories on the origin of the sonnet have gone other ways.[18]

As further support for my interpretation regarding the form of Hofmannsthal's poem, one might mention the fact that, as a Romance scholar, the Viennese poet must have been abundantly familiar with the canzone form. The carryover of the a-rhyme into the *Abgesang* of "Die Beiden"—which is not found in the sonnet—would also seem to point to French poetry of the Middle Ages. Walter Bücheler points out in this respect: ". . . Characteristisch für französische Dichtung [des Mittelalters] ist das Anreimen des Abgesanges an den Aufgesang oder gar das völlige Durchreimen nach provenzalischer Art."[19] In any case, a comment by Hofmannsthal from 1896 concerning poems by Stefan George indicates that the poet must have been—at least fleetingly—familiar with German poetry of the Middle Ages, for he writes: "Es wird niemandem ... ein gewisses Verhältnis der 'Sagen und Sänge' zu dem Tone der Deutschen des dreizehnten Jahrhunderts entgehen" (*Prosa I*, 289–90). Heinz Rölleke's research into the Middle High German lieder in *Jedermann* has shown that Hofmannsthal was not familiar at first hand with the medieval German

---

[16]Karl Bartsch, "Der Strophenbau in der deutschen Lyrik ," *Germania* 2 (1857): 257–98; the quotation is from p. 290.

[17]Heinrich Welti, *Geschichte des Sonettes in der deutschen Dichtung. Mit einer Einleitung über Heimat, Entstehung und Wesen der Sonettform* (Leipzig: Verlag von Veit & Comp., 1884) 35–36.

[18]See Ernest Hatch Wilkins, "The Invention of the Sonnet," *MP* 13 (1915) 463–94; rpt. in Ernest Hatch Wilkins, *The Invention of the Sonnet and Other Studies in Italian Literature* (Rome: Edizioni di Storia e Letteratura, 1959) 11–39; John Fuller, *The Sonnet* (London: Methuen & Co. Ltd., 1972) 1–13; and Paul Oppenheimer, "The Origin of the Sonnet," *Comparative Literature* 34 (1982): 289–304; rpt. in Paul Oppenheimer, *The Birth of the Modern Mind: Self, Consciousness, and the Invention of the Sonnet* (New York, Oxford: Oxford UP, 1989) 171–90.

[19]Walter Bücheler, *Französische Einflüsse auf den Strophebau und die Strophenbindung bei den deutschen Minnesängern*, diss. Bonn, 1928 (Dillingen an Donau: Schwäbische Verlagsdruckerei, 1930) 13.

texts. The poet based his songs on New High German translations.[20] It is also not very likely that the poet was familiar with the canzone form from original texts in French literature of the Middle Ages.

Under these circumstances the question now arises: how could Hofmannsthal have become aware of the canzone form in the first place? The first indication of a theoretically plausible source for the poet's familiarity with this form is to be found in Walter Perl's monograph on Hofmannsthal's early poetry that I cited in another context above. At one point Perl notes:

> Mit dem Jahre 1896 ist der Höhepunkt der lyrischen Entwicklungskurve überschritten, der Dichter wendet sich der dramatischen Dichtung zu. Zugleich verklingt sein eigener lyrischer Ton seltsamerweise allmählich in einer Anlehnung an die überlieferten Formen der alten deutschen Volksliedichtung, die ihm die romantische Liedersammlung "Des Knaben Wunderhorn" vermittelt. (38)

In the secondary literature there has been occasional reference to Hofmannsthal's borrowings from certain lieder in *Des Knaben Wunderhorn*,[21] but not until Heinz Rölleke published his contribution entitled "Hugo von Hofmannsthal und 'Des Knaben Wunderhorn'" was a solid, scientifically supported connection established between the poet and this Romantic collection of folksongs.[22] At one point in this study Rölleke writes: "Es sei nur an Hofmannsthals bekanntes Gedicht 'Die Beiden' erinnert; der Eingangsvers 'Sie trug den Becher in der Hand' ist bis in die Wortwahl hinein dem 'Wunderhorn' Lied 'Das Straßburger Mädchen' verpflichtet: 'Es trug das schwarzbraun Mädelein / Viel Becher rothen Wein...'" (451). One could add to this that the gesture of spilling wine is mentioned explicitly in the second stanza of the lied: "Mein Mütterlein thut schelten / Verschütte ich den Wein...."[23] This lead, however, does not really take us anywhere.

---

[20] Cf. Heinz Rölleke, "Nochmals zu den mitttelhochdeutschen Liedern in Hugo von Hofmannsthals 'Jedermann,'" *Jahrbuch des Freien Deutschen Hochstifts 1979* (Frankfurt am Main: Freies Deutsches Hochstift, 1979) 369–76.

[21] In addtion to Perl, cf. Fritz Adolf Hünisch, "Hofmannsthal und das Volkslied," *Zeitschrift für Bücherfreunde* 2 (April 1910): 145; Jan Aler, "Reminiscenties," *Verzammelde Opstellen: Geschreven door Oud-Leerlingen von Professor Dr. T. H. Scholte* (Amsterdam, 1947) 332–38; Leonard Forster, "Hofmannsthal's Art of Lyric Concentration," *German Studies Presented to Walter Horace Bruford on his Retirement by his Pupils, Colleagues and Friends* (London etc.: George C. Harrap & Co. Ltd., 1962) 218–34.

[22] *Jahrbuch des Freien Deutschen Hochstifts 1976:* 439–53.

[23] Clemens Brentano, *Sämtliche Werke und Briefe, Historisch-Kritische Ausgabe*, ed. Jürgen Behrens, Wolfgang Frühwald and Detlev Lüders, vol. 6: *Des Knaben Wunderhorn: Alte deutsche Lieder*, Part 1, ed. Heinz Rölleke (Stuttgart etc.: Verlag W. Kohlhammer, 1975) 178. Further volume and page references to this edition of the work will be given parenthetically in the text preceded by BA for Brentano Ausgabe. The text of

But noteworthy in regard to our consideration of Hofmannsthal's relationship to the canzone form is the fact that the dedication to Goethe at the beginning of *Des Knaben Wunderhorn* contains a poem taken from Wickram's *Rollwagenbüchlein* (1555) that is written in the seven-line canzone form:

> Ich stund auf an eim Morgen,
> Und wollt gen München gehn,
> Und war in großen Sorgen,
> Ach Gott wär ich davon,
> Meim Wirth, dem war ich schuldig viel,
> Ich wollt ihn gern bezahlen,
> Doch auf ein ander Ziel.

The apparent orphan rhyme in line two is simply an example of how Arnim and Brentano treated the texts they gathered. Heinz Rölleke indicates in vol. 9, 1, which contains the variant readings to this part of the *Wunderhorn*, that line two in Wickram's version originally read "Und wollte gen München *gon*" (my emphasis; BA 9, 1: 72). Arnim's and Brentano's collection, which is a veritable treasure trove of lyrical forms, also contains many other poems written in the canzone form, for example: "Der traurige Garten" (BA 6, 194–95) and especially the love ballad "Der Graf und die Königstochter" (BA 6, 259–63), which because of the nobility and certain features of the love story reminds one vaguely of "Die Beiden." These hints, like the ones above, remain unfortunately inconclusive. Our observations concerning the canzone form and Hofmannsthal remain tentatively on the basis of mere interpretation. It is not possible to establish any closer connections with *Des Knaben Wunderhorn*. But the collection is still not exhausted as a possible source of inspiration for certain formal and acoustical characteristics in "Die Beiden."

The first lied in Arnim's and Brentano's collection, "Das Wunderhorn" (BA 6, 11–12), is germane to our line of argumentation for a number of reasons. It is noteworthy that the source for this ballad, from which the entire collection got its name, goes back to an "altfranzösische Romanze" that freely treats a section from the Anglo-Norman *Lai du Corn*, i.e., it deals with the courtly world around King Arthur.[24] The text of the poem reads as follows:

---

the collection is contained in volumes 6–8, the variants (*Lesarten*) to vol. 6 are found in vol. 9, 1 of the edition, ed. Heinz Rölleke (Stuttgart etc.: Verlag W. Kohlhammer, 1975).

[24] See Karl Bode, *Die Bearbeitung der Vorlagen in Des Knaben Wunderhorn*, Palaestra 76 (Berlin: Mayer & Müller, 1909) 459; and BA 9, 1: 76–77.

DAS WUNDERHORN

Ein Knab auf schnellem Roß
Sprengt auf der Kaisrin Schloß
Das Roß zur Erd sich neigt,
Der Knab sich zierlich beugt.

Wie lieblich, artig, schön
Die Frauen sich ansehn,
Ein Horn trug seine Hand,
Daran vier goldne Band.

Gar mancher schöne Stein
Gelegt ins Gold hinein,
Viel Perlen und Rubin
Die Augen auf sich ziehn.

Das Horn vom Elephant,
So gros man keinen fand,
So schön man keinen fing
Und oben dran ein Ring,

Wie Silber blinken kann
Und hundert glocken dran
Vom feinsten Gold gemacht,
Aus tiefem Meer gebracht.

Von einer Meerfey Hand
Der Kaiserin gesandt,
Zu ihrer Reinheit Preis,
Dieweil sie schön und weis'.

Der schöne Knab sagt auch:
"Dies ist des Horns Gebrauch:
Ein Druck von Eurem Finger,
Ein Druck von Eurem Finger

Und diese Glocken all,
Sie geben süßen Schall,
Wie nie ein Harfenklang
Und keiner Frauen Sang,

Kein Vogel obenher,
Die Jungfraun nicht im Meer

> Nie so was geben an!"
> Fort sprengt der Knab bergan,
>
> Ließ in der Kaisrin Hand
> Das Horn, so weltbekannt;
> Ein Druck von ihrem Finger,
> O süßes hell Geklinge!

Certain formal and textual features remind one of Hofmannsthal's poem: the rhymed couplets of the ballad correspond to the rhyme scheme (aabb) of the first strophe of "Die Beiden." In addition, all four lines of the first stanza in both poems end with exclusively masculine rhymes, which is unusual in a lied or ballad. Der Knabe "auf schnellem Roß" is also reminiscent of the rider "auf einem jungen Pferde" in Hofmannsthal's poem; and the gestures in both poems parallel each other to a certain extent:

Wunderhorn:	Hofmannsthal:
Das Roß zur Erd sich neigt,	Und mit nachlässiger Geberde
Der Knab sich zierlich beugt.	Erzwang er, daß es zitternd stand.

The acoustical similarity between "zur Erd" in the ballad and the rhyme pair "Pferde/Geberde" may be coincidence; but one begins to wonder, for Rölleke points out in regard to this very poem in Hofmannsthal's personal copy of *Des Knaben Wunderhorn*: "Die Bremersche 'Wunderhorn' Edition bietet auf S. 13 das Titelgedicht 'Ein Knab auf schnellem Roß.' Links neben den Gedichttitel hat Hofmannsthal drei kurze Zeilen mit Bleistift notiert, sie aber dann so energisch mehrfach durchstrichen, daß nicht ein Buchstabe zu entziffern ist."[25] Something must have occurred to the poet or at least have struck his fancy. As to the rhyme pair "Pferde/Geberde" it is also worth quoting what Rölleke reports in the next paragraph: "Auf S. 49 unten kennzeichnete Hofmannsthal die Eingangsstrophe des Lieds 'Das Rautensträuchelein' durch einen senkrechten Bleistiftstrich am linken Rand:

> Gar hoch auf jenem Berg allein
> Da steht ein Rautensträuchelein,
> Gewunden aus der *Erden*
> Mit sonderbar *Geberden*.

The emphasis is mine. Toward the end of his study on "Hugo von Hofmannsthal und 'Des Knaben Wunderhorn'" Rölleke returns to this rhyme pair in the poem above and comments: "Den Reim »Erden/Geberden«, den er [Hofmannsthal] im 'Wunderhorn' Lied 'Das Rautensträuchelein' angestrichen hatte, übernahm er nicht weniger als dreimal" (449). He then cites the three instances, beginning with "Lebenslied" (lines 21–22) from 1896, the same year in

---

[25] "Hugo von Hofmannsthal und 'Des Knaben Wunderhorn'" 440.

which "Die Beiden" was written; the other two are "Gesellschaft" (lines 3–4 of the second stanza) and "Der Jüngling und die Spinne" (in this instance in the singular in lines 32–34). Before moving on to the next topic, Rölleke concludes: "Auch dieser von Hofmannsthal offensichtlich besonders geschätzte Reim geht auf die 'Wunderhorn' Herausgeber selbst zurück" (449).

Reading through the entire poem "Das Wunderhorn," one discovers that a number of rhymes in it remind us strongly of similar ones in "Die Beiden." Especially the frequency with which rhymes with "Hand" occur is striking. "Hand" itself is found three times as a rhyme, the same number of times as it is used in "Die Beiden." In addition, two of the three times it occurs in the first line of a stanza; in Hofmannsthal it appears at the beginning of each of the three stanzas. A comparison of the rhymes with "Hand" gives the following result:

"Das Wunderhorn"	"Die Beiden"
Hand/Band (7, 8)	Hand/Rand (1, 2)
Elephant/fand (13, 14)	Hand/stand (5, 8)
Hand/gesandt (21, 22)	Hand/fand (9, 13)
Hand/weltbekannt (36, 37)	

Compare further the similar, although not identical, rhyme pairs that likewise occur in both poems:

Harfenklang/Sang (31, 32)	Gang/sprang (3, 4)
obenher/Meer (33, 34)	schwer/sehr (11, 12)

It is striking that all of Hofmannsthal's masculine rhyme words are monosyllabic.

Besides these similarities there is another basic principle that contributed to the shaping of both of these poems: the way in which the masculine and feminine rhyme words are used. In "Die Beiden" the masculine rhymes of the first stanza symbolize the firm, self-assured demeanor of the maiden. In contrast to this, the otherwise also secure poise of the horseman is momentarily threatened by the almost uncontrollable energy and force of the young horse. The precariousness of the rider's situation is indicated symbolically in the explosive quality of the pf-diphthong at the beginning of the word for horse, "Pferde." Normally one would expect in this context the designation for horse that is found in "Das Wunderhorn:" "Roß." But it is undoubtedly because of the sound quality that Hofmannsthal used "Pferde" instead. The animal is finally forced into standing still, and the feminine rhymes that symbolized the threatening loss of control are embraced by the masculine rhymes again, indicating that a disaster has been averted and a modicum of balance restored. In a similar fashion the feminine rhymes of the third stanza represent the disturbance caused by the emotional reaction of the two young people as they approach one another; in this instance, however, the disruptive emotional effect is not successfully overcome: they fail to make contact and the wine is spilled on the ground.

In "Das Wunderhorn" the feminine rhymes are used in the same way. Except for two places, the poem has consistently masculine rhymes. Only in the seventh and in the final stanza do feminine rhymes occur, and in both instances they are used in connection with the Wunderhorn itself: in the first case, as the boy explains to the empress how one plays the horn: "Ein Druck von Eurem Finger, / Ein Druck von Eurem Finger" (lines 27–28); and in the second, as the empress apparently plays the horn: "Ein Druck von Eurem Finger, / O süßes hell Geklinge!" Both poems therefore end with a feminine rhyme. It is possible that Hofmannsthal found in the acoustical make-up of the poem out of *Des Knaben Wunderhorn* a metrical principle that he then applied in his own poem in a similar—and yet different—manner; likewise rhymes that seem to have appealed to him and that enhance the artistic quality of his "Die Beiden."

In connection with *Des Knaben Wunderhorn*, and especially with the initial poem in that collection, there is another work that one could mention that also reflects certain similarities with "Die Beiden" that have to do with form, acoustical quality, and motivic structure. In the notes to the poem "Das Wunderhorn" Rölleke indicates for line 7: "Das Horn erinnert an Oberons Zauberhorn, das ein Zwerg Hüon überreicht (vgl. Wieland, *Oberon* II, 26–37, 49 und 54)."[26] The material for Wieland's verse epic, which carries the subtitle *Ein romantisches Heldengedicht in zwölf Gesängen* (since 1784), comes, as the poet himself explains in his introduction, "An den Leser," "aus dem alten Ritterbuche von Huon de Bordeaux;" the figure of the fairy king, however, from Chaucer's "Merchant's Tale" and Shakespeare's *Midsummer Night's Dream* (*Oberon*, 162). The close connection between Wieland's work and the Romantic collection of folksongs is therefore clear.

In stanza 49 of the second canto of Wieland's epic the effect of the magical horn is explained in these terms:

> 49. Ertönt mit lieblichem Ton von einem sanften Hauch
> Sein schneckengleich gewundner Bauch,
> Und dräuten dir mit Schwert und Lanzen
> Zehn tausend Mann, sie fangen an zu tanzen.
> Und tanzen ohne Rast im Wirbel, wie du hier
> Ein Beispiel sahst, bis sie zu Boden fallen:
> Doch, lässest du's mit Macht erschallen,
> So ist's ein Ruf, und ich erscheine dir. (*Oberon*, 193)

The rhyme scheme in this stanza, which is one of the four permutations of the stanza form that Wieland uses in this work, is similar to that in "Die Beiden": abbacddc.

---

[26]BA 9, 1: 78. I cite *Oberon* according to the following edition: Christoph Martin Wieland, *Werke*, ed. Fritz Martini and Hans Werner Seiffert, vol. 5: *Verserzählungen 2, Übersetzungen*, ed. Hans Werner Seiffert (Munich: Carl Hanser Verlag, 1968).

The fiftieth stanza of the canto continues the description of the horn and explains the magic goblet and its effect:

> 50. Dann siehst du mich, und wär ich tausend Meilen
> Von dir entfernt, zu deinem Beistand eilen.
> Nur spare solchen Ruf bis höchste Not dich dringt.
> Auch diesen Becher nimm, der sich mit Weine füllet,
> Sobald ein Biedermann ihn an die Lippen bringt;
> Der Quell versieget nie, woraus sein Nektar quillet:
> Doch bringt ein Schalk ihn an des Mundes Rand,
> So wird der Becher leer, and glüht ihm in der Hand." (193–94)

The last rhyme pair is noteworthy, especially the phrase "des Mundes Rand," which reminds us unmistakably of Hofmannsthal's line: "Ihr Kinn und Mund glich seinem Rand." In reading Wieland's *Oberon* one cannot help but notice that the word "Hand" seems to be a favorite of his, for it appears no fewer than 37 times as a rhyme word and is combined with an even greater number of words with which it rhymes. The rhyme pair "Hand / Rand" is used five times alone.

In the fourth canto of *Oberon* the hero, Hüon, encounters a Saracen, to whom he offers the magic goblet in order to test his honesty. At this point the rhyme pair "Hand / Rand" from the stanza cited above returns, almost like a leitmotiv, but this time in close connection with the goblet which is contained in the next couplet:

> 28. Mit scheelem Auge nimmt der Heid aus Hüons Hand
> Den Becher voll, und wie er an der Lippen Rand
> Ihn bringt, versiegt der Wein, und glühend wird der Becher
> In seiner Faust, der innern Schalkheit Rächer! (217–18)

The use of the rhyme pair "Hand / Rand" in relationship to the goblet, again, unmistakably calls Hofmannsthal's text to mind. The desiccation of the wine can also be considered in a certain sense as practically the opposite occurrence to the spilling of the wine in "Die Beiden."

The motif of spilled wine itself plays an important role in another poem in *Des Knaben Wunderhorn*, and indeed in one that is related motivically to "Das Wunderhorn." I refer to the lied "Die Ausgleichung" from the first part of Arnim's and Brentano's collection (6, 366–69) that combines material from two narratives of the Meistersingers, only one of which is of significance here. In "Die Ausgleichung" the horn of the first version (cf. BA 9, 1: 655) has been transformed into a goblet which serves to test the loyalty of a spouse. Here is the *Wunderhorn* version of the text:

> Der König über Tische saß,
> Ihm dienten Fürsten, Herren,
> Viel edle Frauen schön und zart,

So saßen sie paarweis.
Da man das erste Essen aß,
Da kam in hohen Ehren,
Ein Mädchen jung, von edler Art,
Also in kluger Weis.

Den Becher, den sie schwebend hält,
Von Golde ausgetrieben,
Der Königin sie reicht ihn dar,
Die Königin schenkt ein,
Ihn vor den König liebreich stellt:
"Das trink auf treue Liebe!"
Da kommt ein Knab mit gelbem Haar,
Trägt einen Mantel fein.

Der König biethet dar sogleich
Den Mantel weiß und eben,
Der Königin als Ehren-Dank:
"Wie schön wird er dir stehn!"
Drauf will er trinken alsogleich,
Da sprizt der Wein daneben,
Sie will den Mantel legen an,
Der Mantel steht nicht schön.

Der König und die Königin
Verwundern sich gar sehre,
Der König sieht den Becher an,
Den Mantel sie ablegt;
Da fanden sie dann beyder Sinn,
Geschrieben hell und here:
"Nur treue Lieb draus trinken kann."
"Die Treu den Mantel trägt."

Der Königin bracht ein Zwerglein klein,
Des Bechers Goldgemische,
Dem König lehrt die Feye sein,
Des Mantels alten Brauch;
Der Schimpf soll nun auch allen seyn,
Und Herrn und Fraun am Tische
Versuchten auch den Becher Wein,
Den Mantel also auch.

Den Herren wird der Bart so naß,
Der Mantel Fraun entstellet

Bis auf die jüngste Fraue schön,
Dem ältsten Herrn vertraut,
Dem wird der weiße Bart nicht naß,
Der Mantel leicht gesellet
Sich jedem Bug der Fraue schön,
Daß man treu Lieben schaut.

Den Becher läst der König gleich
Dem Ritter voller Treue,
Die Königin das Mäntelein,
Der Fraue, die ihn trug,
Zum Zwerglein ward der Ritter gleich,
Sein Fräulein wird zur Feye,
Den Becher und den Mantel fein,
Sie nahmen voller Trug.

Sie gossen aus den Becher Wein
Ein Tröpflein auf den Mantel,
Und gaben ihn der Königin,
Den Becher leer dem König.
Gleich trank der König daraus Wein,
Der Königin paßt der Mantel,
Vergnügt ward da die Königin,
Vergnügt ward da der König.

Nun prunkten sie noch manches Jahr,
Mit Becher und mit Mantel,
Und jeder Ritter trank ihn wohl,
Er stand wohl jeder Frau.
Doch wuchs mit jedem neuen Jahr,
Der Flecken in dem Mantel,
Der Becher klang wie Blech so hohl,
Sie stellten beydes zur Schau.

If the husband has been disloyal to his wife, "Da spritzt der Wein daneben," as line six of the third stanza explains. In the critical apparatus to *Des Knaben Wunderhorn* (BA 9, 1: 655) Rölleke refers again to Wieland's *Oberon* II, 54, as the source.

The original version of the poem "Die Ausgleichung" was published in 1802 by Paul Jakob Bruns. Of significance about this original version is that it was composed in the bar form that represents an extension of the Minnesang stanza. Rölleke prints the first section of the poem in BA 9, 1 (647–51); it reads this way:

Konig artus uber tysche sass
Im dinten fursten herren
yeglicher mit siner frouwen zart
also in hohem priss

Da man das erste essen ass
Da kam ein hohen ern
ein jungfrawe was von hoher art
also in cluger wiss.

Die truge an von golde ein rich gewande
Ob yrem heupt von stein ein harebande
Sie furt jn yrer hant
ein horn von helffenbeinen gar
es was beslahen vmb sinen rant
mit gulden buchstaben.

Striking in regard to this bar form is the fact that it corresponds in its division into two quatrains and a sestet exactly to the form of "Die Beiden." From this poem one gets the distinct impression that it may well have developed out of a doubling of the seven-line canzone stanza. That seems especially so in relationship to the first two stanzas with their rhyme schemes abcd / abcd.

The close proximity of this poem to "Das Wunderhorn" is not only apparent through the motif of the horn, but also through the similar rhymes that both works have in common, as well as share with Hofmannsthal's "Die Beiden." Hofmannsthal's poem shares even more characteristics with the first section of the Meistersinger work. To begin with, one could point out the corresponding context between the rhyme words "Hand/Rand:" "Sie furt yn yrer hant" and "es [das Horn] was beslahen vmb sinen rant." This impression is backed up by the beginning of the strophe: "Die truge..." and further enhanced by the acoustical similarity in the rhyme words "gewande/harebande." The narrative tone in this early version is also much like that in "Das Wunderhorn" and "Die Beiden." What seems to especially suggest a relationship between "Die Ausgleichung" with its original form and "Die Beiden" is the transformation of the horn from the first version into the goblet in the *Wunderhorn* lied. But there only the two Stollen of the original are retained and combined into one eight-line stanza; the sestet disappeared. Whether Hofmannsthal was familiar with the original version of "Die Ausgleichung" cannot be determined. It is, however, nevertheless noteworthy that "Die Beiden" shares these characteristics with that earlier poem.

Let me now summarize. In the course of this essay I have pointed to a number of works that have certain features having to do with form, acoustical make-up or motivic structure in common with Hugo von Hofmannsthal's "Die Beiden." I dealt in most cases with works that either themselves came out of the

Middle Ages or were at least in some way connected with medieval literature. These were chosen because they seemed to support my interpretation of "Die Beiden" as a symbolic reflection of the canzone form. If the texts I referred to affected in one way or another the composition of Hofmannsthal's poem, then they functioned more as inspirational catalysts than as direct influences, for Hofmannsthal's poem remains unique and unequaled. In its unity and stylistic perfection this work far surpasses the level of artistic quality manifest in the individual texts which may in some way have played a secondary role in the shaping of Hofmannsthal's poem. The connections and contexts that the present study points out are meant simply to deepen the understanding of the text in question and to contribute to the increased appreciation of literary works of art in general.

JAMES M. SKIDMORE

Responding to the Crisis in Leadership: Ricarda Huch's *Der wiederkehrende Christus*

The political situation of the Weimar Republic—the instability of successive governments, the bitterness of the armed forces about the causes of defeat in World War I, the nostalgia of many for the rule of the emperor, and the desire of many others for even more radical shifts away from the democratic reforms—had an impact on all Germans. The citizens of Weimar debated and worried about the future of the country, and many tried to bring about new political formations or restore old ones. The historian and poet Ricarda Huch (1864–1947) was no exception to this trend. A leading figure of letters before the Great War, Huch greeted the postwar period with scepticism and not a little anxiety. Although Huch was no great admirer of Wilhelmine Germany and its very Prussian character that exuded over-enthusiastic, if not chauvinistic, confidence in the German "spirit," Huch was disturbed to see Germany near collapse and in such disarray. But it was in these ashes of chaos that Huch found the possibility of a phoenix of national rebirth. Her letters of the period indicate her sense that renewal could come to Germany:

> Der Zusammenbruch so alter Mächte hat etwas Tragisches, und es kränkte mich anfangs, daß das Tragische im allgemeinen so wenig empfunden wurde. Schließlich muß man aber einsehen, daß sie wohl nicht hätten stürzen können, wenn sie nicht schon innerlich ganz morsch gewesen wären und nicht mehr lebendig im Herzen des Volkes gewurzelt hätten; infolgedessen läßt der Sturz im allgemeinen kalt.
> Ich war schon vor dem Kriege davon überzeugt, daß unsere Kultur auf einem toten Punkt angelangt war und daß eine Erneuerung kommen müßte. Wie so etwas kommt, das weiß man ja aber nicht, und man kann es auch nicht herbeiwünschen, obwohl man es für notwendig hält. Vielleicht kommt nach dem entsetzlich Bitteren, was man hat schlucken müssen, ein neues Leben. Es ist erfreulich zu sehen, mit welcher Intensität sich alles der Bewegung anschließt, das gibt Hoffnung, daß etwas Rechtes daraus wird. (September 17, 1918)[1]

---

[1] Ricarda Huch, *Briefe an die Freunde*, Herausgegeben und eingeführt von Marie Baum, Neubearbeitung und Nachwort von Jens Jessen (Zürich: Manesse, 1986) 79.

In September 1918 Huch was still passive in her critique; she was captivated by the death throes of the culture which she had known her entire adult life (Wilhelm II came to the throne in 1888, just after turning 30; Huch was 22 at the time). She was attracted by the tragic elements of cultural change; her culture was "dead" and in need of "renewal." It is not the collapse of the authority that bothers her so much as the inability of her fellow citizens to perceive this tragic denouement, tragic because the authority structures had been inwardly decaying for years while at the same time retaining a façade of health. In essence Huch was reproaching people for their lack of critical distance; to her mind, the culture was clearly in the final stages of a long decline, and if people had been more critical of the negative aspects of their culture, as opposed to defending it at any cost, they would have seen this passing as inevitable and not have been so surprised by it.

Huch's focus during the Weimar period became the advocation of a renewal within Germany. At first, in a move that was out of character for her, Huch attempted political involvement. She wrote an "Aufruf an die Jugend" for the *Deutsche Demokratische Partei* at the request of a Frau Dr. Kempf, but it was never made public, and no copy of this pamphlet exists.[2] She also tried to get herself nominated to the DDP party slate for the elections of January 1919, but failed in the attempt. These early failures dissuaded Huch from further active involvement, yet her interest in Germany's political situation remained keen, and her letters in the early 1920s indicate that she was following political developments closely.

Two political topics dominated her attention at this time: Bolshevism and leadership. She was attracted by the Bolsheviks because they were able to translate words into actions, something she felt unable to do herself. In an era of political impotence and drift, the leftist revolutionaries gained her admiration for their resolve and the force of their character. According to Huch, such strength of character was lacking in the German people and in their leaders. Huch was convinced of the need for a new beginning for Germany, but worried as early as November 1918 about whether there existed the willpower to carry out such radical change:

> Ich finde, begeistern kann man sich für das Neue nicht, aber man sieht durchaus ein, daß etwas Neues kommen muß, und insofern kann man ja restlos mitgehen. Ich hatte eigentlich Lust, eine, soweit es mir möglich ist, glühende Propaganda zu machen, damit ein Reichsverweser auf Lebenszeit gewählt würde (Prinz Max von Baden), eine Art Wahlkönig, nur daß man den Namen nicht ausspricht. Da sagte Wolfskehl neulich, viele neigten doch zu einer Kollektivregierung, und obwohl ich das im Grunde jämmerlich finde, scheint es mir doch, als hätte Deutschland augenblicklich nicht die Kraft zu einer

---

[2]Frau Dr. Kempf, letter to Ricarda Huch, December 26, 1918, Deutsches Literaturarchiv, Marbach.

Einzelvertretung und als müßte es sich ausruhen, so wie man auch Nervenkranke sich einfach ausruhen läßt. (November 11, 1918)[3]

The idea of an elected-for-life administrator of the empire in the person of Max von Baden might illustrate to some degree the naïveté of Huch's political discernment. But her emphasis on the need for strong leadership would remain with her in the 1920s. Perhaps this is what led her to visit a meeting of the National Socialists in early 1923, some months before the Beer Hall putsch:

> Hitler selber war nicht da. Manches von dem, was gesagt wurde, war vernünftig und sympathisch, aber in dem einen Punkt sind sie verbohrt. Und wenn sie nur verbohrt wären! Ich fürchte immer, Hitler selbst könnte von den Großindustriellen bestochen sein, um durch die Juden von ihnen selbst abzulenken. Ach Gott, ich habe Momente, wo mir der Ekel bis an den Hals geht. Und dann wieder kommt es mir jetzt besser vor als früher,—wir sind jetzt in dem Chaos, aus dem etwas hervorgehen und sich bilden kann.[4]

Her comments here—and her articulate denunciation of the Nazis in March, 1933[5]—show that there was little of Nazi doctrine that interested her. Rather, she appears intrigued by the mystique of Hitler (the first thing she mentions is that he was not present), and was probably eager to see if this man could incorporate the leadership traits she thought necessary to save Germany. She obviously did not find them here, and instead showed herself to be very perceptive about the motives behind industrialist support of Hitler.

Although Huch had been thwarted in her attempt to find a political role, she kept writing, using her historical treatments of various figures from German and European history—*Michael Bakunin und die Anarchie* (1923); *Freiherr vom Stein* (1925); *1848. Die Revolution des 19. Jahrhunderts in Deutschland* (1930)—to extol the values that she felt were absent in the Weimar Republic. The subject matter of the above histories reveals that the heroes of all three share two striking traits. The heroes, as presented by Huch, are all true leaders for they possess a combination of charisma and ideas that serve to define their greatness. But they also all share a similar fate: their "revolutions" fail. Bakunin is never able to establish an anarchist nation, Stein is frustrated by the fact that his reforms went mostly unheeded, and the revolutionaries of 1848 never see Germany united under a liberal constitutional monarchy. Did the failures of her heroes serve to expose Huch's own pessimism about the future of her beloved Germany, or were the studies her attempt, born of optimism, to underscore the positive potential of their leadership?

---

[3] Huch, *Briefe* 80–81.

[4] Marie Baum, *Leuchtende Spur. Das Leben Ricarda Huchs* (Tübingen and Stuttgart: Wunderlich, 1950) 264–65.

[5] Huch, *Briefe* 221–26.

Huch's major fictional account of the Weimar Republic is useful in any effort to understand more clearly Huch's concept of leadership during this troubled period. *Der wiederkehrende Christus. Eine groteske Erzählung* was written in 1925 and published the following year. In a letter to her publisher Anton Kippenberg at Insel Verlag, Huch gives an outline of the story to be used as an introduction on the book's dust jacket:

> Den Inhalt meiner Geschichte bildet die komische Situation, die daraus entsteht, daß eine christusähnliche Persönlichkeit in unserer sich der Humanität befleißigenden, zugleich aber sehr materiellen Zeit erscheint. Die Mächte des Tages versuchen die Persönlichkeit, deren Bedeutung sich geltend macht, für ihre Interessen auszunützen. Da ihnen das nicht gelingt, möchten sie sie beseitigen, ohne daß es aber zu wahrer Tragik oder zum Märtyrertum kommt, was der Zeit nicht gemäß ist. Weil das Komische ins Groteske gezogen ist und wegen der skizzenhaften Ausführung habe ich die Erzählung Schwank genannt; ich würde sie als Komödie bezeichnet haben, wenn das Wort nicht auf etwas Dramatisches schließen ließe. (September 12, 1925)[6]

An author's assessment of his or her own work often leaves much to be desired, even more so in the case of a promotional blurb, and Huch's is no exception. The many attempts which are made to co-opt the Christlike character (Luzius) are the scenes which come together to form the main plot. Luzius is the only natural leader in the story, and many others try to use his popularity and charisma for their own purposes. Huch's précis of her story, however, clearly illustrates that her intention is not to rewrite the story of Jesus, or to present an edifying story of Christian virtue, but to employ the archetype established by the reported life of Jesus in a fictionalized quest for a new perspective on the question of leadership in the Weimar Republic.

How does Huch's Luzius fit into the tradition of the fictionalized Jesus? In his study *Fictional Transfigurations of Jesus*, Theodore Ziolkowski develops a new category of analysis of the fictional Jesus figure. The essential criterion, in Ziolkowski's scheme, that separates fictional transfiguration apart from other treatments of the Jesus story is the presence of formal parallels: for a work to belong to the category of fictional transfiguration, it must be a work in which, "all questions of meaning aside, the events as set down immutably in the gospels prefigure the action of the plot."[7] In other words, the prefiguring occurs at the level of form, not ideology. Ziolkowski demarcates the scope of this new classification by establishing its difference from four previously used categories: the fictionalizing biography; *Jesus redivivus*; the *imitatio Christi*; and the "pseudonym" of Christ. The two former categories have as central characters a historical Jesus, unlike the fictional transfiguration which presents a modern hero, where-

[6]Huch, *Briefe* 143.

[7]Theodore Ziolkowski, *Fictional Transfigurations of Jesus* (Princeton: Princeton UP, 1972) 26.

as the two latter categories veer too far from the Gospel narratives to be considered fictional transfigurations.

For Ziolkowski, the "pseudonym" of Christ presents the scholar with the greatest difficulty for it is so easily confused with fictional transfigurations. This confusion stems from the category's broad scope: a "pseudonym" of Christ includes any novel in which "the hero is felt to be somehow 'Christlike.'"[8] Thus Kafka's *Der Prozeß* is often mentioned as a novel that belongs to this category. Although the story of Luzius has similarities to the story of Jesus found in the gospels, Huch's story is not about the second coming of Christ. Luzius never calls himself Christ; people call him that because of the miracles he performs. In Ziolkowski's scheme the character would fit into the "pseudonym" category. He is not really an example of *imitatio Christi* because there is no indication that he has made a conscious choice to live a life imitative of Christ's.[9] Even so, there are elements of Huch's story which approximate fictional transfigurations of Jesus, or at least of some of the events surrounding his preaching as recorded in the gospels. Luzius is in his early thirties. He heals the rejected and rebukes their oppressors. Luzius sometimes slips away from his followers in order to be alone with his thoughts. He is brought to trial by church authorities on the charge of heresy. Yet these parallels are rather weak, and do not have nearly the same resonance as the example from *Der Zauberberg* which Ziolkowski uses to begin his study.[10]

Despite Luzius's Christlike life, he escapes death at the end, appearing rather to begin his mission anew. Mission may, however, be too strong a word. There is no evidence that Luzius has received instructions from on high to proselytize, and his objective appears to be nothing more than an effort to heal, both physically and emotionally. Luzius "ist eine gewisse Heilkraft angeboren,"[11] and he uses this power mainly for the poor, because it is the poor who need help most. The son of German immigrants to Russia, Adelhart Luzius moves to Germany with his family when only a few months old; his mother, fearing rumors of impending war with Germany, moves the family back to Germany so that no one will have to fight the Fatherland. And his earliest memory is intimately connected with the most basic of elements, water and fire:

> Ferner erzählte er, daß er, obwohl er zur Zeit der Übersiedlung erst ein paar Monate alt gewesen sei, sich noch der großen Wasser der Wolga entsinne, über die sie gefahren wären. Das Wasser und das Feuer in der Schmiede seines

[8] Ziolkowski, *Transfigurations* 26.

[9] Ziolkowski, *Transfigurations* 23.

[10] Ziolkowski, *Transfigurations* 3ff.

[11] Ricarda Huch, *Gesammelte Werke*, ed. Wilhelm Emrich, 11 vols. (Cologne and Berlin: Kiepenheuer und Witsch, 1966–1974) 4: 201. Subsequent references to this edition of Huch's works will be noted parenthetically in the text by volume and page numbers.

Vaters wären seine ersten Eindrücke und gleichsam sein Spielzeug gewesen, indem er sich das Brausen des ungeheuren Stromes oder das lautlose Lodern der Flammen zu vergegenwärtigen gesucht hätte. (4: 225)

This attachment to natural, as opposed to human, habitat remains with him throughout his life. At one point in the story he quietly slips away from the town where he and his small band of companions have been staying and performing good deeds, and travels to the Eifel. There he hurries up a mountainside

> als müsse sein Schreiten in Fliegen übergehen. Oben sauste ein starker Wind und bog die zerfetzten Zweige einer alten Fichte, die vereinzelt neben aufgeschichteten Granitblöcken stand; sie sahen aus wie das Grabmal eines Ruhmgekrönten der Vorzeit. Von hier schweifte der Blick weit durch die bläuliche Septemberluft über Hügel und sanftrauschende Wälder; man hörte nichts als hie und da den wilden Pfiff eines Raubvogels oder das Knarren der windbewegten Fichten. Luzius blieb stehen und breitete die Arme aus. Da bin ich, rief es in ihm, bei euch, meine Brüder! Gefangen war ich, gebunden, geknechtet unter den Menschen, ich Sturm! ich Flamme! Nehmt mich auf, den Sohn der alten Götter, laßt mich frei mit euch brausen. O meine Einsamkeit, wie singst du auf unsichtbarer Harfe, wie duftest du nach welken Rosen! Wiege du mein krankes Herze und füll es mit feierlichen Gedanken! Er warf sich neben den Granitblöcken auf die Knie, schlang den Arm um die Steine und preßte die Stirn dagegen; so blieb er lange. (4: 293–94)

Luzius's emotional return to nature is marked by Germanic and Romantic imagery. The entire scene, the blocks of granite, the human figure dwarfed by the immense expanse around him, remind the reader of German Romantic painting in the vein of Caspar David Friedrich or Johann Dahl, whereas the "Rühmgekrönten der Vorzeit" conjures up images of the Germanic tribal ages. Luzius himself greets his "brothers," and one supposes he means the elements of nature that surround him. But he also addresses his isolation ("Einsamkeit") and asks it to renew his sick heart. Here, among the spruce trees and boulders and crevices, the same formations that painters like Friedrich imbued with a sense of Germanness, Luzius feels at peace, at one with himself and with his truly beloved nature; away from people he can find the solace and calm that he is missing in civilization. This becomes even more obvious during his trial at the Inquisition in Innsbruck. From the courtroom Luzius can see the mountains, and "seine Augen verschlangen die ambrosische Speise, die ihm so lange entzogen war" (4: 361). So intimate is Luzius's involvement with nature that, when he walks into the technological masterpiece that is a modern factory, the machinery stops (4: 217). Moreover, Luzius is able to instill this desire in others. The factory manager's wife describes this influence: "Ich wollte, der Frühling käme endlich, und ich könnte die Natur aufsuchen" (4: 235).

Luzius's work—his vocation of helping the poor—necessarily draws him into the thick of society and its ills. He performs many medical cures, miracles really, such as bringing young Hero, who apparently falls to her death in a factory, back to life. He also cures the farmer's wife, whose stoic belief supports her through all of her trials "denn es ist doch wohl nicht Gottes Wille, daß wir auf Erden schon im Himmel leben." Luzius replies: "Er läßt die, die ihn lieb haben, schon auf Erden davon kosten. Der Himmel ist mit der Erde verbunden durch unsichtbare Gänge, und an manchem Ort, wo es niemand ahnt, sind Pforten, die hineinführen" (4: 206). This statement underscores Luzius's belief that he does not actually perform the cures, but that God intervenes, allowing his grace to be felt by those who believe. Thus he says to Hero's mother: "Gott hat dein Gebet gehört: dein Kind atmet" (4: 218). Both Hero and the farmer's wife are examples of these gates: they are humble people who have been dealt harsh blows by the economic crisis of postwar Germany. Their poverty is also emotional: Hero's mother and the farmer, beaten down as they are by their tragic fate, treat their loved ones unkindly, even cruelly, and it is through the offices of Luzius that they are able to be reconciled to their families.

These reconciliations are Luzius's real miracles. The story opens in a park with Luzius talking to young Lindor, a (former) chemistry student who has taken to hanging around with Luzius. They are discussing the presence of evil and unkindness in the world, which Lindor thinks is the result of an improper education that does not impart Enlightenment ideals. Luzius finds Lindor's idea of goodness to be lacking vitality: "Etwas fade, dieses Gute, das du da aufgepäppelt hast" (4: 197). At this moment a chauffeur-driven automobile crashes into a bridge railing, and the passenger is thrown from the car into the river below. A discharged soldier by the name of Roland leaps to the rescue and saves the passenger, but once Roland notices that the passenger is Jewish, he turns angry and tries to drown him. Luzius then joins the fray and separates the two. He puts his face to the Jew's, and within minutes the Jew regains consciousness. Luzius tells Roland that he should be ashamed of himself:

> "Geh in dich, werde dir bewußt, daß ein Herr über dir ist, dem du verantwortlich bist für dein Denken und Tun. Bitte diesen Mann, den du so gröblich beleidigt hast, um Verzeihung."
>
> Mit dem jungen Manne, der die Ansprache zuerst halb trotzig, halb verlegen anhörte, ging eine Veränderung vor, als er seine dunkelblauen Augen zu dem Fremden aufschlug: er hatte einen solchen Menschen noch nie gesehen. Vor ihm stand ein mittelgroßer, gut gebauter Mann, der im Anfang der dreißiger Jahre sein mochte, mit einem Gesicht, das etwas Wildes und fast Erschreckendes hatte und doch zugleich einen unwiderstehlich hinreißenden Eindruck machte. (4: 199)

Luzius's specialness melts hearts, changes minds, turns foes into friends. He mediates, but subjectively, not objectively, and does not hesitate to chastise those whom he considers guilty of wrongdoing, such as the farmer who refuses to sit beside two Jewish women on a train: "Schäme dich! . . . und ihr andern schämt euch, daß ihr ihm zulacht, anstatt ihn zur Ordnung zu rufen. Was haben dir jene armen Frauen getan? Leicht möglich, daß sie besser sind als du" (4: 292). Eventually the travelers gather round him to listen to what he has to say, and he wins them over. But he wins them over without mincing his words; his message of love, understanding, and tolerance is forcefully, yet eloquently and charismatically delivered.

Luzius does not confine himself to healing personal relationships. His mission has political ramifications as well, if for no other reason than that he is living in times of political crisis, the aftermath of the war still affecting all of Europe. At one village he is able to avert an international incident by getting the inhabitants to disclose the location of a secret cache of arms. Luzius orders the weapons destroyed when he learns that they were intended for use against Germans by insurrectionists:

> Gott hat den Tieren Waffen gegeben, auch die Menschen sollen sie führen können, um Schaden von sich abzuwehren. Solange ihr euch gegenseitig nach dem Leben trachtet, seid ihr der Waffen nicht wert. Schuld habt ihr alle. Lehrte der Hohn und Übermut der Feinde euch nicht, euere Brüder zu ertragen, wer soll's euch lehren? Nicht am Haß des Feindes, am eigenen Haß werdet ihr untergehen. (4: 299)

No one escapes Luzius's wrath. The people as a whole—not just leaders or activists—are guilty of destroying their own society by means of intolerance and hate. Peace returns to the village as Luzius makes the villagers realize that only by loving and tolerating strangers as well as compatriots will they overcome their difficulties.

The gains Luzius makes appear paltry, however, compared with the forces allied against him. Huch's fictional postwar Germany cannot claim sanity for its motto as ever-crazier notions attract people's interest. There is a company which attracts serious investors in its attempts to Christianize Mars (Amach, *Aktiengesellschaft für Mars-Christianisierung*), and the Pope, in order to maintain control of evangelization, is a major shareholder. The company's fortunes rise and fall as new information is gathered about whether or not the civilization on Mars supersedes earthly civilization, even though all of these reports are fictitious. Yet this humorous satire of Weimar culture masks a more serious critique. The willingness to invest in Amach is indicative of society's manic appetite for new ideas and beliefs.

A number of skeptics and opportunists try to take advantage of the situation caused by the appearance of Luzius. A certain Prince Yp, posing as a man of science, is really just a dilettante who pretends to be a serious, objective student of the paranormal and the occult. He believes that everything can be explained in scientific terms, and hopes to find in Luzius a real medium with whom he can conduct controlled experiments.

Another figure of note is the industrialist Strowisch, the owner of the factory where Hero has her accident. A genial man, he is intrigued by Luzius, though not because he believes that Luzius is the son of God. In fact, he does not even believe in God, because a real god would not be lazy and take the seventh day off after creating the world; he would continue working! Despite his atheism, Strowisch attends church religiously, not to worship, but to practice his arithmetic, a habit he picked up as a child. Trying to find a way whereby he can make use of Luzius and his powers, he has dealings with the Pope concerning Amach and the Inquisition. He comes to the aid of the Pope at the end of the story when the Pope decides to burn a straw puppet in Luzius's stead (in the hope that Luzius will become a Bolshevist leader, an opponent the Church could prosecute with impunity and without fear of a popular backlash) by finding a task that can keep Luzius out of the limelight for the short term: Luzius is to be Strowisch's "Strümpfemissionär" in Africa in an effort to find a new market for Strowisch's oversupply of stockings, the result of the changes in fashion in the 1920s.

A more engaging remedy for Weimar's ills comes from what could be called the military reactionaries, who come into direct contact with Luzius by means of Roland. He is sought out by General von Finken, who believes that Germany needs a savior sent by God "um uns aus diesem Saustall zu führen. Erst muß er die Franzosen vernichten und dann den Kaiser wieder auf seinen Thron setzen" (4: 259). Roland must try to win Luzius for the General's plans to reorganize an army and attack France, because Luzius would be Germany's secret weapon: if his presence can stop machinery from functioning, then it could be used to immobilize French tanks. The general is convinced that Luzius is the Christ who has come to fulfill the prophecy spoken by Christ himself at the Last Supper: "Ich werde von nun an nicht mehr von diesem Gewächs des Weinstocks trinken bis an den Tag, da ich's neu trinken werde mit euch in meines Vaters Reich" (4: 258; Mark 14,26). Since, according to von Finken, wine would not be drunk in heaven, Christ/Luzius must mean earth, and "Vaters Reich" is really "Vaterland."

Although von Finken is an exaggerated, fictional portrayal, one would not have to go far in Weimar Germany to find officers who held similar views. The *Freikorps* and the later *Stahlhelm* organization were both led by ultraconservatives who favored authoritarian rule.[12] As much as Huch caricatures the figure of the general, she gives us an honest depiction of the effect of the extreme conservative rhetoric on former soldiers. Roland is easily won over, and he returns home dreamily after meeting the general:

> Was der General gesagt hatte, tönte noch nach in ihm, dazwischen blitzten vergessene Erinnerungen aus dem Kriege und Zukunftsgesichte. Er sah Deutschland siegreich, wiedergeboren, verjüngt, sich selbst zu Pferde, in Uniform, und plötzlich sah er ein weißes junges Gesicht mit Schelmenlächeln

---

[12] For more information on these groups, see Hajo Holborn, *A History of Modern Germany*, 3 vols., 1959–1969 (Princeton: Princeton UP, 1982) 3: 529–31; 587–89.

ihm zur Seite und empfand ein heftiges Glücksgefühl wie einen schmerzenden Stich. Er beschleunigte seine Schritte, als müßte er fliehen; blaß und atemlos kam er in der Herberge an.... (4: 263)

This mixture of happiness and horror at first scares Roland, but he quickly overcomes it to become an active member in von Finken's league. Luzius confronts Roland not long after he starts spending his evenings taking part in secret practices and preparations for war under the guise of "gymnastics for youth," and knows exactly what his follower is up to. When Roland finally works up enough courage to ask Luzius to lead the German troops into battle, Luzius challenges him to forget the idea of attacking France because this plan is straining their friendship. Despite Roland's assertion that nothing could come between him and Luzius (reminiscent of Peter's protestations that he would never forsake Jesus), Luzius wonders what will have been decided if Germany defeats France. Roland's naive, almost programmatic response echoes the nationalist rhetoric of the *Stahlhelm*:

> Was damit entschieden wäre?... Ich bin kein weltblickender Staatsmann, kann dir keinen politischen Ausblick aufrollen. Ich spreche aus meinem Gefühl für mein Volk und mein Land. Ich habe erlebt, wie die Deutschen überall zurückgedrängt wurden, erlebe, wie man über uns hinfährt, als wären wir gewissen. Was in den Sternen über uns geschrieben ist, weiß ich nicht; solange ich lebe, kämpfe ich um das Dasein meines Volkes, damit es weiterlebe, weiterblühe. (4: 276)

Although Luzius understands Roland's emotions, admitting even immediately after the war he might have been persuaded to undertake an attack on France, he refuses to do so now.[13] Luzius is skeptical of Germany's unity of purpose, and worries that Roland and his friends are thinking more of conquering than the consequences of conquest:

> Nur ein Volk, das siegen will, bringt einen Führer zum Siege hervor.... Seid erst einmal ein Volk... habt erst einmal einen Willen! Aber selbst dann, wenn hier ein Volk wäre, das siegen wollte, so kann sein Genius, der es mit dem Geisterreich verbindet, welches allein ewig ist, Untergang, Vergessenheit

---

[13]Luzius's admission that at one time he might have shared Roland's aggressive positions could point to Huch as well; although there is no direct indication in her letters that she wanted to resume the war in order to sue for a better peace, she may well have thought it, considering her disappointment at Germany's submissiveness in the face of defeat. Moreover, during the war Huch gave three or four lectures in Switzerland discussing the idea that the hero develops in the midst of struggle. These talks, now lost, caused a small outcry in the local press. (Cf. Baum, *Leuchtende Spur*, 219.) Yet surely they proposed a similar glorification of the virtue of battle. In *Der wiederkehrende Christus* Huch, through Luzius, demonstrates her realization that such an ethic ignores the suffering endured by those who must fall so that others may glory in the revitalization of their spirit.

und Auflösung wollen. Und du selbst, wenn du nachdenkst, mußt dir sagen: ist nicht das Schönste am Siege das Siegen selbst? Das Hinwerfen der Seele in den Abgrund, der Todesrausch des bekränzten Opfers, das Aufflammen der Erfüllung, wenn die letzte Kraft auf dem rauchenden Altar ergossen ist? An das Einheimsen der Früchte denkst du nicht, an das Verteilen der Beute, an das Elend der Verwaisten, an die Mittagsruhe der Gesättigten. (4: 277)

The exhilaration of victory, of throwing all of one's self into an action that can have the greatest of outcomes or mean certain death, is what Luzius fears in a united people, not to mention the insufferable lot that their victory will impose on others. But then, he is not even sure that the Germans share a common spirit, a common will, anymore. Besides questioning the unity of the German people, Luzius questions the spoils that such a victory would bring: "Besserung der Finanzen—Aufblühen der Industrie—günstige Handelsverträge—Reicherwerden der Reichen, Schwächerwerden der Schwachen" (4: 277)—these are not the goals of his life's work. When later pressed by Roland to join the corps in a renewed struggle against France, Luzius emphasizes his desire to change society fundamentally, to counteract the vengeful nationalism of Roland and his comrades:

> Lösche einmal die Rache aus. Gefällt es euch, wenn die Polen sich rächen? Und wer hätte mehr Ursache als sie? Nein, es muß von Grund aus anders werden. Ich will versuchen, einen neuen Gottesfrieden zu begründen, in den einzelne Personen, Gesellschaften, Fluren und Äcker, Dörfer und Städte eintreten können. Die Allmacht der Staaten muß durchbrochen werden. (4: 306)

Roland's insistence on military action causes Luzius to revise his own plans. He resolves to start preaching a message of tolerance and peace, and prepares to start this "revised" mission in France; Roland, who would follow Luzius into hell, refuses to go west of the Rhine, so strong is his hatred of the French.

The last proposed cure for the troubles facing Germany and Europe is an old-fashioned one proposed by the Catholic Church: the reinstatement of the Inquisition. Huch depicts the church hierarchy as populated by fools: Pope Gregory XIV wants to canonize Brutus, who lived before Christ, because he was the quintessential Roman; none of the cardinals wishes to play chess with the Pope because he is a poor loser, so it falls to Cardinal Sant' Elmo, an incompetent player, to be the Pope's partner; the Cardinal Inquisitor, Donara, travels with all of his belongings to Innsbruck, site of the Inquisition, because it is disadvantageous to purchase anything abroad.

The Church reintroduces the Inquisition for a number of reasons. Donara speaks of ridding the occident of the "Krebs der Irreligiösität" (4: 342): the Church is reacting to the same problems of anarchy, disorganization, and lack of respect for older forms of order that disturb other sectors of society. Ordonelli, the special emissary of the Pope to the German Protestant church, puts the blame for the breakdown of society on the spirit of tolerance that was ushered in by the Age of Enlightenment; people are no longer holy, and the only way to return them to holiness is "mit einer Grausamkeit, die im höheren Sinne Barmherzigkeit ist" (4: 251). Surprisingly, the German Protestants concur wholeheartedly with the Italian Catholics. Justizrat Eierleib responds on behalf of Germany:

> Ich glaube,... daß Deutschland jetzt dafür reif ist, ja, eigentlich danach seufzt. Vor Jahrhunderten verwarfen wir die Inquisition, weil wir einem Zeitalter aufblühender Wissenschaft entgegengingen. Aber wohin hat uns diese geführt? Ins Verderben. Was wir brauchen, ist eine Überzeugung, eine feste, unerschütterliche Überzeugung.... Wir brauchen Unwissenheit, Unwissenheit und Angst. Das viele Wissen und Denken erzeugt den Veitstanz im schwachen Menschengeschlecht. Ein Stand von Priestern und Richtern soll die Wissenschaft pflegen, das Volk soll bescheiden seiner Arbeit und seinen erlaubten Vergnügungen nachgehen. Dahin muß es wieder kommen! Ägypten muß unser Vorbild sein! (4: 253–54)

The Churches want people to worship, not to know, and they see the Inquisition as the ideal means of returning the world to that state of affairs where the pursuit of knowledge, just like the pursuit of pleasure or of work, is strictly controlled. The Church shares the opinion of industrialists in seeing Bolshevism as the root of this evil; as Strowisch puts it, "im Abendlande müsse die Inquisition hauptsächlich dazu dienen, den Bolschewismus zu unterdrücken und Ordnung zu schaffen" (4: 328). The intimate relationship between the Church and commerce is symbolized by the site of the Inquisition: the chosen church being too cold, the tribunal makes its home in a bank that strikes Cardinal Donara as being perfectly suited to the business at hand. When the Inquisition is announced, public opinion endorses its reinstitution.

Luzius is found guilty of heresy by the Inquisition, but the Pope does not wish to execute him, especially after a popular revolt on Luzius's behalf nearly succeeds. As mentioned above, his escape is arranged by Strowisch, but instead of selling stockings in Africa, Luzius, who is accompanied by Strowisch's pilot and Herr Leisegang, a filmmaker who has made documentaries of Luzius's adventures, escapes to the German countryside and walks "durch die schleierweiche Oktoberluft über die braune Heide, das Feuer der Liebe im Herzen" (4: 405). So ends the story.

By the time Luzius heads off across the moors, the reader has traveled through dizzying turns and twists, with some plot strands being resolved and many others remaining dangling. This discordant polyphony evokes a society reeling out of control. Against the forces of authoritarianism—be they military, commercial, ecclesiastical, or technological—that were poised to assert their power stands one man who has discovered God through nature, who by the sheer force of his personality offers an alternative to the reimposition of the status quo, to the usurpation of human freedom through commerce and technology, and to the corruption of the German spirit. The people themselves are seen as weak and suffering, and all of the other figures in the story, whether they be oppressors or victims, lack the strength to withstand the tide of modernity—an era Huch views and depicts as confused, crazed, and dangerous.

Huch wrote *Der wiederkehrende Christus* at the midway point of the Weimar Republic's short democratic life, halfway on the road that led from Wilhelm's abdication to the seizure of power by Hitler. Her protagonist is not a refiguration of Christ, even though he can work miracles and preaches an evangel that many do not want to hear. Huch's lonely "Christ" wishes not to save humanity from its sinfulness, but rather Germany from its anger, hateful intolerance, and disunity. As Luzius makes clear to Roland, he is sceptical about the Germans' unity of purpose and sees that he must devote his energy to healing that ailment; otherwise, the country will never be able to move forward. By creating the story of this character and his travails, Huch was able to give voice to both her hopes and concerns. Luzius is the fictional representation of the charisma which Huch sought without success in Weimar society. Possessing a clear vision of what society ought to be along with a gift for healing people both physically and spiritually, Luzius is Huch's ideal leader: he combines charisma with an ability to renew Germany.

In addition to this utopian characterization, Huch is also realistic enough to portray the near impossibility of Luzius succeeding in a society that is plagued by pernicious *intrigants* and hucksters. Luzius maintains his integrity and independence—it is perhaps his greatest distinguishing feature—but he is not able to overcome the influence of the forces that are allied against him and ripping apart the very fabric of German, and modern European, culture. If scripture had recorded in detail the politics that surrounded the appearance and trial of Jesus, Huch's story could very easily be read as a fictional transfiguration of the machinations of various interest groups which attempted to use Jesus for their own purposes or destroy him.

In the end it appears that Huch is not able to accomplish much more with this fictional narrative than she was able to accomplish with her histories of Bakunin, Stein, and the Revolution of 1848. Luzius, her fictional hero, is as unsuccessful as her historical protagonists, and the leadership question remains unsolved for there is no solution as to where Germany is going to find such leaders. Yet at the same time the story ends on an optimistic note. Luzius is once again free from the mechanical world that is so foreign to this man of nature. As he crosses the German landscape, love burning in his heart, he takes on the mantle of the Romantic hero: one with nature, he will resist a world that has become too mechanical, a world whose rationality has been so sorely overtaxed by hate and intolerance that it no longer functions smoothly or even logically. In short, Luzius preserves by his very existence the true spirit of the German people. As he yelled on the mountaintop, he is the storm and flame, the son of the old gods, the truly *Germanic*: he embodies the intangible essence of Germanness that has been corrupted by war, capitalism, organized religion, and the weakness of the people to withstand these forces. Indeed, Huch has created more than a Romantic hero: Luzius's embodiment of the Germanic reminds the reader of Nietzschean idealism.

In spite of the dangers that come with assuming that a nationality can also possess its own inherent nature, Huch never lost her faith in the goodness and strength of the German character. At the end of the Second World War, as Germany lay divided and in ruins, Huch rose up to defend her conception of the German identity. Responding to Hermann Hesse's public admonition that his Swabian friends should abandon their national feeling ("Nationalgefühl"), Huch countered that it was just at this moment, in Germany's darkest hour, that *Nationalgefühl* was most necessary, for without this sense of patriotism, Germany would never achieve the self-confidence necessary to pull itself out of its misery (5: 950–52). Huch's definition of *Nationalgefühl* was not the jingoistic pride of the Wilhelmine or Hitler eras. It was, rather, the character that Luzius embodies: tolerance of one's enemies and a desire to be united for the purpose of internal well-being, not external advancement.

Der wiederkehrende Christus provides Huch with a site where her optimism and pessimism, her hope for the future and her dissatisfaction with the past and present can counter each other. For as much as Huch would look to particular figures from Germany's past or to her own fictional characters (such as Luzius) to incorporate her ideal German identity, Huch could not find this quality in abundance among her fellow citizens during the Weimar Republic. Huch envisioned a new solution to Germany's woes which did not rely on the old ultranationalistic-militaristic ethic, but which rather consisted of a renewal of the German spirit by turning towards tolerance. The possibility that this reality might be rediscovered filled her with hope and encouraged her to use her pen to promote its existence, but she understood that this turn had many enemies, not the least of which was the country's own despondency and lack of moral courage. In her eyes the country got—and suffered—the leadership it deserved.

SCOTT ABBOTT

Postmetaphysical Metaphysics?
Peter Handke's *Repetition*

> *Pete and Repeat were sittin' on a fence. Pete fell off. Who was left?*
> *Repeat.*
> *Pete and Repeat were sittin' on a fence. Pete fell off. Who was left?*
> *Repeat.*
> *Pete and Repeat were sittin' on a fence. Pete fell off. Who was left?*
> *Repeat.*
> *Pete and Repeat were sittin' on a fence. Pete fell off. Who was left?*
> Bruce Nauman, from "Clown Torture"
> (1987, Amsterdam)
>
> *From desolate repetition to sanctifying repetition: that is, the joy of repetition is only possible when I, having departed into the unknown, am at a loss*
> Handke, *Phantasien der Wiederholung*

Describing Handke and Heidegger in his fine *Der Freudenstoff: Zu Handke eine Philosophie*, Peter Strasser recognizes that the assertions of salvific harmony through art he thinks he reads in both men's work may raise some eyebrows, and he avoids the problem simply by asserting that "I don't want to comment on the sense or nonsense of this perspective."[1] Others, however, have been more forthcoming with their evaluations of Handke as metaphysician. Jürgen Egyptien, for example, says in a discussion of *Repetition* that "Handke's texts pretend to be the words of Moses, the secret Decalogue of our time, the continuation of the holy scripture;" and he disparagingly quotes parts of a sentence from Handke's conversation with Gamper as evidence of Handke's mystical, aesthetic religion: "the final and only rational kingdom . . . will surely be the kingdom of writing, the kingdom of storytelling."[2] There is, perhaps, a mystical feel to this; but it is hardly fair that Egyptien leaves out the word "nonmetaphysical" in his quotation (part of the ellipsis).

[1] (Salzburg: Residenz, 1990) 18. Translation mine unless otherwise noted.

[2] "Die Heilkraft der Sprache: Peter Handkes *Die Wiederholung* im Kontext seiner Erzähltheorie," in *text + kritik*, ed. Heinz Ludwig Arnold (Munich: text + kritik, 1989) 54.

It is not difficult to make Handke sound silly—the "Heino [a cherubic pop singer] of metaphysics," as Walter Jens evidently called him. To do so one simply discounts Handke's suggestion that he is a dialectical writer and focuses on scenes (without reading them closely) that feel metaphysical. Ignoring the material nature of Handke's work, the continuous, insistent, antimetaphysical stance, and the self-consciously constructed, contingent nature of every positive assertion, such "readers" can lament with Manfred Durzak that Handke "has catapulted himself with a *Salto mortale* into salvation and has thereby lost his artistry."[3] Andreas Huyssen, castigating the new romanticism he sees in postmodernism, joins this chorus when he suggests that that "fits in all too well with, say, the celebrations of the prophetic word in the more recent writings of Peter Handke."[4] Peter Sloterdijk is more positive about Handke's recent work (although his statement about nausea and meaning reveals an inability to see Handke's dialectic): "In Peter Handke's development, we can observe the stages subjective positivism can run through: language critique, language-game actions, logical treatment of nausea; then from senselessness to faint-hearted sensuousness, to new narration; circling around the first 'true feeling'; labor of recollection. Nausea and meaning cannot coexist in the long run. In understanding this, Handke is on the way to becoming a significant writer."[5] And although he writes of the pretentiousness of "Peter Handke, who, in the meantime, has set out to give poetry once again the quality of prophetic song," Jürgen Habermas also states the need for such a project, as long, he says, as it arises in the context "of a demystified and demythologized world." Habermas then suggests, in words Handke might have used, that we should "stand firm against the danger of losing the light of the semantic potential once preserved in myth."[6]

I can think of no better words to summarize my discussion of Handke's postmetaphysical metaphysics: Peter Handke writes to regain the "light of semantic potential" in the context of a world he has helped demystify and demythologize.

---

[3] *Peter Handke und die deutsche Gegenwartsliteratur: Narziß auf Abwegen* (Stuttgart: Kohlhammer, 1982) 159.

[4] *After the Great Divide: Modernism, Mass Culture, Postmodernism* (Bloomington: Indiana UP, 1986) 180. He might well take another look at the "prophetic word" of *Die Wiederholung:* ". . . laboraverimus," the simple proclamation that we will have worked, that although we won't have approached some metaphysical telos, we will have created meaning of some sort and will not be suffering the consequences of nihilism.

[5] *Critique of Cynical Reason*, transl. Michael Eldred (Minneapolis: University of Minnesota Press, 1987) 409.

[6] *Nachmetaphysisches Denken: Philosophische Aufsätze* (Frankfurt am Main: Suhrkamp, 1988) 275. Habermas provides a remarkably clear account of the general philosophical debate in which Handke's book and this essay take part. See especially "Metaphysik nach Kant" (chapter 2) and "Motive nachmetaphysischen Denkens" (chapter 3).

Peter Handke's novel *Repetition* (1986) begins with an epigraph from the mystical, Jewish *Zohar*: "'The kings of old died; they could not find their food.'"[7] As the metaphor of a lost and sought-for king unfolds in the novel, it raises the question of metaphysics in the work of an author known for his opposition to metaphysics.[8]

Early in the novel the reader learns that the Kobal family's most important (but perhaps adopted)[9] ancestor, Gregor Kobal, led a peasant revolt against the Habsburg Kaiser in 1713. For his efforts he was beheaded and his family exiled. "It was he who had said . . . that the Emperor was a mere servant and that the people had better take matters into their own hands!" (4). In the context of the

---

[7] *Die Wiederholung* (Frankfurt am Main: Suhrkamp, 1986); *Repetition*, transl. Ralph Manheim (New York: Collier, 1989).

[8] For example, in Handke's early play *Weissagung*, an attempt to demonstrate the empty circularity of metaphor, four actors recite lines like "The flies will die like flies" and "The pig on the spit will scream like the pig on the spit." The following lines from the long poem "Die Sinnlosigkeit und das Glück" similarly reflect Handke's postmetaphysical thinking. Note how Handke discards "meaning" and "meaninglessness" to reside in common, unsystematized sights:

> The opposite of meaninglessness is not
> meaning—
> one no longer needs meaning,
> nor does one seek a philosophical meaning for
> meaninglessness:
> used up words; that ought to be forbidden,
> one thinks.
> . . .
> And with what do you return home
> in the evening?—
> With such sights, for example, answers
> the collector of sights proudly.
> And how do you order them?—
> Because the fear of meaninglessness is past,
> they no longer need an order.

Als das Wünschen noch geholfen hat (Frankfurt am Main: Suhrkamp, 1974) 103–19.

[9] Handke's texts incessantly criticize closed systems of thought and attempt to avoid their own tendency, as texts, toward closure. As a result, even the most innocent assertion, like that made here about Gregor Kobal as an ancestor, must be qualified. The narrator in one place simply states that Kobal is an ancestor, and later repeats and revises that to suggest that perhaps he was adopted. Cf. the following from *Phantasien der Wiederholung*: (Frankfurt am Main: Suhrkamp, 1983): "To hold open emptiness: that would be the highest art" (41); "The constant, necessary, almost-speechlessness of art, of writing, of the art of writing: only this, saying-what-is-the-case-with-halting-voice, the liminal word, will be heard in eternity" (33).

epigraph from the *Zohar* about defunct, mystical, mythical kings, I interpret this eighteenth-century turn from the Kaiser and his authority as the modern age's turn from metaphysics (beginning in the eighteenth century with Kant). That leaves the Kobal family (and Handke's readers) without a comforting philosophical home. Whether the new condition is to be lamented or praised depends on perspective and personal taste.

The Kobals themselves respond diversely to their liminal existence. The novel's narrator, Filip Kobal, reports that for his father the part of this story that counted "was not that his ancestor had been a rebel and guerrilla leader, but that he had been executed and that his family had been banished.... He behaved as if a supreme will, more powerful than that of the emperor who many years ago had ordered the execution of our ancestor Gregor Kobal, decreed that after the disappearance of his eldest son, the last of that name, he must suppress any Slovene sound in his house" (48–49). One response, then, to the condition in which one is cut off or has cut oneself off from metaphysics is absolutely to refuse to speak that language.

In contrast, the mother's response to the same situation is a kind of ritual to reclaim the lost inheritance: "My mother, ordinarily so godless and blasphemous, would lift up her voice and chant names from the [Slovenian] map, syllable after syllable, on a hovering, tremulous high note" (52). "My mother's litany of place names, however faulty her pronunciation, sounded beautiful to me" (52), Filip writes. "From the start my mother's fantasies, remote as they may have been from experience, made a stronger impression on me, the second, late-born son, than did my father's war stories" (54), even though he knows that she is describing a world that does not exist outside her linguistic creation: "a country that had nothing in common with the reality of Slovenia; it was built up exclusively from the names.... This country... became in her mouth a land of peace where we, the Kobal family, would at last recapture our true selves. This transfiguration..." (54).[10]

Despite his personal preference for his mother's creation over his father's begrudging, resentful acceptance of exile and absence, the narrator recognizes both responses to the loss of the metaphysical as human: "When I think back on the image of the two of them, I see one weeping and one laughing storyteller, one standing aside, the other center stage, asserting our rights" (54). He also realizes that both positions are potentially dangerous. If the laughing narrator, the mother, is in the center, she has a position of power from which she can rule: "Then I realized that my mother was not merely self-assured like the waitress but positively imperious. She had always wanted to run a big hotel, with the

---

[10] Cf. from *Essay on Tiredness:* "But isn't it the past that transfigures? If the past was of the kind that transfigures, it's all right with me. I believe in that sort of transfiguration," in *The Jukebox and Other Essays on Storytelling*, transl. Ralph Manheim (New York: Farrar Straus Giroux, 1994) 15.

staff as her subjects. Our farm was small and her demands were great. In her stories about my brother, he was always represented as a king cheated out of his throne" (11). The father, the crying narrator, can likewise exert power, even from the periphery: "His being a stranger in the village made him a domestic tyrant. Because he was nowhere at home, he bullied the rest of us; he drove us from our places or at least poisoned them for us" (54–55). In both positions (the father's post-Slovene liminality and the mother's post-post-Slovene centrality— or, allegorically, the father's emphatic postmetaphysical muttering and the mother's post-postmetaphysical construction) are the possibilities for dominance. But both stances also make possible more humane responses, as in Filip's description of his father's stammered German: "I must own that my father's way of speaking German, serious, graphic, laboriously pondering every word as though intimidated by the presence of foreigners, still sounds in my ears as the clearest, purest, least garbled, and most human-sounding voice I have ever heard in Austria" (49), and in Filip's description of his mother's voice when she frees him from the boarding school: "a light, wingèd, dancing, chanting voice" (26).

The novel describes the travels of 20-year-old Filip through the mountains and Karst region of Slovenia as he searches for his older brother Gregor (named after the ancestor), who went AWOL there during the second world war. Like the extinct kings of the *Zohar* or the now defunct Austrian Kaiser, Gregor represents the truth, essence, presence, center, or metaphysical reality the young Filip desires. In the stories of his mother, for example, Gregor is routinely referred to as a king (11). Or, in a dream, Filip sees his family in the living room of the house with Gregor as the center: "my brother was standing in the middle" (63). Or, in an experience triggered by viewing traces of the old Austrian Empire on a Slovenian building, Filip commands his brother to appear, and when he does: "A shudder ran through me, as though I was seeing my king" (92). Making his own trip to the land of lost inheritance, Filip himself becomes, for his mother, a possible king: "And she saw me as the rightful heir to the throne" (11). With this search for a lost relative who represents truth, Handke again takes up the paradigm of *Short Letter, Long Farewell* in which the narrator, supposing "truth to be a woman," follows his estranged wife across North America.

Surprisingly, Filip's walk through Slovenia achieves its goal (to find Gregor, king, metaphysical presence) fairly early in the novel. The scene is a key one:

> While looking at one of these façades, I suddenly wished with all my might that my missing brother would push open the decrepit terrace door, with its opaque grooved glass, and show himself. I even thought in words: "Forefather, show thyself," and saw the head of the old man beside me turn toward the bay window. And for a moment, as though my call were its own fulfillment, I caught sight of my brother, full-grown (as I had never known him), broad-shouldered, brown-skinned, his thick, dark, curly hair combed straight back, his imposing forehead and his eyes so deep in their sockets that his white blindness remained hidden. A shudder ran through me, as though I were see-

ing my king, a shudder of awe, but even more of terror, which made me leave my place in the hollow without delay and slip into the torrent of passersby on the street above.

It received me at once. My impression from below was false; it was not a torrent at all but an astonishingly leisurely flow in which my excitement over my successful evocation of an ancestor was appeased by an unhurried present.

(92)

In this seemingly mystical moment, and there are others in the novel as well, Filip achieves his goal. The absent becomes present. The lost is found. It would seem that Filip is the exception to Handke's general assertion in *Phantasien der Wiederholung*: "everyone travels at some time to Emmaus, but nothing approaches him except—powerful emptiness" (87). No longer must Filip see "through a glass darkly" (here the opaque glass of the door), for his brother steps through it, visible both to Filip and to the old man next to him. Upon seeing "his king" (like one of the lost kings of the *Zohar*), he experiences the awe, terror, thrill, and solemn shudder of reverence appropriate to a metaphysical vision. But like Hans Castorp when his sees his cousin's ghost during a séance in Thomas Mann's *Magic Mountain*, Filip is more disturbed than edified, and he flees into the company of nonmetaphysical passersby.

Handke undercuts the achieved presence in other ways as well. "The successful evocation of an ancestor," however transcendent the described experience appears on first reading, does not in fact assert and glorify the metaphysical, but rather leads away from the youthful, impetuous desire for the metaphysical and toward the physical.[11] Two subjunctives, for example, relativize the experience. The first, "as though my call were its own fulfillment," might be paraphrased by a semiotician as "as if the signifier and the transcendental signified were the same." But the subjunctive mood signals that this may be contrary to fact. The second subjunctive, "as though I were seeing my king," generally calls the vision into question. Whatever Filip is experiencing as he sees his brother whom he takes to be his king, who is there as if he were his king, who represents his king, is merely a sign. Filip is not in fact experiencing the actual king—that transcendental signified—he has attempted to conjure up.

---

[11]Goethe introduces his journal of art and art history, *Propyläen*, with a metaphoric description of the Greek propylaea: "The youth, when attracted by nature and art, feels capable of entering suddenly, with a lively effort, into the inner sanctum; the man notices, after long travels, that he still finds himself in the outer courtyards.... Stair, gate, entrance, vestibule, the space between the inner and outer, between the sacred and profane—only this can be the place in which we and our friends will usually dwell" Cf. Handke's aphorism from *Phantasien der Wiederholung*: "The determining idea of the child had once been that the visible world was just a dream and would burst, whereupon the real would appear; the determining idea of the adult, however, was: the visible world is it, 'is it already': Being, manifesting itself through the forms" (71).

The achieved peace among the passersby ("in which my excitement over my successful evocation of an ancestor was appeased by an unhurried present"), that turn from the sudden disconnected gap in time to a slow, continuous, humanly shared present, leads away from the metaphysical and connects this scene with the crucial "mystical" blind window at the end of the novel's first part. Likewise, the ghost's eyes (if this is a ghost) also relate to the blind window.

In the scene that gives the first third of the novel its title, "The Blind Window," Filip Kobal waits at the train station for the train that will take him away from home and into the former Yugoslavia where he will search for his brother:

> I raised my head and saw in the end wall of the station a rectangle—a blind window the same whitish-gray color as the wall, but set in from it. Though no longer in the sun, this window shimmered with reflected light from somewhere. In Rinkenberg there was only one such window, and it happened to be in the smallest house, the roadmender's, the one that looked like the porter's lodge of a nonexistent manor.... Whenever I passed, it caught my eye, but when I stopped to look, it always fooled me. Nevertheless, it never lost a certain undefined significance for me, and I felt that such a window was lacking in my father's house.(68)

He tells of a frantic, night train trip his father and brother took from this station to a doctor in Klagenfurt because of an endangered eye, a trip taken in vain, for from that time on

> there was nothing in [the eye's] place but a milky whiteness. But this memory explained nothing. The significance of the blind window remained undefined, but suddenly that window became a sign, and in that same moment I decided to turn back. My turning back—and here again the sign was at work—was not definitive; it applied only to the hours until the following morning, when I would really start out, really begin my journey, with successive blind windows as my objects of research, my traveling companions, my signposts. And when later, on the evening of the following day, at the station restaurant in Jesenice, I thought about the shimmering of the blind window, it still imparted a clear message—to me it meant: "Friend, you have time." (68–69)

A window is generally transparent, as would be a signifier that reveals a transcendental signified.[12] This window, however, is blind, even more opaque than the windowed door Filip hopes his brother will step through. The only window in the village similar to this one is on the roadmender's tiny house, a house that makes Filip think of a nonexistent Lord's or manor house. The double motion of this signifier is characteristic of Handke's work in general—the

---

[12] Cf. Handke's assertion that "The 'mirror of language' should finally be destroyed. One cannot simply look through language to objects. Instead of acting as if one could look through language like a windowpane, one should turn the light on insidious language itself." "Zur Tagung der Gruppe 47 in den USA," in *Ich bin ein Bewohner des Elfenbeinturms,* (Frankfurt am Main: Suhrkamp, 1972) 30.

little house both brings to mind what could be the house of lost kings and reminds one of its nonexistence.[13] This is precisely the novel's stance in relation to metaphysics: it evokes the very thing it simultaneously reveals as absent.

The roadmender was previously described in the novel as a liminal figure in the village. His work as a sign painter (artist, writer) fascinated Filip Kobal and, along with Filip's mentally handicapped sister, he was said to embody in his liminality the (real) center of the village. But just what was the meaning of that decentered centrality? Just what did the so promising blind window express? Whenever Filip stopped to decipher the message it meant, in fact, nothing. But if there was no clear meaning, there was still (undefined) significance. Although Filip wanted a clearer message, the openness of this signifier is as important as the fact of signification. Filip's father's house has no such window of uncertain meaning, because, I suppose, he is a man of defined significance, a tyrant, an oppressive authority figure. Although the narrator suggests that the meaning of the blind window will remain indefinable, Filip nevertheless takes the window as a sign that he should return to his family. But as an indeterminate sign, the window is also interpreted as signifying the exact opposite—as a sign of his travels, of his leaving his family. The next day, in recollection, the contradictory messages give way to a third, enigmatic, statement: "Friend, you have time.'"

As an open signifier, the blind window provides a helpful context for the scene in which Filip perhaps sees and certainly flees the vision of his king / brother. Both scenes involve revelations through blind windows and in both cases the revelation gives way to a final message of slowness and shared humanity: "'Friend, you have time'" and "our slow present." The one scene describes the loss of the brother's eyesight and the resulting milky whiteness of the eyeball, and the other scene has that blind whiteness hidden. Although the empty forms (the blind windows and the empty cow paths) privileged by the narrator over more certain messages are repeated in the brother's blind eye, in the metaphysical vision the blindness is concealed, the ambiguity masked. On this reading, he is unsettled by the gaze that purports transcendent sight but behind the shadow remains the same blind eye.

Another description in the novel further privileges the empty sign:

> But the kingdom of the world that I perceived in this way exceeded the limits of present-day Yugoslavia and all the kingdoms and empires of olden times, and gradually its signs lost their definition. The Cyrillic letters on the newspapers of certain passersby were still clear, the vestiges of an old Austrian inscription on a public building were legible, as was the ancient Greek *Chaire*—Greetings—on the tympanum of a villa; but, on the other hand, the word PETROL on a gas station, which, seen through the branches of a tree, reminded me of a China known to me only from dreams, was ambiguous, and

---

[13]This may be the point of the novel's second epigraph: "I stayed with this one and that one." *Epicharmos*.

an equally exotic Sinai Desert opened up to me behind the high-rise buildings at the sight of a dusty long-distance bus, on the front of which the roller indicating its destination had stopped exactly in the middle between two illegible place names. As it passed, a fragment of a Hebrew scroll struck my eyes—yes, *struck* my eyes, for the landscape that opened up around the script was fraught with terror. (97–98)

"Clear," "legible," "ambiguous," "illegible"—only after this regression does a fragment of a contrived and holy (at least that's how I read "Hebrew" here) text leap into Filip's eyes, open the landscape, and shock him. The sequence culminates in a now familiar empty or open sign: "The vagueness was underlined by a blind window, to which my gaze was now drawn as to the center of the world" (98). Clear, supposedly translucent signification in support of a "kingdom" (cf. the centered Yugoslavian government referred to in the novel: "Marshal Tito was unmistakably there.... I could almost hear him say: 'I know you,' and I wanted to answer: 'But I don't know myself'" [10]) would require debunking. The blind window, however, asserting while questioning itself, can be looked to as the center of a world "kingdom."

The blind window here is part of a large building that Filip takes to be the manor house belonging to the tiny (gate)house of the roadmender back in his village, and is thus the place of metaphysical presence promised by the gate house. In this context the description of the entrance is significant: "A child was on the stairway with his back to me; one foot a step lower than the other, he seemed hesitant; the steps were too big for a child.... [The house] seemed uninhabited. The child on the steps was in the entrance not to a house but to a playground" (98–99). If this is the "lord's" house, then to enter it would be to achieve closure, to find truth. But the child stands on steps too large for it, uncertain. And in fact, the child is not intent on entrance, but stands in a playground. The antithesis of a ruling king yet still in proximity to his house, the child is at play.

Later in the novel playing is defined as the kind of activity that creates its own rights rather than accepting them from an authority: "But from whom could we demand our right? And why did we always demand it of a third, some of an emperor, others of a God? Why didn't we take it for ourselves, essential as it was for our self-preservation, letting no one else intervene? There at last was a game in which we wouldn't have had to measure ourselves against anyone, a lonely game, a wild game—Father, the great game!" (157). If the world is indeed contingent, if truth is best described as Nietzsche's "mobile army of metaphors," if language games are all we have, then those games are our own and the responsibility is in fact ours.

But watching the child at play in front of the lord's house and moved by the blind window's indeterminacy, by its opacity and the absence it represents, Filip Kobal falls out of the determinate world of language: "Thanks to its extreme vagueness, it reflected my gaze; and the muddle of languages, the confusion of voices within me fell silent: my whole being fell silent, and read" (99). Predictably, this state too is ephemeral: "I had never thought it possible that I would lose this blind window; I had felt it to be an unalterable sign. Yet one side glance sufficed: the light emanating from it was gone" (99). And yet the dialectical epiphany returns, notably as Filip finds solace in memory of the healthy *and* blind eyes of his brother: "his good eye studies me with friendly attentiveness and enjoys the sunshine with me, while his blind eye—because it's blind—is none the wiser" (138).

The novel's enigmatic third epigraph, "... laboraverimus," (we shall have worked) relates to the brother's penchant for speaking and prophesying in the future perfect. And what will have been accomplished? the novel asks. We shall have seen the king? We shall have achieved presence? No—simply, "we shall have worked." In this context Filip appoints his brother his protective forebear, knowing all the while that: "Of course I could not when threatened summon him to give me peace; it was the other way around: I found peace by myself, and he was present to bolster me; accordingly it was impossible to lean on my forebears (the only effective forebear, this much I know, is the sentence preceding the one I am writing now)" (138). But with a forebear within him, even if only the appearance of a forebear, he writes, "I am no longer alone; I sit more erect, walk in a different way.... What are facts compared to such appearances? ... Long live appearances! Let them be my subject!" (138).

In the course of the novel Filip learns that "the empty forms both of the cow paths and of the blind windows could be relied on; they were the seal of our right" (159). A seal is the stamp of authority, a sign from above that guarantees or assures. The genius of these particular seals is that they are empty forms, forms that question while asserting, that stimulate a contingent production of meaning. In their blindness, arbitrariness, emptiness, these signs are in fact no different than any other sign. Their power lies in the way their emptiness asserts contingency while they simultaneously act as productive signs.

The experiences that lead to this insight leave Filip in a curious state. He has given up hope that his king would ever appear. He has abandoned metaphysics for the "things and words of this beloved world—for being" (160).[14] And years later as he weakly and carefully narrates his story, as he repeats it to make it myth—"to naturalize myth (repetition)"[15]—he wonders if its sounds will be drowned out by the more urgent, less timid sounds of soldiers. The answer, he decides, is no, for although the soldiers represent one sort of kingdom, the kingdom of the text (whose watermarks are the empty forms) is a recurring kingdom, in fact, the kingdom *of* recurrence (221–22).

---

[14]This is the essential story of *Der Himmel über Berlin*, in which angels leave the metaphysical realm to experience the pleasures, responsibilities, and sorrows of nonmetaphysical existence.

[15]*Phantasien der Wiederholung* 88.

Two scenes late in the novel in which Filip again glimpses his brother add insight to this story of kings. Having decided, because his fantasy can be more creative in places his brother won't haunt, to avoid places his brother mentioned in letters, Filip sees his

> brother stepping through the door to the yard. He appeared to me in a crowd.... Did he really come in? No, he just stood in the doorway, on the threshold ... his deep-sunken eyes—both had their sight—projected an infinite dream. Though I remained seated with my companions, I also had the impression that I got up to make sure it was he.... Neither of us moved; we stood facing each other for an eternity, at a distance, beyond reach, unapproachable, united in grief and serenity, merriment and forlornness. I felt the sun and wind on the bones of my forehead, saw the festive bustle on both sides of the dark passage with my brother's image in it, and knew we were in midyear. Holy forebear, youthful martyr, dear child. (231)

This time the brother remains on the threshold, that interstice that allows both distance and presence in Handke's poetics.[16] Both eyes are seeing, and with them he can dream (not see) into infinity. There is no fear like that of the earlier scene when his blind eye was hidden, for this is clearly a moment of recollection and not a metaphysical vision. When Filip describes getting up to face Gregor he asserts that this too, like the infinity Gregor dreams, is imagined, for he is really still seated. They are separated (at a distance, unreachable, and not able to address one another) and united (by feeling). Filip knows he is seeing an image of his brother, and that image, that creation, helps him situate himself even more securely in the world as he feels the sun and wind, sees the celebrating people around him, and is conscious of being in midyear—a nonmetaphysical, material center quite different from the temporal discontinuity of the earlier vision. He praises the image of his brother's appearance in religious terms because of the earthly meaning it affords, and he can do so precisely because there is no sense of actual metaphysical presence, no religious or political claim that would have to be refuted. Gregor is no longer Filip's king, but a dear child (the child playing earlier between Filip and the entrance to the manor house).

Immediately after this scene Filip once again "sees" ("zu Gesicht bekommen") his brother, but this time it is actually "an empty bed that spoke to me of Gregor" (232). What began as a supposed and threatening real vision has become, as Filip has gained understanding, a story. And with this Filip declares himself "at a goal. My purpose had been not to find my brother but to tell a story about him" (234). Now the brother's prayer that they might one day travel to the marriage of the fabled ninth king of the ninth land can be translated from the realm of metaphysical desire to an "earthly fulfillment: writing" (234). Repeating this idea of earthly, material fulfillment, Handke emphasizes the non-

---

[16] See especially Handke's *Der Chinese des Schmerzes* in which the main character, Loser, is an expert on thresholds.

metaphysical character of the kingdom created in a story: "Thus the final kingdom and also the only rational and not metaphysical kingdom will surely be the kingdom of writing, the kingdom of storytelling."[17] And who will be the king? A smiling narrator, both king and child, inspired by blind windows and other empty signs, repeating and renewing through stories (245–46).

As the epigraphs to this essay suggest, there are two kinds of repetition: the one that tortures the clown (or the crying narrator) who recognizes the contingency of everything and simply despairs, and the one joyfully embraced by a storyteller equally aware of contingency yet anxious to create meaning through repetition. The first is nihilistic. The second resembles the antimetaphysical Nietzschean affirmation of eternal return.

---

[17] *Aber ich lebe nur von den Zwischenräumen: Ein Gespräch, geführt von Herbert Gamper* (Zurich: Ammann, 1987) 158.

KATHLEEN L. KOMAR

Kassandra as a Rebel Against War: The Theme of Heroism in Christa Wolf's Re-Vision of the Trojan War

"Heroism" has become a vexed term in the twentieth century. In an age when death can drop anonymously from a distant sky, the idea of noble individual heroism becomes increasingly untenable. The destructive potential of nuclear weapons forever changed our attitude toward war and "heroism" and robbed warfare of whatever romantic tinge that hand-to-hand combat between males of equal stature might have had. In her essays and narrative focusing on the Trojan War, *Voraussetzungen einer Erzählung: Kassandra* and *Kassandra*,[1] Christa Wolf takes up the theme of heroism and examines it from a uniquely critical point of view—that of the female victim of "heroic" action, the priestess of the losing side, Kassandra.[2] Wolf challenges the traditional male, military vision of "heroism" by attacking it at its roots in the Trojan War, but her critique is pointedly aimed at her own times. By shifting her narrative focus from the male warriors to a female analytic critic, Wolf effectively undermines several aspects of the "heroic" tradition of the west.

Wolf's essays and narrative begin by replacing at least one woman, Kassandra, within the cultural record by giving her the voice she was deprived of in the literary and historical patriarchal tradition of the Trojan War. (Almost totally absent from *The Iliad*, Kassandra is mentioned only twice: once as a promised wife to be given in return for military service [*Iliad* XIII, lines 363–68], and once when she summons the Trojans to mourn for Hektor's returning corpse [*Iliad* XXIV, lines 699–708].[3]) Kassandra gains a literary voice (in Aeschylus's *The Oresteia* and Euripides's *The Trojan Women*) only after the war ends. The bulk of Wolf's text, however, focuses on Kassandra's actions during those war

[1] Christa Wolf, *Kassandra* (Darmstadt and Neuwied: Luchterhand, 1983). *Voraussetzungen einer Erzählung: Kassandra* (Darmstadt and Neuwied: Luchterhand, 1983).

[2] This is not unprecedented, of course, since Euripides also provides a view from the perspective of the defeated women (including Kassandra) in his *Trojan Women*.

[3] See Homer, *The Iliad*, transl. Richmond Lattimore (Chicago: U of Chicago P, 1951) 281 and 493–94.

years in which she is largely missing from the literary record.[4] One of Wolf's major revisions of the Kassandra figure is to restore her as a speaking—and protesting—subject in the history of war where she has often been only an object.

Wolf, in fact, describes how she became interested in the figure of Kassandra: "... [es ist mir] eingefallen, daß um die Kassandra-Figur herum sich etwas Zeitgenössisches machen ließe. Damals habe ich aber an das gedacht, woran Sie vielleicht alle denken: eine Frau, die die Wahrheit sagt, die Zukunft ausspricht und der man nicht glaubt."[5] The initial identification with such a figure for a woman writing today in Europe is obvious. But Wolf soon came to realize that the story of Troy had additional useful ramifications:

> Der eigentliche Grund, warum ich solch einen Stoff wie Kassandra nahm, war die Gefahr der möglichen Vernichtung und Selbstvernichtung unserer Kultur: wie kommen wir heraus? Der Drang nach Macht der patriarchalischen Klassengesellschaften scheint mir, psychologisch gesprochen, in einer furchtbaren Angst der herrschenden Schicht begründet zu sein....Wenn man ihnen diese Angst nehmen könnte, wenn man für diese Aggressivität, die sich angestaut hat, einen ableitenden Kanal schaffen könnte, der nicht Krieg wäre.... Man müßte die Möglichkeit entwickeln zu empfinden, zu lieben und geliebt zu werden, nicht abgelehnt zu werden und nicht ablehnen zu müssen—ein utopischer Weg.[6]

Like Adrienne Rich before her, Wolf perceives that the job of re-vision is truly a matter of survival for women—and for humanity—today.[7] As Rich too sug-

---

[4] Rudolf G. Wagner's "On Christa Wolf's *Cassandra*" in *History: Another Text*, eds. M.D. Birnbaum and R. Trager-Verchovsky (Ann Arbor, Michigan: U of Michigan P, 1988) 87, notes that Lycophron's *Alexandra* also gives Cassandra center stage in a long narrative monologue. Lycophron's text is a notoriously obscure and complex one with passages referring to the glories of Rome which cast doubt as to the authorship and date of the poem. Although Wolf does not refer to Lycophron or the *Alexandra* directly in her *Literaturnachweise* at the close of *Voraussetzungen einer Erzählung: Kassandra*, it is possible that she may have known the text. In any case, Wagner's treatment of the classical material as well as of other East German contexts is quite enlightening.

For an extended discussion of the figure of Cassandra in classical literature, see also Juliette Davreux's *La Légende de la Prophetesse Cassandre d'après les textes et les monuments* (Paris: Bibliothèque de la Faculté de Philosophie et Lettres de l'Université de Liège, 1942).

[5] From "Ein Gespräch über *Kassandra*," an interview with Christa Wolf on June 1, 1983 at Ohio State University, recorded as part of "Documentation: Christa Wolf," *The German Quarterly* 57. 1 (1984): 91–115. This statement is found on 106.

[6] Wolf, "Ein Gespräch über *Kassandra*," 107.

[7] Adrienne Rich, "When We Dead Awaken: Writing as Re-Vision (1971)," originally written for the MLA Commission on the Status of Women in 1971, reprinted in Rich's *On Lies, Secrets and Silence: Selected Prose 1966–78* (New York: Norton, 1979) 3–

gests, the patriarchal culture that glorifies war and hides the inability to feel under a facade of toughness must be critiqued if we are to escape the worst of Western culture and find a better alternative.

In her "Frankfurter Poetik-Vorlesungen," which preceded and conditioned the composition of the narrative of *Kassandra*, Wolf is intensely aware of the possibility of imminent destruction. In the third "Lecture," entitled "Ein Arbeitstagebuch über den Stoff, aus dem das Leben und die Träume sind," she comments directly on the atomic threat to Europe in her diary entry of July 9, 1980:

> Nie sei die Gefahr eines Atomkriegs in Europa so groß gewesen wie heute, erklärt das schwedische Institut für Friedensforschung in seinem Jahresbericht. 60 000 Atomsprengkörper seien auf der Welt gelagert. . . .
> Die Lage Europas ist doch heute grundlegend anders als in den dreißiger Jahren, vor dem Überfall Hitlers auf ungenügend dagegen gerüstete Nachbarländer: Aber selbstverständlich hätten sie sich gegen diesen Gegner rüsten. . . . müssen. Selbstverständlich war Verteidigung gegen den Aggressor sinnvoll in Vietnam; selbstverständlich ist das Gewehr ein Mittel der Verteidigung und der Befreiung in einer Reihe südamerikanischer Länder. . . . Ich aber bin Europäerin. Europa ist gegen einen Atomkrieg nicht zu verteidigen. Es wird nur als Ganzes überleben oder als Ganzes zugrunde gehen. . . .
> (*Voraussetzungen einer Erzählung: Kassandra* 87–88)

Typically, Wolf acknowledges both Germany's past bellicose aggression and the current military intrusions of the United States. She does not merely wish to point an accusing finger at the West; she also looks at nuclear threats from the East such as the Chernobyl disaster described in her 1987 narrative *Störfall: Nachrichten eines Tages*.[8] In fact, Wolf's sometimes direct appeal to her own society to take an antinuclear and antiwar stance raised a good deal of criticism of Wolf's political naiveté.[9] Various political passages in her text were even cen-

---

49. The issue of re-vision in feminist criticism has been discussed by a number of leading feminist critics including Rich, Kolodny, Miller, Schor, and Showalter. Adrienne Rich's programmatic statement concerning re-vision is probably the best known. However, see also Nancy K. Miller, "Arachnologies: The Woman, The Text and the Critic," in *The Poetics of Gender*, ed. Nancy K. Miller (New York: Columbia UP, 1986) 270–96; and Christine Froula, "When Eve Reads Milton: Undoing the Canonical Economy," in *Canons*, ed. Robert von Hallberg (Chicago: U of Chicago P, 1983) 149–75, and Annette Kolodny, "A Map for Rereading: Or, Gender and the Interpretation of Literary Texts," *New Literary History* 2.3 (Spring 1980): 451–67, among many others.

[8]Christa Wolf, *Störfall: Nachrichten eines Tages* (Darmstadt and Neuwied: Luchterhand, 1987).

[9]Ursula Püschel, for example, in her ". . .die Reflexion der weißen Frau auf sich selbst" in *Neue Deutsche Literatur* 32.8 (1984): 132–51, complains: "Christa Wolf kann doch

sored in East Germany.[10] Wolf wants the entire global community to rethink war, and her text makes that clear to both sides. Troy offers her the perfect arena for examining our faith in war at its source and for analyzing women's role in a warlike society. If she can undermine the origin of the Western military and heroic tradition in Troy, she may be able to encourage a re-vision of war in her own world.[11]

Wolf's *Kassandra* is a fascinating modern re-vision of the story of Troy told from the point of view of the ignored percipient, Kassandra. Like Euripides, Wolf narrates from the perspective of the vanquished and suffering survivors of war. And like Dares and Dictys, she depicts an archetypal hero quite different from Homer's complex, musically and medically gifted Achilles.[12] The novel begins with Kassandra waiting before Agamemnon's gates in Mycenae, waiting and speaking. Kassandra's interior monologue as she awaits her imminent death takes her back in memory to her childhood in Troy and to the peaceful times when she would sit at her father's feet as he came into her mother's chamber to discuss politics. Those scenes of the almost constantly pregnant or nursing Hekuba (reputed to have had 50 children) discussing the administering of Troy with her attentive husband, Priam, give Kassandra a glimpse of a society at a moment of balance between the matriarchal and patriarchal traditions. In the

---

nicht denken, wenn die Sowjetunion nackt and bloß wäre, wenn die USA und weitere imperialistische Gruppen zum Beispiel in Afrika machen könnten, was sie wollten, daß sie heute anderes täten als gestern, daß auch nur ein Kind mehr am Leben bliebe, zu einem Menschen heranwachsen könnte" (150). For a variety of positive and negative reactions to Wolf's *Kassandra*, see: Hans Kaufmann, "Wider die troianischen Kriege," *Sinn und Form* 36 (1984): 653–63; Sigrid Bock, Ursule Heukenkamp, Karin Hirdina, Therese Hörnigk, Sigfried Rönisch, and Hans-Georg Werner in their symposium "*Kassandra* von Christa Wolf," *Weimarer Beiträge* 30 (1984): 1353–81; Ingrid Hähnel and Hans Kaufmann, "DDR-Prose der 80er Jahre," *Zeitschrift für Germanistik* 6 (1985): 18–34; and Wilhelm Girnus, "Wer baute das siebentorige Theben?" *Sinn und Form* 35 (1983): 439–47.

[10]For a discussion of the censored passages and the general reaction to Wolf's political program, see Peter J. Graves, "Christa Wolf's *Kassandra*: The Censoring of the GDR Edition," *Modern Language Review* 81 (1986): 944–56.

[11]Alexander Stephan sees Wolf's combination of themes "Frauen und Frieden" as the key to the popular success of *Kassandra* in the early 1980s. See Stephan, *Christa Wolf*, 4th rev. ed. (Munich: C. H. Beck, 1991) 139–54 and his "Frieden, Frauen und Kassandra," in *Wolf: Darstellung, Deutung, Diskussion*, ed. Manfred Jurgensen (Bern: Francke, 1984) 149–73. See also Elise Marks's "The Alienation of 'I': Christa Wolf and Militarism," *Mosaic* 23.3 (Summer 1990): 73–85.

[12]For a thorough and insightful discussion of Achilles's progression through various classical texts, see Katherine Callen King, *Achilles: Paradigms of the War Hero from Homer to the Middle Ages* (Berkeley: University of California Press, 1987).

early days of Troy, when Hekuba and Priam confer jointly for the good of the state, there is no conflict between politics and family, no social wall between men and women. Wolf is, in fact, attracted to the Kassandra story partly by this fleeting moment of political and gender balance in Trojan history.[13] She is looking not for a moment of nostalgia, however, but for a different social structure. "Das Troia, das mir vor Augen steht, ist—viel eher als eine rückgewandte Beschreibung—ein Modell für eine Art von Utopie."[14]

This balance between matriarchal and patriarchal tradition is under attack in Troy however. And Kassandra, priestess of Apollo, is drawn into the fight. She dreams[15] that the moon and the sun struggle for dominance and that she is called upon to decide which shines more brightly. While she senses the question is a trap, she eventually answers logically, as she has been trained to answer, that everyone knows the sun shines more brightly. Upon answering, she hears a voice declaim, "Phoebus Apollo!" whereupon the lady of the moon, Selene, sinks to the horizon lamenting. Kassandra feels herself judged but she is not sure why she is guilty. The wise old woman, Arisbe, leads Kassandra to understand that some questions are perverted and that one is entitled and even

---

[13.]The most exasperatingly perverse reading of the relationship between Hekuba and Priam and its repercussions for Kassandra is presented by Wolfram Mauser in his "Das 'dunkle Tier' und die Seherin: Zu Christa Wolfs *Kassandra*-Phantasie" *Freiburger literatur-psychologische Gespräche* 4 (1985): 139–57 (particularly 145–47). One begins to worry when Mauser labels Hekuba as "herrschsüchtig" (power hungry or tyrannical) on his opening page. This didn't sound like the Hekuba I read in Wolf. Mauser argues that Hekuba is too masculine, strong and power-hungry, and thus that she displaces the weaker but more lovable and loving Priam with whom Kassandra identifies. Kassandra is thus torn between wanting to have her mother's strength and identifying her paternal love with weakness. Sexuality comes to demand dominance and pain, and so Kassandra turns sadomasochist and guilt-ridden about sex. Kassandra cannot go with Aeneas, according to Mauser, because she fears and avoids sex not because she gives her life protesting the heroic tradition. This reading strikes me as so typically patriarchal as to be infuriating. The woman, of course, is at fault—a too strong mother is the cause of all Kassandra's problems. How dare Hekuba want to share in power and thus throw the entire masculine universe off its track? With his Freudian reading, Mauser makes Wolf's text reveal a deep-seated and repressed insight against woman and the matriarchal. Wouldn't Christa Wolf be amazed? There are moments in Mauser's discussion that are fascinating and enlightening, his discussion of Kassandra's relationship to her half-brother Aisakos, for example (151–52). Likewise Mauser's attempt to link the personal to the political without discrediting the political is well intentioned. I must resist, however, the necessarily patriarchal Freudian reading that underlies his essay and that makes it impossible for Kassandra (and Wolf) to support the female despite herself. It again robs her of conscious choice and of a voice.

[14]*Voraussetzungen einer Erzählung: Kassandra* 83.

[15]*Kassandra* 100.

obliged to reject them. This realization gives Kassandra a new sense of freedom. Kassandra's dream symbolizes the struggle between the older, female, maternal goddess Selene and the new, male, Olympian god Apollo. Kassandra's training and position, and her "reason," lead her to side with the patriarchal Apollo and to deny the female and the matriarchal. Only when she escapes her role of priestess and daughter of the ruling house will she be able to affirm the female and to understand issues not controlled by reason.

But Kassandra also remembers the larger destruction of that delicate balance between matriarchy and patriarchy. It begins with Hekuba's alienation and ends with the war. Hekuba's close ties to Priam and to political power begin to weaken when Priam feels compelled to destroy his son Paris because the patriarchal priest, Calchas, has interpreted a dream by Hekuba to mean that Paris would set fire to all Troy. Kassandra realizes that Priam fears the loss of his throne and his patriarchal powers to his son and that he is therefore compelled to destroy Paris. This cruelty begins to harden Hekuba and to alienate her from her husband and from the male power structure. Ironically, Hekuba's dream, that in delivering Paris she was giving birth to a stick of firewood from which countless burning serpents crept forth, was interpreted by the matriarchal representative, Arisbe, to mean that Paris would restore Hekuba's right to the snake goddess as guardian of the hearth. Matriarchal vision versus patriarchal views of the world are thus pitted against one another in Troy through Paris. The struggle between the two social systems would finally be decided during the repercussions of the Trojan war when Orestes is acquitted of his mother's, Klytemnestra's, murder as Aeschylus's *Oresteia* closes. Father right, the right of law and reason, would eventually win out over mother right, the right of blood and emotion. Hekuba's alienation thus symbolizes the alienation of the entire matriarchal social structure and its displacement by the patriarchy.

The military action itself also tips the scales in the direction of the patriarchal tradition as the preparations for war necessitate changing attitudes, moralities and even vocabularies. No longer are the Greeks greeted as "guest friends"; they are seen as spies or provocateurs.[16] Infinitely worse, however, is the war itself. Not content to accept the Trojan War as a battle over beauty and a woman, Wolf depicts the economic underpinning of the war, the battle for control of the Dardanelles and the rich trade that moves through the strait. She also lays bare the lies that help to generate the war and that use women as scapegoats. Kassandra learns early in the war that Helen is not, in fact, in Troy; her inept brother Paris lost Helen to the King of Egypt when returning home. Paralleling Stesichorus's alternate tradition (represented in his "Palinode") of Helen being in Egypt rather than Troy, Wolf implies that the war is fought for a phantom. But she goes one step farther than the ancient tradition in which the phantom of Helen (created by Hera) made the Trojan's believe in her presence. Wolf's

---

[16] *Kassandra* 64.

ruling family *knows* that neither Helen nor her phantom are in Troy. They fight for a bald-faced lie that they themselves sustain. Clearly, male egotism and not female beauty breeds the conflict.

The "heroic tradition," already undermined by these demythifications, rapidly degenerates into bestial cruelty as Wolf indicts the major heroes of the Trojan War. Wolf demonstrates the destructive futility of war and of those who hope to gain either economic profit or social and political standing from it. She lays bare the underbelly of war on a day-to-day level, and she reduces the archetypal military "hero," Achilles, to "Achill das Vieh," a sadistic coward who must literally be dragged into the war and who rapes the corpse of Penthesilea. The most disgusting of his breed, Achilles becomes in Wolf's text and Kassandra's memory the sexually obsessed brute whose first "heroic" action is the sexually perverse slaughter of Kassandra's brother Troilus in the sanctuary of the temple. The Trojan heroes begin honorably, like Troilus, but are rapidly either killed for their naive idealism or changed into the same brutes that the Greeks are. Surrounded by the threat of total destruction in her own historical period, Wolf uses these earlier warriors and war images to warn her own contemporaries.

The remainder of Kassandra's reminiscences trace the degeneration of the government and the people of Troy, their loss of moral stature, their growing war mentality where victory outweighs human value. The narrative ends as Kassandra recalls her rejection of Aeneas's offer of salvation and a new life. She knows only too well that Aeneas will be swept up into a new heroic tradition which he cannot resist. The reader is quite aware that the history of Rome bears out her fears. Kassandra goes to her death partly as a refusal to participate any longer in such a degraded "heroic" world.

Amidst the downhill slide of the Trojan culture and Priam's house, Kassandra also recollects a moment of hope for peace and community during the war. An alternative society of outcasts forms around the benevolent figures of Aeneas's father, Anchises, and the wise old woman Arisbe. This society, composed largely of women, cuts across class and national boundaries. Slave women and noble women of Troy, Greek slaves, Greek women, the remains of Penthesilea's troupes, all gather in the caves by the Scamander River to form a community of mutual support and love. They offer one another the human nurture and tenderness missing from the Troy of the war years. It is this society that Aeneas takes with him to found Rome. A brief utopian moment in the text, this little band will nonetheless be entrapped in the bellicose currents of history once they found the community that will become the Roman Empire.

Wolf's novel focuses on the war situation and on the heroic ethos particularly as embodied in the archetypal warrior, Achilles. Wolf draws not only on

Homer's *Iliad*, Euripides's *Hekuba*, and Vergil's *Aeneid*[17] to create her character of Achilles, but also on the less flattering and more brutal depictions of Achilles in Dictys. It is Dares and Dictys[18] who cite the sexual attraction between Achilles and Polyxena as the eventual cause of Achilles's death and Polyxena's slaughter on his tomb. Wolf also uses Stesichorus's version as seen in his "Palinode" and in Euripides's *Helen* as well as Goethe's *Faust II* to create a Trojan War with an absent Helen at its center. (Wolf's Kassandra shares this feature with H.D.'s *Helen in Egypt*.) The missing Helen and the brutally lustful Achilles allow Wolf to emphasize the futility of war, political pride and the heroic code.

Wolf's novel makes both psychological and political use of the earlier epics and dramas. She even bridges earlier historical periods by having Kassandra be the beloved of Aeneas. This fabrication allows Wolf to link the Homeric and Vergilian worlds. She weaves earlier epic texts and her own imaginative embellishments into a forceful and subtle modern narrative. But Wolf also revises each mediating text; she sees it through a different (female) lens in order to focus upon the heroic tradition's repercussions in her own time as well as on women neglected or not taken seriously in the historical and literary tradition. Wolf thus replaces women as subjects in a history and community in which they

[17] For a discussion of Vergil's view of Achilles's martial career of endless killing, see Katherine Callen King's *Achilles* 121–24.

[18] Oskar Seyffert's *Dictionary of Classical Antiquities* Revised and Edited with Additions by Henry Nettleship & J.E. Sandys (New York: Meridian Library, 1956) describes Dares and Dictys as follows:

> Dares of Phrygia. In Homer the priest of Hephaestus in Troy, supposed to have been the author of a pre-Homeric Iliad. It is doubtful whether there ever was any Greek work bearing this title, but a Latin piece of the 5th century A.D. (*Daretis Phrygii De Excidio Troioe Historia*) bearing a supposed dedication by Cornelius Nepos to Sallust, professes to be a translation of one. This absurd production, and the work of Dictys, was the chief source followed by medieval poets in their stories of the Trojan War (see Dictys). (174)

> Dictys

> (2)Dictys of Gnossos in Crete. Alleged to have been the companion of Idomeneus in the Trojan War, and author of a diary recording his experiences therein. The diary, written in Phoenician on palm leaves, was said to have been found in a leaden box in his grave in the time of Nero, and to have been translated at the emperor's command. The existence of this Greek version was doubted, but a certain Lucius Septimius, of the 4th century A.D., gave out his *Dictys Cretensis Ephemeris De Bello Troiano* as a translation of it. This book and the equally absurd one of Dares..., were the chief authorities followed by the medieval poets who handled the story of Troy. (185)

I find it interesting that Seyffert feels compelled to label "absurd" both of these late versions that are either more critical of the heroic tradition (Dictys) or that see Achilles as thoroughly human (Dares).

were too often placed as objects, and in so doing, she shifts our cultural values away from the masculinely militant and toward a more balanced human totality.

And in her "Frankfurter Poetik-Vorlesungen," Wolf finally places herself as the central subject. The four lectures include a two-part record of Wolf's 1980 trip to Greece during which she explored materials for *Kassandra*; the third essay takes the form of a "work diary" which records contemporary events such as the attempt on President Reagan's life and various political conflicts that terrifyingly parallel the materials of Troy; the last essay is a letter which questions the historical reality of the Kassandra figure and the conditions for the woman writer (or speaker) of the past and present. In first person, Wolf recounts her memories of the trip to Greece and her simultaneous reading of Aeschylus's *Oresteia*; thus, her own experiences as Christa Wolf (rather than as the narrator of a fiction), as well as those of the Greeks, Americans and Germans she meets in her travels, are added to the body of communal memories that make up the text as a whole. This refusal to be bound by any genre definition (either of "novel" or of "formal lecture") contributes to Wolf's re-vision of the tradition she must confront.

The Classical Kassandra[19]

The Iliad is a man's poem. It is about warriors, kings, and clever strategists. It is also about egotism and stubbornness. Women in the tale tend to cause trouble like the feuding goddesses or the beautiful Helen, or to be war prizes like Briseis and eventually Kassandra herself, or to mourn like Hekuba—and Kassandra. Kassandra is almost entirely absent from Homer's great war epic; she is mentioned only twice. In Book XIII, she is the price of military service:

> ... Othryoneus
> ... had asked
> Priam for the hand of the loveliest of his daughters,
> Kassandra, without bride price, but had promised a great work for her,
> to drive back the unwilling sons of the Achaians from Troy land,
> and aged Priam had bent his head in assent. ...
>
> *Iliad* XIII, lines 363–68[20]

---

[19] For an extended discussion of Kassandra's appearance in literary tradition and myth, see Karl Ledergerber, *Kassandra. Das Bild der Prophetin in der antiken und insbesondere in der älteren abendländischen Dichtung* (Buochs: Das Aufgebot, 1940). Wolf herself mentions this work in the bibliography she appends to *Voraussetzungen einer Erzählung: Kassandra* (159). She also mentions several histories of Greek mythology and philosophy as well as the *Lexikon der Antike* (Leipzig: VEB Bibliographisches Institut, 1979) and W.H. Roscher's *Lexikon der griechischen und römischen Mythologie* (Hildesheim, 1865). For a superb reading of Kassandra and her function in the *Oresteia*, see Robert Fagles and W.B. Stanford's introductory essay, "The Serpent and the Eagle" in *The Oresteia* transl. Robert Fagles (New York: Viking, 1975), particularly 28–40.

As bartering material without a voice regarding her own fate, Kassandra is only a passing justification for another warrior to enter the fray. Although she (like Helen) is thrown the bone of beauty, Kassandra's true value is that of property to be traded. Only Othryoneus's death forestalls a marriage in which Kassandra has no say.

In her re-vision of Kassandra, Wolf, who was very familiar with the classical texts,[21] gives Kassandra a much more active role in the prewar and war years. During precisely those years when Homer absents Kassandra, Wolf will allow her to view and analyze and narrate the slow disintegration of Troy. Wolf will, however, retain the idea of selling Kassandra for military support and even allow the warrior to live long enough to engender twins. Wolf's version is more biting than Homer's however in that Wolf has Kassandra given to Eurypylos in marriage late in the war, after Hektor's and Achilles's deaths, when the gesture seems already futile. Wolf's Kassandra will take her children with her into death.

The second mention of Kassandra in the *Iliad* comes in Book XXIV, lines 692–708[22] when she calls the Trojans to mourn the returning body of Hektor, who had so often protected them. The only time she is given voice in Homer's record of the war years, her words are lament: "Come, men of Troy and Trojan women; look upon Hektor if ever before you were joyful when you saw him come back living from battle; for he was a great joy to his city, and all his people." Neither prophetess nor madwoman, the Kassandra of Homer's *Iliad* is a woman in mourning. She retains the role in Wolf's *Kassandra* where she mourns not just for her brother but for her entire civilization. The role of mourner was one designated especially for women in the classical tradition,[23] and as priestess, Kassandra was doubly suited to fill it. This feature of the Kassandra figure is crucial to Wolf. But there is also a prophetic moment in Kassandra's being the first to glimpse the returning body of Hektor, as Seth Schein points

---

[20]Homer, *The Iliad*, transl. Richmond Lattimore (Chicago: U of Chicago P, 1951) 280–81.

[21]In *Voraussetzungen einer Erzählung: Kassandra*, Wolf appends a Bibliography of the many classical texts she has read in preparation for her writing of *Kassandra*. These include among others an anthology of classical literature, Aeschylus's *Oresteia* (in several translations and adaptations), Euripides's collected works, Homer's *Iliad* and *Odyssey*, Aristotle's *Poetics*, Herodotus's history, Sappho's poetry, as well as several scholarly texts which comment upon these works. See 156–60 of *Voraussetzungen einer Erzählung: Kassandra* for a complete list.

[22]*Iliad*, Lattimore translation, 493–94.

[23]See Meg Alexiou, *The Ritual Lament in Greek Tradition* (Cambridge: Cambridge UP, 1974) 12, 21, and 212 n.107 on women's role in rituals of mourning.

out.[24] The death of Hektor foreshadows the fall of Troy as a whole since he is its heroic soul. What Homer's Kassandra is seeing in Hektor's corpse, then, is the future death of her civilization. This symbolism intensifies her lament and anticipates her full prophetic powers which appear only in Aeschylus's *Agamemnon* and Euripides's *Trojan Women.*

Wolf's Kassandra, too, will have a voice of mourning as she watches her young brother Troilus slaughtered before her eyes. She will have a *body* of mourning as she empathizes physically with her brother Hektor's death:

> In der tiefsten Tiefe; im innersten Innern, da, wo Leib und Seele noch nicht geschieden sind und wohin kein Wort, auch kein Gedanke reicht, erfuhr ich alles über Hektors Kampf, Verwundung, seinen zähen Widerstand und seinen Tod. Ich war Hektor, das ist nicht zuviel gesagt, weil: ich war mit ihm verbunden, viel zu wenig sagte. Achill das Vieh hat ihn, hat mich erstochen, verstümmelt, am Gehenk das Aias viele Male um die Burg geschleift. Ich war lebend, was der tote Hektor wurde: ein Klumpen rohes Fleisch. Fühllos.
> (*Kassandra,* 127–28)

Whereas Homer's Kassandra bewails a returning corpse, Wolf's Kassandra lives—and narrates—his death and degradation. Wolf's Hektor is a gentle, likable but not overly bright young man ill-suited to become the chief warrior of Troy. Not willing to shirk his responsibility however, Hektor trains to become the warrior Troy needs and comes as close as Wolf allows to being a hero when he and Ajax exchange arms. Kassandra does not just mourn "Hektor dunkle Wolke," as Wolf dubs him, she suffers with him as he is slaughtered and brutalized by Achilles. Again, Wolf goes several steps farther than Homer to produce a female figure who participates sympathetically (in the literal sense of "feeling with") in the action of the war rather than just reacting to it.

In order to fill in those many years of Kassandra's absence from Homer's epic, Wolf must imaginatively re-member the Kassandra that might have been and provide her with a voice. One of Wolf's primary re-visions, then, is to give Kassandra a place in the history of the Trojan War, to return her to the stage of epic tradition in order to let the absent female voice surface and reevaluate the heroic tradition and the place of women in it.

The classical Kassandra does find voice powerfully and eloquently, however, in Aeschylus's *Oresteia.* Her roughly 300 lines in the *Agamemnon* give Wolf more to work with. Here we find the Kassandra's prophetic power and the intensity of madness. This Kassandra first captivates Christa Wolf with her cry to and against Apollo. Apollo is invoked by Kassandra in his opposition to the Earth, the Mother: "Aieeeeee! Earth—Mother—Curse of the Earth—Apollo Apollo!" And again, "Aieeeeee! Earth—Mother—Rape of the Earth—Apollo

---

[24]Seth L. Schein suggests a number of such symbolic foreshadowings in his *The Mortal Hero: An Introduction to Homer's "Iliad"* (Berkeley: U of California P, 1984). See particularly 14–15 and 189.

Apollo!"²⁵ This opposition remains a crucial one throughout the *Oresteia*. It comes to the fore again when Apollo testifies in favor of Orestes's acquittal of his mother's, Klytemnestra's, murder in *The Eumenides*. In perhaps one of the most male chauvinist statements of all times, Apollo argues:

> The woman you call the mother of the child
> is not the parent, just a nurse to the seed,
> new-sown seed that grows and swells inside her.
> The *man* is the source of life—the one who mounts.
> She, like a stranger for a stranger, keeps
> the shoot alive unless god hurts the roots.²⁶

Hardly an advocate of Mother Right, Apollo attempts to prove his argument by producing Athena as a motherless wonder. Sprung full-blown from the head of Zeus, Athena is not born of woman. As happens so often in history and myth, however, this logic simply suppresses the fact that Athena did, in fact, have a mother—Metis ("Wisdom" or "counsel")—from whom she inherited the talent of persuasion she would need to bring the *Oresteia* to a harmonious close. Zeus, in a less than fatherly show of lack of affection, swallowed Metis whole when she conceived because he feared she would bear a son who would overthrow him. Priam would repeat this same attempt to destroy his offspring in order to retain power in the *Iliad* as well as in Wolf's *Kassandra*. In any case, Apollo shows himself hostile to the mother principle and staunchly in favor of male sexual and judicial dominance. He creates a counterweight to Klytemnestra's assertion of Mother Right when she kills Agamemnon in vengeance because he sacrificed her daughter Iphigenia.

In narrating her visions of the House of Atreus and its horrors of murder and cannibalism, Aeschylus's Kassandra rises to the intensity of madness. Her words produce isolated images of horror, of children slain and served to their unwitting fathers, of bonds broken and oaths violated. The old men of Argos begin to fear the truth of her visions. Unlike the Trojans, the men of Argos recognize Kassandra as a true seer. They cannot, however, bring themselves to envision that a woman could kill the King. In a powerful vision of sexual and political role reversal, Kassandra reveals Agamemnon reduced to a slaughtered animal:

> Ai, drag the great bull from the mate!—
> a thrash of robes, she traps him—
> writhing—
> black horn glints, twists—
> *she gores him through!*

---

²⁵Aeschylus, *The Oresteia*, transl. Robert Fagles (New York: Viking Press, 1975) 150, *Agamemnon* lines 1070–71 and 1074–75.

²⁶*Oresteia*, 288, *The Eumenides* lines 666–71.

> And now he buckles, look, the bath swirls red—[27]
> [emphasis in the original]

Here Klytemnestra, the woman, seizes power, and hers is the act of penetration now perverted from an act of love to one of death. Kassandra recalls the events in the dreadful fall of the House of Atreus, and in doing so, reveals that history is a process of action and reaction. For the self-devouring house that sacrifices loved ones, someone must always plot revenge. The honesty of this perception would appeal to Christa Wolf with her solidly Marxist underpinnings; it mixes fate with human response to produce a more anthropocentric vision.

After foretelling Agamemnon's death, Aeschylus's Kassandra throws off the regalia that marks her as Apollo's seer. She finally rejects Apollo's voice for her own and declares herself "free at last." Christa Wolf reacts directly to this moment of freedom in her sympathy with Kassandra:

> Und ich fühle ihr eine Erleichterung ab, die vielleicht durch ihre bloßen Worte nicht zu belegen ist. Einer drückenden Berufung endlich zu sein, nichts dem Gott mehr schuldig ("Jetzt führt der Seher seine Seherin zum Beil"), nichts ihren Landsleuten ("Sie haben Ilion zerstört. Ich hab's gesehn, wie es geschah"); unberufen, wenn auch nicht vom Zwang zu "sehen" frei, schuldet sie noch sie selbst—was eigentlich? Selbsterkenntnis, Distanz, Nüchternheit glaube ich, bei innigster Betroffenheit, aus ihrer Stimme herauszuhören....
> (*Voraussetzungen einer Erzählung: Kassandra* 13)

Only at this point, after throwing off the god and gaining her *own* voice can Wolf's Kassandra begin to narrate her story of Troy. Aeschylus's Kassandra too seems to take on a new clarity of vision about the future once she has escaped Apollo. Unfortunately, what Kassandra so clearly sees is the coming of Orestes and the eventual triumph of the patriarchy as he is acquitted of his mother's murder—the triumph of the male right of law over the female right of blood.[28] Christa Wolf sees Orestes's acquittal as patriarchal rationalization that must make woman hateful in order to justify itself.

> Das alte Blutrachegesetz, in dem Orest sich verfängt: Nie durfte der Sohn sich an der Mutter vergreifen.... Aischylos scheint damit zu rechnen, daß Nachklänge der heiligen Scheu vor der Frau auch sein männliches Publikum ... noch beunruhigen. Ein Chor von Frauen bekommt die Aufgabe, die Frau als das größte Übel unter dem Himmel zu brandmarken....—Gräßliche Bei-

---

[27] *Oresteia*, 154, *Agamemnon*, lines 1127–32.

[28] In their insightful and moving introductory essay to *The Oresteia*, Robert Fagles and W.B. Stanford argue that a balance between male and female, the Olympian gods and the Furies is achieved to produce a new Athenian democracy built upon law. See 1–99 "The Serpent and the Eagle" in Fagles's translation of *The Oresteia*. While I personally would prefer their reading, the more feminist reading informs Wolf's text. And even in the *Oresteia*, I must admit that the female, though indispensable, does not seem to me to exit on equal footing with the male.

spiele werden zum Beweis zitiert, es gibt schon eine lange Geschichte der Umdeutung der einst unberührbaren Frau in ein Ungeheuer. Die Frau muß weg! heißt es jetzt, ohne Umschweife. Und, als es getan: Doch denkt auch, daß Orest kein Mörder ist. Dies soll als Wahrspruch dem Publikum eingehämmert sein, doch daran ... ist der Grieche gescheitert.

(Voraussetzungen einer Erzählung: Kassandra 81–82)

Wolf associates the triumph of Orestes and the patriarchy with the general suppression of women. Orestes declares in *The Eumenides* that he has suffered into truth (line 274); Wolf takes this policy as typically male as she echoes Horkheimer's and Adorno's *Dialektik der Aufklärung* (1947):

"Lernen durch das Leid"—dies scheint das Gesetz der neuen Götter zu sein, der Weg des männlichen Denkens auch, das die Mutter Natur nicht lieben, sondern durchschauen will, um sie zu beherrschen und das erstaunliche Gebäude einer naturfernen Geisteswelt zu errichten, aus der Frauen von nun an ausgeschlossen sind; Frauen, die man sogar fürchten muß, vielleicht, weil sie— dem Denkenden, Leidenden, Schlafenden unbewußt—weil *auch* sie Urheberinnen jener Gewissensangst sind, die sein Herz wachklopft. Weisheit wider Willen. Kulturgewinn durch Naturverlust. Fortschritt durch Leid: die Formeln, vierhundert Jahre vor unsrer Zeitrechnung benannt, die der Kultur des Abendlands zugrunde liegen.

(Voraussetzungen einer Erzählung: Kassandra 75–76)

Wolf obviously believes this strategy of suffering into knowledge is a mistake on Aeschylus's part, a mistake that structures all of Western culture and that leads us to the edge of our own annihilation in this nuclear age.

Wolf suggests that Aeschylus makes two other "mistakes" as well. The first is to think that Kassandra would mourn for Agamemnon: "Nie hätte sie gesagt: Auch drinnen kann ich/ Agamemnons Los beweinen.—Agamemnon—der letzte in der Reihe der Männer, die ihr Gewalt antaten (der erste war Apoll, der Gott)—ihn beweinen? Da müßte ich sie schlecht kennen."[29] Wolf's Kassandra knows Agamemnon for the weak and abusive man that he is. His pitiful actions act as another indictment of the hero since Agamemnon is both a king and the military leader of the Trojan expedition.

Wolf's Kassandra even sympathizes with Klytemnestra, who must kill her husband, Agamemnon, or return to a repressed condition upon his homecoming. Kassandra knows that she and Klytemnestra could have been allies, sisters, under other circumstances; she also knows that Klytemnestra has no choice in the logic of power but to kill her. Wolf thinks Aeschylus's second mistake—that he has Kassandra and Klytemnestra detest one another—is a mark of his prejudice against Mother Right.[30] Kassandra and Klytemnestra would, perhaps, have been too terrifying as allies. Having predicted Orestes's coming, Aeschylus's

[29] *Voraussetzungen einer Erzählung: Kassandra* 15.

[30] *Voraussetzungen einer Erzählung: Kassandra* 41.

Kassandra accepts her fate and goes to her death. Wolf's Kassandra too accepts death when she has finished the tale that echoes with the realities of our century as well as hers.

Finally, the classical Kassandra appears briefly in Euripides's *The Trojan Women*. A prophetess here as well, Kassandra prepares to be the "bride" of Agamemnon who she knows is returning them both to their fates in Mycenae. Among the women being returned to Greece as prizes of war, Kassandra has been chosen to accompany Agamemnon while her mother Hekuba must follow Odysseus. We learn also from Euripides that Kassandra, like Helen before her, is a classical rape victim. Torn from Athena's altar and raped by one of the Greek "heroes," Ajax the Lesser, Kassandra's sexuality becomes another indication of her defenseless and degraded state. In league with Poseidon, however, Athena will exact some vengeance for the defilement of her sanctuary. She asks Poseidon to make the voyage home a painful event for the Greeks. Given the trials of Odysseus, which Kassandra predicts in the play, and the marital welcome of Agamemnon, her wish seems duly fulfilled.

In a painful irony in praise of "heroism" (a scene which Wolf must have admired), Euripides's raving Kassandra thanks the Achaeans for coming to Troy in order to enable Hektor and the Trojans to die heroes. She argues that had Paris not married Helen, "fame in our house would sleep in silence still."[31] One could only wish that it did. Here too, Kassandra's last vision is of her own death. Envisioning herself as a Fury who will accompany Agamemnon to Mycenae, she foresees her reunion with her brothers and fathers beneath the ground. Their reunion will be a happy one, since Kassandra's death also signifies the wreck of the House of Atreus.

Kassandra Re-Membered

Wolf begins her *Kassandra* with a third-person narrator who is clearly a contemporary of the reader and who we suspect is Wolf herself. By the end of the first paragraph, however, Wolf's third-person narrator becomes the classical Kassandra in her own historical period at the time of the fall of Troy. This merging of narrator and subject takes place in the first few lines of the text. In the final lines of the narrative, Wolf closes the modern frame of her text by returning to the ruins of Mycenae: "Hier ist es. Diese steinernen Löwen haben sie angeblickt. Im Wechsel des Lichts scheinen sie sich zu rühren."[32] The stone lions that seem to move in the shifting light remind us that the "heroic" and destructive tradition still threatens to reanimate itself in our own time. The lion in *The Iliad* figures Achilles in his rage. These ancient petrified lions that threaten

---

[31] *The Complete Greek Tragedies.* Vol. 3, *Euripides,* eds. David Greene and Richmond Lattimore (Chicago: U of Chicago P, 1959) 627. *The Trojan Women* line 399.

[32] *Kassandra* 157.

to stir again remind us that Achilles's spirit (and Wolf's Achilles "The Beast") lives on in our own era. Should the lion rage today, however, the results would be annihilation.[33]

By immersing herself in Kassandra's consciousness, Wolf merges her personal memory with that of her subject. Together, the modern narrator and her classical character re-member the cultural tradition itself; and they dismember many of the patriarchal myths as well as institutions of heroism and valor associated with war. Wolf's Kassandra reassembles the pieces of her past life in order to define a new self that breaks with all of the cultural institutions that enslave both her and the males of her world. Through her re-vision of Kassandra, Wolf inscribes a *new* cultural tradition and unwrites that earlier male tradition that holds her character captive.

Wolf's Kassandra struggles to find a voice for the self that she has so long repressed into the role of daughter or priestess. What she finds first is not a voice, but a long and tortured shriek that echoes the "Aieeeeee!" of her opening line in Aeschylus's *Agamemnon* (lines 1070 ff.).[34] The birth pangs of a painful self-knowledge, Kassandra's opening cry captivated Wolf as she read the *Agamemnon* and realized that Kassandra was the only person in the play who knew herself.[35] When she learns that the Trojan priest Calchas has chosen to stay with the Greeks when his prediction of success for the second ship sent to Greece fails, Kassandra comes to understand the political machinations that impinge upon ritual and prophecy. The epiphany triggers her first experience of her "voice."

> Und ich, hörte ich mich zu Aineias sagen, ich habe es von Anfang an gewußt. Die Stimme, die das sagte, war mir fremd, ... Willentlich ließ ich sie frei, damit sie mich nicht zerrisse; was dann kam, hatte ich nicht in der Hand..... mein Mund, außer daß er den Schrei hervorstieß, erzeugte diese Art von Schaum, der sich auf Lippen und Kinn absetzte.... unbeherrschbar ich.
> (*Kassandra* 45–46)

---

[33]Ironically, however, the lion is also one of those symbols usurped from the matriarchal tradition. Lions are often seen to flank Kybele as she sits on her throne (see Merlin Stone, *Mirrors of Womanhood* 199, and illustration #3 of *When God Was a Woman*). Merlin Stone, *When God Was a Woman* (New York: The Dial Press, 1976); originally published in Great Britain under the title *The Paradise Papers: The Story of the Suppression of Women's Rites* by Virago Limited in association with Quartet Books Limited. *Ancient Mirrors of Womanhood: A Treasury of Goddesses and Heroine Lore from Around the World* (Boston: Beacon Press, 1984); originally published by New Sibylline Books, New York, 1979.

That the lion comes to be tied rather to Achilles's rage and Agamemnon's gate is an indication of how thoroughly the earlier female goddess rituals were in fact subsumed by the later patriarchal tradition.

[34]See Aeschylus, *The Oresteia*, transl. Robert Fagles 150.

[35]See *Voraussetzungen einer Erzählung: Kassandra* 10.

The voice that rends Kassandra's body is the long-suppressed voice of her own recognition of truth. She is forced to acknowledge that Troy is living a series of political lies that draw it closer and closer to war. The seizure that follows this newly released voice will recur several times in the story at points when Kassandra is forced to confront a truth she has suppressed in order to remain loyal to her family and to Troy. Her society will label her mad in order not to have to confront the truth that she speaks. The voice, and the seizure, will come again as Kassandra cries "Woe" and tries to stop Paris's ill-fated ship, bound for Greece and Helen.

Only after long years of political analysis and personal conflict does Kassandra finally master the famous voice that is so despised by her fellow Trojans. When trying to dissuade her father, Priam, from using her sister Polyxena as sexual bait to trap Achilles late in the war, Kassandra does not lapse into madness. Trying to save Polyxena from becoming a mere sexual pawn to be used to "win" the war, Kassandra maintains a cool rationality that infuriates her father and his toadies. This time she is not held by men who restrain her flailing body from its seizure; she is seized by men who imprison her, appropriately enough, in the graves of the heroes. As she attempts to scrape her way out of her tomb, Kassandra thinks, "Jemand winselte: Jetzt nicht den Verstand verlieren, jetzt nicht—. Meine Stimme. Ich blieb bei Verstand."[36] Having faced the worst, and in defense of her sister, Kassandra finds a voice of truth that does not force her into madness and that eventually leads her to the alternative society of women who live in the caves along the Scamander river. It is there that Kassandra finally becomes herself.

Kassandra must struggle to find the discrete self that is often lost to categories and labels. The location and maintaining of this self against a hostile outer world is what western tradition has so highly prized in its history. But Kassandra, having located this individual self, must move on to the next level of selfhood in which one finds meaningful community. Kassandra comes to realize this as she looks for a new "we" to complete her "I," her personal voice. Kassandra comes to realize this necessity for community as she joins the society of the women who dwell in the caves. After being unable to say "we" throughout the text because of her alienated state, Kassandra finally accepts "we," the sign of community, from Arisbe, the wise old woman of the alternate society.

After this first experience of community, of "we," Kassandra dreams of a unified existence in which life and death do not struggle against one another, but constantly metamorphose into new and beautiful shapes. Characteristically, however, Kassandra is awakened from this utopian vision by the harsh realities of the war and of her father's plan to use Polyxena as bait to capture Achilles. The unity and community are fleeting, then, but undeniably important.

---

[36] *Kassandra* 146.

But Kassandra must also struggle against silence in the war. War itself threatens to silence her as history will later. The symbol first used to figure the silencing is unavoidably sexual—i.e., the forcing of something into the mouth. In the dream in which Kassandra is given the gift of prophecy, Apollo in the form of a wolf, spits into Kassandra's mouth when he cannot overpower her sexually. This moment of sexual retribution figures the pollution of Kassandra's true words by the military machine of war. In myth Kassandra is silenced because of a moment of sexual refusal. Wolf adds to this the silence enforced by Troy's leaders because they need to keep the war propaganda positive in order to incite the people to fight.

Kassandra is also silenced early in the story however by her own position as priestess born of the royal house and expected to show allegiance to it. Her warnings are held in check by her own unwillingness to believe in the insanity of war (in the absence of Helen, for example). As the palace shifts from matriarchy and peace to patriarchy and war, Kassandra finds it increasingly difficult to fall into line politically. She is finally driven to speak. Ironically, however, Kassandra's rebellious speaking would save the most guilty of all the war figures, Achilles.[37] But Kassandra wants to sound a moral as well as military alarm by warning "Achilles the Beast" rather than let her own people be reduced to his disgusting level. Kassandra is silenced by her family and the patriarchal structure that it rules. She is not killed outright, but is symbolically enclosed in a beehive-shaped basket (symbolic of the womb), which is hidden in the Tomb of the Heroes, while Achilles is being slain. Forced back into the womb and buried among the moldering bones of past wars, Kassandra's humane protest is silenced before it can have any effect. Kassandra is doubly silenced because of the war—once by her "duty" as priestess to support the war propaganda and once by her courage in opposing it.

Only in the telling of her own tale does Kassandra regain her voice. Wolf's narrative restores to Kassandra what war and "duty" have necessarily robbed her of. That she tells her tale at all is an act of revolt against the heroic tradition. Kassandra even fantasizes about begging Klytemnestra to give her a slave girl who might remember her tale and pass on her voice through generations of women:

> Klytaimnestra, ... Schick mir . . . eine junge Sklavin mit scharfem Gedächtnis und kraftvoller Stimme. Verfüge, daß sie, was sie von mir hört, ihrer Tochter weitersagen darf. Die wieder ihrer Tochter, und so fort. So daß neben

---

[37] Kassandra threatens to warn Achilles of the trap being set for him using the alluring Polyxena as bait. The fact that Kassandra hates Achilles (for his sadistic and cowardly murder of her brother Troilos and the later murder of Hektor) and will nonetheless warn him underlines Wolf's point about the unconditional resistance to the war mentality.

dem Strom der Heldenlieder dies winzge Rinnsal, mühsam, jene fernen, vielleicht glücklicheren Menschen, die einst leben werden, auch erreichte.

(*Kassandra* 93)

The hopes of creating an alternative to the heroic tradition, a society built not upon war but upon community and love and passed down through a matriarchal oral tradition, fires Kassandra's imagination. She envisions a new voice in history, a female counterpoint to the heroic code. She has, however, seen too much reality to become a utopian thinker. Her imagined plea is followed immediately by the lines: "Und daran könnt ich glauben, auch nur einen Tag? Erschlag mich, Klytaimnestra. Töte mich. Mach schnell." We have, of course, never produced those happier non-warlike nations, but in Wolf's text, Kassandra's voice does indeed live on.

Ironically, in repossessing her own voice, Kassandra is also forced to perpetuate what she hates most—the fame of Achilles. Her fondest wish is to eradicate the name of Achilles from all human records, but she cannot even utter the wish without recalling his name to the text. Like Kassandra, the contemporary woman writer who would re-write or un-write the earlier heroic tradition embodied in history and literature is condemned to repeat it in order to change it. She experiences a kind of forced collusion even in the attempt at re-vision. Unless she wants to step entirely outside of the tradition and overthrow it wholesale as Monique Wittig tries to do in *Les Guérillères*, the modern woman author must confront the tradition that suppresses her and continues to glorify the "hero." But even Wittig draws upon earlier myths and tales in *Les Guérillères*. The ideal of an entirely new tradition is illusion. Kassandra knows that she cannot eradicate Achilles's name; it has been inscribed too long on the roles of the heroic tradition. She can, however, redefine that name to be synonymous with all the monstrosity and perversion of war. No one who has read Wolf's *Kassandra* will ever again recall Achilles as a hero. If Wolf's Kassandra cannot erase Achilles's name, at least she blackens it.

Christa Wolf is out to remake thousands of years of the literary tradition, to displace the hero from its center, to make a place for women in it. She also demystifies myth by laying bare its rationalizing pragmatism (such as Achilles's circulation of the rumor of his divine parentage, or Panthous's declaring the dead Troilus to be older than his years so that a prophecy of Troy's fall could not be fulfilled). Wolf does not want to inscribe new female myths; she wants reasonableness to replace the need for myth. Her Kassandra constantly suggests the course that would save Trojan lives even if it means losing face politically. She resists the propaganda poured into Panthous's and Helenus's prophecies. Her madness, ironically, is the constant insistence on the truth and on what is reasonable. But displacing the hero proves a contradictory task; in order to revise heroic myth and female roles in it, Wolf must also re-collect the story. Achilles's name must be spoken in order to be undone. This painful irony is the recurrent and unavoidable problem of all contemporary women re-visionists. Through her rebellious Kassandra, however, Wolf turns her forced participation in the myth into a powerful protest against its ideology.

DAVID DOLLENMAYER

The Search for "Another Face of Germany" in Kay Boyle's *The Smoking Mountain*

In the years immediately following the end of the Second World War, Americans and Germans encountered one another in greater numbers and across a broader spectrum of social classes than ever before. The extreme circumstances under which this encounter took place were bound to throw the differences between the two cultures into sharp relief. The absolute victors confronted the utterly vanquished amid the ruins of their cities. From 1948 to 1952 the American expatriate writer Kay Boyle lived in occupied Germany. In a series of stories and articles written during those years for American magazines, she reflected on this extreme and unwilling encounter between two peoples and in 1951, collected and published the best of these under the title *The Smoking Mountain*. The volume is an extraordinary document of one American writer's attempt both to understand the terrible German past and to find cause for hope in the German future.

In her introduction Boyle states her mission with brutal frankness: "I came to live here, and, by so doing, committed myself to a painstaking and almost completely loveless search for another face of Germany."[1] The trope of two Germanies, one with a good and one with an evil face, informs Boyle's search as well as some of the volume's central images. Again and again in these stories, particular faces are scrutinized as mirrors of the person within.

The opening story "Begin Again" exemplifies several of Boyle's techniques and preoccupations. It is less a story than a panoptic sketch. An American woman drives the Hessian autobahn and talks in turn to four representative Germans to whom she gives rides: a medical student, a fräulein who has a GI boyfriend, a one-legged veteran, and a former judge.

Since these are the immediate postwar years the hitchhikers can plausibly represent a fairly broad spectrum of social and educational background. They are nevertheless united by their refusal to take responsibility for what has happened. The title "Begin Again" thus proves to be a bitter double entendre, rais-

---

[1] Kay Boyle, *The Smoking Mountain: Stories of Germany during the Occupation* (New York: Knopf, 1963) 4. All references to this volume will be given in parentheses following the quotation.

ing hopes only to dash them. The aesthetically sensitive medical student cannot believe that it was the Germans, not the Allies, who blew up the bridges of Florence. The amputee, having acquired a Norwegian wife during the German occupation of Norway, still thinks that 1943–44 were "the good years ... There was more than you could eat up there—milk, butter, eggs, for everyone—no war, no fighting. Those were the good years for everyone" (83). The girl has absorbed both the substandard English and the racial bigotry of her GI boyfriend. Only the monarchist judge seems a possible candidate for "good German." He has been persecuted by the Nazis, yet these positive credentials are immediately invalidated by his aristocratic contempt for the "common people" (85): "If Hitler had been a university graduate ... there could never have been a Nazi movement. There would have been no means of communication between him and the folk" (86). He may scorn the Nazis out of class pride, but he shares their anti-Semitism, despising Roosevelt's sons as "salesmen" and their father as having "Jewish blood" (86).

The moral ugliness of these postwar Germans—their unregenerate bigotry and arrogance—is unsubtly figured forth in their faces. The medical student is "a sharp-faced young man, wary as a cat" with "thin lips" and "long, fleshless hands" (78). The girl wears "Post Exchange nylons on her heavy German legs" (80) and her made-up face is a "sullen, bewildered mask, the blank flesh on which had been painted brightly and viciously a child's stubborn despair" (81). The former judge is described as "small-skulled and as vindictive as an eagle, with an eagle's cold, belligerent eye" (84). (To be sure, the internal corruption of some characters is occasionally belied by their handsome exterior: the "light eyes" of the tall, blond, sun-tanned ten-year-old Horst in "Fife's House" look "without emotion" at a younger American child whose gold wristwatch he covets [92].)

In contrast to the Germans, the woman who picks up the hitchhikers in "Begin Again" is described simply as "an American woman driving past" (78). Some version of this woman, either alone or in the company of a young child, is the center of consciousness in many of the stories in *The Smoking Mountain* and has clear autobiographical characteristics. Her observing eye is apparently dispassionate, even sympathetic (she after all does give the Germans a lift), but the narrator is quick to intervene whenever a German threatens to make too good-natured an impression. For instance, instead of letting the irony of history itself contradict the amputee's prattling about the "good years" in Norway, the narrative interjects: "Those were the years when the gas chambers burned the brightest, the American woman thought..." (83). This figure suggests the urgent immediacy with which Boyle often transferred her own experiences into her fiction.[2] When reading the proofs of *The Smoking Mountain*, she wrote to her

---

[2]Such direct transferral of Boyle's personal experience into fiction is a frequent theme of both Sandra Whipple Spanier, *Kay Boyle: Artist and Activist* (Carbondale and Ed-

agent, "I hate the figure which emerges—the eternal 'I'—from these pages, and I hope to efface her wholly in all the future writing that I do."[3]

Boyle's provocative, partisan descriptions encompass not just the Germans themselves, but the whole country which in these stories seems constantly bathed in "bleak Teutonic twilight" (163). The VWs on the autobahn remind her not of beetles but of "the hard, bisected shells of cockroaches" (77–78). A village church "seemed, in its austerity, vowed to relinquish nothing either to the grace of the rolling wooded country or to the homage of erring man" (217), while even the village geese have been infected by the moral miasma, walking past "in stiff-necked bigotry" (218).

Except for the few surviving direct victims of Nazi persecution in Boyle's stories, her occupation-era Germans fall into two unequal groups. By far the largest is made up of people like those in "Begin Again:" Germans of various social classes "beginning again" their interrupted careers and studies, but also reweaving the torn social fabric of postwar Germany with the threads of bigotry, xenophobia, arrogance, and resentment that allowed the rise of National Socialism in the first place.

The second group is smaller, more fragile, endangered. It consists of those who can't find their footing in postwar Germany: the returning soldiers and the young. There are only a few of them in these stories, and they bear a family resemblance to the heroes of Heinrich Böll's postwar stories: they are misfits without respectable occupation, sometimes physically maimed, often would-be artists or performers. Like Böll, Boyle exploits the ironic possibilities in the reversal of "good" and "bad," "law-abiding" and "criminal" inherent in the clash of these figures with a majority culture which has survived the transition from criminal fascism to nascent democracy with its respectability intact. The title character of "The Criminal," for instance, is a starving, skeletal *Wehrmacht* returnee hired by a former Nazi *Blockwart* to dig potatoes in his garden. The *Blockwart*, a "heavy man" with "heavy-limbed daughters" (202–3) has been permitted continued use of the garden although his house has been commandeered for an American officer and his family. The suffering of the returnee is particularly visible in his sunken, cavernous eyes, where the Americans "saw the lurking thing come furtively to life and wait in trembling, bleak pain" (204). When the starving man breaks into the house and steals some food while leaving all valuables untouched, the *Blockwart* tells the Americans, "It is a mistake to deal with anyone who hasn't a roof over his head . . . I would be quite willing to relieve you of the matter and turn him over to the police myself" (216).

---

wardsville: Southern Illinois UP, 1986) and Joan Mellen, *Kay Boyle: Author of Herself* (New York: Farrar, Straus & Giroux, 1994).

[3] Quoted by Mellen 326.

In "Cabaret," a troupe of young actors led by a veteran with maimed hands stages a satirical review mocking both the allied occupiers and Goebbels, Hitler, and the Germans who had followed them like sheep. The prospering audience of tradesmen, officials, and black-marketeers rock with laughter at both kinds of skit, "even those who had believed in it all once ... And, having laughed, they seemed relieved, as if they had broken a mirror set before them, and now it could no longer bear their completed image" (145).

But the stories in *The Smoking Mountain* are at least as much about the occupiers as the occupied. Only "Cabaret" is peopled exclusively by Germans; all the others grow out of encounters between Germans and Americans. The motto of the book, a quote from Theodor Plievier's *Stalingrad*, indicts the militarization that has turned German society into a "monstrous, smoking mountain" in which "the individual became nothing but wood, peat, fuel oil, and finally a black flake spewed up out of the flames" (vii). Thus from the outset there is a built-in irony, for most of the Americans belong in one way or another to the military.

As she does with the Germans in "Begin Again," Boyle surveys the occupiers early in the collection, in the story "Summer Evening," in order to establish a basic typology. The majority reveal themselves to be politically naive, careerist, and venal (another story is entitled "The Lovers of Gain"), but also daunted by the lowering, hostile atmosphere of Germany. At a cocktail party in a requisitioned villa American officers get drunk, flirt with each other's wives, and discuss how to acquire German antiques at bargain prices. Across the valley from their manic, superficial chatter looms the symbol of the "Teutonic twilight" Germany they occupy with such unease:

> On the opposite hill, the ancient *Schloß* rose, sombre and monumental, above the treetops, its façade and turrets turned toward the widening river valley, appearing to watch, as it had watched century after century, for armored knights on horseback to take shape in the twilight of the distance, or for armored vehicles and low-flying planes to advance, as they had come in April, four years before, out of the area of perpetual dusk that lay fifteen or twenty miles away.
> (99–100)[4]

The only even vaguely sympathetic figure at this party, a young captain named Pete Forsythe, contemplates this scene from the villa's terrace and remarks to a passing guest, "I'm against it. I'm against organized, uniformed annihilation" (105). He and his childlike wife stand in sharp contrast to the other guests: they possess the same youth, vulnerability, and aesthetic sensibilities as Boyle's good

---

[4] Boyle is so obsessed by this scene (a view of the unnamed Marburg where she lived with her husband) as a stage for the confrontation of America and Germany that she repeats it almost verbatim both in the story "The Criminal" and in her novel *Generation Without Farewell*, where the castle is described as having a "heart made of the coldest stone" (New York: Knopf, 1960) 10.

Germans. They contemplate with melancholy the imminent extinction of the whooping crane "like man himself" (108) as an image of a larger fate that has befallen the world, but also the more particular fate probably in store for their kind in the postwar world.[5]

But there is one figure in "Summer Evening" who belongs neither to the insouciant and superficial majority nor the sensitive and delicate minority. He is a young intelligence officer "with cool, dark, diabolical eyes" (103, repeated 104), recently arrived from Berlin. While pursuing one of the women with "controlled hot passion" (106) he is also monitoring the drink-loosened tongues around him and closes the story by remarking to his host, "Seems a bit on the appeasing side—Captain Forsythe—doesn't he, Major?" (115). In a masterful bit of dialogue Boyle reveals the full significance of this sinister figure: chatting about the ease of obtaining works of handicraft from the impoverished Berliners, he remarks "They'll part with their back teeth if you have coffee or lard" (112). Herself very soon to be overtaken by the wave of McCarthyism,[6] Boyle in this image connects the casual discourse of one of its agents directly to the most shocking images of the Holocaust, suggesting that fascism is neither a unique nor a uniquely German phenomenon. Its symptoms are evident in the representative of the power that has nominally vanquished it.

But Boyle locates the most glaring contradiction to triumphal American democracy not in McCarthyism but in the "American dilemma" meticulously described by Gunnar Myrdal only a few years earlier, in 1944. The intersection between German and American racism is announced early in the collection when the GI's German fräulein in "Begin Again" says she "won't have nothin' to do with niggers . . . They're just like animals. They ain't like men" (82). This dilemma is central to two of the most moving and tightly structured stories in *The Smoking Mountain*. Both exploit the same basic situation: a black GI encounters a child victim of the war and an epiphany of individual human kindness occurs.

In "Home," a black soldier from Mississippi finds a German urchin standing in the rain outside the PX. He brings him into the store reserved for US Army personnel and buys him a set of clothes over the protests of the priggish German saleswoman. While he picks out clothes,

> the soldier dreamed the brief, clear dream of love about the boy. For the duration of the dream, the boy was his, the authority of family, of country, of Occupation even, having discarded him; and the soldier, who had known only

---

[5] It is not always easy to tell whether Boyle is slipping inadvertently into purple prose or whether she means her characters to seem a little silly: "'My wife has been crying,' said Captain Forsythe, with the contemplative smile on his tilted mouth. 'We read Proust until late last night, and the world was recreated. Then you come awake'" (107).

[6] See Spanier 177–79 and Mellen 327–41.

leaning Negro shacks, became the provider, the protector at last, the dispenser of white-skinned charity. (159)

When it becomes clear that the boy gets stationed at the PX door by his mother every morning in a scam to appeal to the sympathy of the Americans, the saleswoman cries out a distortion of Boyle's implicit diagnosis of the "average" Germans in "Begin Again" and other stories: "Don't you see how it is with the people of this country? Don't you see they don't know the difference between good and evil any more?" (162). But her idea of evil, it has already been made clear, is anything that deviates from bourgeois propriety: "'He says he doesn't know where he lives,' she said . . . saying these words in condemnation of him and of the people from which he came, her voice grim, relentless, in its yearning for the decency, the order, they had, as a country, known before" (160–61). When she refuses to remove the boy's rain-soaked socks, the soldier stoops to do it himself in what Boyle constructs as a saintly act of abasement and charity, discovering that the boy's feet have suffered frostbite, "the grief of it stabbing his heart . . . and he held the boy's feet cradled in his long, dark hands" (159).

"The Lost" is set on a baronial Bavarian estate, used by the Nazis as a selection camp. Boyle is fond of such symbolically dense environments and makes the most of this one. The place shares the stony gloom of the *Schloß* in "Summer Evening" and all other historic buildings in these stories: "Even before the Americans had mounted the cathedral-like steps, and opened the massive door of the stone-winged house, they felt the chill of winter and silence and death that stood like a presence in its feudal halls." The former library contains the official records, "neatly and alphabetically filed" and including photographs, of the Jews and slave laborers who passed through this place: "It was the eyes of these men and women, who were there no longer, which looked now at the Americans, and beyond them, upon some indescribable vista of hopelessness and pain" (174).

Boyle sets the story up as a perfectly symmetrical transformation of hopelessness into hope, of evil into good, for the Americans have converted the estate into a Children's Center for war orphans from all over Europe. At the beginning of the story, three new boys are dropped off at the Center by an army jeep. They are "Unaccompanied Children" (175), orphaned boys who during the course of the war became adopted as mascots by American soldiers. The MPs have caught them trying to slip onto the transport in Bremerhaven in order to return to the States with their GI adopters.

The central character, the Czech orphan Janos, "a tall, dark-haired boy of fifteen or sixteen maybe" (175), has acquired the army name of Johnny Madden. He has witnessed the hanging of his parents by the Germans, has no surviving relatives, and hopes to be adopted by Sergeant Charlie Madden of Chattanooga who taught him English, how to repair cars, and also ". . . the names of all the stars there is . . . They might be one place in winter, and another place in the summertime ... but he'd call them for you. We was in three countries together, and the same stars was usually there" (192).

Johnny's childhood, like those of his two younger companions, has been brutally curtailed by the war. They have been forced to become boy-men who have already seen more horrors than the director of the center can imagine, and she addresses them accordingly, with diplomatic respect, as "you men" and gives them time to get used to this place. Her charge is to either find surviving relatives they can be returned to or, for the lucky few, arrange adoptions in the US.

Johnny's hopes of adoption by Charlie Madden are doomed from the beginning, however, by the fact that the GI is black. The director resignedly attempts to explain the "color question" (196) to him, and when he realizes there is no chance that he can be adopted by Charlie, he disappears from the center, leaving behind a letter to be forwarded to his friend:

> Yessitdy I talk to the US consil Charlie and what do ya think now? Seems my fammillys jus as good as they ever waz so Charlie I make up my mynd sudden to go back whar they waz waiting for me Im shure ya thinks its for the best Charlie so I says so long. (198)

So Boyle unbalances the symmetry she has led us to expect at the beginning of the story, namely, that American kindness will cancel Nazi cruelty. The focus shifts from Nazi crimes to the ongoing crime of American racism. Even the center's maternal director, the embodiment of the very highest ideals of American warmth, charity, and generosity, is powerless against it: "I cannot explain to you why it is like this, but it *is* like this" (196).[7]

Thus it is Boyle's simple black GIs who come closest to a universal ideal of humanity trying to reassert itself after the horrors of the war. Charlie Madden's familiarity with the stars that are the same from country to country suggests his connection to the universality of the natural world. The nameless GI from Mississippi in "Home" is associated with another universal archetype as he kneels, Christ-like, cradling the frost-bitten feet of the boy. Yet their individual acts of kindness and love, as well as those of the director of the Children's Center and indeed of Janos himself, are at the same time perceived in these stories as more the exception than the rule. They stand under threat of extinction like the whooping cranes adduced in "Summer Evening." Boyle's postwar German settings lead her inevitably to her urgent exploration of the struggle between good and evil. The terrible lessons of the war and the Holocaust are universally applicable, but in these stories, it is above all the Germans who are called upon to prove that they have learned them. Whether they have or not hangs in the balance. In the stories, this question gets both asked and answered indirectly, but in Boyle's introduction it is starkly direct. Her "Stories of Germany during the Oc-

---

[7] Boyle had difficulties selling this story because American magazine editors were skeptical that such a thing could happen, but it is in fact, like many of the stories, based on a real incident that Boyle witnessed. See Mellen 325 and Spanier 190.

cupation" (thus the book's subtitle) are introduced by a report which takes up almost the first third of *The Smoking Mountain* and chronicles the murder trial in early 1950 of Heinrich Baab, the first Gestapo official to be convicted by a German court in the young Federal Republic for crimes committed in course of his duties during the Third Reich.

The modest title "Introduction" obscures the central importance of this piece of reportage to her project in *The Smoking Mountain*.[8] It is almost three times longer than the longest story. In fact, Boyle writes, the stories are paradoxically "the introduction to the trial" because they are "the record of that painstaking search through time and emotion which led eventually to a court of justice" (74). Her stories of a defeated and occupied Germany prepare the ground for the trial's test of the moral fiber of the young Federal Republic. The trial—at which Baab was convicted of fifty-five counts of murder and sentenced to hard labor for life for his role in carrying out the deportation of Frankfurt's Jews—represents the culmination of her loveless investigation of the German soul, a last chance for the Germans to redeem themselves, to show "another face" that might outweigh Boyle's chilling description of Baab. Twelve years before Hannah Arendt's *Eichmann in Jerusalem*, Kay Boyle had already limned the banal face of evil:

> He had a pallid, bloated face, this forty-one-year-old Frankfurt citizen, and he wore a khaki shirt, the collar of which seemed tight around his fleshy neck. His broad rayon tie, which had apparently been striped in yellow and brown in its time, was now faded, and his heavy head, with the front half of the skull naked of hair, hung sideways. For, despite the fact that he was on trial for the murder of fifty-six other Frankfurt citizens, he was concerned with some kind of tidbit, some kind of nut, which his fingers kept shelling out of sight below the panels of the dock. . . . his blunt-fingered heavy hand could be seen only at those moments when he contrived to slip a nut into his mouth. As he prepared the next morsel of food for consumption, his sagging jowls went surreptitiously into motion . . . His slightly bulging, heavily lidded eyes looked slowly and without expression over the occupants of the two benches which seated the press . . . (8)

Boyle the novelist, the shaper of individual faces and fates, refuses to accept both the idea of collective guilt and thus also the collective exoneration being promoted by Adenauer: "The moral decision each German made then is still, in 1950, burningly alive in the consciousness of every German" (6). Two years after the foundation of the Federal Republic, Boyle frames the significance of the trial as a test of the cumulative weight of those individual moral decisions. "Of what, and of how many, was this man Baab a representative?" (10).

---

[8] The piece was originally published in *The New Yorker* (September 9, 1950) as "A Reporter in Germany—The People with Names."

The outlines of her answer match precisely the groupings that emerge in the stories: the evil, the good, and the majority that is neither one nor the other and thus abetted the triumph of the former:

> Before this spectacle of one element of a nation's people brought to trial by another element of that same people, the inevitable and unanswerable question arises as to how strong in Germany each of those elements now is. If this Germany for which Baab stands as symbol can be dismissed as a mere handful of madmen, then does it follow that the members of the Court, and the spectators in it, must likewise be dismissed as a mere handful of sane men who do not speak for the multitudes of Germany? Are the multitudes of Germany something quite different from either of these two groups of which I write? (33–34)

Boyle records with an acute and indignant eye the conspicuous absence at the trial of both the renascent German business and government establishment and the representatives of the American military:

> No handsome German cars, driven by chauffeurs in livery, waited outside the courthouse as they wait outside the Bad Homburg casino . . . [no] German businessmen who are to be seen every day entering the former I. G. Farben building (now used by the American, British, and French occupation authorities . . .), in well-cut overcoats of imported wool, carrying leather briefcases in their smartly gloved hands . . . Not only was there no American in that crowd, but no representative of the West German government in Bonn . . . Those who were the spectators at Baab's trial were, in the main, Baab's victims as well. (9–10)

Several times she contrasts French resistance to German acquiescence and asks why Germans so timidly allowed the Nazi persecution of the Jews. It is particularly interesting that as an answer to that question Kay Boyle, herself a successful and celebrated writer, adduces her conversations with two professional women to whom under other circumstances she would surely have felt a close affinity. One is a philology professor who unexpectedly unburdens herself to the American writer, describing the step-by-step imposition of anti-Jewish laws and ending with the words, "Perhaps there was something else we could all of us have done, but we never seemed to find a way to do it, either as individuals or as a group, we never seemed to find a way" (37).

The other is the Riefenstahl-like aviatrix Hannah Reitsch, a former test pilot for the Luftwaffe and the last person to fly out of besieged Berlin on April 27, 1945, after having accompanied Field Marshal Greim to Hitler's bunker. This woman had dined with Boyle in the summer of 1948 and embodied the kind of dashing romanticism that surely would have appealed to the American writer did it not serve as a pretext for the denial of knowledge about the genocide carried out by the Nazis: "You see, I was a flying woman, a birdwoman, I only knew what was taking place in the sky. I was not even a member of the Nazi Party, for I scarcely knew what the whole thing was about. If you belong to the air, you do not know what is taking place on earth. How can you know?" (43).

While not as analytical as Hannah Arendt commenting on the trial of Eichmann twelve years later,[9] Boyle had lived in Germany long enough and talked to enough Germans to appreciate the complexities and paradoxes that could arise from the collision of class, race, and national arrogance in an individual: "A Nazi-classified 'mongrel,' a lady of breeding, said to me recently: 'Of course, if you had ever had anything to do with Polish Jews you would understand how the Nazis felt. They were an uneducated, grasping people, not at all like the cultivated German Jews'" (50). This woman is representative of "that genteel and confused intelligence that judges persecution and extermination to be less grave matters when storekeepers and insurance salesmen are concerned than when the victims are people of intellectual distinction" (50).

The half-Jewish prosecutor Dr. Kosterlitz, whose mother was killed in Auschwitz, becomes perforce the central figure in Boyle's narration of the trial; he is the chief representative of the good face of Germany. She likes him so much, in fact, that she includes him *honoris causa* in her Francophilia:

> Dr. Kosterlitz can perhaps best be described by the French word *fin*, which means that he is subtle and quick of mind, and exact and light of speech; although German, he had acquired, through intelligence, an almost exclusively Gallic fusion of shrewdness and lucidity... He was not only the appointed conscience of the state, but likewise the playwright and the producer of this drama in which he played. (26)

But Boyle's search for another face of Germany ultimately takes place neither among the educated bourgeoisie like the philology professor nor among the survivors of persecution like Kosterlitz and the surviving victims who testify against Baab, people whose opposition to Nazism goes without saying. She searches rather among the middle and working classes, the ordinary Germans for whom the former judge in "Begin Again" shows such contempt. The jury in the Baab trial ranges from a minor official of the Frankfurt municipal government to a manual laborer and a tobacconist. In spite of her skepticism toward the probability of any genuine remorse or sorrow on the part of the "multitude of Germans," Boyle insists that these six jurors "are representative of a potential majority" (21). For the majority they potentially represent, the Baab trial—not the Nuremberg Trials—provides the first inescapable opportunity to realize Nazi crimes. The victims of those crimes become "the people with names" (thus Boyle's original title):

> For the first time, with the names and addresses of commonplace citizens crowding the scene, many in Frankfurt came finally to believe that vast numbers of other commonplace citizens, with names and addresses as commonplace as theirs, had, in the Nazi years, been systematically and deliberately de-

---

[9]Joan Mellen makes the same point, 321.

stroyed. The photographs of the massed naked dead that were shown to the Germans in 1945 had been dismissed by most of them as propaganda... (55)[10]

Boyle the novelist still requires a particular face to embody this new insight and overcome Baab's blandly evil countenance, an individual cipher of hope for the future to cancel the despair at the past he represents. And near the end of her report, she finds it:

> During the weeks of the trial, a young green-uniformed court guard had sat at times at the end of the bench on which the defense counsel sat below the prisoner in the dock... and, because of the composed earnestness and intelligence of his young face, one's eyes repeatedly sought him out. When one glanced from the defendant's countenance to his, it was as if one turned from darkness to light, from the opacity and muteness of death to the clarity and eloquence of life. (69–70)

This young court guard even attends the trial in civilian clothes on his day off, and on the day of sentencing, he and his colleague

> ... did a singular thing. They opened one half of the press door wide enough to let first one, and then another, and finally a total of six scrubwomen, hatless and wearing their soiled aprons, slip in and stand among the others who had waited since seven in the morning for the doors to open, and who were packed into the courtroom now to hear the few words that were about to be said. (73)

By concentrating on the face of this individual guard which is at the end "for an instant turned toward the press bench, as clear as light with vindicated pride" (74), Boyle assuages her own clearly articulated fear that he may *not* represent the majority of Germans.

If the unambiguous verdict of the trial allows hope to outweigh fear, the cumulative verdict of the fictional stories is more equivocal. Although Boyle calls the stories the "introduction to the trial," this is really true only in a temporal sense: they all occur during the Occupation, while the trial takes place in the young Federal Republic. In an aesthetic and emotional sense however, their inverted sequence in *The Smoking Mountain* as well as their generally pessimistic view of both Germans and Americans modify the stirring optimism engendered by the Baab verdict and the young guard's face.

In the volume's last and longest story, Boyle once again marshals her iconography of faces in order to suggest that in the end, only individual acts of sorrow, repentance, and reconciliation are assured. The story's title "Aufwiedersehen Abend" is an intentional solecism on Boyle's part, the nonce invention of

---

[10] Ruth Klüger, an Auschwitz survivor living in Straubing in Bavaria after the war, makes the same point, although she locates the turning point as the later Auschwitz trials. The Baab trial was perhaps not widely publicized in Germany. See Ruth Klüger, *weiter leben: Eine Jugend* (Göttingen: Wallstein Verlag, 1992) 200–201.

the American Information Services Officer Rod Murray as he tries to describe in his inadequate German a "farewell evening" he is arranging for a departing colleague. The story recounts Murray's bumbling attempts to hire entertainers for the party, his attendance at a *Spruchkammer* proceeding, and finally the party itself.

The somewhat disjointed story is held together by the central figure and a series of extraordinary faces he encounters. In Boyle's classification of Americans, Murray is one of the endangered "odd ones" who "might be disposed of as fanatics" (234). In the war he was a bomber pilot who took part in air raids on Kassel, and now he has returned to Hesse as one of the "civilians with a mission, having accepted both war and peace as their responsibility" (235). He is the only figure in all the stories who explicitly shares Boyle's quest for the good German, "this fateful seeking in an alien country for men with whom free men might have affinity" (235). On his own time after work, he visits village assemblies in a vain attempt to turn them into the critical, democratic community meetings he has known at home in the Midwest. He finds only docile villagers who accept without question the pronouncements of the *Bürgermeister* or *Landrat* and when he excitedly urges them to ask questions, they "turn their heads to stare at him, not in censure, or in ridicule, but merely stare, their bland eyes vacant even of curiosity" (236).

These placid bovine faces contrast sharply to the three extraordinary faces that constitute the nodal points of this story. They show Boyle out to shock us by unexpectedly reversing the conventional correspondences of her physiognomic iconography, namely, that good is attractive, evil repulsive. To be sure, the first face seems rather to reinforce than to reverse these correspondences. It is the face of the aged proprietress of the *Berufsschule für Bewegungs-Ausdruck-Kunst-Rhythmik und Gesellschaftstanz* (sic) where Murray has gone to seek dancers for the party. The face seems like nothing so much as a direct transcription of a George Grosz portrait:

> Her brow was covered by a smooth, oiled, ebony bang which a green silk ribbon held in place, and from under this fringe, her black eyes watched him narrowly. Two spots of rouge, as dark as bruises, stood high upon her cheekbones, and within the shadow of the grotesquely hooked nose, the thin lips of a medieval lackey were painted mauve, and given a shape that was not theirs, so that they might seem athirst for sensuality. A green brocaded neckcloth kept the disaster of her throat from sight, but the fleshless cartilage of her ears was visible through the dyed black tassels of her hair. (240)

The narrator leaves no doubt that this grotesque woman is as "bowed and evil" (239) as her face would suggest. She lewdly misunderstands what Murray is looking for and parades before him three of the girls who work for her in what is obviously a brothel. Their sample song is "Deep in the Heart of Texas." The shocking reversal comes only later, when he learns by chance that this expressionist nightmare of a madam is Jewish. We do not find out how she has survived the Holocaust, nor much else about her, only that she "used to have a big house in Hamburg" and "a fine selection of pupils, girls from decent families" (238). The shocking description of her face would seem then almost gratuitous except that as a specifically Jewish face, it subverts the *fin* Dr. Kosterlitz and reminds us that persecution does not automatically make the persecuted into good people. In any event, Murray knows instinctively, even before seeing her face clearly, that "it would not be she who had cupped in her bare hands, and shielded through the years, the small, hot, eager flame of individual intent, keeping it clear of the collective blasphemy" (238).

The second face shocks in a different way; it is indeed an iconographic reversal. It belongs to the principal prosecution witness in the *Spruchkammer* trial of the former editor of the town's newspaper.[11] This trial lends a certain symmetry to *The Smoking Mountain* by echoing the Baab trial at the beginning of the volume. Again an accused Nazi is being judged in a proceeding run by Germans and—except for Murray—attended only by Germans. But in fact this trial subverts Boyle's hopes for a "potential majority" of penitent Germans. In contrast to Baab, this defendant is "a lean, distinguished, white-haired gentleman" who smiles "discreetly, under his clipped moustaches, at his wife and his three daughters," a man "celebrated and respected" (243) in the town and who shamelessly claims to be an anti-Nazi.

The genuinely anti-Nazi editor called to testify against him, on the other hand, is "a broad, short young man with thick-lensed glasses on his nose, wearing a suit that was too tight for him" (245), who shows no emotion on his "smooth, fat, fair-skinned face" (247). While he speaks, "a crescent of flesh, which lay pink and fresh beneath his chin, shrunk and expanded, deflated, inflated, as if made of rubber" (245). This peculiarity is explained when he testifies that during his internment in Dachau, he was beaten so badly that his windpipe has been broken. The narrator, who has earlier poked gentle fun at the good American Rod Murray's quixotic ineptitude and slight portliness (236), again pulls the rug out from under her readers by presenting us with a comparably good German being mocked and ridiculed by both the genteel defendant—who offers sarcastically to take up a collection "to enable this needy man to buy himself a hearty meal" (247)—and the jeering public crowding the courtroom. Their unruly tumult rises into cries of "Heil Hitler!" (248) and finally forces the young and inexperienced *Spruchkammer* judge to clear the court. Unable to overcome the language barrier and express his solidarity with judge, prosecutor, and witness, Murray can only silently shake their hands.

---

[11] Again, the unnamed town strongly resembles Marburg, which Boyle called a "bigoted little town" in an October 1, 1948 letter to her agent Ann Watkins, quoted by Spanier 175.

Into the third and most extraordinary face of the story Boyle has poured all the ambiguities of her feelings about the Germans and their American occupiers. It belongs to a young medical student and member of the local symphony orchestra who has been hired to play violin at the farewell party. Boyle surrounds him with the emblems of a good German. He is artistic, cultivated, and idealistic, but also self-deprecating: "'We will be doctors. We will cure humanity,' saying it partly in humor to the American" (258). More than that, she is at pains to make him a bringer of hope for the future. He smiles at the party decorations of paper wisteria, "as if he had recognized in these tokens that a long, cold season was about to change" (257) and recommends to Murray a "quite lonely[12] statue of Schiller . . . among the lilacs" on the castle hill. And his face seems to mirror his goodness: "The head was a classical, rather noble head, constructed of long, solid bones, and crowned with a mane of lightish, lively hair." But this is only as long as he keeps his right profile toward Murray. When he finally turns fully toward him, Murray sees

> . . . the face of a broken statue, for a scar ran hideously from the lobe of the left ear, slashed into the shattered temple, and crossed the forehead, a welt that served to seam the cavity where the hinge of jaw and cheekbone had functioned once, but where hinge and cheekbone were no longer, and mounted to stitch the empty temple closed. (258)

Although the young man says his father was an Army surgeon specializing in turning such a broken face into "a warrior's face," in his case they

> . . . knew they could make it look the way they wanted, and then in six months, eight months, it would betray them again. It would look like a musician's face, or a poet's face. It would have the old mark of loneliness on it, and this they could not have. (259)

So paradoxically, in spite of its ghastly disfigurement, this face confirms Boyle's iconography. It is a good face that cannot be made evil, only broken. And what of Rod Murray? His fortitude is tested by this face, but his naive, American self-confidence is shattered by Boyle's final revelation: the student received his wound not at the front, but rather during the air raid on Kassel, the raid in which Murray himself participated.

In this double face, at once handsome and horribly broken, Kay Boyle's search for another face of Germany—and its attendant scrutiny of Germany's American occupiers—reaches its uncertain conclusion. Only as individuals might Rod Murray and the disfigured medical student, the best representatives of their respective nations, be able to reach each other across the abyss of violence, suffering, and guilt: "If the others, the Germans and the Americans alike,

---

[12] Probably a misprint for "lovely."

were to go away and leave them together for a little while, it was possible that something quite simple and comprehensible might still be said" (261).

ALAN KEELE

Walter Kempowski: Tinker, Tailor, Chronicler... *Spy?*
A Note on the Margins of Fact and Fiction

Goethe reportedly first used the title of his autobiography as a retort to visitors in Weimar who asked whether his writings were "Dichtung *oder* Wahrheit." "Dichtung *und* Wahrheit" the sage is said to have replied, which reminds us that not only is truth stranger than fiction, but fiction is often truer than truth.[1]

So perhaps it is immaterial, ultimately, whether the works of any literary author contain objective, historical truth in the mundane sense of Goethe's guests, as long as they contain poetic truth in the more cosmic, Goethean sense of *Grundwahrheit*.

Still, it is instructive to examine the interplay between literary work and historical event, especially if the literary work expressly purports to belong to a genre known as "faction" (fact + fiction), and is styled a *chronicle* of Germany, as is the case with Walter Kempowski's "Deutsche Chronik," which consists to date of six novels: *Schöne Aussicht, Aus großer Zeit, Tadellöser & Wolff, Uns geht's ja noch gold, Ein Kapitel für sich* (an earlier but substantially different version of which is entitled *Im Block*), and *Herzlich willkommen*, as well as three related "Sachbücher": *Haben Sie Hitler gesehen?, Immer so durchgemogelt: Erinnerungen an unsere Schulzeit,* and *Haben Sie davon gewußt?* (the latter a collection of narratives revealing, around the edges and in the cracks of the stock denials, how well known to ordinary people in Germany concentration camps were during the Third Reich).

In addition to Kempowski's own claims for the historicity of his chronicle, at least two scholars, Franz Josef Görtz ("Walter Kempowski als Historiker,"

---

[1] Cf. Erich Trunz's comment: "Goethe wußte, wie viel an dem ganzen Werk Form, schriftstellerische Kunst sei. Das alles nannte er *Dichtung*. Er setzte freilich voraus, daß Dichtung nicht Gegensatz, sondern eine besondere Form der *Wahrheit* sei. Ein Polizeiprotokoll oder ein Arztbericht kann mehr an tatsächlicher Wahrheit enthalten; aber das, was Goethe das *Grundwahre* nannte (an Zelter 15.2.1830), das lebt in der Dichtung, denn sie ist nicht nur Mitteilung, sondern zugleich Symbol." (*Goethes Werke*, Hamburger Ausgabe, [Hamburg: Wegener, 1967], vol. 9, p. 615).

Akzente 1973, pp. 243–54) and Volker Hage ("Walter Kempowski: Eine Art Gedächtnistraining," *Akzente* 1972, pp. 340–49) have compared Kempowski's novels with some of Kempowski's own sources, with his mother's letters, for example. They note only minor variations and conclude that Kempowski's literary works are also very reliable historical documents.

My investigation focuses on one episode from the chronicle and compares it with independent documentation of the same episode, documentation which Walter Kempowski did not know existed. And though the episode is brief, it is arguably one of the most important and most interesting of the entire chronicle: the events described therein lead directly to the arrest and eight-year incarceration of the Kempowski family on charges of espionage by the NKVD, the Soviet Secret State Police.

I will first sketch the story as Kempowski relates it in the chronicle, that is, at the end of the novel *Uns geht's ja noch gold* and at the beginning of *Ein Kapitel für sich* (as well as in the earlier version of the latter, *Im Block*):

At the end of World War Two, during the last days of which his father had been killed on the eastern front, and with their family shipping business ruined, Walter Kempowski, his mother Margarethe, and his older brother Robert reluctantly decide to leave their home in Rostock in the Soviet zone and go to the West. They are in no particular hurry, since Robert has a job at a shipping firm and is in a position to ship their possessions to relatives in Hamburg, which must be done over a period of some months to avoid raising suspicion.

In due time, on November 29, 1947, eighteen-year old Walter illegally crosses the inner-German border to make preparations for the others to follow. In his suitcase he carries a number of bills of lading, collected by his brother at the port, which document the shipping of German reparation goods to the Soviet Union and which he hopes might open certain doors for him in the West.

Walter goes to Wiesbaden where he has a friend named Fritz Legeune, who has some vague connections to the American intelligence community. Sometime after Christmas, with Fritz' help he makes contact with the CIC, the US Counter Intelligence Corps. When he arrives at their office in the Bierstadter Straße, Special Agents Weinschenk and Seeschaf interrogate him. After some small talk about life in the Soviet zone, Walter finally says: "Und dann holen sie ja alles raus."

> "Was denn?" "Babywäsche, Kupferplatten, Zement, Nähmaschinen...." Eine Ladung Zement hätten sie in Leningrad einfach auf den Kai geschüttet, Regen drauf, aus." "Woher ich das alles wisse?" "Von meinem Bruder, der wär am Hafen und aus den Frachtbriefen." "Frachtbriefe? Was denn für Frachtbriefe?—" Sie standen auf. "Die Frachtbriefe, die ich in meinem Koffer habe." "Sofort holen!" ("Junge sieh dich vor!")
>
> Ich holte das Paket, und in der Bierstadter Straße war schon alles bereit. Da war sogar der Chef gekommen aus seinem Zimmer. Eine graue Gesichtsfarbe hatte er, vermutlich von nächtlichen Verhören. Sie zeigten sich die ein-

zelnen Positionen. Großartig! Aber natürlich an sich gar nichts Besonderes. Völlig wertlos, aber immerhin. Ob sie das haben könnten?" Deshalb hätte ich das ja mitgebracht, damit das Unrecht hier bekannt wird. . . . OK, OK. Die Frachtbriefe könnten sie wohl verwenden. Hier, für meine ehrliche Gesinnung: 2 Stangen Camel. Und wenn Sie was brauchen, dann kommen Sie zu uns (*Uns geht's ja noch gold*, 346–49).

When he tells them he needs a job, the CIC agents immediately find him one as a checker in an American commissary grocery store, "eine Art Schlaraffenland," as Walter describes it, where what is called "Broken Stuff," including dented cans of food, is smuggled out in imaginative ways after work by the hungry German employees.

In the middle of February, 1948, Kempowski's friend and roommate Fritz Legeune goes off to Augsburg to visit a certain Lerche, someone described only as a former Nazi from Rostock. Upon his return, his pockets now inexplicably full of money, Fritz mentions to Walter that Lerche now works for the CIC, and that Lerche is going to Rostock the following week.

That gives Kempowski an idea: He, too, will go back to Rostock, legally now, with an interzone passport. He can discuss with his mother and brother their final plans for coming to the West, he can share with them some of his treasure-trove of coffee, cigarettes, and salted peanuts, and he can get the latest batch of bills of lading, which might then help his mother and brother find jobs and living quarters as the earlier batch had helped him.

On the first of March he boards the train in Wiesbaden. Inexplicably, Fritz Legeune strongly objects to him going. "'Ich würde nicht fahren,' sagte Fritz. 'Fahr nicht!' 'Bleib hier, komm, steig aus.' Am liebsten schlüge er mich K.O. und zöge mich aus dem Zug heraus. Ich sei ja wie besessen" (*Uns geht's ja noch gold*, 363).

Kempowski visits relatives in Hamburg for a few days before arriving in Rostock on March 7th. He stays at home only a few minutes before telling his mother he needs to go into town. He takes the tram to the Hopfenmarkt where he meets—mirabile dictu—none other than Mr. Lerche, the man from Augsburg:

Früher war er Fähnleinführer gewesen. Nun war der bei der CIC. Wenn ich zu Fuß gegangen wäre, hätte ich ihn nicht getroffen. Oder eine Bahn später oder eine früher. Aber dann wäre ich ihm vielleicht am nächsten Tag begegnet. "Na, hast DU schon was?" fragte er. —Fritz habe ihm erzählt, daß ich auch für die Freiheit sei. "Pro re III" sollte ich mich nennen, wenn ich ihm mal eine schriftliche Nachricht zugehen ließe (*Uns geht's ja noch gold*, 367).

Later that evening, Kempowski finds himself at home with his mother and brother. While regaling him with tales of the strange goings-on in the Soviet zone recently, they happen to mention that one of their acquaintances, a Herr Mathes, had come over some time before, late at night, had paced nervously around in the apartment, and had finally blurted out that he was in danger, that he had to leave East Germany because of some unspecified political matter Walter was involved in at Wiesbaden. He had refused to say anything more and had abruptly left the apartment. Robert and his mother had shrugged their shoulders and written off the incident as just another freak event (*Uns geht's ja noch gold*, 368).

After a few more anecdotes about bizarre conditions in the Soviet zone, Robert goes out for the evening to visit a girlfriend, and Walter and his mother retire for the night. The next words, the last paragraph in *Uns geht's ja noch gold*, and the first of *Im Block* read: "Im Morgengrauen holten sie mich aus dem Bett. Zwei trugen Lederjacken. Da hast du was zu melden, wenn du wieder rüberkommst, dachte ich."

Walter is arrested immediately, Robert a few moments later as he returns home from his girlfriend's house. One of the three Russians, the interpreter, stays behind and searches the apartment. In the typewriter he finds a letter which Walter had only just started the night before: "'Lieber Fritz' stand da drauf. 'Aha!' sagte der Russe. 'Fritz Legeune in Wiesbaden.' Der wußte ganz genau Bescheid" (*Ein Kapitel für sich*, 11).

This happened on March 8, 1948. A few months later, sometime in late July or early August, while an acquaintance of Robert—a black marketeer of sorts—happens to be visiting Mrs. Kempowski, there is a knock at the door and a young man with wire-rimmed glasses and a trench-coat comes in. "Sein Name wär Katzberger...." Margarethe Kempowski later reports:

> er komme aus Wiesbaden, sagte der Mann—es war ein Amerikaner, man konnte es hören—und er habe den Auftrag, nachzufragen, was mit meinen beiden Söhnen wär. Sie hätten doch Nachrichten über die Plündereien der Russen liefern wollen, und nun habe man nichts mehr von ihnen gehört? Ich erzählte, was passiert war, und er hörte sich das an. Und dann sagte er: die da in Wiesbaden, die täten sicher alles, um meine beiden Jungen zu retten. Die hätten ja ganz andere Mittel, auf höchster Ebene. Eines Tages wären beide wieder da, Robert und Walter, ich sollt mal sehen (*Ein Kapitel für sich*, 41).

Frau Kempowski is surprised that a CIC agent would speak so openly in front of her visitor, a shady character, but later, when the black-marketeer is arrested, her surprise changes to the apparently well-founded fear that he might tell the police about her American guest: Shortly thereafter, in September, 1948, she, too, is arrested.

The Kempowskis are tried for espionage and sentenced to 25 years at hard labor. After five-and-a-half years, in June, 1954, Mrs. Kempowski is released from the infamous women's prison at Sachsenhausen. After eight years, in March, 1956, Walter is freed from the equally infamous men's prison at Bautzen. Robert is allowed to leave Bautzen in December.

When I encountered this episode in Kempowski's novels, I happened to recall from James K. Lyon's *Bertolt Brecht in America* that Lyon had invoked the Freedom of Information Act to get access to FBI files on Brecht, so I conceived the idea of writing to the US Army Intelligence and Security Command at Fort Meade, Maryland, asking them to declassify and release to me any extant documents pertinent to the Kempowski case. Within a few weeks, to my surprise, I received a rather fat file of materials and began to peruse them.

Later, undoubtedly to his surprise as well, I sent copies of some of the most interesting ones to Walter Kempowski, whom I had met some time before, in 1981, during one of his trips to America. From these documents and from Kempowski's letters to me in response to them I have been able to glean the following:

Much in the documents corroborates the historicity of Kempowski's story: According to the CIC documents, he was indeed interrogated by the CIC in Wiesbaden during December 1947. Most of the reports are signed by Special Agent Fritz Weinschenk, the exact (sur)name of one of the agents mentioned in the novels. (The other name mentioned by Kempowski, Seeschaf, does not appear in the CIC documents.)

According to the CIC, Kempowski did indeed obtain a position with the 2009th Labor Supervision Company housed at the Hotel Prinz Nickolas, and was employed as a checker at the Wiesbaden Sales Commissary.

So far, so good. But now the matter gets a bit more complex: According to Special Agent Weinschenk's reports, Kempowski is "first routinely interviewed as a border crosser about December first, 1947," and then returns several times to the CIC during December 1947, January and February, 1948. (The novels make it sound like he made just one visit to the CIC after Christmas to give them the bills of lading.)

According to the documents, Kempowski also told the CIC he had left the Soviet zone to "escape political pressure being exerted against him by one fnu [first name unknown] KOMMISSAROV, political officer of the Rostock SMA [Soviet Military Administration]," something not mentioned in the novels nor in Kempowski's subsequent responses to me about the matter.

The perhaps most substantive difference between the accounts is that in the CIC version, Kempowski did not actually have in his possession any bills of lading at all. Rather the reports read that he "volunteered information which was of no apparent CI value, but which might be considered to incriminate Subject from a Soviet viewpoint." Kempowski confirmed this in a letter to me: "Ich hatte keine Frachtbriefe, ich wollte sie beschaffen."

Surprisingly, there *are* 92 pieces of shipping data, labeled exhibit A, in the file, but Weinschenk's reports state that a certain friend of Kempowski named Hans Siegfried (whom Kempowski acknowledged is identical to the figure of Fritz Legeune in the novels) came to this office about 8 April, 1948, with the attached shipping lists, stating that Subject [Kempowski] had been arrested at his parent's [sic] home in Rostock. Siegfried stated that subject had made arrangements with him prior to leaving Wiesbaden, that in case something happened to him, Siegfried would aid him in his self-appointed mission.[2] Upon the receipt of a telegram from his brother informing him of Kempowski's arrest, Siegfried wrote his girlfriend in Rostock, instructing her to secure the shipping lists. The girlfriend contacted a clerk in the Rostock office of Derutra [Deutsch-Russische-Transport-Agentur] who removed the lists from the safe and gave them to Siegfried's girlfriend. She took the lists to Hamburg, from where she sent them by registered mail to Hans Siegfried in Wiesbaden.[3]

Agent Weinschenk also claims to have learned from Hans Siegfried's telegram that, along with Walter Kempowski and his brother, a man named Merk had been arrested as well. According to Weinschenk's reports, Hans Siegfried

> admitted having visited fnu Merk in Wuerzburg shortly before Merk's departure for the Soviet zone, and stated that he had known Merk's and Kempowski's intentions. Both were known to him from schooldays in Rostock. He stated that Merk knew that he (Merk) was wanted in the Soviet zone because his contact with an American intelligence agency had leaked out, but that Merk departed in spite of emphatic warnings.

In his correspondence with me, Kempowski confirmed that Merk is identical with the mysterious Lerche whom Hans Siegfried, alias Fritz Legeune, visited (the novels say it was in Augsburg rather than Würzburg) shortly before Lerche left on a CIC mission for Rostock. This is also the man Kempowski happens to meet in Rostock the day of his arrival.

In language replete, in my view, with transparent deniability disclaimers, the CIC documents tell us further that in February 1948,

> Kempowski offered to obtain general information in Rostock, which he intended to revisit. He was told that any effort he made to collect information in the Soviet zone would be done on his own initiative and that he would not be considered as on assignment from this office nor connected with this organization in any way. Subject departed with this understanding[4] and left Wiesbaden about 25 February, 1948.

---

[2] Such phrases as "self-appointed mission" cause me to suspect that the CIC agents were careful to add an element of "credible deniability" to their reports in order to limit their responsibility for what happened to Kempowski and the others.

[3] Weinschenk felt—and I agree—that this whole story about the girlfriend sounded fishy, and he suspected that the 92 shipping lists may not have been legitimate.

[4] The novels rather masterfully portray the agents' keen interest in the bills of lading, as Kempowski's treatment of the dialogue allows us to glimpse their excitement emerging from beneath the veneer of their studied professional insouciance. This creates an interesting paradox: even though it is *fiction* that he actually had the documents in his

Given the desirable job in the commissary and other substantial payments by the CIC to Kempowski, methinks Agent Weinschenk—in a report written AFTER the arrest—doth again protest too much that Kempowski was acting on his own, especially when one also considers that an American CIC agent apparently later risked exposing himself in East Germany in order to visit Mrs. Kempowski and inquire about the boys. (Kempowski confirmed in his letter to me that the Katzberger character is factual, and that his real name was Oky or Okey.)

Kempowski's letters say that he went back to Rostock primarily because of homesickness, but one is still left to wonder about his secondary and even tertiary motives. When he says he accidently meets Merk, alias Lerche, at the Hopfenmarkt, for example, he makes it sound in the novels like a quirk of fate. Yet Hans Siegfried tells Agent Weinschenk that "he had known Merk's AND Kempowski's intentions" in Rostock, and even the novels themselves record the clearly conspiratorial question: "Hast DU schon was?" as well as the code-name pro-re III. Here again, though they obfuscate much, the novels at times reveal even more evidence of Kempowski's serious involvement with the CIC than the CIC documents do.

And some of the omissions in the novel, like the mysterious visit of Herr Mathes to Robert and Frau Kempowski during the time Walter is residing in Wiesbaden, may be explained by certain things Kempowski did not know, something which emerges from a chilling statement with which Agent Weinschenk concludes one of his earlier reports: "It is the opinion of this agent that subject [Hans Siegfried] and RILKE [another roommate from the Hotel Prinz Nickolas] are low-level informants of the MVD [the secret police] in Rostock and that they contributed to the arrest of Kempowski and Merk."

Acting on this suspicion, Weinschenk requests and receives from other agents more information about Siegfried. A report written thereafter reads:

> From the contents of the enclosed SRI, it appears that the suspicion voiced against subject [Hans Siegfried] in the above-referenced MOIC may be well founded. This further raises the question as to whether the shipping lists submitted to our sub-region Wiesbaden as having been "lifted" from the Rostock offices of Derutra are legitimate or not.

After he received copies of the CIC documents from me, Kempowski's letter contains a spontaneous denial that Hans Siegfried could have had anything to do with his arrest, ("Siegfried hat mich ganz sicher nicht angezeigt"), but in the same letter he added a statement which seems to hint at the possibility of

---

possession, that the CIC was deeply interested in what he had to offer is probably portrayed more *factually* in the novels than in the CIC documents themselves, certainly there is more Goethean *Grundwahrheit* in the fiction than in the documents.

Siegfried's complicity: "Siegfried sollte in der Tat nach Rostock fahren, hat aber im letzten Augenblick Abstand genommen davon."

When Kempowski learned from the documents that his friend had given the shipping lists to the Americans after his arrest, he quite angrily wrote "*Siegfried hat mir nie etwas davon erzählt* [underlined by Kempowski in his letter], und daß ich dahintergekommen bin, daß er so eine Art Leichenfledderei begangen hat, als mein guter Freund—das könnte unserer Freundschaft den Rest geben."

So where is this taking us? I'm not sure one could ever write this cloak-and-dagger hi/story "wie es eigentlich gewesen," nor am I clear where the point of diminishing returns in the matter lies: if I had discovered something like this about Shakespeare or Homer or Wolfram, no doubt it would be different than for Walter Kempowski.... Perhaps a few interim conclusions will help to take our minds off that injustice:

As Görtz and Hage already demonstrated, the espionage episode confirms that Kempowski's story does have a very strong basis in fact, in actual historical occurrences. That comes as no surprise. The inclusion of corroborated names, places, dates and events does tend to lend credibility to the work's role as chronicle.

But accuracy can be a double-edged exegetical tool. The accuracy with which so many events are portrayed in the Chronicle, including exact details such as names and dates, suggests that departures in the novels from actual events may also be attributable to factors besides lapses of memory on Walter Kempowski's part.

And there remain clear differences between what Kempowski apparently knew and what he writes, when he makes it appear in the novels, for example, as though his one-time visit to the CIC was a kind of *Dummerjungenstreich*, and his meeting in Rostock with Merk (alias Lerche) a kind of bad karma.

To the extent the CIC documents can be believed, and in this regard I think they can, he apparently conferred with the CIC on a number of occasions over a period of three months, went back to Rostock with the clear intention of procuring shipping lists for the CIC, and met his contact man Merk according to some plan prearranged in all probability in Würzburg by his (false?) friend Hans Siegfried.

So quite aside from things he may not have known about, like the presumptive double-agent role of his friend, why did Kempowski alter or obscure in his chronicle things he knew to be facts? Perhaps it was done unconsciously? Almost everyone embellishes or tightens up stories in the retelling. Contemporary theory and research into the subjectivity of memory, that of the neurology of storage and retrieval alone, suggest that this is an extremely complex, unconscious, and *inevitable* process, over which we do not entirely have control.[5]

But one can also alter facts consciously. I believe some of these changes were made very consciously, in part, apparently, to prevent the Kempowski family from incurring even more grief from their incursions into the murky and dangerous world of cold-war espionage. These practical reasons I will briefly discuss before turning, finally, to what I consider more interesting, if more vexing, symbolical considerations, which may, however, if my conjectures are correct, shed a bit of new light on the literary and aesthetic qualities of the German Chronicle.

The former are soon told: In 1956, when Walter was released from Bautzen, he applied for a kind of reparations payment from the West German government, available at that time to refugees who could show they had been persecuted for political reasons in East Germany. But as he filled out the complex application forms, he encountered, he says, one innocent-looking question near the bottom left on page 23, which asked if the applicant had ever had any contact with a Western intelligence agency. Without thinking about it, Walter wrote *yes*. Consequently his application was at first denied, though later he did receive 6,347 Marks in reparations (cf. *Herzlich willkommen*, 37–38, 328–29). His brother, however, released some months later and thus forewarned of the consequences of writing *yes*, wrote *no*.

I believe one reason for the relative *Verharmlosung* of the events as described in the chronicle, the attempt to downplay the extent of the actual espionage activities of Walter and his brother, is because Walter Kempowski, who suffered terrible guilt for his responsibility in the imprisonment of his mother and his brother in the first place, understandably wished to prevent his brother from getting into any further difficulties with any governmental agency, even years after the fact, over the complete truthfulness of his answer to that crucial question.

But if Kempowski had really wanted to cover up the facts to avert blame from his brother or from himself, for that matter, he could have done it simply by further acts of omission: he could have included an account of the arrest without mentioning in the novels his involvement with the CIC, nor Fritz Legeune's unexplained money, nor his meeting with Lerche, nor the visits of the mysterious Herr Mathes or the American agent Katzberger, nor the fact that it was his brother Robert who got the shipping lists for him in the first place.

---

[5] I refer to such work that by David E. Rumelhart on "Schemata: The Building Blocks of Cognition," in *Theoretical Issues in Reading Comprehension. Perspectives from Cognitive Psychology, Linguistics, Artificial Intelligence, and Education*, Rand J. Spiro, Bertram C. Bruce, and William F. Brewer, eds., (Hillsdale, New Jersey: Lawrence Erlbaum Associates, 1980).

Kempowski seems to walk a kind of tightrope between two competing desires: on the one hand he appears careful not to incriminate himself or his family beyond a certain point, and on the other he includes the espionage story, in considerable incriminating detail, in his narrative.

Perhaps the reason for this is simple and obvious: the episode is so central to his narrative, and so interesting an event in itself, that it would have been unthinkable to leave it out. So he included it, leaving out just enough detail to preclude further calamity. This explanation is possible, but not entirely satisfying.

Another possibility, also not entirely satisfying, but more intriguing, is that Kempowski wished to *universalize* his experience, without removing his or his family's culpability in the matter, yet making it into something that was in fact a bit more like bad karma, a bit more like the kind of trap any German could have stumbled into in the charged climate of the cold war.

My working hypothesis is that for symbolic and universalizing reasons Kempowski may have wanted to portray himself as a bit more of a victim of global politics and a bit less of an active spy (at least relative to the view given by the CIC documents), a clue to which is found in the novels, in the paragraph just before his encounter with the CIC, in a description of the hotel where he and Fritz Legeune live in a kind of boarding house milieu. With a reference to Thornton Wilder's *The Skin of Our Teeth*,[6] Kempowski writes: "Immer mehr Leute kamen ('Nun mach doch die Tür zu!'), und schließlich saßen wir wie Mr. Anthropos und seine Familie beim Nahen der Eiszeit. Nur die Dinosaurier fehlten" (*Uns geht's ja noch gold*, 346).

Is it possible that though Kempowski narrates the history of our century on the basis of details drawn from the lives of his family and from his own life, he is in fact raising himself, his associates, and the Kempowski family to the symbolic level of *everyfamily*? Can he be subtly portraying them as a microcosm of the human family, the family of Mr. Anthropos, certainly the German branch of the Anthropos family, fated to experience in our century two world wars, the division of their country, and their role as a pawn between two superpowers? Neither innocent bystanders nor solely responsible for it, they personally suffer all the grief our century has to offer.

This universalizing symbolic tendency is made a bit clearer in *Herzlich willkommen*, when Walter, only recently released from prison (and as a more-or-less random substitute for a clergyman who has two competing invitations and decides to take the more exotic one to California), is invited to Locarno for six weeks to attend an all-expenses paid ecumenical conference. Here, in the Casa Zwingli (Walter is expressly pigeonholed by this group as a Lutheran, thus

---

[6]The German title of this play, *Wir sind noch einmal davon gekommen*, is uncannily similar in style to the titles of the books in Kempowski's German Chronicle, causing me to speculate that in some ways it may have served as their model, perhaps not only in its title.

underscoring by that juxtaposition with Zwingli a *division* among religious groups, not their unity), people of all faiths gather from all over the world, ostensibly to foster the cause of global understanding. In the event just the opposite happens: as a personification of collective guilt, Walter is ostracized and made a scapegoat simply because he is a German. He is blamed, as a microcosm of all Germany, for the war and the Holocaust, and, more subtly, for Germany's more recent history: the narrative emphasizes that the Swiss newspaper his judgmental associates see Walter holding at breakfast just happens to display the incriminating headline: "Wiederbewaffnung der Bundesrepublik macht Fortschritte."

Like the family of Mr. Anthropos in the hotel, the Casa Zwingli community is also essentially a microcosm of our planet, in this case a microcosm of a divided humanity, unable and unwilling to communicate, a significant symbol for which Walter believes he sees in a tapestry prominently displayed on the dining-room wall:

> Über der Anrichte hing ein Wirkteppich, auf dem der Babylonische Turm dargestellt war mit Menschen davor, die die Hand hinter das Ohr hielten. Nach dem Essen der gemeinsame Choral in aller Welt Zungen — was da die Leute wohl gedacht haben, die draußen grade vorübergingen (*Herzlich willkommen*, 98).

When finally his turn comes to say the Lord's Prayer at supper, Walter decides to employ his Rostock Low German dialect:

> Unse Vadder du, in'n hogen Hewen....
> Da war aber schlagartig Ruhe im Aufenthaltsraum! Dieser junge Mann, dieser lutterische oder lutheerische Mensch, der sprach da ja in einer Sprache, die irgendwie bemerkenswert war. Die babylonischen Bauleute auf dem Wirkteppich hielten die Hand hinters Ohr, und dasselbe taten die hier Anwesenden nun allesamt (*Herzlich willkommen*, 103–4).

In this passage, by the simple device of juxtapositioning two groups of people holding their hands up to their ears, Kempowski's poetic imagination raises an unremarkable, practically random private historical event to the symbolic level of the entire world's population, still as incapable of communication as it had been at the Tower of Babel. Like the family of George Anthropos, humanity, with culpable/innocent Walter Kempowski as its scribe, again experiences the approach of the ice-age.

I realize that I have only sketched out here the beginnings of this universalizing everyfamily motif in Kempowski, and the related symbolism of its eschatological and apocalyptic fears of our century as ice-age. The everyfamily/ice-age topic deserves a separate investigation, which I know would be beyond the scope of this paper because I have already done some work on it. My preliminary investigations on the subject, aided by my concordance[7] of the German Chronicle, reveal that these symbols run like red threads through the entire complex tapestry, picking up associative biblical and mythic dimensions as they go: The family of Kempowski/Anthropos confronts mythic signs of the coming ice-age from Noah's Ark to the Tower of Babel as they experience history from the Kaiser to Hitler to the cold war.

In the end I remain convinced that it is such universalizing symbolic literary concerns, structural and aesthetic, that most thoroughly shape Kempowski's narrative, including the espionage episode, and account for the most significant differences between fact and fiction. To play their role as everyfamily, the Kempowski/Anthropos family has to tend toward the typical, not toward the unique or outstanding, as they experience history. Thus they tacitly support the Kaiser with their conservative, chauvinistic views, but they are not fiendish warmongers. As fellow travelers they passively tolerate Hitler, yet do not stand apart as evil Nazis. Their lives are disrupted by the cold war, but they are not *really* spies. . . .

Paradoxically, one misses this dimension of the German Chronicle precisely if one is misled by its aura of *historicity*. It is easy to overlook Kempowski's "Dichtung" if we believe we are reading a *mere* chronicle, mere "Wahrheit."

---

[7]Published in 1994 by Georg Olms Verlag, Hildesheim.

CECILE CAZORT ZORACH

Home Territory:
The New Germany in Recent American Fiction

Toward the end of Joyce Carol Oates's short story "My Warszawa: 1980" in *Our Wall*, her collection of pieces set in Central Europe, the American visitor anticipates her imminent departure from Warsaw as follows:

> In another day they will be leaving Warsaw—in another day they will be gone. They will fly out of Poland to Frankfurt, to the West; immediately they will recognize their home territory. Posters of left-wing *Terroristen* are prominently displayed in the Frankfurt Airport—sad sullen intelligent, faces, the eyes rather like Judith's own—and young German guards stroll about in pairs, their submachine guns cradled casually in their arms. A journalist friend of Judith's who once interviewed West German soldiers reported that the young men had never heard of Auschwitz, Belsen, Dachau... they'd never even heard the names.
>
> Along with standard signs for restaurants, restrooms, telephones, and first aid there will be, in the Frankfurt Airport, signs for sex shops: cartoon drawings of the female figure. Home territory, the West.[1]

This passage conveys an ironic discrepancy between the reassuring and the disturbing in the familiarity of West Germany to the American visitor. "The West" contrasts with the East Bloc as a familiar part of our own experience, visually distinguished by the signs of a rich, industrialized, capitalist society. This familiarity, however, arises in part from the threat of violence and of exaggerated police intervention, the dangers of short historical memory, and the misogyny of consumer culture. These qualities of Germany, an alien, "foreign" country, characterize the United States as well. Finally, though, there is Auschwitz, permanently dividing "us" from "them"... or not? The tension between the reassuring and the disturbing, in a country which after nearly five decades of strong American influence has come to seem familiar, "home territory," permeates texts by American writers as diverse as William F. Buckley, Joyce Carol Oates, Walter Abish, and Ward Just. In these texts the various faces of the Federal Republic mirror aspects of our own culture's concerns and anxieties about our place in the

---

[1] Joyce Carol Oates, "My Warszawa: 1980," *Last Days*. NY: E. P. Dutton, 1984. 185.

world: our relationship to our history, the implications of our economic power, our international position, and other nations' perception of us.

Surely no non-anglophone country has dominated the American literary imagination in the last half of this century as Germany has. And, of course, the twelve years of Hitler's rule have generated a disproportionately greater number of fictional works than has the half-century of the Federal Republic. Even when one sets aside literature of the Holocaust as a completely distinct category, one confronts a huge body of fiction surrounding the Third Reich.[2] Supermarket bookshelves regularly feature pulp thrillers about descendants of Nazis scheming to overthrow Western civilization.[3] The New Germany, that is, the Federal Republic after the success of the Economic Miracle, by contrast, shows a much lower profile. Indeed, its profile sometimes seems so flat, as in the Oates passage, as to appear barely noticeable at all, until enhanced by resonances of past and present political terror. This "depthlessness"[4] itself comes to dominate a text like Abish's *How German Is It*, written before its author ever set foot in the Federal Republic. Even as a setting for espionage novels or international thrillers during the Cold War, pitted against the German Democratic Republic, West Germany lacks the presence in American fiction that it occupies in British novels, for example those of John Le Carré or Len Deighton. In general, it is probably true that to the literary imagination of other industrialized countries, a sta-

---

[2] For definitions and discussions of "Holocaust literature" see Lawrence Langer, *The Holocaust and the Literary Imagination*. New Haven: Yale U. Press, 1975; Saul Friedlander, ed. *Probing the Limits of Representation; Nazism and the "Final Solution."* Cambridge: Harvard U. Press, 1992; Alvin Rosenfeld, *A Double Dying. Reflections on Holocaust Literature*. Bloomington: Indiana U. Press, 1980; and S. D. Ezrahi, *By Words Alone: the Holocaust in Literature*. Chicago: U. of Chicago Press, 1980. Rosenfeld's *Imagining Hitler*, Bloomington: Indiana U. Press, 1985, examines one aspect of the Nazi legacy and includes pulp fiction. In many ways distinct from Holocaust literature is the considerable body of postwar American fiction reflecting the war years and their aftermath in Germany, an American *Trümmerliteratur*, e.g., Vonnegut, Pynchon, Thomas Berger, John Hawkes (*The Cannibals*). See Martin Meyer, *Nachkriegsdeutschland im Spiegel amerikanischer Romane der Besatzungszeit*. Tübingen: Gunter Narr, 1994. This Germany, however, has little in common with the New Germany examined in this essay.

[3] This phenomenon is just as pronounced in British espionage fiction. In 1978 Melvin distinguished five eras of British spy novels, the last of which emerged with détente and the waning of the Cold War and entailed "the attempts of unregenerate Nazis to create the Fourth Reich and apolitical super-criminals." David Skene Melvin, "The Secret Eye; The Spy in Literature; The Evolution of Espionage Literature—a Survey of the History and Development of the Spy and Espionage Novel." *Pacific Quarterly* 3 (1978), 15.

[4] Fredric Jameson, *Postmodernism, or, The Cultural Logic of Late Capitalism*. Durham: Duke U. Press, 1991, 12.

ble and prosperous Federal Republic appears lackluster, justifying the remarks of one German commentator in 1986, "daß eine ökonomisch gesunde Bundesrepublik in der Rolle des Klassenprimus in Europa wenig Farbe hat."[5] Nonetheless, the New Germany, with its eruptive violence, expansive consumerism, dubious history, and frequently awkward international alliances, has in recent decades entered American fiction to cast light—and sometimes shadow—on our own sense of cultural identity.

Although most American espionage fiction situates the Federal Republic either as a background of international intrigue, or as a source of neo-Nazi conspiracy or sometimes even of international intrigue managed by people who could just as well be Nazis, a few have focused explicitly on the crucial historical and political situation of the New Germany. Of particular note for their treatment of the West German dilemma are William F. Buckley, Jr.'s two spy thrillers about political events in the Federal Republic, *Stained Glass* (1978) and *The Story of Henri Tod* (1984).[6] Less suffused with the paranoia and conspiratorial intrigue developed in the labyrinthine plots of mainstream espionage novelists such as Robert Ludlum, Buckley's novels nevertheless use conspiracy theory "to think the impossible totality of the contemporary world system" (Jameson 38). Both works deal with the precarious position of the Federal Republic between the US and the USSR during the Cold War: *Stained Glass* reflects the consolidation of the German division in the early 1950s, while *Henri Tod* focuses on the construction of the Berlin Wall in 1961. On a superficial level, both books appear to reflect a simplistic, indeed Manichaean, view of the Cold War as the struggle between the freedom-loving West and the evil, repressive Soviet Union; as one reader has observed, it is even possible to read them in the context of "Reagan's . . . (spectacularly successful) remythologization of American post-Vietnam foreign policy."[7] But through the portrayal of the Germans, the East-West conflict comes to appear more problematic. In both works Buckley pairs his slick, Yalie CIA agent Blackford Oakes, unabashedly, in his words, "engaged in the organic job of maintaining peace and freedom," with an enigmatic, visionary young German bent on saving his country from the Communist threat

---

[5]Peter Hasenberg, "'The Teuton's inbred mistake—'; Das Deutschlandbild im britischen Agentenroman," Hans-Jürgen Diller; Stephan Kohl; Joachim Kornelius; Erwin Otto; Gerd Stratmann, eds. *Images of Germany. Anglistik und Englischunterricht* 29–30. Heidelberg: Carl Winter, 1987, 236. In this connection Hasenberg also quotes Karl-Heinz Bohrer's essay "Die europäische Dekadenz und Wir. Warum die Westdeutschen nach außen so gesichtlos wirken" in Bohrer's *Ein bißchen Lust am Untergang. Englische Ansichten*. Munich, 1979. 121–28.

[6]William F. Buckley, Jr., *The Story of Henri Tod*. Garden City: Doubleday & Co., 1984. *Stained Glass*, Garden City: Doubleday & Co., 1978.

[7]Barry Sarchett, "Unreading the Spy Thriller; The Example of W. F. Buckley," *Journal of Popular Culture* 26:2 (Fall, 1992), 128–29.

and doomed in the end to fall foul of Soviet belligerence and American timidity. In both novels, however, the German hero's apparently impeccable anti-Nazi credentials—one fought in the resistance in Norway and has a Jewish best friend while the other is a Jewish survivor—are coupled with a peculiarly selective reading of German history which calls into question his understanding of the New Germany's position.

In *Stained Glass* Count Axel Wintergrin in 1952 restores a thirteenth-century chapel in his family's Westphalian castle, bombed by the Allies in the War, and at the same time campaigns successfully throughout Germany for his political party, the single-minded purpose of which is the unification of both Germanys. In *Henri Tod*, the Jewish survivor Tod in Berlin, 1961, plots a campaign, code-named "Rheingold," with his secret "Bruderschaft" to sabotage the imminent construction of the Wall. Tod, an ascetic teetotaler, lives in a building which had housed Graf von Stauffenberg shortly before his arrest; wounded during a foray into East Berlin, he recovers in the Führer's own bed in Hitler's private railroad car, which has been meticulously restored by Walter Ulbricht's nephew. Both Germans, Wintergrin and Tod, show troubling signs of messianic zeal and impatience with normal procedures of a democratic state. Tod's many quirks include a proclivity for secret societies with Teutonic names and an intense relationship with his sister worthy of a Thomas Mann text. Before the war, he and his sister (who as young adolescents "had privately sworn never to sleep other than in a single room," 45) form their own secret society called "Valhalla"(45), predating his Bruderschaft and his operation Rheingold by several decades. Both Tod and Wintergrin are charismatic personalities who attract devoted "disciples" (*SG*) prepared to follow them anywhere in their missions. Both gradually win first the respect, then the love of the American Oakes. Yet, despite the American's personal affection for them, both of these heroic figures end up sacrificed to the preservation of balanced power in the Cold War, with Washington bowing to the inexorable Moscow. The obtrusive intermingling of real, historic personalities with the fictional characters signals the rupture between public exigencies and private ethics driving the plot as in so much espionage fiction of the late twentieth century. *The Story of Henri Tod*, which begins on the Kennedy yacht, ends with the President at a state dinner offering almost *sotto voce* a toast to "Rheingold." *Stained Glass* ends years after the CIA-engineered accident that killed Axel Wintergrin with a conversation between Blackford Oakes and Allen Dulles. Here, too, the government spokesman confesses a private belief in the rightness of the patriotic German's cause. Yet he raises the issue of ambiguity and its risks that lies at the core of both novels. The tension between individual idealism and government ideology takes on added poignancy in Germany, where history has encumbered eccentric idealism with explosive potential.[8]

Buckley's two German novels go beyond simply positing a Federal Republic as a pawn in the Cold War. More interesting is the ambiguity of the two respective German freedom fighters and their brand of patriotic nationalism, which the American protagonist senses but avoids confronting. For Oakes and even more for the reader, nostalgia for unqualified heartfelt allegiances struggles with a dawning recognition that modern politics and history render such allegiances untenable and, in Germany, downright alarming. In *Stained Glass* Oakes never allows himself to reflect on the implications for fledgling German democracy of a new party founded by a charismatic aristocrat who poses a serious threat to Adenauer's power and who talks publicly about Germany's potential economic and nuclear military strength (181). In *Henri Tod* Oakes does find himself in the uncomfortable position of having to explain his inability to aid the German's struggle for "the future of Berlin and of millions of Germans . . . the future of the West," by explaining the processes of democratic bureaucracy:

> How in the hell *can* I? I'm an American citizen and an agent of the Central Intelligence Agency, and we get our instructions from the President of the United States, and he gets his from Congress, and Congress gets its from the voters. Now you people have put on one hell of a show. But you also write your own rules. You go out and kill people as required. I'm not saying the people you do this to don't deserve it. I'm not even suggesting that if I lived here I wouldn't join your organization. I'm just saying that I'm an American citizen, and when I got into this job I made certain *commitments*— (218–19).

A free-floating idealist like Tod shows little interest in the grounding of political activity in law, indeed in the whole concept of the *Rechtsstaat*, so carefully articulated in the West Germany's Basic Law. The reader has a troubling sense of *déjà vu*.

Detached from the rule of law, the idealistic visions of eccentric individuals can become coupled with idiosyncratic political platforms, based on perverse interpretations of German history. Wintergrin, for example, lauds "the genuine idealism of the German people who had become united less than a hundred years earlier, and now were sundered by a consortium of powers." He proposes further that "only Germans can reshape their own destiny. Only Germans can

---

[8] Writing specifically with regard to British secret agent fiction, Hasenberg notes since the 1960s a widening gap between the private morality of the hero and the ideology of his government; Sarchett senses a related development in Buckley's novels, which, in his words "represent the recuperated heroic-romantic spy story at the end of its tether, barely managing, if at all, to suppress a counter-narrative of ambiguity and male-fantasy-destroyed. Buckley's spy thrillers may then report the demise of dominant ideological structures in a much more compelling manner than the 'realistic' works of 'serious' writers such as Greene and Le Carré" (137).

come, would come, to the aid of their brothers in the East. Faced with such resolve, the Russians would necessarily yield; even as, eventually the Nazis had yielded" (12–13). Wintergrin glibly links German idealism and the unification of 1871 to the position of Germany in the 1950s as though Hitler were a minor blip in a smooth and grand historical continuum. His suggestion, in 1952 (!), that the Nazis had yielded before the idealism of fellow Germans guarantees Wintergrin's popularity at home and explains the skepticism of American officials, who have the whole denazification process fresh in their memories. Tod, likewise, a decade later, through his identification of Communism with Nazism, conveniently removes from his countrymen the burden of trying to understand their own history, encouraging them to see themselves simply as victims, just as their poor cousins in the East continue to be victims. He strives to get his countrymen "to see that Nazism continues only under another name" (133). Again, this fellow's popularity with his countrymen is not hard to understand, nor is the skepticism of both the US and the USSR. The good-hearted Oakes—devoted as he is to the fight against evil Communism—regards both these figures with unquestioning admiration and, no doubt, also with a wistful longing for such grandly schematic visions of his own nation's history.

In these two books Buckley's skill lies largely in his ability to create engaging German heroes and yet insure that the reader breathes a sigh of relief, although tinged with regret, when they meet the doom toward which they so implacably rush. Here the ambiguity of the "good German" arises less from his personal flaws than from the historical position of the Federal Republic, struggling for recognition as a good team player in the international community and trying to allay worldwide fears of resurgent nationalism. Buckley's spy novels, however, leave it to the reader to see through the official rhetoric of both the US and the USSR and the well-meaning blindness of the American protagonist and reflect upon the uncertain position of West Germany, both with regard to the US and with regard to its own history.[9] Other more complex texts, such as Joyce Carol Oates's "Ich Bin Ein Berliner" (1982) and Walter Abish's *How German Is It* (1978), with their very titles place the political and historical ambiguity of the Federal Republic squarely at the center of their focus, as does, in a different way, Oates's 1984 story "Master Race," also set in contemporary West Germany.

"Ich Bin Ein Berliner" is one of several of Oates's pieces dealing with Germany and Central Europe.[10] In this story the first person narrator recounts his experiences and ruminations while visiting Berlin in the early 1980s to investigate the death of his older brother a year earlier; the brother had apparently been shot by East German border guards while attempting to cross the Wall illegally

---

[9] Sarchett is surely correct in his insistence that Buckley's novels should not be read exclusively as expressions of the ideas in his political journalism.

[10] Joyce Carol Oates, "Ich Bin Ein Berliner." *Last Days*. NY: E. P. Dutton, 1984, 97–112.

on June 17. The story enacts an American variant of "Mauerkrankheit," that pathological blend of depression, paranoia and claustrophobia documented by psychologists in some residents of West Berlin. What distinguishes this story from others of progressive mental deterioration is the way in which, through the disorientation of a foreigner in 1980s Berlin, it conveys metaphorically the madness and inexplicability which so many outsiders have seen in German history of the twentieth century and in the geopolitical situation of West Berlin in particular.

The title itself already suggests disjuncture on several levels. The narrator, from the beginning ill-at-ease with his own identity in Berlin, emphatically rejects the statement of the title: "For the record, I am not a Berliner. Nor can I be called a tourist. And I am not an *American* [italics the narrator's]—in the allegorical sense" (100). John F. Kennedy, an American in the "allegorical" sense, has made an assertion which has no bearing on his real identity. Moreover, the narrator's expropriation of the quotation—insofar as one can attribute a title to a narrator rather than to an author—establishes an ironic disjuncture between the empathy behind Kennedy's statement, which so endeared him to the Berliners, and the narrator's own profound alienation from the city.

Berlin itself, by virtue of its bizarre geographical and political position, epitomizes qualities of the narrator's mental state. In its hectic modernity it blurs the distinction between Old World and New, both reflecting and engendering his disorientation: "Automobiles, taxis, the usual amplified music. It is America. But no it is Berlin. West Berlin. Germany. But no it is America. No? Yes? America? But with such strong accents?" (100). For the protagonist even the points of the compass become relativized by the troubling political division: "Since West Berlin is a walled city in the East, an escape from "East" to "West" might involve an attempt to scale the Wall in an *easterly direction*" (104). In such passages the use of quotation marks and italics underscores the elusiveness of meaning and the narrator's dissociation from language. The frequent contradictions in his assertions, the nonsequiturs, and the increasingly arbitrary use of language all underline the gradual unhinging of his perspective: the narrator, for example, repeatedly designates sexual encounters as "research" and misstates, then restates, what should be self-evident: "The anniversary of his birth is approaching. 17 June. An error: I meant to say, the anniversary of his death is approaching. 17 June" (107).

Thus to fault the text for its "obviously stereotyped images of the Germans" and for an excessive emphasis on Germany's suppression of the Holocaust is to ignore the madness defining the narrative perspective.[11] The dead brother's statements "Hitler is forever—he has made the rest of us fiction" (109) and

---

[11] Hanspeter Dörfel, "Images of Germany and the Germans in Some of Joyce Carol Oates' Short Stories," Peter Freese, ed., *Germany and German Thought in American Literature and Cultural Criticism*. Essen: Die Blaue Eule, 1990, 277–78.

"The Wall is forever" simply reflect the radical disjuncture between past and present, between reality and fiction, ultimately between life and death, which presumably drove him to suicide and threaten to destroy the surviving brother. Such statements reflect a loosening of the grasp on historical reality, on the very concept of history, on which the ironic significance of the brother's choice of June 17th for his suicide depends. For a supposed leftist, who had once penned an elegy on the suicide of Ulrike Meinhof, to choose the West German national holiday commemorating the Soviet suppression of the East Berlin workers' uprising to have himself killed by East German border guards suggests a radical overturning of political and historical distinctions. Meinhof's death—a suicide which looks like foul play, or is it the other way round?—becomes a model for the American's death, an image without clear political dimensions.

Admittedly, the narrator's own disoriented ramblings inevitably pick up clichés about Germany and its past, some of which may come "pretty close to the presentation of German SS-officers in American postwar movies" (Dörfel 279). Thus his hotel room becomes a "sealed bunker" and at one point he fantasizes about poisonous gases coming into the room. But these images occur in an indiscriminate hodgepodge, side-by-side with icons of American or international culture:

> X-rated Playtime, Colonel Sanders Kentucky Fried Chicken. I move on to prescribed tourist pleasures, baby prostitutes in platform open-toed shoes, robust singing in beer gardens, Old World charm, marching songs, Salon Massage ("Boys & Girls All"), a floor show called "Welcome to Hell" in helpful English. (102)

Nevertheless, the American's receptivity to certain images, enhanced by his delusional state, does manifest itself as a misreading, or sometimes a paradoxical reading, of specific cultural signs. Hence the brother's acquaintance Rudi is "a thug who is in fact a university student, a male prostitute, who is in fact only a waiter at the Flash Point" (198). The story's concluding sentence, which follows the insertion of a folk tale about imprisonment and the irrational yearning for release—"Such is the folk wisdom my tireless research daily yields. Unless Rudi, or one of the others, is telling me lies. Unless they are confusing me with someone else." (112)—punctuates both the narrator's paranoia and his projection of his own confusion onto others.

The narrator's ranting, nevertheless, bears the mark of a specifically American identity. Undoubtedly the US media have shaped his perceptions of Berliners, for example, in the "aura of brutality" and similar corresponding motifs of thuggishness noted above. References to St. Ursula's School in Detroit, where he and his brother were taught by nuns, raise the issue of Catholic education's effects on his perspective, for example in his designation of "the Mercedes-Benz cross, rotating nobly overhead! A sacred vision..." (100) and his sardonic response to Berlin nightlife as "a tonic dose of the pagan" (101). The nightlife also brings out the lurid and misogynist side of the narrator's repressed sexuality: "I am standing in that street or in another shouting after two German girls who have passed me by, bitches, pigs, cunts, I shouted, krauts I shouted, I'll make you regret laughing at me!—laughing at an American!" (107). Desperately pursuing release from the sexual repressiveness of his Midwestern Catholic upbringing, the narrator imagines himself following in his brother's footsteps:

> Perhaps his research took him to the Internationale Spitzengirls Salon, and to the Cabaret Chez Nous, and the Big Eden Peep Show, and the Chalet Noir, Non-Stop Sex-Shop. Drugged teenaged girls, very pretty. But skeletal-thin. Something has happened to the robust Aryan mammalian form. (101)

Research indeed! Such passages illustrate both the tourist appeal of "decadent" Berlin for puritanical Americans, in the postwar era as in the 20s, and the prurience in the obsession with Fascism in general noted by Sontag and others.[12] The narrator now shows traces of the obsessiveness catalyzed by Berlin which also drove his brother up the Wall. Gradually the reader comes to credit the remarks of the State Department official, superciliously dismissed by the narrator: "Young Mr. G—the seemingly helpful State Department lackey..." (99) implies that the brother's original interest in "certain subjects—Berlin now, Berlin in the Forties, Berlin in the Thirties. Berlin when it became *Berlin*, in 1920" and in "Germany, and the Germanys, and the Reich, and the Republic, and of course the Wall" (100) became "morbid," "disturbed," "obsessive," a "fixation" (100).[13]

Oates continues to explore the American fixation on German history in "Master Race."[14] The story recounts the brief sojourn of two American academics in Mainz in 1983, during which the woman is assaulted by a black GI and then chooses to keep the incident private, even refusing to discuss it with her male companion. The incident and her response to it seal the growing distance between the two, Philip Schoen and Cecilia Heath. Schoen, respected historian and grandson of German immigrants, travels to Germany as to the Homeland; his much younger colleague, a historian of nineteenth-century American art, confesses to an ignorance of German culture. The two characters thus already posit the duality of familiarity and strangeness. The story's particular twist lies in its application of the title not to the New Germany, as the reader

---

[12]Susan Sontag, "Fascinating Fascism." *Under the Sign of Saturn*. NY: Farrar, Straus & Giroux, 1980, 100–2.

[13]The American official, of course, is not alone in his judgment. The enormous popularity of many of Robert Ludlum's works is explicable, in part, by the "morbid fascination" that Nazi Germany holds for readers. See L. K. Donaldson-Evans, "Conspiracy, Betrayal, and the Popularity of a Genre: Ludlum, Forsyth, Gérard de Villiers and the Spy Novel Format." *Clues* 4:2 (1983), 103.

[14]Joyce Carol Oates, "Master Race." *Partisan Review*. 51:4 (1984), 566–90.

might expect, but to the male American professor and his relationship to his colleague.

At first the reader tends to dismiss as ironic such remarks of Schoen's as "The Germans really are a master race—even when they—or do I mean we?—pretend humility" (571). Gradually, however, as his character unfolds in the story, the professor, confirming the vanity implied in his surname, evinces an overbearing egotism, contemptuous of vulnerability and bent on stifling the voices of others. Schoen regards the New Germany with scorn as a vulnerable, vulgarized society. Claiming to base his historical judgment on "facts,"

> he believes he knows the German soul perfectly... but by way of scholarly investigations and interviews primarily: not (or so he hopes) by way of blood. Historical record is all that one can finally trust, not intuition, not promptings of the spirit.

Yet this purportedly disinterested view of German history shows striking bias. Schoen describes how the "catastrophic Treaty of Versailles... forced [the Germans] into an outlaw mentality... outside, beyond, *beneath* the law," adding "Perhaps Hitler was no more than the scourge of God" (576). Schoen also relativizes the Holocaust by calling attention to anti-Semitism in Poland and, implicitly on the same level, "the cruelty of the Czechs toward any number of defenseless minorities" (576). In the light of such statements, his pat retort at cocktail parties to inquiries about his current scholarly projects, "You don't really want to know," assumes sinister dimensions. One suspects a questionable revisionist history of World War II in progress.

Schoen's perspective on German history owes a great deal to his family's mythology about the "natural superiority of the Homeland," demonstrated by an uncle who was a German bomber pilot. His older relatives' concessions regarding Nazism and Hitler, like his own attitude to history, focus on feasibility rather than morality. "Of course, if hard pressed my father and uncles would admit that Hitler was a madman, the Reich was doomed, the entire mythopoetics of Germanness was untenable" (571). The dissociation of moral evaluation from scholarly endeavor, part of Schoen's insistence on challenging "liberal pieties" (575), baffles Cecilia, who is disturbed by a similar tendency among other male academics. She has attended a symposium, all-male, on contemporary philosophical trends in the US, which ignored altogether the areas of aesthetics, ethics, and metaphysics. The chairman's opening statement, voicing his expectation "evidently without irony"... that "certain key problems might finally be solved" (571), with its chilling and utterly unsocratic suggestion of "final solutions," connects the story's Germanic title to patriarchal thinking in authoritarian institutions at home. Here, too, the narcissistic egotism of Schoen characterizes the philosophers; the group never seek common terms, never achieve any consensus; "each speaker wanted to wipe the slate clean and begin again" (572).

The "clean slate," however, is yet another two-edged metaphor with ramifications for German history. Toward the end, Schoen and Cecilia attend a dinner with Mainz intellectuals where the conversation inevitably turns to Germany. The German participants express the concerns of many West Germans in the early 80s about their country: the presence of US nuclear missiles, the scandal of the fake Hitler diaries, the fascist tendencies of the left. Of the Germans, the one for whom Schoen feels the greatest affinity is the writer Rudolph, a self-proclaimed leftist, born in 1955, who would like to ban all books written before 1949; for him, as for Schoen, the world is coexistent with his own ego as circumscribed by the existence of the Federal Republic. His choice of 1949 places him in a different political category from those who, like Thomas Mann, believed simply that all books written during the Reich should be burned. Rudolph's declarations about the US role in postwar Germany as one of imperialist aggression and his embracing of "German destiny" (586) reveal a chauvinistic passion which strikes sympathy in the American. In a heated discussion the two lament "the folly of German submersion in 'European civilization' on a continent where most nations are doomed to be 'slave states'" (587). The evening culminates with Schoen's avowal of "sympathy solely for the West Germans, amnesiac for so many years, and made to be on perpetual trial in the world's eyes ... made to feel shame for being German. Indeed, words like 'shame' and 'guilt' strike the ear, Philip says, as distinctly hypocritical. Is German 'shame' indigenous, for instance or a matter of import? And 'guilt' . . .?"(588). With this diatribe Schoen gives vent to his distaste, expressed earlier to Cecilia, for "self-loathing" among the Germans (571). His expropriation of a particular Germany as his own home territory, his denial of shame and guilt to the New Germany, reveals the amorality and ahistoricity of his perspective, which construes human society largely in terms of power relationships.

Relationships of power and status, underlined by the two references to Faßbinder, pervade "Master Race." They define the plight of the black GIs and Cecilia's attempts to befriend them, the structure of Cecilia's and Schoen's professional world, and the problematic sexuality of their relationship. Schoen's own identification with Germany, rather than with the US, reflects his determination to align himself with a "superior" culture. His scorn for the US manifests itself in various ways. He sees Mainz largely under the imprint of "blatantly vulgar" US influence: coarse English graffiti, blaring American rock music, the Chagall windows in St. Stephen's church "like a Disney heaven," even the Dom as "old teutonic *kitsch*, preserved for German and American tourists" (572–73). Schoen's perverse image of Germany thus reflects a hatred of his own country and a search for an heroic, hierarchically composed, elitist homeland.

As the title suggests, however, the most troubling side of Philip's search emerges in his condemnation of the black soldiers. Cecilia sees tragedy in their plight in Germany as earlier in Vietnam: "an army consisting of many impoverished blacks, very young and ill-educated men, men who probably know little about why they are where they are, or even, precisely, where they are" (575). Her companion, on the other hand, claims that "the 'tragedy' is Germany's," and cites various crimes and disruptions attributed to the soldiers. In contrast to Cecilia, he lacks historical perspective on his own country; his deliberate amnesia about American race relations and about Vietnam explain his ready embrace of a clean slate for Germany.

Oates's "Master Race" uses Germany as the twentieth century's emblem of guilt and malfeasance to illuminate America's lost innocence, the innocence captured in the nineteenth-century American art which Cecilia studies. Cecilia's own flight from sexuality, like her recurrent recollections of her parents and aunts in her rural American home territory, her decision to abandon Schoen and return home, and her concluding dream of childhood all show a desperate clinging to a frozen past, just as her approach to the black soldiers marked an attempt to return to a world of simpler human intercourse. Her dream at the end, however, recapitulates motifs of pursuit, assault, disorientation, a flood and the final surfacing of a sunken foreign city "partly in ruins, blackened by fire . . . a cathedral of massive dimensions, its highest tower partly crumbled, its edifice stark and grim" (590). This final architectural image suggests the Berlin *Gedächtniskirche*, a postwar monument to not forgetting, and thus, like the motifs of the flood, implies an irreversible destruction of innocence.

In Oates's two stories, psychological conflicts and unresolved tensions of American characters emerge through the encounter with the West Germany of the 1980s. The nation's troubled history speaks to specific aspects of the American characters' background as they respond to a Germany both reassuringly familiar and disturbingly alien. Walter Abish's *How German Is It*, though ending in a psychiatrist's office, replaces the psychology of individual characters with bleakly humorous interplay of familiar and alien, of expected and disruptive.[15] One can read Abish's novel as a transparent parable of how the prosperous New Germany has constructed itself over an unregenerate and poorly concealed evil past. The novel's often ignored epigraph, however, taken from Jean-Luc Godard, "What is really at stake is one's image of one's self," summons the reader to examine Abish's New Germany in the light of his own self-image—raising for the reader questions of his own national and cultural identity. Abish himself has asserted elsewhere that his book is about Germany as a "preoccupation," permitting a "glimpse of a society".[16] Germany, then, as a preoccupation resembles Switzerland as an idea from the character Ulrich Hargenau's book *The Idea of Switzerland* mentioned in the novel, an abstraction, a "catchword," except that "Germany" in the twentieth century is a much more loaded catchword than

---

[15] Walter Abish, *How German is it; Wie Deutsch ist es. A Novel.* New York: New Directions, 1979.

[16] Sylvère Lothringer, "Interview with Walter Abish." *Semiotext(e)* IV: 2 (1982), 160–61.

"Switzerland." Through this catchword Abish comments on the difficulty of coping with ambiguity, specifically on contemporary America's rejection of ambiguity with regard to contemporary Germany.

Among the works considered here, Abish's alone, with its shifting, elusive narrative perspective, does not explicitly establish an American perspective from which to view Germany. Indeed, it opens with the question, "What are the first words a visitor from France can expect to hear upon his arrival at a German airport?" (1). One could raise the question, "How American is it?" with regard to Abish's perspective. It is largely the obsessiveness of the text toward Germany, the grotesquely exaggerated, almost "morbid" concern in Oates's terms, a cultural obsessiveness with typically American clichés about Germany, rather than an individual, pathological obsession, which makes the book, despite its affinities with the French *nouveau roman*, seem so American.

The issue of hermeneutic ambiguity emerges explicitly in many passages in the novel, for example in Ulrich and Daphne's exchange about a Dürer drawing, the *Double Goblet*:

> As the title indicated it offered the viewer a view of two extremely ornate goblets, one balanced head down on the other, as well as revealing upon closer scrutiny an entirely different picture, one that disclosed an explicit sexual content.
> You like that, don't you, she said challenging him.
> What? The sexual content?
> No, the duality in the picture. Seeing something that others may overlook.
> She looked startled when he said: Why are you attacking me? (24)

Ulrich's own writing is said to be permeated by an "air of ambiguity ... as if some vital piece of information is being withheld" (52). The ambiguity appears in the irony of his name, deceptive in someone unable and unwilling to take anything "haargenau." Abish's text, too, on the level of plot withholds many vital pieces of information, while at the same time providing descriptions of the New Germany in anything but ambiguous terms.

The reference to Dürer's *Double Goblet* as an icon of duality revises an earlier association of Dürer with depiction of the "typically German:"

> It was a German face, like his own. A determined and somewhat obdurate face, a face that Dürer might have taken a fancy to and painted or sketched. (12)
> It seemed likely that a young, earnest-faced American woman when visiting Würtenburg could not help but see the world of Albrecht Dürer come to life. (18–19)
> ... a familiar face, no doubt a German face, a Dürerlike face of an acquaintance or friend. (21)

Such remarks implicitly question the extent to which one artist's works capture general characteristics of a society, a race or a nation. The same question arises for the reader later in the photography of Rita Tropf-Ulmwehrt, published in the glossy magazine *Treue* and introduced with the comment, "an invitation—what else?—to reinterpret Germany. A new Germany" (129): how faithful to the new Germany can this photography be?

Abish's novel raises the hermeneutic question whether it is really possible to perceive duality and ambiguity, without necessarily rejecting one meaning in favor of another. Ulrich's own conviction that "nothing is what it first appears to be" implies seeing through the surface of things into their inner essence, the mass grave beneath the new street. In bringing to the surface this newly discovered reality, one risks forfeiting duality and ambiguity. This is the point of the book's final sentence, "Is it possible for anyone in Germany, nowadays, to raise his right hand, for whatever the reason, and not be flooded by the memory of a dream to end all dreams?" (252). Rather than insisting on latent Nazism in contemporary Germany, the words challenge the reader to examine his own Hollywood-generated image of all Germans as latent Nazis.[17]

How, then, is one to read the epigraph? It suggests that how I read the novel is directly connected to what I think of myself; how an American or non-German reads Abish's Germany is connected with how he or she views his or her own country. Do I need an image of modern West Germany as a cold, shallow slick surface covering a bestial violent essence? Does such a reading enable me to congratulate myself on my own country's moral superiority, nonviolent history, frank and open social structures? Or should I be prepared to entertain different answers to the questions (such as the final one) raised by the novel and simultaneously accommodate a more problematic image of my own society? The continual process of "defamiliarization" which many readers note in the novel applies to the reader's relationship to his own society as well.[18] A passage recounting several Germans' smug comments on a Turkish restaurant implicitly warns the reader against a similar condescension vis-à-vis Germany:

> Some people Franz knew once visited the Turkish restaurant and reported to him that the food was quite good and the decor, in general, surprisingly attractive, and that for a *foreign* place, they stressed the "foreign," it was remarkably clean and the service quite up to standards, not what you might ex-

---

[17]Martin quotes Abish himself with regard to this final passage and its connection, in the author's own mind, with Hollywood: "To me the salute contains an ikonic position in a time frame. Hence, it is a gesture that cannot be made innocently. The memory of a dream to end all dreams is a vague statement. I had Hollywood in mind." Richard Martin, "Walter Abish's Fictions; Perfect Familiarity, Familiar Imperfection," *Journal of American Studies* 17:2 (August, 1983), 241.

[18]See Paul Wotipka, "Walter Abish's How German Is It; Representing the Postmodern." *Contemporary Literature* 30:4 (Winter, 1989), 503–17 and Maarten Van Delden, "Walter Abish's How German Is It; Postmodernism and the Past." *Salmagundi* 85–86 (Winter-Spring, 1990), 172-94.

pect from the Turks. All the same, they would not go back, but they had enjoyed it, and what is more it was not terribly expensive. On the walls, they had said, there were large not too badly painted murals of Istanbul, and there were also candles on each table. (69)

The tension between the reassuringly familiar (good food, attractive decor, cleanliness, good service, etc.) and the alien—the Turkish, foreign quality, Istanbul, and so on—here reflects an anxious need to confirm the preeminence of the familiar and its capacity to subsume the foreign. The passage provides an ironic commentary on much of Abish's novel, which, despite its rhetoric of ambiguity, wittily conveys a world which looks very attractive to the foreign tourist but which educated, historically aware Americans compulsively need to see as menacing. There is, after all, Auschwitz.

A number of allusions to the visual arts sharpen the focus on ambiguity and "image" in the Godard quotation while linking it to the German past. References to film and photography, for example, suggest the possibility, sometimes the necessity, of unambiguous interpretation.[19] A chapter which begins with the caption "Past riches," followed by a passage on concentration camps in Germany, raises the question as follows:

> And then, of course, there are the films and photographs. What is one to make of them? The viewers, young and old alike, are faced with the grim problem of whether or not to accept the old film footage of the skeletonlike men and women in their striped prisoner's uniforms, vacuously staring at the camera. Did this really occur or have these photographs been carefully doctored, ingeniously concocted simply in order to denigrate everything German? (190–91).

The proper response to these photographic documents, however, appears clear; one must accept them as accurate depictions of reality. A later passage describes, presumably from the government perspective, the goals of an anti-terrorist police film: "Admittedly, the film is also an attempt to further escalate the continuous overreaction and over-response of one side to the actions of the other... In order to clarify, to make evident a terrorist threat, the film has to distort, fabricate and often lie" (243). In the question of truthfulness of images, Abish's text occupies an unclear and shifting position between the two extremes of documentation and propaganda. Here again one suspects an ironic self-reference, for Abish's novel, unlike the photos and films mentioned, self-consciously doctors and concocts its picture of Germany, distorts and fabricates (like all fiction), creating an overreaction in its reader.

Many of the photographs described appear to reveal Germany's "hidden" or "suppressed" past: "A shot of Jonke [collector of photos from the Nazi era] in his store window, beaming ... a single railroad boxcar on a siding next to an

---

[19]Wotipka's essay contains thoughtful remarks on the use of photography in the novel. Oddly enough, however, he does not address the epigraph.

unloading platform... Rita seems to like railroads, said Gisela.... a shot of Franz, stiffly at attention, next to his partially completed matchstick model of the Durst concentration camp" (200). Then, however, comes a photo "of a horse standing in a lake, in one or two feet of water, with its muscular erect bareback rider wearing a visored military cap and looking into the camera's lens" (201), the same image which has appeared in a coloring book titled *Unser Deutschland* which Daphne sends to Ulrich: "a drawing of a young man wearing a visored military cap and a striped jersey astride a horse that was standing in the shallow part of a lake. The rider was barefoot and riding the horse bareback" (178). Helmut's indignant identification of the rider as the sniper who had fired on him and Ulrich out in the woods (an event apparently engineered by Helmut) adds a twist to the "plot" by linking Helmut to the terrorist Daphne. Such a photo, however, also appears on the book's cover, credited to the author's wife, Cecile Abish, thus, like the epigraph and the bilingual title, drawing the reader beyond the text, summoning him or her to abandon a fixed perspective within the text. Yet the novel also questions the prospect of any fixed perspective (hence its connection to the *nouveau roman*), a tendency apparent in the exchange between Ulrich and Gisela about some ruined fortifications on the beach left over from the war:

> I thought they're all destroyed, he said as he reluctantly joined her.
> Well, you can still see bits and pieces.
> If you insist...
> What you need is a new perspective, she said.
> Are you sure that's what you mean? (232–33).

This dialogue recapitulates the reader's persistent search for a stable perspective on the text, a search which, however, always leads only to new questioning of any and all perspectives. Abish's novel challenges the reader to resist a fixed perspective and to resist forging the bits and pieces together into a whole based on predetermined cultural expectations; at the same time it seems to exploit such expectations. As Maarten Van Delden observes, "The urge to tie things together, to uncover analogies and produce explanations, is, in *How German Is It*, at once acknowledged and assiduously undermined" (179).

The reality of the New Germany in the 1970s and the specifics of its problematic history play a more urgent role in Abish's novel, with its motifs of truthfulness, reliability, and photographic representation, than does the reality of Mainz or West Berlin in Oates's stories. Yet one could not substitute any other country nor any other historical epoch without radically changing the impact of each work. Still, in these works the New Germany functions essentially as the self-consciously artificial construct of one narrative consciousness. Two sociopolitical novels of Ward Just, neither of which is set primarily in the Federal Republic, appear to create a more "realistic" West Germany but as a component of commentary on the United States.

Just's Germany is the Federal Republic shaken by the terrorism of the 70s, and then later by the trauma of a disintegrating East Bloc, but it is always primarily a context within which to investigate American society and its traditions of democracy. *The American Ambassador* (1983) presents its protagonist Bill North against the triadic configuration of the United States, Germany, and sub-Saharan Africa.[20] Within this configuration a sharp distinction emerges between the New Germany and older, traditional Germany, with North occupying an intermediate generation between the two. The son of a cultivated Berlin Jew who established himself comfortably in Boston in the interwar period, Bill represents a conventional immigrant's success story. As a mid-level, middle-aged professional diplomat, he envisions the US in the mythic terms of a carefully crafted Pilgrims' story (Thanksgiving, his favorite holiday, is mentioned several times in the book) and of its prominent leaders, especially his hero, the self-made-man Abraham Lincoln. When explaining his professional ambitions to his skeptical father (himself a "German of the 19th century and a Jew of the 20th," 249), North, a self-defined pragmatist, declares his intention of "moving on," i.e., turning his back on the Old World and specifically on the legacy of the Holocaust. North achieves full assimilation into American society, marrying into a moneyed Chicago WASP family, and advancing through the ranks of the foreign service.

The novel's Prologue, however, a monologue of North's only child, Bill, Jr., to his mildly retarded but beautiful German girlfriend Gert, reveals a seriously troubled reality under the smooth surface. In addition, North himself is developing disturbing medical symptoms, pain and loss of feeling in his right hand, suggesting a loss of touch, a loss of grip. Young Bill, like the American Daphne in *How German Is It*, belongs to a West German terrorist group; he is preparing and rehearsing the murder of his father as the latter prepares to assume a new post in the Federal Republic. West German terrorism in these novels has little in common with the historical Rote Armee Fraktion (the Baader-Meinhof gang) which, seeking to effect its political agenda with bombings, kidnappings, and murders, wreaked havoc with life in the Federal Republic in the 1970s. Whereas RAF cells had ties to Third World revolutionary movements as well as to the GDR, Bill's group, like Abish's *Einzieh* group, lacks either clear goals or political consciousness, resembling Faßbinder caricatures of terrorism more than any real groups. As in the Oates quotation opening this essay the aesthetics of violence more than the political agenda for the Federal Republic is what compels the Americans' interest.

Just's West Germany is a land dominated by the past, not just by vague, picturesque tradition but by specific political history, whereas sub-Saharan Af-

---

[20] Ward Just, *The American Ambassador*. Boston: Houghton Mifflin, 1987. It is interesting to note a similar configuration with Abish, whose first novel was the experimental *Alphabetical Africa*.

rica, on the other hand, represents a world on the threshold, waiting to enter modern political history. In this novel, as in Just's *Translator*, middle-aged German men with memories of the war voice this acute awareness of their nation's history. The Ambassador's friend Kleust from his African tour of duty, a man whose name—with its proximity to Kleist—conjures up venerable Prussian tradition, describes Germany as "a glass house, the world pressing in on all sides, everything visible" (211). This metaphor echoes Abish's uses of glass as an architectural motif typical of the New Germany, but now with a genuine transparency insuring against amnesia. Kleust had gone to Africa to escape the immense burden of the German past, hoping to find a fresh, in his words a "chaste" (210), political climate. To his dismay, he discovers among the African politicians an appalling fascination with Hitler and Nazi systems of control, and an indifference to the horror of genocide:

> Kleust explained about the Jews, their role in history, their dispersion, their prominence in the cultural and commercial life in Germany, but still the Africans didn't get it. Were the Jews like colonialists, then? Clannish, mysterious, racist, rich, taking what they wanted, promulgating their own laws, cuisine, clothing, religious customs, raping the land? Insulting the majority race! Could they be compared with the Indian merchants who held every African town and village in thrall—in a Hindu stranglehold? ... Kleust preached the virtues of a benign anarchism, but the Africans were not impressed. They wanted control and authority, and there was also a thirst for revenge. The German model seemed convenient, so many lessons to be learned. (211)

This naive appropriation of another culture's history is, however, no more questionable than the American tendency to fabricate its own history at will.

Germany, as a "glass house," a nation open to the world's constant scrutiny, becomes an admonition to the US, built on a selective historical memory that exalts the great heroes and neglects less glorious episodes. The fragile transparency of the Federal Republic contrasts with the manufactured images which the US successfully projects of itself. This particularly American substitution of images for political-historical context defines the young terrorist's values. Bill, Jr. reflects that:

> Americans were not reluctant to tamper with their own history, trying to make things nice, and that was why living in America was an adventure—a world of science fiction, a lake one day was a forest the next and a desert the day after. And no one was in charge. America reinvented itself each day, why couldn't the world do likewise? (124)

Bill, Jr.'s postmodernist attitude contrasts markedly with Kleust's analysis of German terrorism, freighted as it is with the language of history, tradition and legend. Kleust, describes the terrorists as "good haters," adding,

> They've been stunned, by the memory of the Nazis, and the advent of the Americans. They see the Americans as barbarians, the great colonialists; peo-

ple like me are weaklings and traitors, American puppets, Fausts. The governments of Europe are only the creatures of the Americans. American money, American culture, American CIA. They see a world out of control and want only to hasten the process, start it spinning faster and faster until it melts. . . . Like your own children's story, Sambo, and the tigers turned into butter. A kind of Sambo as if it were written by the Brothers Grimm. Except they don't know what kind of butter they want. (254–55)

Viewed against the tortured relationship of Just's German characters to their nation's past, Bill Jr.'s proclamation of a fluid national identity marks an unwholesome culmination of his family's immigrant tradition. The Ambassador himself, for example, responding to Kleust's ambivalence toward Germany, declares his own zesty, naive patriotism as follows: "I love my country, my dream of it. I love the freedom of it, its impulsiveness. The buffoonery, the instability, the romance of money, the loneliness, and the grab. It's a fictional country, arising deep from the imagination" (212). The American, unlike the German, can delude himself that his part of the twentieth century has been "particularly benign" (212). Whereas Bill, Jr.'s early encounter with Africa and friendship with an urban black schoolmate have given him a sense of racial injustice, his father's shallow but peculiarly American insistence on "moving on" has blinded him to his country's failings.

Bill, Jr., for all his perspicacity in identifying the flaws of the older generation, fails to provide a positive model for political action. His allegiances are essentially nihilistic, driven by a hatred of America rooted in oedipal rage. Absolute in his condemnation of the older generation—both of the West Germany of the Economic Miracle and of the US which engineered it—, he offers no alternative except destruction. The most dangerous aspect of Bill, Jr.'s terrorist program is its nationalism, now divorced from any sense of history and out of step with the West German mainstream. Thus, in a passage recalling Rudolph's diatribe in Oates's "Master Race" about the American Imperialist aggression and the need for Germany to embrace its destiny, Just's terrorist imagines West Germany's future in the following terms:

Wasn't it only a matter of time before the Germans began to think again, and the nation slowly move its shoulders, uncomfortable in the American jacket. Ostpolitik, Deutschpolitik. Germany had a right to control its own affairs. Germany had a right—no, a duty—to sit at the head table, as the strongest power in Europe. Germany had done its penance, had reconciled its past, and the new generation insisted on charting its own future, having suffered long enough for the sins of the fathers. *Ja?* (125)

The American's ahistorical proclamation departs from earlier modes of revolutionary opposition, represented here by Gert's father, Max Mueller, also eventually murdered by the two. An unattractive, ruthless old-style Marxist revolutionary now presumably operating at the bidding of the Soviets, Mueller nonetheless espouses clear political goals within a defined historical perspective. As a consequence he earns the young terrorists' contempt for having "too much ideology, too little passion, too much history." In Bill, Jr.'s mind, "He still distinguished between ends and means, failing to understand that the means were the ends; often the means were more expressive, more elegant, than the ends" (167).

The question of memory central to Abish's examination of the New Germany forms the crux of Just's juxtaposition of the New Germany to the US of the 1980s: "Germans had long memories, history was with them every day; no day so bright that darkness was not visible. Everything in Germany was approached with profound ambivalence. Germans were afraid of themselves" (211). Kleust and the missionary doctor Burkhalter uphold the imperative of seeing the present through the past. The United States, exemplified by the three generations of the North family, has, on the other hand, generated a culture based on fabulation and forgetting. The Ambassador's own response to conflict suggests the American dream of consumption and oblivion, decried by his radical son, "Their solution to everything is to have an expensive meal and drink champagne" (2). The merging of the ahistorical American view of politics with the young German resentment toward oppressive memory creates the murderous potential of Bill, Jr.'s group.[21] By linking and contrasting problems of contemporary German politics with American political and historical misapprehensions, Just's novel projects different models of political engagement, all based on different responses to historical realities and all faulty in some way. In provoking the reader to reexamine his own national heritage, *The American Ambassador* recalls Abish's epigraph: what is really at stake is one's image of oneself.

The concern with images and self-images of Germany and the US pervades Just's 1991 novel *The Translator* as well, one of the first American novels in which the fall of the Wall figures prominently.[22] The protagonist, Sydney van Damm, a German living with his American wife and severely autistic child in Paris, ekes out a meager existence as a translator, working sporadically for the affable yet unscrupulous American Junko Poole and his CIA-funded publica-

---

[21]Jameson's remarks about the "delirious non-stop monologue" of the "new free play with the past" aptly describe Bill, Jr.'s perspective: "equally allergic to the priorities and commitments, let alone the responsibilities, of the various tediously committed kinds of partisan history" (368–69).

[22]Ward Just, *The Translator*. Boston: Houghton Mifflin, 1991. Another example of American *Wende* fiction is Theodore Weesner's academic novel *Novemberfest*, (NY: Knopf, 1994) in which a middle-aged Germanist experiences a negative tenure review, a debilitating job search, the dissolution of marriage, and the opening of the Berlin Wall while wallowing in fantasies of a failed love affair in occupied Germany. Weesner's novel is ultimately about the shallowness of many Americans' experience of Germany. Here the troubling complexities of German history—the Holocaust, the Wall, unification—simply dissolve before private fantasies of an academic New World voyeur looking for a belle époque in which to escape the perpetual present which seems to constitute American culture.

tions, then more steadily for the publisher of a fellow expatriate German novelist, Josef Kaus. Set in 1989–90 as the old European configuration of powers crumbles, the novel repeatedly raises the question of individual and cultural identity. Van Damm's own first name reflects the partial conquest of one national identity by another, arising when GIs after the war misunderstood "Siggi" as "Sydney." The novel's plot consists of Sydney's struggle in Paris to support his family in the light of his wife's declining family fortune. The troubled flux of political alliances provides the background against which the translator, as a linguistic mediator between cultures, is drawn into a venture involving the illegal purchase of Soviet weapons. In the end he falls victim to a senseless tussle with Stasi agents when he journeys briefly to his mother's house in the GDR.

Through the three main characters, Sydney, his wife Angie, and Poole, the friend who brought them together, the novel asks the reader to reflect on Germany and the US in the light of contemporary political changes. In *The Translator*, as in *The American Ambassador*, Vietnam marks a major turning point in US consciousness. After Angie's brother dies in Vietnam, the family fortune, generated and maintained for generations by the Yankee entrepreneurial spirit, disintegrates. Her brother's death alienates Angie from her father, who becomes increasingly unable to handle his money, and the family dynasty comes to an end. When Angie returns to Maine to claim her only valuable family possession, a Winslow Homer watercolor, she finds that her feckless father has sold it. Compared with the ambiguous *Double Goblet* and the other allusions to Dürer in Abish's novel, the Homer painting functions as a more conventional metaphor for Just, though also as an icon of national identity. The presence of Homer, remembered for his paintings of the Civil War as well as for his seascapes, adds depth of perspective on a Germany riven by division yet striving for unity. Angie's particular painting depicts a mariner alone in a boat, "the wind rising, the mariner troubled" (287), suggesting the loss of orientation which both the postwar German generation (Sydney) and the post-Vietnam American generation (Angie) in the novel feel as they vainly seek a horizon.

The Translator goes beyond Just's *American Ambassador* in its emphasis on the impotence of politics and the mercenary power of money to solve problems. The resilient Junko Poole, although his first name conveys the shabby, tarnished quality of his endeavors, in many ways exemplifies even more than Ambassador North, the pursuit of the American Dream. To Sydney, who wryly sees himself as "a degenerate monk from the Middle Ages" (250), Junko seems

> ... a pillar of the Enlightenment, prosperous, Godless, and confident. . . . Junko's world was more spacious, altogether more unpredictable, various, and fun, absorbed as he was in the great task of capital formation, working at it with the protean intensity of Voltaire on *Candide*, and to a roughly similar subversive end, except that Junko's scientific garden was the wide world. (250)

This is a new, ruthless, international twist on the entrepreneurial spirit which created Angie's fortune.

In this world, works of art have become primarily indicators of wealth. Just as the loss of the Homer emphasizes the sagging fortunes of the US economy, a French Impressionist sketch which Sydney admires one night in a gallery window highlights the surging fortunes of the New Germany. As he contemplates the piece, a prosperous young couple, cultivated, polite with "the complacent faces of the new Germany" (206), come up to the window and discuss buying it the next morning—with their American Express card. Sydney reflects on the conversation:

> So why not take it? An Impressionist, no less, whose work was in great museums everywhere on the continent and in America. The picture was for sale, so why not buy it? They had as much right as anybody, they worked hard, and the deutsche mark was firm. It was a better investment than shares in Siemens. (207–8).

In this Americanized European world art has become a commodity, akin to stock shares in major industry.

Although Junko's illegal arms turn out to be just as hollow a financial prospect as the Homer painting, Junko, having recognized the international primacy of money over politics, will move on to other schemes and continue to prosper. The younger generation of Europeans appears to follow his lead. Even the international bevy of "casually predatory" (153) stewardesses, neighbors of the Van Damms, are "not part of any community, except the common market of Europe" (153). The Austrian one laments to Sydney,

> It is beyond us to construct a new society, something different and something better and more hopeful, because we are all one body now. We draw from the same wallet. Our sheiks have bank accounts in every capital in Europe and accountants to keep track of them, Swiss francs and French francs, lire, deutsche marks, escudos, kroner, guilders, rials, dollars. Maybe the experiment in the East will bring us all down. But so what. Do we have so far to fall? (153)

The constant uprootedness of the stewardesses and the easy touring habits of the young rich West German couple, who readily alter their itinerary in order to accommodate the art purchase, contrast markedly with the Van Damms' sessile existence.

The traditional integrity characterizing Sydney and Angie is associated in Just's novel with rootedness in a particular place and in a particular culture. Hence, once the traumas of their respective nations' histories (Nazism or Vietnam) disrupt this tradition, the characters desperately try to create a coherent world of their own elsewhere. The whimsical epithet "Fortress America" with which they and their friends designate their apartment building in Montmartre suggests this artificial homeland. Sydney and Angie, critically detached from their roots, cannot indulge in even the sense of national solidarity which the cosmopolitan young German tourists display when the man says to Sydney: "It has been a pleasure speaking with you. I did not recognize you as a countryman. It does not matter so much which of us buys the Vuillard, then. It is either us or the Japanese" (107). For the younger generation of the New Germany, national allegiance has become largely a feature of economic rivalry, especially against the Japanese.

The primacy of international economic activity over traditional nationalism defines the various characters' response to the imminent German unification. The most enthusiastic praise for unification comes from the American Junko, who sees in it his own advantage:

> No winners, no losers, only survivors. It's time at last to think about a Europe free of rivalry, where everyone has a community of interest. The modern European choir: basses, tenors, sopranos, all singing the same song. The economy, for example, the mighty engine of Western civilization. And what is the bottom line of this civilization? Sell the people what they want! When the people have what they want, there's a spirit of public happiness. (261)

Undoubtedly, the young German couple will join this modern European choir, so long as it guarantees them American Express and money for Impressionist art. Sydney, a man of simple wants standing outside this community of interest, does not share his friend's enthusiasm:

> You could draw a common boundary and call it unification, but it wasn't unification in any sense other than economic, an arrangement supervised by Düsseldorf banks. It was only a common skin. (264)

With a mother who, in her old age fled the Economic Miracle and returned to her native village in the GDR (recalling a similar move by Burkhalter in *The American Ambassador*), Van Damm views German unification as a superficial scheme of businessmen and politicians.

Those Germans like Sydney and the novelist Kaus who have tried to come to grips with the questions of national identity will find no solace in the new Federal Republic. Yet at the same time even Sydney is able to speak of Germany as seeking a "Rightful Place," from which it has presumably been banished. He recapitulates the legend with which the novel has opened, the story of a dwarf who leads the inhabitants of a village to a pyrrhic military victory and then disappears, leaving them to wonder about him and his dubious legacy. In a conversation with the melancholy East German functionary Erich, Sydney recalls the legend:

> the itinerant dwarf who with his raised sword was the height of a normal man. He and Erich and the dwarf, too, sought a Rightful Place. . . . (264)

This legendary Germany, the Germany of the past, has attained stature only through military might, which has left its heirs exhausted, doubting themselves, and vowing "never again to follow one who claimed divine inspiration" (2). The new commercially-engineered Germany will have as little place for Germans of conscience like Sydney, condemned to remain expatriates, as for East German Marxists like Erich. The legend is open-ended, the fate of the dwarf uncertain; similarly, the novel, ending before the actual unification, withholds judgment about the German future. But the scenario of international commercialism sketched with increasing intensity throughout the novel does not bode well for future political and historical accountability—to paraphrase Bill, Jr., too little history, too little ideology, and passion only for consumer goods. In *The Translator*, as in *The American Ambassador*, the singularity of recent German history leaves no satisfactory historical models for the "good Germans" (Kleust, Burkhalter, Sydney), melancholy expatriates trying to come to grips with the nation's historical and political situation. The present is for them a dead-end. Leaving no heirs to uphold a tradition, they are replaced by a culture of international entrepreneurs.

These works subvert the clear-cut political morality with which West Germany has appeared in much American popular culture—for example in espionage novels and television series— where American-inspired democracy and capitalism unequivocally represent the triumph of good over the evils of Nazism and Communism.[23] Germans no longer figure prominently as arch-villains, except in international thrillers featuring old Nazis and their descendants. The New Germany of the 1990s nevertheless remains a source of sinister qualities, often as an emblem of amorality rather than of evil. For example, a 1991 novel of industrial espionage, *Endgame in Berlin*, set in a reassuringly sober and humane unified Germany, where anti-Semitism is the exclusive domain of the Russian KGB, nevertheless presents a specifically German antagonist: "Kurt Horst Steiner... what made that kind of man? Tobin [the CIA protagonist] stared into his eyes, and what he saw was the end of Western civilization. Steiner was the kind of man Hitler had made. Was it only the Germans who could do it? Was it only the Germans who could be turned into what this man was?"[24] And the KGB agent who kills the villain remarks. "Basic defect in the German character... Why they always lose. They always obey orders" (307). America's sense of a basic defect in the "German character" lurks in many of these works, from the gratuitous assumption of "thuggishness" by Oates's disturbed narrator to the ambiguous insinuation about Ulrich's raised right arm at the end of *How German Is It*. Such a flaw, a malleability comprised of the absence of any values except obedience to the stronger, also appears a component of German terror-

---

[23]John Nelson's observations from the mid-70s about the image of Germany in American television as an agent of cultural destruction suggest some parallels with the fiction discussed here. "Das Bild des Deutschen im amerikanischen Fernsehen." Wolfgang Paulsen, ed. *Die US und Deutschland. Wechselseitige Spiegelungen in der Literatur der Gegenwart*. Bern: Francke, 1976, 176–77.

[24]William Harrington, *Endgame in Berlin*. NY: Donald I. Fine, 1991, 306.

ism as it is treated in these works. Wotipka's comments on terrorism's capacity to create ambiguities and inhibit immediate interpretation help explain its attractiveness to Just's young terrorists as well as to Abish's *Einzieh* group.[25] All these characters share with Oates's anarchic leftist Rudolph a remarkable paucity of political commitment or ideology. German terrorism thus becomes violence as violence, postmodernist ahistoricity, surface, image, a source of Jameson's "euphoria;" in this capacity it presents a glamorous counter-model to the pervasive violence in the US, where analysis of its economic and sociological roots has led only to despair and cynicism.

Continued American anxiety toward the Federal Republic centers on that nation's economic power, the legacy of postwar US aid, rather than on any feared military designs for world domination emerging from a supposed indigenous tradition. In *The Translator* the illegally imported arms themselves pose no immediate threat; the danger arises from the disintegration of law and justice precipitated by economic opportunism. A more extreme case of amoral German commercialism comes out in John Irving's *A Son of the Circus* (1994), where Dieter, the degenerate and manipulative drug-dealer, is made to appear particularly heinous through his major prop, a huge pink dildo stuffed with drugs and deutsche marks. With such figures, as with the descriptions of Berlin nightlife in Oates's "Ich Bin Ein Berliner," the American perception of Germany harks back to Weimar: for the now poorer, but still puritanical, world west of the Atlantic the thrill of decadence and amorality is intensified by the slick patina of wealth in the New Germany.

Yet economic success has still not obscured the critical issue, explicit or implicit, in many of these works, i.e., whether the taint of Nazism still places the Federal Republic permanently beyond the pale of "civilized" humanity and conclusively deprives the New Germany of a Rightful Place in the European, or North Atlantic, community. What connection is there between Germany's economic power and "the end of Western Civilization"? At the same time some of these works also examine the other side of the coin, namely the question whether the German historical experience is unique and lacking common themes with American tradition. Buckley's two spy novels superficially emphasize commonality of the two nations and establish the New Germany as a home territory. Only gradually does the reader sense disturbing tendencies in the German heroes Henri Tod and Axel Wintergrin, both of whom reveal, to paraphrase Ward Just's terrorist again, too little history, too much passion, too much ideology. With them the ostensibly straightforward "American" ideal of freedom, when absorbed by a Germany with an imperfect grasp of its own history, takes on inappropriate and then positively dangerous dimensions. The lethal potential of the New Germany, at least of the New Berlin, becomes internalized in

---

[25]Martin, 512, refers to Sloan's *Simulating Terrorism* (Norman: U of Oklahoma Press, 1981) 14–15.

Oates's "Ich Bin Ein Berliner." Here brutality as a specifically German characteristic, a legacy of the nation's history, dominates the narrator's perceptions, psychotic though they are; yet this psychosis clearly feeds on images of Germany in American popular culture—still bent on distancing "us" from "them—and is in some passages indistinguishable from such images. The Nazi racial ideology implied in the title of Oates's "Master Race" similarly dominates the psyche of an American character in this story. The encounter with Germany intensifies Philip Schoen's "secret gloating pride in... blood,... race—in sin, guilt, history..." which he projects onto his hosts in Mainz. The experience of this society, in which blacks do not fare much better than at home, confirms Cecilia's wish to withdraw from the twentieth century and avoid growing up. The attempts of the German hosts to draw the two American visitors into discussions of such topical contemporary issues as gay readings of Hart Crane and Whitman, black Marxist street poetry, the placement of Pershing II missiles, and so on, fail because such topics demand political engagement with an unacceptably complex modern world; Philip prefers to remain stuck brooding in his protofascist fantasies, and Cecilia retreats to her dream world, seeking in vain a lost American childhood. Philip, the historian, and Cecilia, the art historian, fail to integrate an understanding of history with their individual grasp of contemporary reality: perhaps Rudolph really is right in simply ignoring history.

The critique of "certain ahistorical tendencies of contemporary culture at large," which Wotipka (516) finds in Abish's novel characterizes all these texts in different ways. *How German Is It*, however, presents a particularly compelling critique, for, through its persistent references to the Holocaust, it suggests the moral urgency of finding some kind of historical perspective.[26] With their emphasis on historical memory as an ambiguous process, Ward Just's two novels recapitulate threads from Abish but hint at some kind of intelligibility in history; Just's New Germany explicitly raises the question of the American tradition. Although his Germany initially appears more reassuringly familiar and thus less disturbing than the Germanys of the other works, its parallels with Just's America are troubling: two nations saddled with grand mythic pasts rudely destroyed and a present floundering to stabilize its identity. His middle-aged German characters Kleust and Sydney Van Damm ("self-respecting, self-hating German[s]")[27] suggest a moral historical consciousness lacking in the pragmatic American self-made men (Junko Poole) dominating the popular imagination of the US. Yet Just's New Germany appears imperiled: its citizens of conscience are dying without heirs and being replaced by the forces of international greed and anarchy.

[26] Van Delden treats this question thoughtfully in his discussion of postmodernism and history in Abish's novel.

[27] 148. This self-designation of Sydney's contrasts markedly with Philip Schoen's vocal distaste for "self-loathing Germans."

At play in all these works are variations of the anxieties and hopes in American culture of the late twentieth century which also make Nazi Germany a persistent topic of popular culture. The turning of American writers in the 1970's and 1980's toward the New Germany undoubtedly owes something to the same factors which Karl-Heinz Bohrer in the mid-70s noted in Hollywood's persistent focus on an earlier Germany: the "Verlust an einem Sinn für nationale Werte" and a consequent "Bedürfnis nach Kontrast und Erleichterung;" he adds, ". . . das Land mit seiner wachsenden Angst um die politische, moralische und besonders die ökonomische Gegenwart fürchtet sich, seinem eigenen komplexen Ich ins Gesicht zu sehen."(123) Behind the focus on the New Germany in all these works lies the question of our own country's Rightful Place, the stability of our society, the purity of our historical tradition, and the legitimacy of our political and economic power. In short, "What is really at stake is one's image of oneself."

Notes on Contributors

Scott Abbott is Associate Professor of German at Brigham Young University. He is the author of *Fictions of Freemasonry: Freemasonry and the German Novel* and has published articles on Handke, Grass, Rilke, Thomas Mann, and Goethe. He is currently one of the Directors at Large of the North American Goethe Society. The essay on Handke is a chapter of the forthcoming book *Pragmatic Dreams: Peter Handke, Contingency, and the Dialectic*.

Geoffrey Atherton is lecturer at Princeton University in the Department of Germanic Languages and Literatures and the Program in Humanities Studies, where he also is a Ph.D. candidate. The title of his dissertation is *Disiciendi membra poetae: Vergil and the Germans in the Eighteenth Century*.

David Dollenmayer is Associate Professor of German at the Worcester Polytechnic Institute in Worcester, Massachusetts. He is the author of *The Berlin Novels of Alfred Döblin* (1988) and co-author of *Neue Horizonte: A First Course in German Language and Culture* (4th edition, 1996). He has published articles on Döblin, Christa Wolf, Joseph Roth, and Ingeborg Bachmann and has translated Brecht's *Flüchtlingsgespräche*.

Ellis Finger is Director of the Williams Center for the Arts at Lafayette College, a position he has held since 1983. He came to Lafayette in 1973 as assistant professor of German, and has continued to serve as a member of the Lafayette faculty and to teach courses on the arts. He is a 1966 graduate of Davidson College and holds an MA degree from Duke University. He has published articles on Goethe, Schiller, and the Romantic novel, and was translator for *The Calov Bible of J.S. Bach*, published by UMI Press in Ann Arbor (1985). He has taught workshops and conference presentations on the aesthetics of performance.

Kathryn Shailer Hanson is Assistant Professor of German at the University of Western Ontario in London, Canada. Following completion of her Ph.D. in 1978, she spent a dozen years as a marketing executive in Vancouver, British Columbia, before returning to academic life in 1990. Her research interests are

European Romanticism, modern German cultural history, and German film. She has published articles on Adam Oehlenschläger, Henrich Steffens, and German-Canadian history. In preparation: *Rethinking Romantic Allegory: Tieck's Kaiser Octavianus and Oehlenschläger's Aladdin*.

Hildburg Herbst is Associate Professor of German at Rutgers University, New Brunswick, NJ and a second-term Chairperson of her Department. She is the author of *Frühe Formen der deutschen Novelle im 18. Jahrhundert* and editor of *Was nicht in dem Geschichtsbuch steht: Oral History 1930-1950*. She has published and lectured on Goethe and Schiller and the eighteenth century in general, on short prose forms, contemporary cinema and pedagogy.

Otto W. Johnston is Professor of German and past Chair of the Department of Germanic and Slavic Languages and Literatures at the University of Florida at Gainesville. He is the author of *The Myth of a Nation. Literature and Politics in Prussia under Napoleon* (Columbia, SC: Camden House, 1989) and *Der deutsche Nationalmythos. Ursprung eines politischen Programms* (Stuttgart: Metzler, 1990). He has also contributed numerous articles to professional journals in Germany and the United States.

Alan Keele is Professor of German Language and Literature at Brigham Young University in Provo, Utah. His research interests include postwar German literature, German opera, and the resistance to Hitler. His books include: *Paul Schallück and the Postwar German Don Quixote* (1976), *The Apocalyptic Vision, A Thematic Exploration of Postwar German Literature* (1983), *Understanding Günter Grass* (1988), and *When Truth Was Treason: German Teenagers Against Hitler* (1995). With poet Leslie Norris he has translated Rilke's *Sonnets to Orpheus* and *Duino Elegies* (1989, 1993).

Kathleen L. Komar is Professor of German and Comparative Literature and Associate Dean of the Graduate Division at the University of California, Los Angeles where she received the 1989 Distinguished Teaching Award. She chaired the Program in Comparative Literature from 1986 to 1989. She has published articles on contemporary women writers from several cultures (including among others Christa Wolf, Monique Wittig, Christa Reinig, and Ingeborg Bachmann) as well as on a broad range of modern German and American literature. Her articles have appeared in *Euphorion, Monatshefte, Comparative Literature Studies, Comparative Literature, The German Quarterly, The Germanic Review, Modern Austrian Literature*, and *Twentieth Century Literature*. In addition to her two books, *Transcending Angels: Rainer Maria Rilke's "Duino Elegies"* (1987), and *Pattern and Chaos: Multilinear Novels by Dos Passos, Faulkner, Döblin and Koeppen* (1983), she is currently completing a book entitled *Re-*

Visions of the Women of the Trojan War: Contemporary Women Authors' Rewriting of Helen and Klytemnestra.

Paola Mayer received a Ph.D. in Germanic Languages and Literatures from Princeton University in 1993 and now holds a Killam Postdoctoral Fellowship in the Department of Germanic Studies at the University of British Columbia. She is at present revising her dissertation *The Reception of Jakob Böhme in Early German Romanticism,* for publication. Her research interests include: Romanticism's relationship to Neoplatonic mysticism; Romantic metaphysics and Natural Philosophy; theory and literature of the uncanny. An article, "Die unheimliche Landschaft: Ein Aspekt von Eichendorffs lyrischer Dichtung," will be appearing in *Athenaeum* 1995.

Clark Muenzer is Associate Professor of German at the University of Pittsburgh, where he served as the department's chair from 1987 to 1995. His research and teaching interests include German literary and cultural studies from the eighteenth through twentieth centuries. He has written a book on Goethe's novels (1984), as well as essays on Lessing, Herder, Goethe, Schiller, Kleist, Kant, and Kafka. Currently he is completing a book on Goethe's hermeneutical discourse of monuments entitled *Wandering among Obelisks: Topics in Goethe's Historical Reconstruction of Knowledge.* The essay published here will be a chapter in his study.

James M. Skidmore is Assistant Professor of German at Wilfrid Laurier University, Waterloo, Ontario, Canada. His research interests are German Cultural Studies (specifically questions about identity), women's writing, C.M. Wieland, and Ricarda Huch.

Alexander Stephan taught at Princeton University and at the University of California, Los Angeles. He is currently Professor of German at the University of Florida. Major book publications: *Christa Wolf* (Munich, 4th enl. and rev. ed., 1991), *Die deutsche Exilliteratur* (Munich, 1979), *Max Frisch* (Munich, 1983), *Anna Seghers im Exil* (Bonn, 1993), *Im Visier des FBI. Deutsche Exilschriftsteller in den Akten amerikanischer Geheimdienste* (Stuttgart, 1995), *Anna Seghers: 'Das siebte Kreuz'. Welt und Wirkung eines Romans* (Berlin, 1997); (ed.) *Peter Weiss. Die Ästhetik des Widerstands* (Frankfurt, 3rd ed. 1990), *Schreiben im Exil* (Bonn, 1985), *Exil. Literatur und die Künste nach 1933* (Bonn, 1990), *Christa Wolf. The Author's Dimension* (New York, 1993; London, 1993; Chicago, 1995); *GDR Short Stories* (New York, in press, 1997). Some 65 articles on modern German literature. Produced for German television a documentary film titled *Im Visier des FBI. Deutsche Autoren im US-Exil* (ARD, 1995). Editor of the book series *Exilforschung Exile Studies.*

Maria Tatar is Professor of German at Harvard University. She is the author of *Spellbound: Studies on Mesmerism and Literature* (1978), *The Hard Facts of the Grimms' Fairy Tales* (1987), *Off with Their Heads: Fairy Tales and the Culture of Childhood* (1992), and *Lustmord: Sexual Murder in Weimar Germany* (1995).

George C. Tunstall is Associate Professor of German and Classical Languages at Kansas State University in Manhattan. His research interests are German poetry, German literature and philosophy, Jahrhundertwende, and Latin and Greek metrics. He has published on Georg Kaiser, Nietzsche, Hebbel, and Kokoschka.

Walter D. Wetzels is Professor of German at The University of Texas at Austin. He has taught and published on German literature of the eighteenth and early nineteenth centuries. The focus of his research for some time now has been the relationship of literature and the natural sciences. In recent years his interests were concentrated on the literature which attempts to popularize the new physics of Copernicus, Kepler, and Newton. He has published a number of articles on aspects of the influence of the natural sciences on German writers of the eighteenth century such as Herder and Goethe. The scope of his research on the popularization of the natural science has broadened in the last years to include writers such as Fontenelle and Algarotti and the translations of their works into German by Gottsched and others. He is the author of *Johann Wilhelm Ritter: Physik im Wirkungsfeld der deutschen Romantik* (1973). He has edited *Myth and Reason* (1973), and co-edited (with Leonard Schulze) *Literature and History* (1983).

Cecile Cazort Zorach is Professor of German at Franklin and Marshall College in Lancaster, PA. She has published essays on twentieth-century German literature and on German-American literary relations.

Selected Writings by Theodore Ziolkowski

I. Books

A. Monographs

Hermann Broch, Columbia Essays on Modern Writers 3 (New York: Columbia UP, 1964).
  Extensively revised in *European Writers: The Twentieth Century*, ed. George Stade, vol. 10 (New York: Charles Scribner's Sons, 1990) 1385–1408.
  Reprinted with abbreviations in *Europe: revue littéraire mensuelle* 741/742 (1991): 75–86.

The Novels of Hermann Hesse: A Study in Theme and Structure (Princeton: Princeton UP, 1965).
  Trans. Gerardo Espinosa Wellmann: *Las novelas de Hermann Hesse* (Madrid: Punto Omega, 1976).
  Chapter 8 reprinted in: *Hesse Companion*, ed. Anna Otten (Frankfurt: Suhrkamp, 1970) 71–100.
  Chapter 9 translated by Ursula Michels-Wenz in *Materialien zu Hermann Hesses Der Steppenwolf*, ed. Volker Michels (Frankfurt: Suhrkamp, 1972) 353–77 ("Steppenwolf: Eine Sonate in Prosa"); rpt. *Steppenwolf: Erläuterungen und Dokumente*, ed. Friedrich Voit (Stuttgart: Reclam, 1992) 122–24.
  Chapter 8 translated by Ursula Michels-Wenz in *Materialien zu Hermann Hesses Der Steppenwolf*, ed. Volker Michels (Frankfurt: Suhrkamp, 1976) 133–61 ("Siddhartha: Die Landschaft der Seele").
  Chapter 11 translated by Tsai Chin-Song in Chinese translation of Hermann Hesse, *The Journey to the East* (Taiwan, n.d.).
  Chapter 9 reprinted in *Hermann Hesse: A Collection of Criticism*, ed. Judith Liebmann (New York: McGraw-Hill, 1977) 90–109 and in *Literature and Music*, ed. Nancy Anne Cluck (Provo: Brigham Young UP, 1981) 195–212.

Hermann Hesse. Columbia Essays on Modern Writers 22 (New York: Columbia UP, 1966).

Extensively revised in *European Writers: The Twentieth Century*, ed. George Stade, vol. 9 (New York: Charles Scribner's Sons, 1989) 833–58.

Dimensions of the Modern Novel: German Texts and European Contexts (Princeton: Princeton UP, 1969).

  Trans. Beatrice Steiner and Wilhelm Höck: *Strukturen des modernen Romans: Deutsche Beispiele und europäische Zusammenhänge* (Munich: List, 1972).

  Chapter 4 reprinted in *Zu Alfred Döblin*, ed. Ingrid Schuster (Stuttgart: Klett, 1980) 124–48.

  Chapters 1, 3, 4, 9 and 10 reprinted in *Twentieth Century Literary Criticism* (Detroit: Gale Research, 1982, 1986, 1993, 1994).

  Trans. Ihsan Abbas and Bakr Abbas: *Abad al-riwayah al-hadithah: nusus Almaniyah wa-qarain Urubbiyah* (Bayrut: al-Muassasah al-Arabiyah lil-Dirasat wa-al-Nashr, 1994).

Fictional Transfigurations of Jesus (Princeton: Princeton UP, 1972).

  La Vida de Jesus en la Ficción Literaria (Caracas: Monte Avila Editions, 1982).

  Korean translation, 1989.

Disenchanted Images: A Literary Iconology (Princeton: Princeton UP, 1977).

  Imagenes Desencantados, trans. Aurelio Martinez Benito (Madrid: Taurus, 1980).

Der Schriftsteller Hermann Hesse (Frankfurt: Suhrkamp, 1979).

The Classical German Elegy, 1795–1950 (Princeton: Princeton UP, 1980).

Varieties of Literary Thematics (Princeton: Princeton UP, 1983).

German Romanticism and Its Institutions (Princeton: Princeton UP, 1990).

  Das Amt der Poeten: Die deutsche Romantik und ihre Institutionen, trans. Lothar Müller (Stuttgart: Klett-Cotta, 1992).

  Rpt. Munich: Deutscher Taschenbuch Verlag, 1994.

  Recorded for Talking Books by Royal National Institute for the Blind (1993).

Virgil and the Moderns (Princeton: Princeton UP, 1993).

The Mirror of Justice: Literary Reflections of Legal Crises (Princeton: Princeton UP, 1997).

B. Translations (with Yetta Ziolkowski)

Herman Meyer, *The Poetics of Quotation in the European Novel* (Princeton: Princeton UP, 1968).

Hermann Hesse: A Pictorial Biography, ed. Volker Michels (New York: Farrar, Straus & Giroux, 1975).

C. Editions with Introduction

Hermann Hesse, *Späte Prosa* (New York: Harcourt, Brace & World, 1966).

Hermann Hesse, *Stories of Five Decades* (New York: Farrar, Straus & Giroux, 1972).

Hermann Hesse, *Autobiographical Writings* (New York: Farrar, Straus & Giroux, 1972).

Hesse: A Collection of Critical Essays (Englewood Cliffs: Prentice-Hall, 1973).

Hermann Hesse, *My Belief: Essays on Life and Art* (New York: Farrar, Straus & Giroux, 1974); paperback reprint 1975.

Hermann Hesse, *Tales of Student Life* (New York: Farrar, Straus & Giroux, 1976).

Hermann Hesse, *Pictor's Metamorphoses and Other Fantasies* (New York: Farrar, Straus & Giroux, 1982).

Hermann Hesse, *Soul of the Age: Selected Letters 1891–1962* (New York: Farrar, Straus & Giroux, 1991); paperback reprint 1992.

II. Scholarly and Critical Articles

"Goethe's *Unterhaltungen deutscher Ausgewanderten*: A Reappraisal." *Monatshefte* 50 (1958): 57–74.

"Hermann Hesse's *Steppenwolf*: A Sonata in Prose." *Modern Language Quarterly* 19 (1958): 115–33.

"Hauptmann's *Iphigenie in Delphi*: A Travesty?" *Germanic Review* 34 (1959): 105–23.

"Rilke's *Portal* Sonnets." *PMLA* 74 (1959): 298–305.

"Camus in Germany, or the Return of the Prodigal Son." *Yale French Studies* 25 (1960): 132–37.

"Heinrich Böll: Conscience and Craft." *Books Abroad* 34 (1960): 213–22.

"Heinrich Böll und seine Dichtung." *Universitas* 16 (1961): 507–16.

"Heinrich Böll—the Man and the Writer." *Universitas* (English-language edition) 5 (1962): 183–92.

"Napoleon's Impact on Germany: A Rapid Survey." *Yale French Studies* 26 (1960–61): 94–105.

"Hermann Hesse's Chiliastic Vision." *Monatshefte* 53 (1961): 199–210.

"Agenda for Translators and Publishers: German." *The Craft and Context of Translation*, eds. William Arrowsmith and Roger Shattuck (Austin: University of Texas Press, 1961) 202–06.

"James Joyces Epiphanie und die Überwindung der empirischen Welt in der modernen deutschen Prosa." *Deutsche Vierteljahrsschrift* 35 (1961): 595–616.

"Der Karfunkelstein." *Euphorion* 55 (1961): 297–326.

"The Odysseus Theme in Recent German Fiction." *Comparative Literature* 15 (1962): 225–41.

"Albert Camus and Heinrich Böll." *Modern Language Notes* 77 (1962): 282–91.

"Max Frisch: Moralist without a Moral." *Yale French Studies* 29 (1962): 132–41.

"Gerhart Hauptmann and the Problem of Language." *Germanic Review* 38 (1963): 295–306.

"Zur Entstehung und Struktur von Hermann Brochs *Schlafwandlern*." *Deutsche Vierteljahrsschrift* 38 (1964): 40–69.

> Reprinted in abbreviated form in *Materialien zu Hermann Brochs 'Die Schlafwandler'*, ed. Gisela Brude-Firnau (Frankfurt: Suhrkamp, 1972) 126–51.

"Contemporary German Drama." *Books Abroad* 38 (1964): 239–47.

"Language and Mimetic Action in Lessing's *Miss Sara Sampson*." *Germanic Review* 40 (1965): 261–76.

"German Literature." *New International Yearbook 1964* (New York: Funk & Wagnalls, 1965) 235–36.

"German Literature." *New International Yearbook 1965* (New York: Funk & Wagnalls, 1966) 221–22.

"Gruppe 47: Thumbnail Sketch." *American-German Review* (Special Supplement, April 1966): 8–11.

"German Literature and the Prize." *Books Abroad* 41 (1967):13–17.

"Der Blick von der Irrenanstalt: Zur Verrückung der Perspektive in der modernen deutschen Prosa." *Neophilologus* 51 (1967): 42–54.

"Hermann Hesse: *Der vierte Lebenslauf*." *Germanic Review* 42 (1967): 124–43.

> Reprinted in German translation in Hermann Hesse, *Der vierte Lebenslauf Josef Knechts: Zwei Fassungen* (Frankfurt: Suhrkamp, 1986) 163–205.

"Hermann J. Weigand and a Letter from Thomas Mann: The Critical Dialogue." *Yale Review* 56 (1967): 537–49.

> Reprinted in Hermann J. Weigand, *Critical Probings: Essays in European Literature from Wolfram von Eschenbach to Thomas Mann*, ed. Ulrich K. Goldsmith (Bern: Lang, 1982) 11–24.

"Hermann Broch and Relativity in Fiction." *Wisconsin Studies in Contemporary Literature* 8 (1967): 365–76.

> Trans. Paul Michael Lützeler in *Hermann Broch: Perspektiven der Forschung*, ed. Manfred Durzak (Munich: Fink, 1972) 315–27 ("Hermann Broch und die Relativität im Roman").

"Hans Fallada." *Encyclopedia of World Literature in the 20th Century*, ed. W. B. Fleischmann, vol. I (New York: Ungar, 1967) 369–70.

"Paradigms of the Recent German Novel." *Modern Language Journal* 52 (1968): 28–31.

"The Crisis of the Thirty-Year-Old in Modern Fiction: Toward a Phenomenology of the Novel." *Comparatists at Work*, eds. Stephen G. Nichols, Jr., and Richard B. Vowles (Waltham: Blaisdell, 1968) 146–65.

"Saint Hesse among the Hippies." *American-German Review* 35 (1969): 19–23.

"Methodologische Überlegungen." *Das Nachleben der Romantik in der modernen deutschen Literatur*, ed. Wolfgang Paulsen (Heidelberg: Stiehm, 1969) 15–31.

"German Literature." *Encyclopedia of World Literature in the 20th Century*, ed. W. B. Fleischmann, vol. II (New York: Ungar, 1969) 16–29.

"Art: Creation or Participation?" *Dimension* 2 (1969): 238–39.

"Toward a Post-Modern Aesthetics." *Mosaic* 2 (1969): 112–19.

"Foreword." Hermann Hesse, *The Glass Bead Game* (New York: Holt, Rinehart & Winston, 1969) vi-xix.

> Trans. Ursula Michels-Wenz in *Materialien zu Hermann Hesse 'Das Glasperlenspiel* 2 (Frankfurt: Suhrkamp, 1974) 204–15 ("Zur Aktualität des Glasperlenspiels").
>
> Updated revision (New York: Henry Holt, 1990) vii-xix.

"An Ontology of Anxiety in the Dramas of Schiller, Goethe, and Kleist." *Lebendige Form. Festschrift für Heinrich E. K. Henel*, eds. Jeffrey L. Sammons and Ernst Schürer (Munich: Fink, 1970) 121–45.

"Der Hunger nach dem Mythos: Zur seelischen Gastronomie der Deutschen in den Zwanziger Jahren." *Die sogenannten Zwanziger Jahre*. First Wisconsin Workshop, eds. Reinhold Grimm and Jost Hermand (Berlin: Gehlen, 1970) 169–201.

"Hesse's Sudden Popularity with Today's Students." *University: A Princeton Quarterly* 45 (1970): 19–25.

"Vom Verrückten zum Clown." *In Sachen Böll*, ed. Marcel Reich-Ranicki. 3rd ed. (Cologne: Kiepenheuer & Witsch, 1970) 345–57.

"The Life and Works of Hermann Hesse." *Nobel Prize Library: Hemingway, Hamsun, Hesse* (New York: Helvetica, 1971) 367–75.

"Reflections and Notes on the Teaching of German Lyric Poetry." *Die Unterrichtspraxis* 4 (1971): 3–11.

"Form als Protest: Das Sonett in der Literatur des Exils und der Inneren Emigration." *Exil und Innere Emigration*. Third Wisconsin Workshop, eds. Reinhold Grimm and Jost Hermand (Frankfurt: Athenäum, 1972) 153–72.

"Hesse, Myth, and Reason: Methodological Prolegomena." *Myth and Reason: A Symposium*, ed. Walter D. Wetzels (Austin: University of Texas Press, 1973) 127–55.

"Heinrich Böll: The Inner Veracity of Form." *Books Abroad* 47 (1973): 17–24.

"Cultivating Hesse." *Times Literary Supplement* 31 August 1973: 989–91.

> Reprinted in *T.L.S. 12: Essays and Reviews from The Times Literary Supplement* (London: Oxford UP, 1974) 175–89 ("The Hesse Cult").
>
> "Die Kultivierung Hermann Hesses." *Über Hermann Hesse* 2, ed. Volker Michels (Frankfurt: Suhrkamp, 1977) 148–65.

"Nonpartisan Thoughts on Politics and Literature." *Yearbook of Comparative and General Literature* 22 (1973): 7–19.

"The Quest for the Grail in Hesse's *Demian*." *Germanic Review* 49 (1974): 44–59.

"The Imperiled Sanctuary: Toward a Paradigm of Goethe's Classical Dramas." *Studies in the German Drama. A Festschrift in Honor of Walter Silz*, eds. Donald H. Crosby and George C. Schoolfield (Chapel Hill: University of North Carolina Press, 1974) 71–87.

"Typologie und 'Einfache Form' in *Gruppenbild mit Dame*." *Die subversive Madonna: Ein Schlüssel zum Werk Heinrich Bölls*, ed. Renate Matthaei (Cologne: Kiepenheuer & Witsch, 1975) 123–40.

"The Author as *Advocatus Dei* in Heinrich Böll's *Group Portrait with Lady*." *University of Dayton Review* 12 (1976): 7–17.

"Foreword." *The Hesse-Mann Letters: The Correspondence of Hermann Hesse and Thomas Mann, 1910–1955* (New York: Harper & Row, 1975) ix-xx.

"Thomas Mann as a Critic of Germany." *Thomas Mann 1875–1955* (Princeton: Princeton University Library, 1975) 17–23.

"Thomas Mann and the Emigré Intellectuals." *Thomas Mann 1875–1955* (Princeton: Princeton University Library, 1975) 24–38.

"The Telltale Teeth: Psychodontia to Sociodontia." *PMLA* 91 (1976): 9–22.

Trans. Cho Hyo-Je in *The Journal of Dental Clinics* (Korea), 1987 (no. 3: 72–74; no.4: 76–79; no. 5: 57–59; no. 6: 76–78; no. 7: 72–74; no. 8: 62–65; no. 9: 81–83).

"Die Natur als Nachahmung der Kunst bei Goethe." *Wissen aus Erfahrungen. Festschrift für Herman Meyer* (Tübingen: Niemeyer, 1976) 242–55.

"Some Features of Religious Figuralism in Twentieth-Century Literature." *The Literary Uses of Typology*, ed. Earl Miner (Princeton: Princeton UP, 1977) 345–69.

"The Literature of Atrocity." *Sewanee Review* 85 (1977): 135–43.

"Die Säkularisation der Bibel." *Jahrbuch Deutsch als Fremdsprache* 3, ed. Alois Wierlacher (Heidelberg: Groos, 1977) 137–49.

Reprinted and expanded "Zur Unentbehrlichkeit einer vergleichenden Literaturwissenschaft für das Studium der deutschen Literatur." *Fremdsprache Deutsch* 2, ed. Alois Wierlacher (Munich: Fink, 1980) 486–506.

"Jesus between Theseus and Procrustes." *Bulletin of the Midwest Modern Language Association* 11 (1978): 53–61.

Rpt. in *The Horizon of Literature*, ed. Paul Hernadi (Lincoln: University of Nebraska Press, 1982) 307–317.

"Otherworlds: Fantasy and the Fantastic." *Sewanee Review* 86 (1978): 121–129.

"Religion and Literature in a Secular Age: The Critic's Dilemma." *Journal of Religion* 59 (1979): 18–34.

"Versions of Holocaust." *Sewanee Review* 87 (1979): 676–686.

"Hermann Hesse in den USA." *Hermann Hesse Heute*, ed. Adrian Hsia (Bonn: Bouvier, 1980) 1–24.

"Broch's Image of Vergil and Its Context." *Modern Austrian Literature* 72 (1980): 1–30.

Rpt. in *Vergil*, ed. Craig Kallendorf. The Classical Heritage 2 (New York: Garland, 1993) 87–111.

"Science, Frankenstein, and Myth." *Sewanee Review* 89 (1981): 34–56.

"Medicine and Literature." *Sewanee Review* 89 (1981): 652–59.

"Figuren auf Pump: Zur Fiktionalität des sprachlichen Kunstwerks." *Akten des VI. Internationalen Germanisten-Kongresses Basel 1980*, eds. Heinz Rupp and Hans-Gert Roloff (Bern: Lang, 1981) 166–76.

"Die Auferstehung: Ein geistesgeschichtliches Motiv des 19. Jahrhunderts im Roman des 20. Jahrhunderts." *Literaturwissenschaft und Geistesgeschichte. Festschrift für Richard Brinkmann*, eds. Jürgen Brummack et al. (Tübingen: Niemeyer, 1981) 616–34.

"Mörike's *Die schöne Buche*: An Arboreal Meditation." *A Tribute to Hermann Weigand on the Occasion of His Ninetieth Birthday*, eds. A. Leslie Willson and Jeanne Willson (Austin: The Dimension Press, 1982) 107–123.

Rpt. *German Quarterly* 56 (1983): 4–13.

Trans. Hartmut Fröschle in *Beiträge zur schwäbischen Literatur- und Geistesgeschichte* 3 (1985): 75–91.

"Anatomies of Holocaustics." *Sewanee Review* 90 (1982): 592–604.

"Heinrich Heine." *Hudson Review* 36 (1983): 217–23.

"Literature and the Bible: A Comparatist's Appeal." *Art/Literature/Religion: Life on the Borders*. JAAR Dramatic Studies 49/2, ed. Robert Detweiler (Chico: Scholars Press, 1983) 181–89.

"The Existential Anxieties of Engineering." *The American Scholar* 53 (1984): 197–218 (frequently reprinted for classroom use, e.g. at North Carolina State).

"Mines of the Soul: An Institutional Approach to Romanticism." *English and German Romanticism: Cross-Currents and Controversies*, ed. James Pipkin (Heidelberg: Winter, 1985) 365–390.

"Theologie und Literatur: Eine polemische Stellungnahme zu literaturwissenschaftlichen Problemen." *Theologie und Literatur: Zum Stand des Dialogs*, eds. Walter Jens, Hans Küng and Karl-Josef Kuschel (Munich: Kindler, 1986) 113–29.

"Der Wanderer über dem Nebelmeer: Caspar David Friedrich und Goethe." *Form und Formgeschichte des Streitens: Der Literaturstreit*. Akten des VII. Internationalen Germanisten-Kongresses Göttingen 1985, vol. 2 (Tübingen: Niemeyer, 1986) 201–208.

Rpt. *Wochenendbeilage der Hannoverschen Allgemeinen Zeitung* 17–18 May 1986.

"Modes of Hesse's Political Allegory: A Platonic View." *Hermann Hesse: Politische und wirkungspolitische Aspekte*, eds. Sigrid Bauschinger and Albert Reh. 14. Amherster Kolloquium zur deutschen Literatur (Bern: Francke, 1986) 187–203.

"Five Theses on Generic Transformation." *Neohelicon. Acta comparationis litterarum universarum* XIII/1 (1986): 9–35.

"The Uses and Abuses of Romanticism." *The Sewanee Review* 95 (1987): 276–87.

"Hermann Hesse and Novalis: A Portrait of the Artist as a Young Dilettante." *Echoes and Influences of German Romanticism. Essays in Honour of Hans Eichner*, eds. Michael S. Batts, Anthony W. Riley, and Heinz Wetzel (New York: Lang, 1987) 115–32.

"Hermann Brochs *Tod des Vergil* und Thomas Manns *Lotte in Weimar.* Zwei Exilromane." *Hermann Broch: Das dichterische Werk. Neue Interpretationen*, eds. Michael Kessler and Paul Michael Lützeler (Tübingen: Stauffenburg, 1987) 263–72.

"Schinkel's Museum: The Romantic Temple of Art." *Proceedings of the American Philosophical Society* 131/4 (1987): 367–77.

"Kleists Werk im Lichte der zeitgenössischen Rechtskontroverse." *Kleist-Jahrbuch 1987*, ed. Hans Joachim Kreutzer (Berlin: Schmidt, 1987) 28–51.

"Goethe in English." *The Hudson Review* 41 (1988): 499–511.

"*Faust* and the University: Pedagogical Ruminations on a Subversive Classic." *Texte, Motive und Gestalten der Goethezeit. Festschrift für Hans Reiss*, eds. John L. Hibberd and H. B. Nisbet (Tübingen: Niemeyer, 1989) 65–79.

"The Lure of the Law in German Romanticism." *Historical and Cultural Contexts of Linguistic and Literary Phenomena.* Proceedings of the Seventeenth Triennial Congress of the Fédération Internationale des Langues et Littératures Modernes, ed. G. D. Killam (Guelph: University of Guelph, 1989) 73–92.

"Vergil und die Moderne: Politisierte Bukolik." *Poetik und Geschichte: Viktor Zmegac zum 60. Geburtstag*, ed. Dieter Borchmeyer (Tübingen: Niemeyer, 1989) 136–49.

"Rhetorik der Revolution in Jena: Schlegels drei Tendenzen." *Geist und Gesellschaft. Zur deutschen Rezeption der Französischen Revolution*, ed. Eitel Timm (Munich: Fink, 1990) 83–97.

"Literature and Law." *The Sewanee Review* 99 (1991): 122–32.

"Wagner's *Parsifal* between Mystery and Mummery: or Race, Class, and Gender at Bayreuth." *The Return of Thematic Criticism*, ed. Werner Sollors (Cambridge: Harvard UP, 1992) 261–86.

"The Cultural Landscape of Berlin." *Along the Royal Road: Berlin and Potsdam in KMP Porzellan and Painting, 1815–1848*, ed. Derek E. Ostergard (New York: The Bard Graduate Center for Studies in the Decorative Arts, 1993) 19–33.

"The Flying Dutchman: From Phantom Vessel to Demon Seaman, or The German Ahab and His Trance Maiden." *Muse and Reason: The Relation of Arts and Sciences 1650–1850*, eds. B. Castel, J. A. Leith, and A. W. Riley (Queenston: Royal Society of Canada, 1994) 157–77.

"The Limits of Comparison." *The Sewanee Review* 102 (1994): 459–71.

"Introduction." *Thematics Reconsidered. Essays in Honor of Horst S. Daemmrich*, ed. Frank Trommler (Amsterdam: Rodopi, 1995) 5–11.

"Judge Bridoye's Ursine Litigations." *Modern Philology* 92 (1995): 346–50.

"Das Neueste aus USA: Der Text als Feind." *Jahrbuch der Deutschen Schillergesellschaft* 39 (1995): 454–59.

"August Böckh und die Sonettenschlacht bei Eichstädt." *Antike und Abendland* 41 (1995): 161–73.

"Friedrich Schlegel und seine drei Tendenzen: krank oder gesund?" *Goethe-Jahrbuch* 112 (1995): 121–34.

"The Art of the Essay." *Sewanee Review* 104 (1996): 295–304.

"Kafkas 'Der Prozeß' und die Krise des modernen Rechts." *Literatur und Recht. Literarische Rechtsfälle von der Antike bis in die Gegenwart*, ed. Ulrich Mölk (Göttingen: Wallstein, 1996) 325–40.

III. Incidental Pieces

"Hesse and Film: The Seduction of a Generation." *Chronicle of Higher Education* 1 October 1973: 9.

"Scholarship Redefined." *University: A Princeton Quarterly* 64 (1975): 25.

"Background: Jesus of Nazareth." *TV Guide* 2 April 1977: 24–25.

"Talking Dogs from Kafka to Snoopy." *TV Guide* 25 June 1977: 22–23.

"Yesterday's Model for Today's University." *Chronicle of Higher Education* 24 April 1978: 44.

Rpt. *University: A Princeton Quarterly* 76 (1978).

"The Seventies: 'Verweile doch! Du bist so schön!'" *Monatshefte* 72 (1980): 245–53.

"The Graduate School and Its Implications for the College." *Princeton Alumni Weekly* 19 May 1980: 6–7.

"The Responsibilities of Knowledge." *University: A Princeton Magazine* 85 (1981): 1–4.

"The Presidential Task Force on the Arts and Humanities: A Skeptical Humanist's View." *Proceedings of the Thirty-Eighth Annual Meeting of the Midwestern Association of Graduate Schools* (1982) 5–12.

Rpt. *CGS Communicator* 15 (1982): 1–4.

"Today's American Scholar." *Key Reporter* 48 (1983): 2–4.

"Doorways to Literacy." *Hun Today* 4 (1983): 2–4.

"Hermann J. Weigand: A Memorial Note." *PMLA* 101 (1986): 110–12.

"Hermann Weigand: A Eulogy." *The Hermann J. Weigand Fellowship* (North Haven, 1986) 3–10.

"Presidential Address 1985. A Rhetoric of Ritual: Or, Crisis and Community." *PMLA* 101 (1986): 314–23.

"Heinrich Böll: A Biographical Memoir." *Yearbook 1985 of the American Philosophical Society* (Philadelphia, 1986) 95–101.

"Max Frisch: A Reminiscence." *World Literature Today* 60 (1986): 555–57.

(Edited with introduction) "Current Issues in Scholarship and Graduate Education in Languages and Literature." *Proceedings of the Twenty-Fifth Anniversary Meeting of the Council of Graduate Schools in the United States* (December 11–14, 1985) 1–17 ("Introduction," pp. 1–3).

"The Living Legacy of Andrew Fleming West." *Princeton Alumni Weekly*, November 9, 1988: 8.

"Some Modest Proposals for the Ph.D." *The Chronicle of Higher Education* April 12, 1989: B4.

"The Ph.D. Squid." *The American Scholar* 59 (1990): 177–95.

"Was heißt und zu welchem Ende studiert man Germanistik? Oder Schizophrenie als Lebensform." *Germanistik*. Sonderheft: *Germanistische Fachinformation international*, ed. Wilfried Barner (Tübingen: Niemeyer, 1990) 9–23.

"The Shape of the PhD: Present, Past, and Future." *ADE Bulletin* 97 (1990): 12–17.
    Rpt. *The Grad Student's Guide to Getting Published*, eds. Alida Allison and Terri Frongia (New York: Prentice Hall, 1992) 219–24.

"Princeton in *Whose* Service?" *Princeton Alumni Weekly*, January 23, 1991: 11–16.

"Testimony before Senate Subcommittee on Education, Arts, and Humanities." *CGS Communicator*, 24 (May-June, 1991): 9–10.

"Reflections of Dean Quixote." Circulated as Presidential Address by the Association of Graduate Schools, 1991.

"On the Polysyllabification of Learning." *Ideas for the University*. Proceedings of Marquette University's Mission Seminar and Conference, ed. Ed Block (Milwaukee: Marquette UP, 1995) 73–89.

"Nachruf: Victor Lange (1908–1996)." *IVG Mitteilungsheft* 1996/97: 3.

Index*

* Entries for the Index were prepared by the contributors.

Abish, Cécile, 296
Abish, Walter, 281, 286, 292–97, 300–301, 305–306; *How German Is It*, 282, 286, 292, 296–97, 304, 306
absolutism, 80, 89
Adenauer, Konrad, 261, 285
Adorno, Theodor, 247
Aeschylus, 234, 239, 242, 244–47, 249; *The Oresteia*, 234, 239, 242, 244–45; *(Agamemnon)*, 244, 249; *(The Eumenides)*, 245, 247
Agnesi, Maria Gaetana, 38; *Analytical Institutions for the Use of Italian Youth*, 38
Algarotti, Francesco, 22, 29–33, 35–38; *Il Newtonianismo per le Dame (Newtonianism for the Ladies)*, 22, 29
allegory, 95, 97–98, 135–36, 144, 151
Anakreontik, 125
anti-Semitism, 214, 255, 290, 304
archetype, 260
Arendt, Hannah, 261, 263; *Eichmann in Jerusalem*, 261
Aristophanes, 69
Arnim, Ludwig Achim von, 117, 198, 203
Auschwitz, 281, 295

Baab, Heinrich, 261–64
Baader, Andreas, 297
Baden, Prinz Max von, 209–10
Bakhtin, Mikhail, 176
Bakunin, Mikhail, 210, 220

ballad, 191–92, 200
Barbapiccola, Giusippa Eleonora, 38
Bartok, Bela, 114
Bautzen prison, 272, 277
Becker-Neumann, Christiane, 48, 50–52
Berg, Alban, 114
Berlin Wall, 283–84, 286–9, 300
Bernstein, Leonard, 116
Bethge, Hans, 116, 134; *Die Chinesische Flöte*, 134
Blei, Franz, 168–69
Boccaccio, Giovanni, 79
Böhme, Jakob, 94, 96–100, 104–105, 110–112
Böll, Heinrich, 2, 256
bolshevism, 209, 216, 219
Borchardt, Rudolf, 190; *Rede über Hofmansthal*, 190
Börne, Ludwig, 80
Boyle, Kay, 254–68; *The Smoking Mountain*, 254–55, 257–58, 261, 264, 266
Brecht, Bertolt, 84, 181, 273; *Flüchtlingsgespräche*, 84
Brentano, Clemens, 115, 117, 198, 203
Bruns, Paul Jakob, 205
Büchner, Georg, 114–15; *Wozzeck*, 114
Buckley, William F., Jr., 281, 283–86, 305; *Stained Glass* 283–85; *Story of Henri Tod*, 283–5

canzone form, 193–98
Castera, M. Dupperon de, 29–30
Catholic Church, 27, 218
Chagall, Marc, 291
Châtelet, Marquise du, 38; *Institutions of Physics*, 38
Chaucer, Geoffrey, 202; *The Merchant's Tale*, 202
Chernobyl disaster, 236
christian faith, 23; fundamentalism, 26, 28, 36
christianity, 7, 95, 99–100, 113
CIA (Central Intelligence Agency), 283–85, 299, 300, 304
CIC (Counter Intelligence Corps), 270–78
Cicero, Marcus Tullius, 7
classicism (Weimar), 43, 48–50, 64, 66, 69, 75–76
cognition, 100–105
Cold War, 278, 280, 282–85
communism, 283, 286, 304
concentration camps, 269, 295–96
consciousness, 96–98, 102–105, 107–108, 112
Copernican system, 21–23, 25–27, 29, 38
Copernicus, Nicolaus, 21–22, 25, 29, 38
cosmogony, 97, 100, 102–104, 106, 108, 110–12
Crane, Hart, 306

Dachau, 281
Dahl, Johann, 213
Dannecker, Johann Heinrich, 63
Dante, Alighieri, 7
Deighton, Len, 282
Derrida, Jacques, 2
Deruda (Deutsch-Russische Transport Agentur), 274–75

Descartes, René, 23, 27, 29–30, 32, 38; *Principia philosophiae*, 38
Deutsche Demokratische Partei (DDP), 209
dialectic, 223, 231
Diderot, Denis, 37, 69
divinity, 100, 104–105, 108, 110, 112
D(oolittle), H(ilda), 241; *Helen in Egypt*, 241
Dulles, Allen, 284
Dürer, Albrecht, 293, 301

East Bloc, 281, 291, 297
Eckermann, Johann Peter, 54, 90, 93; *Gespräche mit Goethe in den letzten Jahren seines Lebens*, 90, 93
economic miracle, 283, 299, 303
elegy, 49
Eliot, T.S., 114; *Tradition and the Individual Talent*, 114; *The Waste Land*, 114
emanation theory, 96–97, 104, 106, 108, 111
empiricism, 32, 35
empty form, 224, 229–31
enlightenment, 21–22, 35, 219
epistemology, 64–65
Erzählung, 144, 148
Euripides, 69, 234, 237, 241, 244, 248; *Hekuba*, 241; *Helen*, 241; *The Trojan Women*, 234, 244, 248
Eve, 166, 169, 171–73, 175

Farbensymbolik, 150–151, 159
fascism, 256, 258, 289
Faßbinder, Rainer Werner, 291, 297
FBI (Federal Bureau of Investigation), 273

Federal Republic of Germany, 261, 264, 281–83, 285–86, 291, 297–98, 303, 305
femme fatale, 169, 176
feudal system, 91
Fichte, Johann Gottlieb, 94, 96–97, 102–104, 111, 113, 136–37, 141, 143; *Wissenschaftslehre* (1794), 102
fin-de-siècle, 116, 118
folklore, 157–58
Fontenelle, Bernard de, 22–30, 32, 36, 38; *Conversations on the Plurality of Worlds*, 22–23, 27, 29, 36
Förster, Friedrich, 92
Foucault, Michel, 2, 41
frame (also Rahmen), 79, 82, 84–85, 88, 90–91, 93
Freedom of Information Act, 273
Freikorps, 216
French Revolution, 78–79, 82–89, 92–93
Friedrich, Caspar David, 130, 213
Frisch, Max, 2
Fürstendiener, 80–81, 93

Galilei, Galileo, 21, 24, 32; *Dialogue Concerning the Two Chief World Systems*, 21, 24
Gasbarrone, Lisa, 37
George, Stefan, 196
Gestapo, 261
ghosts, 40–41, 45, 48, 52–53, 56, 58, 65–66, 72
Godard, Jean-Luc, 292, 295
Goebbels, Joseph, 257
Goethe, August von, 54
Goethe, Johann Wolfgang von, 14–15, 16, 20, 39–76, 78–93, 115–16, 119, 121, 137, 156, 158, 170, 198, 241, 269; *Die Aufgeregten*, 78; *Ausgabe letzter Hand*, 39, 46, 64, 77; *Der Bürgergeneral*, 78; *Dichtung und Wahrheit*, 80, 269; *Elegien II*, 47, 76; *Der Erlkönig*, 121; *Euphrosyne*, 47, 50–52, 69, 71, 76; *Faust*, 45, 52–7, 62, 66, 68–69, 74, 116, 121, 241; *Gott und Welt*, 46, 77; *Götz von Berlichingen*, 89; *Der Groß-Cophta*, 78; *Hefte zur Morphologie*, 47, 50–51, 77; *Die Metamorphose der Pflanzen*, 46–52, 69–72; *Parabase*, 52, 77; *Die Propyläen*, 69; *Reise in die Schweiz 1797*, 54, 62; *Roman über das Weltall*, 77; *Über den Granit*, 67; *Unterhaltungen deutscher Ausgewanderten*, 78–84, 86, 88–93; *Versuch die Metamorphose der Pflanzen zu erklären*, 42, 45, 47–48, 70–71, 73–74; *Wahlverwandtschaften*, 88; *Weissagungen des Bakis*, 69; *Werther*, 66; *Westöstliche Divan*, 115; *Zum Shakespeare-Tag*, 60, 68
Gotthelf, Jeremias (Albert Bitzius), 158; *Die schwarze Spinne*, 158
Gottsched, Johann Christoph, 22
Greim, Robert Ritter von, 262
Grimm, Jacob, 299
Grimm, Wilhelm, 299
Grosz, George, 265
guillotine, 82, 88

Habermas, Jürgen, 223
hades, 158
Hammer-Purgstall, Joseph, 115
Handke, Peter, 135–37, 145, 148, 222–28, 232; *Als das Wünschen noch geholfen hat*, 224; *Die Literatur ist romantisch*, 135; *Phantasien der Wiederholung*, 222, 227; *Short Letter, Long Farewell*, 226; *Die Wiederholung* (*Repetition*), 135–36, 144, 222, 224
Harrington, William, 304; *Endgame in Berlin*, 304
Hartmann von Aue, 195

Heidegger, Martin, 222
Heino, 223
Herder, Johann Gottfried 43, 52, 66
hermeneutics, 43, 51–52, 59, 62, 64–65, 70, 72
Herodotus, 69
heroism, 234, 240, 249; hero, 237, 240, 244, 247–48, 250–252; heroic, 234, 237, 240–41, 244, 248, 251–52
Hesse, Hermann, 2, 221
Hitler, Adolf, 210, 220–21, 236, 255, 257, 262, 266, 280, 282, 284, 287, 290–91, 298, 304
Hofmannsthal, Hugo von, 188–98, 200–203, 206–207; *Die Beiden*, 188–98, 200–203, 206–207; *Gesellschaft*, 201; *Jedermann*, 196; *Der Jüngling und die Spinne*, 201; *Lebenslied*, 200; *Poesie und Leben*, 188; *Sonett der Seele*, 191; *Sonett der Welt*, 191; *Vorfrühling*, 191; *Weltgeheimnis*, 191
Holocaust, 258, 260, 266, 279, 282–83, 287, 290, 297, 306
Hölty, Friedrich, 119
Homer, 39, 69, 114, 158, 237, 241–44, 276; *The Iliad*, 234, 241–43, 245, 248; *Nausicaa*, 39; *Odyssee*, 43, 114
Homer, Winslow, 301–302
Horatius, Flaccus Quintus, 7, 10
Horen, 58
Horkheimer, Max, 247
Huch, Ricarda, 208–212, 215–16, 220–21; *1848. Die Revolution des 19. Jahrhunderts in Deutschland*, 210; *Freiherr vom Stein*, 210; *Michael Bakunin und die Anarchie*, 210; *Der wiederkehrende Christus*, 208, 211, 221
Huelsenbeck, Richard, 169
Huygens, Christian, 35

Ibsen, Henrik, 176

idealism, 95–102, 107–108, 110, 112–13
Insel Verlag, 211
intellect, 94, 98–99, 105
Irigary, Luce, 176
Irving, John, 305; *A Son of the Circus*, 305

Jack the Ripper, 164–66, 168, 180–81, 186
Jean Paul (Richter), 116
Jesus, 211–12, 216–17, 220
Joyce, James, 114; *Ulysses*, 114
Just, Ward, 281, 296–302, 305–306; *The American Ambassador*, 297, 300–301, 303–304; *The Translator*, 298, 300–301, 304–305

Kafka, Franz, 114, 150, 212; *Der Prozeß*, 212
Kandinsky, Wassily, 114
Kant, Immanuel; 41–3, 96–97, 100–103, 106–107, 113, 225; *Kritik der reinen Vernunft*, 106, 113; *Kritik der Urteilskraft*, 42
Karl August Duke of Weimar, 78, 80, 83
Katzberger (see Oky)
Keller, Gottfried, 149–163; *Romeo und Julia auf dem Dorfe*, 149–50, 152, 156, 162
Kempf, Frau Dr., 209
Kempowski, Margarethe, 270, 272, 275
Kempowski, Robert, 270–72, 275, 277
Kempowski, Walter, 269–80; *Aus großer Zeit*, 269; *Deutsche Chronik*, 269; *Haben Sie davon gewußt?*, 269; *Haben Sie Hitler gesehen?*, 269; *Herzlich willkommen*, 269, 277–79; *Im Block*, 269–70, 272; *Immer so durchgemogelt: Erinnerungen an unsere

Schulzeit, 269; *Ein Kapitel für sich*, 269–70, 272; *Schöne Aussicht*, 269; *Tadellöser & Wolff*, 269; *Uns geht's ja noch gold*, 269–72, 278
Kennedy, John F., 284, 287
KGB, 304
Kippenberg, Anton, 211
Klee, Paul, 174
Kleist, Heinrich von, 298
Des Knaben Wunderhorn, 117, 197–98, 200, 202–203, 205; *Die Ausgleichung*, 203–206; *Der Graf und die Königstochter*, 198; *Das Rautensträuchelein*, 200; *Das Straßburger Mädchen*, 197; *Der traurige Garten*, 198; *Das Wunderhorn*, 198–203, 206
Knebel, Karl Ludwig von, 47
Kommissarov, 273
Körner, Christian Gottfried, 82
Körner, Justinus, 119
Kosterlitz, 263, 266
Kraus, Karl, 164
Kutscher, Artur, 166

Lai du Corn, 198
Lalande, Jérôme de, 22–23; *Astronomie des dames*, 23
Laocoon, statue and story, 5–6, 10–15, 17–20
Le Carré, John, 282
Legeune, Fritz (see Hans Siegfried)
Lerche (see Merk)
Lessing, Gotthold Ephriam, 18–19, 150
Lettre moderne, 27
lied, 191, 196–206
Lincoln, Abraham, 297
Linnaeus, Carolus, 41–42
love, 97–100, 103–105, 111–12
Lucretius, 69

Ludlum, Robert, 283
Lukács, Georg, 2
Lustmord, 164–65

MacPherson, James, 66
Mahler, Alma Schindler, 129
Mahler, Gustav, 115–19, 129–34; *Blicke mir nicht in die Lieder*, 129; *Ich atmet einen linden Duft*, 117, 131; *Ich bin der Welt abhanden gekommen*, 130; *Kindertotenlieder*, 116–117, 129; *Liebst du um Schönheit*, 129; *Das Lied von der Erde*, 116, 134; *Lieder aus der Jugendzeit*, 117; *Lieder eines fahrenden Gesellen*, 117; *The Titan*, 116; *Rückert Songs*, 117, 129–130; *Um Mitternacht*, 130; *Wunderhorn Lieder*, 117
Mahler, Maria, 129
Malebranche, Nicolas de, 29, 35
Malerdichter, 150
Mann, Thomas, 115, 227, 284, 291; *Doktor Faustus*, 115; *Der Zauberberg* (*The Magic Mountain*), 212, 227
Märchen, 144–45
Marx, Karl, 2
Marxists, 299, 304
mathematics, 26, 30, 35
Mathes, 271, 275, 277
matriarchal tradition, 237–39, 251
matter, 97–98, 100, 107, 111–112
Matthisson, Friedrich von, 119
McCarthyism, 258
Meinhof, Ulrike, 288, 297
Meistersinger, 203
Mengelberg, Wilhelm, 116
Merck, Johann Heinrich, 80
Merk (alias Lerche), 271, 274–77
metamorphosis, 42–43, 45, 71–72, 75–76

metaphysics, 222–33
Meyer, Heinrich, 53, 55, 61
Milton, John, 32–34; *Paradise Lost*, 32–33
Minnesang, 193, 195, 205
Minnesangs Frühling, 195
modernism, 130, 133
monument, 62, 65, 67–68, 72–73, 75
moon(s), 23, 25, 27
Möser, Justus, 80; *Patriotische Phantasien*, 80
Moses, 28–29
Müller, Wilhelm, 119
Myrdal, Gunnar, 258
mystical, 222, 224, 228
mysticism, 107–108
myth, 95–97, 223, 231
mythology, 94–97, 110, 158

nation, 86–87
National Socialism, 210, 256, 271, 280, 286, 294, 298, 302, 304–306
Nationalgefühl, 221
natural sciences, 21; as barbarism, 24, 30, 37; popularization of, 21–23, 34, 38
Naturphilosophie, 28, 136, 139, 141
Nauman, Bruce, 222; *Clown Torture*, 222
Neoplatonic mysticism, 95, 98
New Germany, 282–83, 289–292, 296–97, 300, 302- 307
Newes (Wedekind), Tilly, 181–87
Newton, Isaac, 21, 23, 27, 29–32, 35–36, 38; *Opticks*, 29; *Principia*, 23, 29, 38
Nietzsche, Friedrich, 174–75, 230; *Die Geburt der Tragödie aus dem Geiste der Musik*, 175; *Jenseits von Gut und Böse*, 174–75; *Von Wahrheit und Lüge im aussermoralischen Sinn*, 175
nihilism, 233
NKVD, Soviet Secret State Police, 270
nouveau roman, 293, 296
novella (Novelle), 79, 82, 91, 144, 150, 152–53, 155, 159
Nuremberg Trials, 263

Oakeshott, Michael, 51
Oates, Joyce Carol, 281, 286, 289, 292–93, 296–97, 299, 304–306; *Ich Bin Ein Berliner*, 286, 305–306; *Master Race*, 286, 289, 291–92, 299, 306; *My Warszawa 1980*, 281; *Our Wall*, 281
Oky (alias Katzberger), 272, 275, 277
organic, 56, 68, 73, 75
orientalism, 115
Ossian, 64–66, 119

Pabst, Georg Wilhelm, 170, 186
Pandora, 171–75
pastourelle, 193
pathos, 9, 11–14, 16, 19–20
patriarchal tradition, 234–35, 237–39, 249, 251
Pergolesi, Giovanni, 114
Picasso, Pablo, 114
Pirandello, Luigi, 114
Plato, 24, 96–100, 105, 111
Plievier, Theodor, 257; *Stalingrad*, 257
Pliny, 69
Pope, Alexander, 29, 31, 33, 36
Portal, Pierre Paul Frédéric de, 151–52, 155, 159–60, 162–63; *Des couleurs symboliques dans l'antiquité, le moyen-age et les temps modernes*, 151
prismatic symbols, 150

Proust, Marcel, 114
Provençal poetry, 193
Ptolemy, 23

racism, 258, 260
Reagan, Ronald, 242, 283
realism, 152–53
Reitsch, Hannah, 262
religion, 27, 94, 96–97, 108, 112
re-vision, 234–35, 237, 242, 244, 249, 252–53
Revolution of 1848, 210, 220
Richter, Johann Paul Friedrich (see Jean Paul)
Riefenstahl, Leni, 262
Rilke, Rainer Maria, 275
romanticism, 135, 213; romantische Poesie, 148
Roosevelt, Franklin D., 255
Rote Armee Fraktion, 297
Rückert, Friedrich, 114–27, 129–34; *Blicke mir nicht in die Lieder*, 129; *Du bist die Ruh*, 120; *Geharnischte Sonetten*, 115; *Ich atmet einen linden Duft*, 117; *Ich bin dein Baum*, 127; *Ich bin der Welt abhanden gekommen*, 132; *Kindertotenlieder*, 116–117, 129; *Lachen und Weinen*, 122–23; *Liebesfrühling*, 115; *Liebst du um Schönheit*, 129; *Schön ist das Fest des Lenzes*, 124, 126; *Sei mir gegrüßt*, 120; *So wahr die Sonne scheinet*, 126; *Um Mitternacht*, 130

Sachsenhausen prison, 272
Sadoleto, Jacopo, 15–17; *De Lacoontis statua*, 15
Scheffauer, Philipp Jacob, 63
Schelling, Friedrich, 69, 136–37, 141
Schiller, Friedrich von, 14, 18–20, 46–50, 52, 56–58, 63–64, 69, 79, 81–82, 89, 93, 119, 137, 267; *Horen*, 79, 81; *Das Ideal und das Leben*, 19; *Musen-Almanach für das Jahr 1799*, 46–49, 51, 69, 76; *Über das Pathetische*, 18; *Über naive und sentimentalische Dichtung*, 58; *Wallenstein*, 48, 50–51
Schindler, Alma (see Alma Mahler)
Schlegel, August Wilhelm, 119
Schlegel, Friedrich, 69, 94–113, 119, 135, 141; *Gespräch über die Poesie*, 94; *Zur Entwicklung der Philosophie in zwölf Büchern*, 95
Schönberg, Arnold, 114
Schubert, Franz, 116, 119–24, 133; *Du bist die Ruh*, 120, 122, 124, 133; *Der Erlkönig*, 121; *Lachen und Weinen*, 120, 124; *Die schöne Müllerin*, 119; *Sei mir gegrüßt*, 120; *Die Winterreise*, 119
Schumann, Clara, 123–24
Schumann, Robert, 116, 123–129, 131, 133; *Ich bin dein Baum*, 127, *Schön ist das Fest des Lenzes*, 124, 128, *So wahr die Sonne scheinet*, 126
scientific method, 25–26
Seeschaf, 270
sentimentality, 14, 16–17
Shakespeare, William, 60, 68, 115, 152, 160, 202, 276; *A Midsummer Night's Dream*, 202
Siegfried, Hans (alias Fritz Legeune), 270–78
Socrates, 24, 31; Socratic dialogue, 24, 31
sonnet, 190–95
Sontag, Susan, 289
Sophocles, 18; *Philoctetes*, 18
Soviet Military Administration, 273
Soviet Union, 270–71, 283
Soviet Zone, 270–75

Spinoza, 94, 113
spirit, 97–98, 105, 107, 111–112
Spruchkammer, 265–66
Stahlhelm, 216–17
Stasi (Staatssicherheitsdienst), 301
Stauffenberg, Klaus Schenk von, 283
Steffens, Henrich, 136–42; *Beyträge zur innern Naturgeschichte der Erde*, 137, 139; *Was ich erlebte*, 137
Stein, (Heinrich Friedrich Karl) Freiherr vom (und zum), 210, 220
Stesichorus, 239, 241; *Palinode*, 239, 241
stoicism, 9, 17, 20
Stolberg, Friedrich, 119
Storm and Stress, 80, 86
Stravinsky, Igor, 114; *Pulcinella*, 114
substance, 96, 100–102, 107, 111
symbolic representation, 54–61, 63–64

Tasso, Torquato, 33
teleology, 41–42
terrorism, 281, 297–99, 304; terrorist, 281, 296–97, 305
Third Reich, 261, 269, 282
Thucydides, 69
Tieck, Ludwig, 135–37, 139, 141–42, 144; *Kaiser Octavianus*, 141; *Der Runenberg*, 135–37, 139, 144, 146–47; *William Lovell*, 141
time and space, 97, 100–101, 105–108, 112
Tito, Josip, 230
topos, 59–62, 71, 75
transfiguration, 225
Trojan War, 234, 239–41, 244
Trotsky, Leon, 165

Uhland, Ludwig, 93
Ulbricht, Walter, 284
understanding, 101–102, 104–105
Urpflanze, 40, 42–44, 50, 52, 63–64, 66
US Army Intelligence and Security Command, 273
utopia, 240, 250, 252

Velazquez, Diego, 114
Vergilius, Publius Maro (Virgil), 2, 6–17, 19–20, 69, 241; *Aeneid*, 6, 10, 13, 241; *Eclogue IV*, 7; *Georgics*, 10
Vico, Giambattista de, 37
Vietnam, 283, 291, 301–302
Voltaire, François 69, 301; *Candide*, 301

Walser, Martin, 90
Walter, Bruno, 116, 118
Wedekind, Frank, 164–70, 172–79, 181–87; *Büchse der Pandora*, 164, 167, 170, 178, 183, 186; *Erdgeist*, 164, 167, 170, 174, 176, 178–81, 183; *Frühlings Erwachen*, 167, 179; *Mine-Haha oder Über die Erziehung der jungen Mädchen*, 168, 185; *Das Opferlamm*, 185; *Rabbi Esra*, 183; *Tod und Teufel*, 185; *Totentanz*, 173; *Über Erotik*, 167; *Die Zensur*, 184–85, 187
Weimar Republic, 208–11, 215–16, 220–21
Weinschenk, Fritz, 270, 273–75
Werner, A.G., 137
Wharton, Edith, 175; *The House of Mirth*, 176
Whitman, Walt, 306
Wickram, Jörg, 198; *Rollwagenbüchlein*, 198
Wieck, Clara (see Clara Schumann)
Wieland, Christoph Martin, 202–203; *Oberon*, 202–203
Wilder, Thornton, 278; *The Skin of our Teeth*, 278

Wilhelm II, German Emperor, 209
Wilhelmine Germany, 208, 221
Winckelmann, Johann Joachim, 5–12, 15–20; *Florenzer Manuskript*, 10; *Gedanken über die Nachahmung der griechischen Werke in der Malerei und Bildhauerkunst*, 5, 7, 10; *Geschichte der Kunst des Altertums*, 10
Wittig, Monique, 252; *Les Guérillères*, 252
Wolf, Christa, 234–249, 251–53; *Frankfurter Poetik-Vorlesungen*, 236, 242; *Kassandra*, 234, 236–37, 242–45, 248–49, 252; *Störfall: Nachrichten eines Tages*, 236; *Voraussetzungen einer Erzählung: Kassandra*, 234, 236, 246–47
Wolff, Caspar Friedrich, 51
Wolfram von Eschenbach, 276
Wolfskehl, Karl, 209
women and science, 23–24, 36–38
World War I, 208
World War II, 145, 221, 226, 254, 270, 279
world-ego, 107–109, 111–12

Zohar, 224–26
Zumsteeg, Johann Rudolf, 65–66
Züricher Post, 184
Zweig, Stefan, 177
Zwingli, Ulrich, 279

OHIO UNIVERSITY LIBRARY

Please return this book as soon as you have finished with it. In order to avoid a fine it must be returned by the latest date stamped below. All books are subject to recall after two weeks or immediately if needed for reserve.

CF